Institutional Investing: Principles and Practices

ONLINE COURSE PORTAL

The LOMA 357 Course Portal, available online at www.LOMANET.org via your "My Learning" page, includes numerous multi-media features designed to reinforce and enhance your learning experience and help you prepare for the exam. Among these features are numerous "Learning Aids" that illustrate key concepts presented in the assigned course materials, the Test Preparation Guide's popular interactive Practice Questions and Sample Exam with answer feedback, and the "Top 10 Tough Topics" review of the most challenging topics in this course. If you are not already using the online Course Portal but would like access to the many additional study resources for this course, please follow the log-in instructions provided in your Enrollment Confirmation e-mail, or call 1-800-ASK-LOMA or e-mail education@loma.org for assistance.

LOMA (Life Office Management Association, Inc.) is an international association founded in 1924. LOMA is committed to a business partnership with the worldwide members in the insurance and financial services industry to improve their management and operations through quality employee development, research, information sharing, and related products and services. Among LOMA's activities is the sponsorship of several self-study education programs leading to professional designations, including the Fellow, Life Management Institute (FLMI) program. For more information on all of LOMA's education programs, please visit www.loma.org.

Statement of Purpose: LOMA Educational Programs Testing and Designations

Examinations described in the LOMA Education and Training Catalog are designed solely to measure whether students have successfully completed the relevant assigned curriculum, and the attainment of the FLMI and other LOMA designations indicates only that all examinations in the given curriculum have been successfully completed. In no way shall a student's completion of a given LOMA course or attainment of the FLMI or other LOMA designation be construed to mean that LOMA in any way certifies that student's competence, training, or ability to perform any given task. LOMA's examinations are to be used solely for general educational purposes, and no other use of the examinations or programs is authorized or intended by LOMA. Furthermore, it is in no way the intention of the LOMA Curriculum and Examinations staff to describe the standard of appropriate conduct in any field of the insurance and financial services industry, and LOMA expressly repudiates any attempt to so use the curriculum and examinations. Any such assessment of student competence or industry standards of conduct should instead be based on independent professional inquiry and the advice of competent professional counsel.

Institutional Investing: Principles and Practices

LOMA Education and Training
Atlanta, Georgia
www.loma.org

Information in this text may have changed or been updated since its publication date.
For current updates visit www.loma.org.

PROJECT TEAM

Project Manager:	Julia K. Wooley, FLMI, ACS, ALHC, HIA, MHP
Content Developers:	Jo Ann S. Appleton, FLMI, PCS, ALHC, HIA, CEBS Susan Conant, FLMI, CEBS Rosemary Thomas Cunningham, Ph.D. Patricia Wilson Fridley Mary B. Naismith, J.D., FLMI, FFSI, CLU, AIRC, ACS, AIAA, PAHM, AAPA, ARA Steven Silver, J.D., FLMI, AFSI, ACS, AIRC, AIAA
Manuscript Editors:	Jo Ann S. Appleton, FLMI, PCS, ALHC, HIA, CEBS Susan Conant, FLMI, CEBS Steven Silver, J.D., FLMI, AFSI, ACS, AIRC, AIAA
Examinations Editor:	Yanhua Xun, Ph.D., FLMI, FFSI, AIAA, ARA, AAPA, PCS
Permissions Editor:	Steven Silver, J.D., FLMI, AFSI, ACS, AIRC, AIAA
Copy Editor:	Robert D. Land, FLMI, ACS
Indexer:	Robert D. Land, FLMI, ACS
Consultant:	Barbara Foxenberger Brown, FLMI, ACS, AIAA, AIRC

Text Production:

Figure Designers:	Nick Desoutter, FLMI, PCS, AAPA Amy Stailey, ACS, ALMI
Typesetter:	Amy Stailey, ACS, ALMI
Production Coordinator:	Amy Stailey, ACS, ALMI
Production Proofreader:	Natalie K. Cape Sanders
Workflow Coordinator:	Kelly W. Neeley, FLMI, ALHC, AIAA, ACS, PAHM
AVP, Marketing:	Paul Wilson
Product Marketing:	Kathryn Brown, ALMI, PCS
Graphic Designers:	Marlene McAuley Amy Stailey, ACS, ALMI
Cover Design:	Amy Stailey, ACS, ALMI

Portal Production:

Project Management:	Gene Stone, FLMI, ACS, CLU
Portal Design:	Brian Laframboise, ALMI
	Marlene McAuley
Portal Text Editor:	Gene Stone, FLMI, ACS, CLU
Videos:	Bill Maura
	Frank Robinson
	John Rocchetti
Learning Aids:	Susan Conant, FLMI, CEBS
	Brian Laframboise, ALMI
	Monica R. Maxwell, J.D., FLMI, AIRC, ARA, ACS
	Tonya Vaughan
Top Ten Tough Topics:	Sean Schaeffer Gilley, FLMI, ACS, AIAA, AIRC, FLHC, AAPA, ARA, CEBS, HIA, MHP, PAHM
	Elizabeth A. Mulligan, FLMI, FLHC, PCS, PAHM, AAPA, AIRC, ARA, AIAA
	Yanhua Xun, Ph.D., FLMI, FFSI, AIAA, ARA, AAPA, PCS
TPG Online Conversions:	David A. Lewis, FLMI, ACS
TPG Authors:	Vivian Heeden, FLMI, FFSI, CLU, FLHC, AIRC, AAPA, AIAA, PCS, ARA
	Lisa M. Kozlowski, FLMI, FFSI, CLU, ChFC, FLHC, ACS, AIAA, AIRC, ARA, AAPA
	Elizabeth A. Mulligan, FLMI, FLHC, PCS, PAHM, AAPA, AIRC, ARA, AIAA
	Yanhua Xun, Ph.D., FLMI, FFSI, AIAA, ARA, AAPA, PCS
ISA	David A. Lewis, FLMI, ACS
Manager, Product Sourcing:	Carol Wiessner, ACS
Product Sourcing Coordinator:	Natalie K. Cape Sanders
Administrative Support:	Mamunah Carter

21 20 19 18 17 16 15 14 13   10 9 8 7 6 5 4 3 2 1

ISBN 978-1-57974-418-2

Contents

Module 2: Portfolio Management Principles for Institutions (Chapters 4–7)

Module 3: Investments for Institutional Investors (Chapters 8–10)

Chapter 8: Bonds and Bond-Related Investments 8.1

Chapter 9: Investments Based in Real Estate 9.1

Preface

Institutional Investing: Principles and Practices provides a primer on asset types and investment principles, describes the investment environment of financial institutions, and describes institutional practices for portfolio management in contexts including separate accounts and the general account of a life insurance company. The text is divided into three modules:

■ Module 1: Institutional Investments Overview (Chapters 1–3)

■ Module 2: Portfolio Management Principles for Institutions (Chapters 4–7)

■ Module 3: Investments for Institutional Investors (Chapters 8–10)

Acknowledgments

Institutional Investing: Principles and Practices is the result of the combined efforts of industry experts who served on a text development panel and LOMA staff and consultants. The LOMA 357 authors wish to express gratitude for the dedication, knowledge, expertise, and guidance provided by all of these individuals throughout the writing of this text.

LOMA 357 Text Development Panel

On behalf of LOMA and its membership, we would like to thank all of the LOMA 357 text reviewers and the companies that supported their efforts. Text reviewers are busy industry professionals who actively support the educational needs of current and future industry employees and generously volunteer their time and expertise to review a text's content. The LOMA 357 text development panel made many substantive contributions, commented on the developing chapters, provided suggestions for additional content, submitted relevant research materials, and answered numerous questions posed by LOMA staff. Text developers are responsible for the accuracy and clarity of the text, and take responsibility for any errors.

The following individuals participated in every aspect of this text development project, from reviewing the course outline to reviewing all chapters:

Matthew J. Budenz, CPA, FLMI
Manager, Finance
Consumers Life Insurance Company

Ivan Francis, CFA, FLMI/M
Vice President, Fixed Income
Standard Life Investments Inc.

Donna Gagnon
Vice President & Chief Technology Officer
Liberty Mutual Group Asset Management Inc.

Daniel C. Leimbach, CFA, FLMI, CLU, ChFC
Vice President
Director of Research
United Services Automobile Association (USAA)

James McClure
Vice President, Investment Accounting and Reporting
Prudential Investment Management

Leon Osborne, CFA, MBA
Due Diligence Consultant
MML Investors Services, LLC (Mass Mutual)

Barbara Seith, FLMI, MBA, MSIS, PMP
Director, Key Portfolio Initiatives
Genworth Financial

Jane Zhao, MBA, FLMI, ARA, ACS
Senior Retention Management Analyst, Reinsurance Division
Pacific Services Canada Limited

The following individuals provided expert guidance or other substantive assistance with this text development project:

Silas H. Allen
Senior Investment Performance Analyst, USAA Chief Investment Office
United Services Automobile Association (USAA)

Mark Bursinger, CFA, FSA
Investment Leader
Nationwide Insurance

James C. Craft
Portfolio Manager, Portfolio Management Group
Allstate Investments, LLC

Douglas Dupont, ASA, CFA
Vice President and Managing Director, Portfolio Management Group
Allstate Insurance

Luke McLaren, J.D., MBA, CLU, CPCU, RHU, FFSI, FLMI, AAPA, AIAA,
ACS, AIRC, ARA
Executive Director, Insurance Compliance
United Services Automobile Association (USAA)

John A. Zelinske, CPA, CGMA, CMA, CFM, FLMI
Assistant Vice President
Alternative Investments & Real Estate Accounting & Reporting
MetLife, Inc.

The following individuals participated in some aspects of this text development project, from reviewing the course outline to reviewing several chapters:

Wendy Chase, CLU, FLMI, ChFC, CRPC, AIAF, AIRC, AIAA, PCS, FFSI
Vice President
Life Client Solutions
Partner Solutions for Life, Claims & Distribution
Lincoln Financial Group

Scott Hintz, CFA
Assistant Vice President, Securities Products
State Farm

James Hix, FLMI
Unit Manager, Broker-Dealer Transitions, Orphaned Reassignments,
and Imaging for the Broker-Dealer
Allstate Financial Services, LLC

The following individuals reviewed portions of the course outline or text or provided expert guidance or other assistance with this text development project:

Diane Bellas, Allstate Corporation; Damon Buckwalter, Nationwide Insurance; Mark W. (Sam) Davis, Allstate Investments, LLC; Kathrina-J. Dizon, Philippine American Life; Sarah Donahue, Allstate Life Insurance Company; Joan S. Freedman, LifeComps Commercial Mortgage Index; David Hayter, Liberty Mutual Group Asset Management Inc.; Yussri Ibrahim, Penn Mutual Life Insurance Company; Paul McCullough, Thrivent Financial for Lutherans; Jason Pandolfo, MetLife, Inc.; Tonya Sweeden, State Farm; Chuck Taylor, Allstate Financial; George Wahle, Allstate Life Insurance Company.

Special Thanks

The LOMA 357 Institutional Investing: Principles and Practices course is the result of the dedicated efforts of a project team of LOMA staff members and consultants who were responsible for writing and editing the text's content; developing learning aids and study materials to accompany the text; and overseeing the production of the text and the course portal.

LOMA wishes to thank the LOMA 357 course project team members for all of their hard work.

In addition, we thank LOMA staff members who graciously provided other support and expert advice: Olivia Blakemore, ALMI, ACS; Linda Cobb; Curtis Conner, FLMI, ACS, ARA, CIA, CPA; Mallory Eldridge; Harriett E. Jones, J.D., FLMI, ACS, AIRC; Angie Norman, CTP, ALMI; and Stephen Quina, ALMI, PCS.

Finally, LOMA extends a very special thank you to Julia K. Wooley, FLMI, ACS, ALHC, HIA, MHP, Assistant Vice President, Learning Content Development, who served as project manager and provided guidance and support throughout the project; and Katherine C. Milligan, FLMI, ACS, ALHC, Vice President, Education and Training Division, who served as the project's executive sponsor and provided leadership, guidance, resources, and support for this project.

Jo Ann S. Appleton, FLMI, PCS, ALHC, HIA, CEBS

Susan Conant, FLMI, CEBS

Rosemary Thomas Cunningham, Ph.D.

Patricia Wilson Fridley

Mary B. Naismith, J.D., FLMI, FFSI, CLU,
AIRC, ACS, AIAA, PAHM, AAPA, ARA

Steven Silver, J.D., FLMI, AFSI, ACS, AIRC, AIAA

Introduction

The purpose of *Institutional Investing: Principles and Practices* is to provide industry employees with an overview of how financial institutions, including insurance companies, their investment affiliates, and pension plans invest within today's global environment. To enhance your learning experience, LOMA makes available for this course a Course Portal that is accessible upon course enrollment in LOMANET. A LOMA Course Portal is an online resource from which learners access everything they need to study and prepare for the course examination. The Course Portal organizes the assigned text material into convenient Modules—chapter clusters that help to focus the learning process by breaking up the course content into meaningful sections. In addition to the assigned study materials, the Course Portal provides access to an array of blended learning resources, including multimedia features designed to enhance the learning experience. The LOMA 357 Course Portal provides access to

- An introductory course video

- PDFs of the assigned text and Test Preparation Guide, which can be printed or read online

- The interactive version of the Test Preparation Guide's Practice Questions and Sample Exam

- Review tools, including Learning Aids—animations of important concepts—and a "Top Ten Tough Topics" tutorial

- Recommended study plans to help you set goals and manage your learning experience

- Related links which help you apply the course instruction to the real world

LOMA 357 is part of the Fellow, Life Management Institute (FLMI) program. Students preparing to take the examination for LOMA 357 will find that the assigned study materials—the protected PDFs of the text and Test Preparation Guide—include many features designed to help learners more easily understand the course content, organize their study, and prepare for the examination. These features include lists of Learning Aid topics available on the Course Portal, chapter outlines, chapter learning objectives, key terms, figures containing real-world examples of course content, and a comprehensive glossary. As we describe each of these features, we give you suggestions for studying the material.

- **Learning Aids and Top Ten Tough Topics.** A list of Learning Aids is provided in the PDF for the entire text as well as for each Module. Review this list to become familiar with topics for which an animated learning aid is available on the Course Portal. Viewing these Learning Aids allows you to see topics in action or to view topics from a different perspective than from simply reading about them in the text. Also included is a Top Ten Tough Topics tutorial. This tutorial contains animations and study tips for topics that learners often find difficult when answering questions on the examination. Both the Learning Aids and the Top Ten Tough Topics tutorial enhance the learning experience, appeal to a variety of learning styles, and offer a great way for learners to advance their understanding and retention of course content.

- **Learning Objectives.** The first page of each chapter contains a list of learning objectives to help you focus your studies. Before reading each chapter, review these learning objective s. Then, as you read the chapter, look for material that will help you meet the learning objectives. The interactive version of the Test Preparation Guide's Practice Questions and Sample Exam questions (accessible from the Course Portal) are linked to the learning objectives to give you an idea of how the learning objective might be measured on an examination, as well as to help you assess your mastery of the learning objectives.

- **Chapter Outline.** Each chapter contains an outline of the chapter. Review this outline to gain an overview of the major topics that will be covered; then scan through the chapter to become familiar with how the information is presented. By looking at the headings, you can gain a preview of how various subjects in each chapter relate to each other.

- **Key Terms.** This text explains key terms that apply to the text material and, where appropriate, reviews key terms previously presented in LOMA courses. Each key term is highlighted with **_bold italic type_** when the term is defined and is included in a list of key terms at the end of each chapter. All key terms also appear in a comprehensive glossary at the end of the PDF of the text. As you read each chapter, pay special attention to the key terms.

- **Figures.** We include figures throughout the text to illustrate and bring a real-world perspective to the text's discussion of selected topics. Information contained in figures may be tested on the examination for the course.

- **Glossary.** A comprehensive glossary that contains definitions of all key terms appears at the end of the text. Following each glossary entry is a number in brackets that indicates the chapter in which the key term is defined. The glossary also references important equivalent terms, acronyms, and contrasting terms.

LOMA may periodically revise the assigned study materials for this course. To ensure that you are studying from the correct materials, check the current LOMA _Education and Training Catalog_ available at www.loma.org or on the Course Portal. Also be sure to visit the Announcements page on the Course Portal to learn about important updates or corrections to the assigned study materials.

Using the Test Preparation Guide

LOMA's _Test Preparation Guide for LOMA 357 (TPG)_ is assigned reading for students preparing for the LOMA 357 examination. It contains Practice Questions organized by chapter and a full-scale Sample Exam. The TPG is available in two versions, both accessible from the Course Portal: (1) a printable PDF that includes answer keys for all questions, and (2) an interactive version that can be used online or downloaded for offline use. The interactive version has the added advantage of answer-choice explanations for all Practice Questions and Sample Exam questions. The TPG is designed to help you learn the course content and prepare for the examination. Used along with the assigned text, the TPG will help you master the course material. **Studies indicate that students who use LOMA TPGs consistently perform significantly better on LOMA examinations than students who do not use TPGs.**

Learning Aids

The LOMA 357 Course Portal, available online at www.LOMANET.org, includes several Learning Aids designed to reinforce concepts covered in the assigned text. If you are not already using the online Course Portal but would like access to the Learning Aids for this course, please follow the log-in instructions provided in your enrollment confirmation email, or call 1-800-ASK-LOMA or email education@ loma.org for assistance. **PLEASE NOTE:** Examination questions will be based only on content presented in the assigned text.

Module 1: Institutional Investments Overview (Chapters 1–3)

- ✓ Work in the Investment Function
- ✓ Investment Words
- ✓ Capital Markets and Financial Institutions
- ✓ Regulatory Structures
- ✓ Securities Regulation
- ✓ Risk Controls in Investments
- ✓ Questionable Practices

Module 2: Portfolio Management Principles for Institutions (Chapters 4–7)

- ✓ Return Concepts
- ✓ Investment Risk and Return
- ✓ Fund Styles
- ✓ Due Diligence for Fund Options
- ✓ Measures for Fund Analysis
- ✓ Selecting Portfolio Asset Classes
- ✓ Risk, Return, and the Efficient Frontier
- ✓ ALM Risk Policies
- ✓ Debt Investment Strategies

Module 3: Investments for Institutional Investors (Chapters 8–10)

✓ Government Bonds

✓ Bond Categories

✓ Trading Corporate Bonds

✓ Real Estate Appraisals

✓ Mortgage Types

✓ Stock Valuation and Ratios

✓ Derivative Securities

Chapter 1

Overview of Investments

Objectives

After studying this chapter, you should be able to

1A Explain how the job environment in the investment function differs from the job environment in other areas of a financial services company and describe and differentiate between the jobs of investment professionals in a financial services company

1B For investment operations in a financial services company, differentiate between front-office operations, back-office operations, and middle-office operations

1C Identify and describe important software systems for data management in investment information technology, including investment accounting information systems, trade management systems, and risk management and analysis systems

1D Identify important interactions of noninvestment functions with investment functions

1E Describe and differentiate between asset classes for institutional investors, including stocks, bonds, mortgages, and real estate

1F Explain the usual role of financial institutions in a basic model of capital markets, and describe the role of rating agencies

1G For a general account and a separate account of a life insurance company, describe the movement of funds from a customer, through a financial services company, and into the capital markets; then back from the capital markets to the company; and finally from the company to the customer in the form of a benefit payment

1H Describe the purposes of management systems for enterprise risk management, asset-liability management, asset allocation, and portfolio management in financial services companies

Outline

Investment Professionals in Financial Institutions

Organization of the Investment Function

Investment Management Data and Software

Units That Interact with the Investment Function
- Treasury Operations and Cash Management
- Product Development
- Investment Marketing
- Customer Service

Investment Types and Concepts
- Equities
- Bonds
- Mortgages
- Accounting Classifications for Assets

Capital Markets
- An Overview of Capital Market Transactions
- Capital Market Participants

Path of Funds in the Investment Process
- General Account
- Separate Accounts

Investment Goals and Investment Portfolios

Regulation Affecting the Investment Function

Corporate Alignment, Governance, and Control for Investments
- Enterprise Risk Management
- Asset-Liability Management
- Asset Allocation
- Portfolio Management

Insurance and financial services companies, as well as other types of financial institutions, typically have an investment function.[1] In that respect, they are all classified as institutional investors. An ***institutional investor*** is any organization devoted to holding financial assets and trading securities in large volume.

Examples: Institutional Investors

- Insurance companies
- Mutual funds
- Banks
- Trust departments
- Hedge funds
- Brokerages
- Pension and retirement funds
- Labor union pension and retirement funds
- University endowments
- Charitable foundations

This text is designed to help you better appreciate the investment function in financial services companies. An investment is any use of resources that is intended to generate a profit or positive return. In this text, we focus on the investments of financial resources by financial services companies—in particular, insurance companies.

Investment activities are very similar in any of these institutions. Institutional investors, including insurance companies, act on behalf of the institution itself for some portions of their business; for other portions of their business, some of these institutions also invest for the benefit of their clients' accounts. For instance, insurance companies invest both to support their insurance products and to support client investment accounts. Mostly to support these different needs, insurance companies divide their assets into two main types of accounts—a general account and separate accounts.

Although every functional area within a financial services company has some distinctive terminology and practices, the language and operations in the investment function are markedly different from those in other functional areas.

Example: Jargon in Press Clipping

S&P 500 index—for "Standard and Poor's" index of the top 500 listed stocks on the New York Stock Exchange

ZGFX—The stock market ticker symbol for Zouse Global Financial

assets under management—A measure of the size of Zouse's investment business

asset bubbles—Asset markets with irrationally high and inflated market prices

M&A—"Merger and acquisition" or ways of combining forces with an existing business

Zouse Global Financial Executive Expresses Positive Outlook

Kalamazoo, December 20, 201X. Despite projections that the S&P 500 index will perform only slightly better next year than it did this year, and that interest rates will remain low, Zouse Global Financial's (ZGFX) analysts expect total assets under management to grow 8% to 10% during the year.

Zouse economic analysts see increased activity among institutional investors around the world, and foresee a benefit to Zouse's investments arm in the near term.

Speaking to analysts and investors yesterday, CEO Axel Schwartz expressed a bright outlook for Zouse's growth in the coming year:

"We see new opportunities for expansion into emerging markets, where we anticipate that inflation will be slower to emerge in the early phases of economic recovery.

"Containing inflation and avoiding asset bubbles in emerging markets depends largely on sound government policies."

Schwartz anticipates M&A opportunities to pick up existing asset managers based in Latin America or the Asia-Pacific region.

If you already understand all of the investment terminology used in this news item, that's great. If not, you should be able to after you've learned the material in this course. This text provides you with an understanding of investment terms and concepts so that you better appreciate the work of the investment function in financial services companies, and in other contexts as well.

We can start to address the investment function by considering the following facts about investment professionals:

- **Compensation of investment professionals emphasizes performance incentives.** The maximum potential incentive compensation bonus for investment jobs is much greater than for any nonsales job or nonexecutive position outside of investments. A large percentage of an investment professional's incentive compensation is tied to the profitability of the assets under that person's management. Because of this compensation structure, investment professionals are motivated to grow customers' account values. In turn, having satisfied customers can improve a company's profitability and customer retention.

Example: Incentive Compensation

Logo Financial's employee compensation strategy incorporates performance-based incentive bonuses for management employees as well as investment professionals. (Company executives have individual compensation agreements, and are outside of this system.)

At Logo Financial, these incentive bonuses are limited to the following maximum percentages of base pay:

Employee Class	Compensation
Management, not in investments	Base pay plus up to 15%
Investment professionals	Base pay plus 50% up to 100%

- **Investment professionals work primarily with data generated externally.** In contrast, many other financial services professionals, such as accountants, actuaries, information technology professionals, marketing analysts, and customer services representatives, work primarily with data generated internally.

- **Investment professionals require current information.** Although many areas of a financial services company require current information about customers or processes to operate successfully, the need for real-time financial market price information is critical. In the investment area, even small movements in market prices can significantly impact revenues or profits. Financial markets are fluid, with prices changing throughout the day, so investment professionals face urgency to act on current financial market pricing. To do so, investment professionals must have immediate access to the most current financial market prices in all relevant markets, and special care must be taken to ensure that external data feeds continue without interruptions.

Example: Movements in Market Data

At 9:30 a.m., Mario authorized a purchase order for 100,000 shares of GoldenCoins Inc. at the market opening price, but not to exceed $116 per share. In the first hour of trading, the price moved between $114 and $117. To Mario's satisfaction, the order was fulfilled at $115 per share.

Throughout a trading day, market data crawlers provide investment professionals with continuously refreshed information. You've probably seen market data crawlers—such as the ones pictured in Figure 1.1.

Investment Professionals in Financial Institutions

The following professional jobs are typically found within the investment function of insurance and financial services companies.

- *Traders* are investment professionals responsible for executing purchases and sales of publicly traded securities under instructions from portfolio managers. A stock trader, also known as an *equities trader*, executes orders to purchase or sell stock shares.

- *Portfolio managers* are investment professionals with broad authority and accountability for fulfilling the mission and objectives of an investment portfolio. A *portfolio* is a collection of assets, such as stocks and bonds, assembled to support a common objective and, typically, to spread the investor's risk exposure over a variety of risk classes. A portfolio may contain only one asset, several assets, or many more assets.

- *Asset-liability managers* monitor the company's assets supporting a specified product line, such as annuities. For a specified product line, the asset liability manager monitors the investment cash inflows, cash outflows, increases in value, and decreases in value, and ensures that sufficient funds and assets are on hand at all times.

- Some companies have *asset-class managers* who specialize in managing a particular class of assets, as defined later in this chapter. The responsibilities of an asset-class manager differ from one company to another, and depend on the asset class involved.

- *Investment accountants* ensure (1) accurate and timely recording of all investment transactions and values and (2) compliance with complex financial reporting standards related to investments of financial services companies.

- *Investment risk management professionals* focus on measuring and identifying relevant risks, statistical analysis of risk, economic capital calculations, setting investment diversification criteria, and setting investment policy statements. In many companies, investment risk management reports to the board.

- Investment information technology professionals maintain the information technology for software and information processing packages, data reporting, data communications, information feeds, and data storage.

- *Analysts* are investment professionals responsible for monitoring issuers of securities and making buy-hold-sell recommendations as to future trading activity. Some analysts are generalists, whereas others specialize in a specific asset type or industry.

Figure 1.1 Market Data Crawlers

Source: Photo by Alex Wong / Getty Images News / Getty Images

Examples: Investment Analysts

A *quantitative analyst* studies the measurable factors associated with businesses that issue securities.

A *credit analyst* studies the business data of corporate bond issuers to evaluate the issuers' creditworthiness and then makes buy-hold-sell recommendations. Also, credit analysts in a company assign a proprietary bond credit rating to corporate bond issuers—for use within the financial institution only.

An *equity analyst,* also called a *stock analyst,* studies issuers of stock, evaluates the issuers' expected future growth, and then makes buy-hold-sell recommendations.

A *real-estate analyst* within the investment operation studies the real estate markets and evaluates income-producing properties in order to (1) make buy-hold-sell recommendations, (2) estimate market values of properties, or (3) evaluate commercial mortgage investments.

An *industry analyst* studies the economic and financial prospects of an industry and evaluates the industry's prospects for growth.

Due-diligence analysts evaluate issuers of securities—specifically investment companies and investment management companies—and externally managed investment funds to ensure that these parties can reasonably be expected to meet their objectives or perform their functions.

Organization of the Investment Function

Insurance companies make a variety of arrangements for their investment function, as follows:

- Some insurance companies operate the investment function in a department within the company. Such insurance companies sometimes obtain specialized investment management services from external sources.

- Some insurance companies formerly had an internal investment department, but years ago they established it as a separate company that retains a corporate affiliation with the insurance company. In these cases, the separate investment management company performs most investment services for the insurance company, while providing these services to other clients also.

- Some insurance companies obtain most of their investment services from external providers—investment management companies—that have no past or current affiliation with the insurance company.

- Institutional investors provide services to one another in a variety of situations. In such arrangements, clients of institutional investors often are other financial institutions. Sometimes an institutional investor and its client company have a corporate affiliation. In other words, they are owned by the same holding company. Sometimes an institutional investor provides investment services to its parent corporation.

Example: Financial Holding Company

Algo Financial Group, a financial holding company, has several subsidiaries, including Algo Global Investment Management, Algo Life Insurance, and Algo General Insurance. Algo Global Investment Management performs the investment function for all other subsidiaries of Algo Financial—including Algo Life Insurance, and for clients that are not part of the Algo Financial family of companies.

Regardless of the client-and-provider relationships or corporate affiliations involved, investment operations themselves are similar across many types of institutions.

As illustrated in Figure 1.2, operations in the investment function are often divided into either (1) front- and back-office operations, or (2) front-, middle-, and back-office operations. Although industry professionals often refer to these concepts, each company has a unique organizational design. Here, we describe the typical understanding of these terms for the investment function:

■ *Front-office operations* typically comprise all investment administration operations that deal directly with the securities marketplace, trade negotiations, and trading securities. For control purposes, front-office operations have a separate chain of command from middle- and back-office operations. Investment administration functions encompass portfolio management, asset management, asset trading, portfolio analysis, and investment research. This usage contrasts with "front-office operations" in insurance administration, which deal directly with external customers.

■ When applicable, *middle-office operations* consist of trade-support operations, including investment forecasting, securities regulatory compliance, trade settlements, funds disbursement, investment risk management, and portfolio performance reporting. If investment operations are divided into only front- and back-office operations, then middle-office operations are classified instead as back-office operations.

■ Back-office operations differ on the basis of how the investment operations are divided. When investment operations consist of only front and back offices, *back-office operations* of the investment function encompass all operations other than the front-office operations. In a system that includes front, middle, and back offices, back-office operations all tie into the official company records, including investment accounting, investment reporting, investment information technology, data governance and security, and management of vendors.

Figure 1.2 Investment Operations in the Corporate Culture

This figure illustrates the usual schemes for naming operations within the investment function, as well as the division between true investment operations and other relevant operations that are not viewed as investment operations.

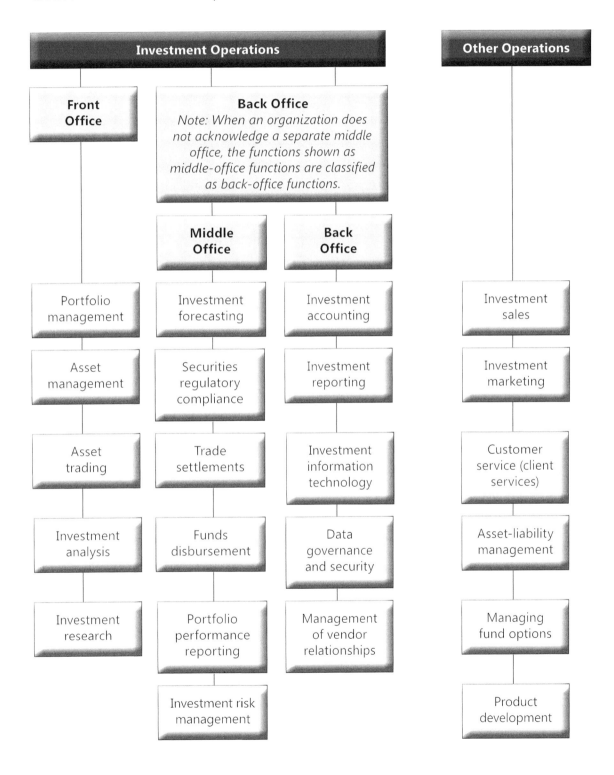

Investment Management Data and Software

Because investment data are complex, companies must merge information from multiple internal and external data sources. External databases provide financial data about issuers of securities; prices for publicly traded securities; complex cash flow projections for mortgage-backed securities; public credit ratings; and actions initiated by securities issuers, such as stock splits, spin-offs, and unscheduled debt prepayments. Typically, internal processing systems track accounting and credit data. Accounting data relevant to investment operations include account balances, costs, book values, coupon rates, dividend rates, maturity dates, and projected cash flows. Credit data relevant to investment operations include nonpublic credit ratings, credit watch data, and compliance data.

Investment software refers to several types of investment information systems:

- *Investment accounting information systems* support general ledger processing, reporting to clients, and compliance with internal and external financial controls. Such systems also generate sales proposals to institutional clients.

- *Trade management systems*, also known as *order management systems*, are associated with trading platforms and support the processes of trade initiation, trade execution, and transaction recording. These systems allow traders to monitor and execute trades online in real time.

- *Risk management and analysis systems* support the processes for risk management, asset analysis, asset-liability management, scenario analysis, and portfolio performance measurement and analysis. Many risk analysis systems are dedicated to a single asset class.

Units That Interact with the Investment Function

Many functional areas within an insurance company interact with and provide important support to the investment function. Although these activities are critical to the success of the investment function, they are not typically part of the investment function.

Treasury Operations and Cash Management

The treasury function is an essential company financial function responsible for managing a company's cash resources and maintaining them at needed levels. A company's treasury function is usually separate from the investment function, although the two functions must be closely coordinated. Cash management activities include cash forecasting, bank relations, and bank account administration, as well as short-term lending and borrowing activities. Cash forecasting involves tracking and predicting the movement of money into and out of the company.

Product Development

Product development in life insurance companies requires bringing together a broad team of professionals, including actuaries and investment professionals. To create a product's financial design, this team requires information from an investment professional. Investment professionals also participate in product planning and development to support long-term matching of assets and liabilities—that is, identifying asset classes available to match the characteristics of a given insurance product. Investment professionals also must evaluate any product design assumptions involving the assets backing a product.

Investment Marketing

A company's investment marketing function is responsible primarily for the marketing and sales of investment services. Thus, the investment marketing function provides marketing support for the investment function. In performing this function, it relies heavily on information provided by investment professionals working within the investment function. A company's sales representatives frequently make presentations designed to (1) place the company's message in front of potential institutional investment clients or (2) convince the potential institutional investment clients to select the company as their provider for investment management services.

When an insurance company's sales representatives communicate with potential institutional investment clients, they use marketing materials such as those found on their company's website, in brochures, and in advertisements. Marketers also communicate detailed data about selling points, such as records of successful investment performance. Staff in an investment marketing communications unit may also support training programs for an institutional investment product. For example, the insurance company educates its own sales staff or the institutional investment client's staff about the operation of a guaranteed investment contract (GIC).

In addition, an investment marketing communications unit develops all of the information for use in product or service descriptions and promotional information about the company's institutional investment management services. The unit then develops, produces, and helps to distribute the communications pieces. A unit within client communications prepares all responses to requests for proposal (RFPs) from potential clients.

Sales representatives connected with the insurance company's investment marketing operation pursue new institutional clients. Sales representatives in a life insurance company's investment marketing operation typically specialize in consultant relations or the broker-dealer distribution channel.

Consultant Relations. Many large insurance companies or their investment management affiliates provide investment management services to retirement plans and similar financial institutions that do not perform these functions internally.

These client institutions, including employee retirement plan sponsors, public pension funds, and union funds, hire consultants to advise them in their relationship with the insurance company or other service provider. These consultants typically come from employee benefits consulting firms, actuarial consulting firms, or accounting firms. These consultants strongly influence the client's choice of an investment services provider.

For providing service to these institutional clients, companies often have a type of investment marketing unit, sometimes known as a *consultant relations unit*. A consultant relations unit can be a part of an insurance company's sales unit. The consultant relations unit is responsible for maintaining close ties with employee benefits and retirement plan consultants, both during a sales opportunity and after a sale has been closed.

Broker-Dealer Distribution. Some insurance companies distribute their investment products and services through a broker-dealer to the broker-dealer's retail clients. A *broker-dealer* is a financial institution that buys and sells securities either for itself or for its customers and provides information and advice to customers regarding the purchase and sale of securities. Such a distribution effort is sometimes classified as broker-dealer distribution or third-party distribution. For insurance companies with such programs, a broker-dealer distribution unit presents the company's marketing message to broker-dealers who are interested in offering the company's services to their retail clients. This unit offers sales support to the broker-dealers affiliated with the insurance company.

Customer Service

Companies employ customer service representatives (CSRs) to answer questions, provide information, suggest new solutions, and help customers initiate or complete a variety of transactions after a product is sold. Some CSRs handle sales as well as service, and such CSRs must be properly registered to sell securities. CSRs who provide service on behalf of investment-type products are not necessarily part of the investment function.

Investment Types and Concepts

Institutional investors make a wide variety of investments in various assets. *Assets* are things of value that are owned. An asset class is a grouping of assets having similar risk and return characteristics, such as stocks, bonds, or real estate. Some assets, such as real estate, may be owned directly. For example, a company can purchase an office building.

Stocks and bonds, along with derivatives, are types of financial securities. A *financial security* can be (1) an equity security, which is an ownership interest in a business, (2) a debt security, which is an obligation of indebtedness owed by a business, a government, or an agency, or (3) a derivative security, as we discuss shortly.

An equity security, such as a share of common stock, provides evidence of the equity holder's ownership share in the issuing company. To grow and maintain their businesses, corporations and other business entities issue stocks to sell equity stakes and use bonds to borrow funds. A debt security, such as a bond, provides evidence of the owner's financial interest in a loan made to the issuer of the security. For a bond, the investor has legal recourse to seek satisfaction of the debt. A debt holder's claim on assets in the event of the debt issuer's financial distress is superior to any equity holder's position.

Examples: Securities

Stocks are equity securities. Stocks are issued by corporations, such as Wal-Mart, PepsiCo, Volkswagen, Apple, and Starbucks.

Bonds are debt securities. They are issued by governments, government agencies, and corporations.

Investments can also be classified as fixed-income investments, equity investments, derivative securities, and hybrid securities.

Fixed-income investments typically provide a predictable stream of income. Fixed-income investments include bonds, mortgages, mortgage-backed securities, and some types of equity investments.

Equity investments represent ownership of assets. Equity investments typically include ownership of common stock, real estate, commodities, limited partnerships, joint ventures, and private equity investments. ***Commodities*** are primary products traded in bulk on commodities exchanges or in spot markets and comprising natural resources that have been mined or extracted—such as metals, coal, and petroleum—and agricultural products and livestock—such as grains, coffee, sugar, orange juice, and pork.

Derivative securities are financial securities that derive their values from other securities. One type of derivative security, an *option*, provides an investor with an opportunity to buy or sell another security at a specified price for a specified period of time. Insurance companies typically use derivatives to manage their risk exposures. Types of derivatives include put and call options, swaps, futures, rights, and warrants.

Hybrid securities are financial securities having characteristics of both equity and debt securities. Examples are preferred stock and convertible bonds.

Securities are also classified as public or private, depending on how they were issued. Specifically, methods of offering newly issued securities for sale are classified as public offerings or private placements:

- A ***public offering*** of securities is a method of issuing securities in which they are sold to the public, usually through the services of an investment banking firm. Securities sold in this manner are often called *public securities, public stocks, public equities,* or *public bonds.*

- A ***private placement*** of securities is a method of issuing securities in which the issuer sells the entire issue directly to one or more qualified investors. Securities sold in this manner are often called *private placement securities,* such as *private placement stocks, private equities,* or *private placement bonds.* An institutional investor in private placements can potentially earn a higher return than would be available from investing only in public securities. Private placement bonds tend to put more requirements on the borrower than do otherwise comparable public bonds.

Equities

Insurance companies own equities in the forms of stocks, real estate, and venture capital. Owners of stocks, referred to as *stockholders* or *shareholders*, can earn returns in two forms: dividend income, and, if the stock is sold for more than its original purchase price, the difference between the selling price and the purchase price. Insurance companies hold stock mainly in their separate account portfolios, where the stock supports variable products and retirement account deposits. Insurance companies also hold publicly traded stock in the general account.

Real estate assets consist of real property, buildings, and fixtures on the property. Insurance companies often own their office buildings. Some institutional investors invest directly in other commercial real estate, for the purposes of earning rental income or selling the property at a price higher than the purchase price, or both. Real estate generally is considered to be an equity investment. Although most equity investments are not classified as fixed-income investments, some institutions classify real estate held for producing rental income as a fixed-income investment.

Venture capital refers to an investment of capital in a new and usually risky enterprise. Institutions invest most venture capital funds in private equities in the medical, technology, and retail sectors. A potentially high return on private equity investments balances the high investment risks these ventures represent.

Bonds

As debt securities, bonds represent loans made by the purchaser of the bond to the issuer of the bond. We discuss bonds in greater depth in Chapter 8.

An insurance company purchases bonds to earn the steady investment returns needed to meet future obligations to customers. The bond issuer generally makes interest payments on a regular schedule and then repays the original loan value of the bond on a specified maturity date.

Bonds are usually issued by corporations or governments. Bonds issued by corporations are called **corporate bonds**. **Government bonds** are bonds issued by governments. Governmental issuers of bonds include federal, sovereign, state, provincial, county, city, and other local governments, and local government agencies or projects. In the United States, federal government bonds are usually classified as Treasury bonds or agency bonds, depending on the issuer. States, counties, cities, local government agencies, and other local governments issue municipal bonds.

Some bonds are traded in public bond markets, whereas others—private placement bonds—are placed directly between a lending institution and a borrowing corporation.

Mortgages

Mortgages are a type of long-term, fixed-income investment. A **mortgage** is a loan secured by a pledge of specified real property. Institutional investors may hold large commercial mortgages in whole, or they may own shares in portfolios of residential or commercial mortgages. We discuss mortgages and mortgage-related investments in Chapter 9.

Accounting Classifications for Assets

To organize a company's assets into a meaningful order for accounting records, the company assigns its assets to various classifications.

The following asset classifications are used in accounting for invested assets:

- *Short-term assets* (*current assets*) consist of cash and assets that a company expects to convert to cash within one year. Short-term assets are also sometimes called *liquid assets. Liquidity* refers to the ease with which an asset can be converted into cash for an approximation of its true value. Short-term assets include cash and cash equivalents.

- *Long-term assets* (*noncurrent assets*) are those that a company expects to hold for more than one year. Any asset, such as a stock or bond, that an investor plans to hold for more than a year is a long-term asset.

- **Tangible assets** have physical form. Examples of tangible assets include cash, real estate, automobiles, collectibles, commodities, equipment, and machinery.

- **Intangible assets** represent ownership of a legal right or another nonphysical resource. Important examples of intangible assets are securities, patents, copyrights, computer software, leases, and licenses.

- In the United States, *admitted assets* are assets for which the full value may be reported on the Assets page of an insurance company's Annual Statement. Assets may be admitted in full or in part.

- In the United States, *nonadmitted assets* are assets for which no value may be reported on the Assets page of an insurance company's Annual Statement.

Note that a specified asset can be assigned to several different classifications. For example, a short-term asset is either tangible or intangible. Figure 1.3 presents examples of asset classifications.

Figure 1.3 Asset Classifications

	Tangible	Debt	Equity
Stocks	✗	✗	✓
Bonds	✗	✓	✗
Mortgages	✗	✓	✗
Direct real estate investments	✓	✗	✓

Yes = ✓   No = ✗

Capital Markets

Capital markets are the aggregate of all marketplaces, participants, and activities that move funding in a given economic system from net suppliers of capital to net users of capital. Stock markets and bond markets are components of capital markets. (*Capital* has a number of potential meanings. In this context, we're discussing financial capital.) Households and businesses can participate as suppliers of funds in the capital markets.

In the aggregate, households are net suppliers of funds to capital markets. Financial services sold to individuals and households are classified as *retail* financial products. When households and individuals purchase retail financial services or products, these entities are supplying funds to capital markets.

Examples: Retail Financial Products That Provide Funds to Capital Markets

Mutual fund shares
Certificates of deposit
Life insurance policies
Disability income policies
Retirement savings accounts
Retirement income accounts
Accumulation and payout annuities

Although businesses overall are users of capital, some businesses supply funds to the capital markets. For instance, some businesses enter into investment contracts supported by insurance companies and, thus, are clients of insurance companies.

■ Insurance companies provide investment support for employee benefits and retirement benefits through such products as guaranteed investment contracts, corporate-owned life insurance, and bank-owned life insurance arrangements.

■ Insurance companies, through their investment products and services, support current income and wealth accumulation for endowment funds.

■ Insurance companies provide investment contracts to support lottery payouts and structured settlements.

In the role of capital market suppliers, institutional investors first gather funds from many households, retirement funds, and businesses. Then, through investment activities, institutional investors move the supply of funds into the capital markets.

By supplying funds to capital markets, institutional investors provide an important service to the global economy: they move available funding from the economic units that supply capital to the economic units where capital is needed for productive projects. The scale of these combined institutional investing activities is vast, as illustrated in Figure 1.4.

Figure 1.4 Economic Scale of Assets Held by Financial Institutions

Our bar chart shows the economic scale of assets held in various countries by financial institutions—including banks, insurance companies, and other institutions—compared to those countries' gross domestic product (GDP). The chart reflects 2010 data for several large member countries of the Organisation for Economic Co-operation and Development. (A number of important countries are not members of this organization.)

In several cases, the assets held by financial institutions are far greater than the country's annual production. For several countries on this list, the scale of capital considerably exceeds the country's GDP.

2010 Total Institutional Assets as a Percentage of Gross Domestic Product (GDP)

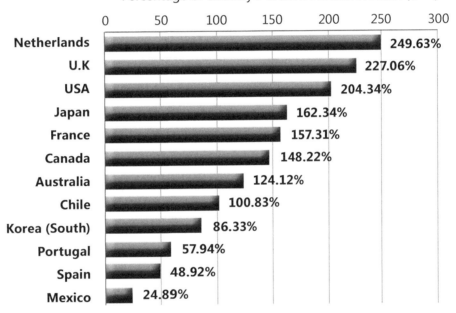

Percentage of Country's Gross Domestic Product (GDP)

Country	Percentage
Netherlands	249.63%
U.K	227.06%
USA	204.34%
Japan	162.34%
France	157.31%
Canada	148.22%
Australia	124.12%
Chile	100.83%
Korea (South)	86.33%
Portugal	57.94%
Spain	48.92%
Mexico	24.89%

Source: Based on data from OECD (2012), OECD.Stat Extracts, (database). doi: 10.1787/data-00285-en (2 July 2012). © OECD. Used with permission.

An Overview of Capital Market Transactions

As background for understanding a capital market transaction, first we consider the elements present in any purchase-and-sale transaction. In such a generic market transaction, the two parties to the transaction are a seller and a buyer. Sellers interact with buyers, and the parties exchange items of value:

- Typically, a seller provides a good, service, or financial security, and obtains funds from a buyer.

- A buyer parts with funds and obtains a good, service, or a financial security from a seller.

A generic market transaction may have support from such facilitators as a sales representative, an auction forum, a retail outlet, an appraiser, and others. Figure 1.5 illustrates a generic marketplace transaction and a transaction in a bond market.

Example: Corporate Bond Market Transaction

In a bond sale and purchase through a public bond market, a corporation retains an investment bank and, through the services of the bank, issues and sells bonds to a bond purchaser. The bond seller promises to pay the bonds' face amount in the future and to pay interest periodically. The bonds' original purchaser in effect provides funds to the seller. A bond purchaser, also called a bondholder, exchanges the current use of money for the bond seller's future repayment of the bonds' face amount and regular interest payments.

Several parties typically take part in such a transaction. An investment bank underwrites the bond issue. A broker-dealer may take part in making the sale. A custodian might hold the bond certificates and record the transfer of ownership. A settlement service might hold the purchaser's funds for disbursement until the ownership of the bond certificates has been recorded and potentially after the bond certificates have been delivered.

Figure 1.5 Capital Market Transactions

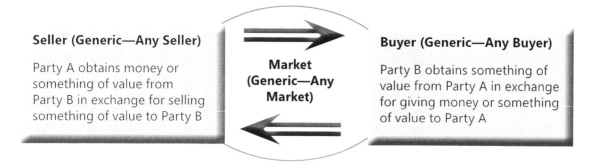

Seller (Generic—Any Seller)

Party A obtains money or something of value from Party B in exchange for selling something of value to Party B

Market (Generic—Any Market)

Buyer (Generic—Any Buyer)

Party B obtains something of value from Party A in exchange for giving money or something of value to Party A

Example: Bond Market Transaction

Seller: Corporation

Dynamic Equipment Company needs funds to build a new manufacturing plant, so the company issues and sells bonds to investors through the bond market.

Bond

Bond Market

Cash

Buyer: Bond Purchaser

Pleasant Life Insurance Company needs high-quality corporate bonds to back its life insurance products. The insurer purchases bonds in the bond market.

Capital Market Participants

Capital markets represent a complex marketplace where users of capital enter into transactions with suppliers of capital, as depicted in Figure 1.6. Capital markets perform an important role by rationing scarce supplies of available funds and providing those funds to users of capital. Normally, investors seek a level of return consistent with the level of risk they perceive in an investment. (We discuss the importance of perceived risk and expected investment return in Chapter 4.) Investors generally prefer to invest in existing projects and organizations with a record of successful performance rather than in new or untried projects and organizations.

Capital markets include many different physical and virtual markets. Numerous specific entities represent each of the roles—capital market sellers, capital market facilitators, and capital market buyers.

- Capital market sellers include governments, government agencies, and business corporations, among others. They sell financial securities to capital market buyers in exchange for new funding. Capital market sellers compensate capital market buyers for use of the funds generated by sales of securities, typically by granting the buyer an ownership interest in a business venture or promising to repay the buyer with interest.

- *Capital market facilitators* consist of the securities exchanges and other mechanisms and forces that enable a buyer and seller to complete a securities transaction. Investment banks, broker-dealers, regulators, custodians of securities, and trade settlement agents participate in the issuance of new securities. Custodians of securities keep physical or virtual custody of securities, maintain controls, and keep a current inventory of an investor's securities owned. Settlement agents hold securities while a transaction is in process, ensuring that ownership is formally transferred from the seller to the purchaser only after the purchaser has tendered payment for the securities.

- Capital market buyers comprise mutual funds, hedge funds, insurance companies, banks, endowment funds, charitable trusts, retirement funds, pension plans, governments, and reinsurance companies. Overall, through their investment activities, these entities inject funds into the capital markets. As we stated earlier, individuals and households are investors, too, although households generally make retail investment transactions through financial services companies rather directly using capital market mechanisms themselves. Although insurance companies, mutual funds, retirement plans, and pension funds are institutional investors, they are investing for the benefit of individual investors. If an individual purchases shares in a mutual fund, the mutual fund must purchase securities for its portfolio.

Figure 1.6 Capital Market Roles

Capital Market Sellers	**Capital Market Mechanisms**	**Capital Market Buyers**
Governments	Securities exchanges	Banks
Government agencies	Securities broker-dealers	Mutual funds
Business corporations	Custodians	Insurance companies
	Settlement services	Hedge funds
	Rating agencies	Pension funds
	Regulators	Retirement funds
		Endowment funds
		Private wealth funds
		Sovereign wealth funds

Private rating agencies, although not direct capital market participants, use their proprietary standards to assign and publish a rating, grade, or score, to indicate how closely the rated entity fits their standards. The companies rated enter into agreements to undergo the rating process and permit publication of the ratings. The following types of external ratings agencies influence activity in capital markets:

■ Several private (nongovernmental) financial rating services, notably including Standard and Poor's (S&P) and Moody's, rate the credit quality of financial securities and their issuers. Issuers of securities pay for these ratings and agree for them to be published. Both buyers and sellers in an investment transaction are typically customers of the rating agencies. Institutional investors use these services for ratings of public securities.

■ Quality ratings of insurance companies are provided mostly by the same rating agencies that rate financial securities. These ratings are essential for companies to attract customers or sales producers. A company without a reasonably high rating finds it difficult to issue new business or keep existing business. Three areas considered in such assessments are capital position, customer service practices, and claims-paying ability.

■ Morningstar, Value Line, Lipper, and numerous other publishers analyze, rank, and rate mutual funds, providing summary information about their attributes. Investors in mutual funds generally consult these mutual fund ratings and the accompanying analysis as a partial basis for selecting a mutual fund. Insurance companies and other institutional investors use public ratings and analysis as resources for confirming their internal evaluations of external mutual funds.

- Within investing institutions, securities analysts perform proprietary analysis of investments securities and mutual funds. Such analysis is important for verifying the published ratings of public securities, when such ratings are available, and is critical for fully understanding the risks in private placement securities.

Path of Funds in the Investment Process

Let's follow the movement of an insurance customer's premium or deposit into the company, then into the investment process, and finally into the capital markets. Then, we examine the path of benefit payments or withdrawals to a customer in fulfillment of the company's contractual obligation as the funds come from the capital markets, back through the company, and finally to the customer.

As mentioned earlier, insurance companies generally operate a general account and separate accounts. The movement of funds through the investment process can differ markedly between products based on the general account or those based on a separate account. When managing the general account portfolio, insurance companies are acting on behalf of their own asset account. However, when managing a separate account portfolio, insurance companies are typically acting on behalf of their clients.

General Account

For the general account, the company bears the investment risk and also the risk attached to paying the insurance benefits or other product guarantees to customers. Products typically backed by general account assets include fully guaranteed life insurance or annuity products, individual universal life insurance products, fixed fund options under a variable product, or guaranteed minimum benefit riders under variable products. The general account supports all general obligations of the insurance company.

When a policyholder pays a premium for a fully guaranteed product, the money is usually invested through the company's general account. There, the company grows the money over time through investments. Although the customer has a claim against the company under an insurance or annuity contract, the customer does not own a unit share in the general account, and does not have a direct interest in the financial success of general account investments.

After a customer's premium is in the company's accounts, the company uses the funds to purchase assets for the general account. The company's front-office investment operations undertake a number of steps to accomplish the purchase or sale of securities. Insurance companies and other institutional investors may make trades directly or place orders through a securities broker. Asset trades typically incur transaction fees.

After the company reaches an agreement to purchase securities, the seller of securities provides a written confirmation of the agreement. Then the insurance company arranges to transfer a payment to the seller or the securities to a purchaser.

For most institutional trades, a *settlement agent*, also known as a *clearance agent*, is the external service provider who transfers the payment of funds and the ownership of securities.

Similarly, for some institutional trades, a *custodian* is the external service provider that holds any physical certificates and makes arrangements for their transfer. In most cases, however, a separate institution known as a *clearinghouse* holds the physical stock certificates on deposit for institutional investors. These certificates are held in *street name*—the name of a broker or other nominee—rather than in the name of the investor who actually owns the stock.

Insurance policy benefits eventually become payable, and the company draws from the general account to pay those benefits. Sometimes, incoming cash flows from investments can fund outgoing cash payments of benefits. Other times, the company may sell noncash assets in the capital markets to raise cash to fund the benefit payments.

The movements of a customer's funds into and out of a general account are illustrated in Figure 1.7. Because the general account is an asset account, this chart reflects only the assets side of the balance sheet; it does not illustrate the reserves associated with the assets. Each movement of assets typically has a corresponding accounting entry affecting the company's reserves or capital or both.

Separate Accounts

Traditionally, a separate account is an asset account designated for supporting an insurance company's financial products for which the performance is linked to investment results. The customer, not the company, directly bears the investment risk for assets held in these accounts. Some traditional distinctions between the general and separate account have evolved recently, however, and continue to evolve.

The term "separate account" is primarily used in the United States. Products for which performance is linked to investment results and that are supported by specific assets are sometimes referred to as a segregated fund, in Canada, or a unit-linked portfolio in many other countries. For this course, the term "separate account" also refers to its non-U.S. counterparts, including *segregated fund* and *unit-linked portfolio.*

When the owner of a variable contract pays a premium into a variable fund option, the money is invested with the company's separate account assets. For an individual separate account product, the customer typically elects one of several fund options wherein the customer typically bears the investment risk on the assets. In these cases, the company sets up an account specific to the customer, and the customer has a direct interest in the fund assets. The company tracks the market value of the assets attributable to the specified customer, and the customer's account value rises or falls according to the market value of a specified portfolio or portfolios. A variable product may have contractual guarantees that cushion a customer's direct experience of investment risk.

Under variable account products, the company is typically obligated to pay benefits in the form of surrender benefits, withdrawal benefits, loans, death benefits, survivor benefits, and potentially other benefits. Typically, the benefit amount depends directly on the value of the assets in the customer's account.

Eventually, when the benefits come due, the company draws funds from the separate account assets to pay the benefits.

Figure 1.7 General Account Movements of Funds

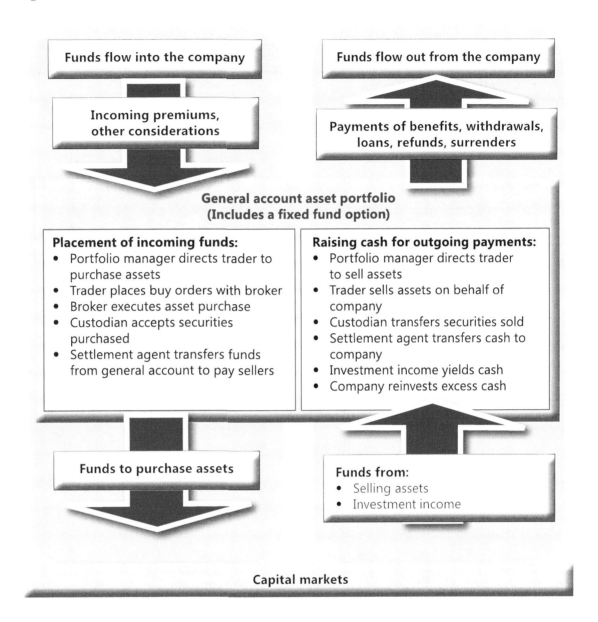

The movements of a customer's funds into and out of a separate account are illustrated in Figure 1.8. (This flow chart does not illustrate the reserves associated with the assets.)

Figure 1.8 Separate Account Movements of Funds

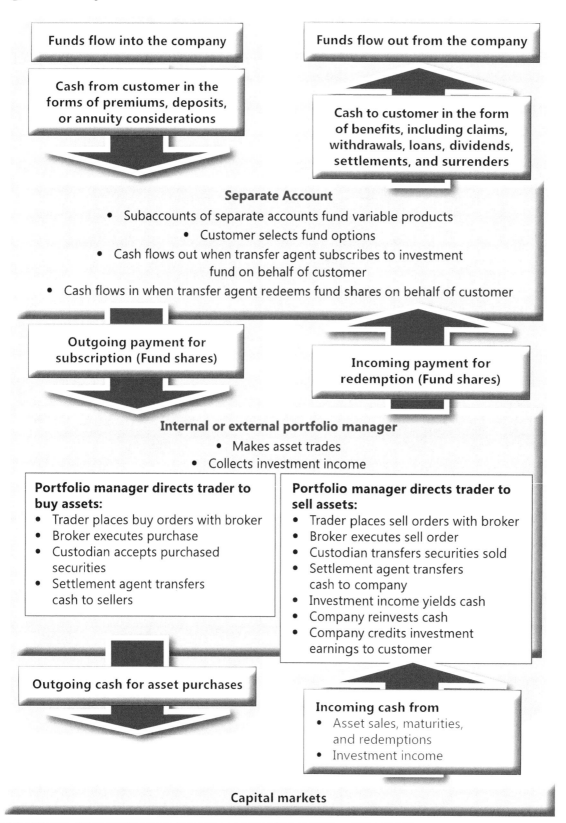

Funds flow into the company

Cash from customer in the forms of premiums, deposits, or annuity considerations

Funds flow out from the company

Cash to customer in the form of benefits, including claims, withdrawals, loans, dividends, settlements, and surrenders

Separate Account
- Subaccounts of separate accounts fund variable products
  - Customer selects fund options
- Cash flows out when transfer agent subscribes to investment fund on behalf of customer
- Cash flows in when transfer agent redeems fund shares on behalf of customer

Outgoing payment for subscription (Fund shares)

Incoming payment for redemption (Fund shares)

Internal or external portfolio manager
- Makes asset trades
- Collects investment income

Portfolio manager directs trader to buy assets:
- Trader places buy orders with broker
- Broker executes purchase
- Custodian accepts purchased securities
- Settlement agent transfers cash to sellers

Portfolio manager directs trader to sell assets:
- Trader places sell orders with broker
- Broker executes sell order
- Custodian transfers securities sold
- Settlement agent transfers cash to company
- Investment income yields cash
- Company reinvests cash
- Company credits investment earnings to customer

Outgoing cash for asset purchases

Incoming cash from
- Asset sales, maturities, and redemptions
- Investment income

Capital markets

Investment Goals and Investment Portfolios

As we have seen, business organizations, households, and individuals rely on institutional investors to pursue specific financial goals on the customers' behalf. An institutional investor's portfolio is also designed and constructed to support specific investment goals. Typically, these goals include wealth accumulation and preservation of principal.

Various types of institutions have characteristic investment goals.

■ Life insurance companies invest to provide financial security to their customers. Insurance companies must accumulate funds over many years to support the benefits provided under life insurance policies, annuity contracts, retirement funding contracts, long-term disability and long-term care policies, and structured settlement contracts. Under many of these products, one investment objective is to build wealth, and another is to preserve the value of assets already accumulated.

■ Property and casualty (P&C) insurance companies, also known as general insurance companies, provide financial protection against various risks to property. P&C insurance companies invest on a shorter-term basis than do life insurance companies

■ Pension funds accumulate funding for future payouts of pension liabilities. These funds focus on capital preservation and income accumulation.

■ Retirement funds invest to preserve the principal value of the fund and accumulate wealth for individuals at the end of their working years.

■ College endowment funds invest to sustain an educational institution beyond the lifetime of current students and alumni by building wealth and providing income for the institution.

■ Charitable foundations sustain a social program beyond the lifetime of the founder. To do so, their investments must grow the value of the endowment and generate current income.

■ Sovereign funds invest to build and sustain government services and public infrastructure over many years.

Regulation Affecting the Investment Function

All investments are heavily influenced by securities regulation. Insurance company investments are also affected by insurance regulation. Investments on behalf of retirement products are sometimes affected by regulations designed to protect investments for retirement accounts.

■ Securities regulators, acting to maintain orderly financial markets, provide oversight and rules regarding the issuance of securities. The primary objective of securities regulation is to require the disclosure of full and accurate information needed to protect investors against fraud.

- Insurance regulators, acting in the interest of insurance policyholders, focus on safeguarding the overall financial health of insurance companies to protect policyholders. The primary objective of insurance regulation is to ensure fulfillment of the insurance companies' obligations.

Each government has defined which companies are considered insurance companies for regulatory purposes. These companies are subject to some form of supervision by insurance regulatory authorities. Typically, insurance companies are subject to insurance regulation as well as other regulations applicable to businesses in their relevant jurisdictions, sometimes including securities regulations.

The strength of securities regulation, regulatory oversight, and enforcement varies by jurisdiction.

Corporate Alignment, Governance, and Control for Investments

As we discuss at length later in this text, a company's investment function must be aligned with and support many other organizational initiatives. Companies have many required and voluntary provisions for ensuring that all company undertakings are directed toward common goals and objectives. These provisions include establishing the board of directors, oversight committees, and the organizational chain of command; strategic plans; corporate policies, including codes of conduct; controls, such as audits; regulations for public companies; and professional standards. Within this control structure, a number of management programs and systems are important, including enterprise risk management, asset-liability management, asset allocation, and portfolio management.

Enterprise Risk Management

Enterprise risk management (ERM) is a cross-functional and comprehensive management system for coordinating management of all corporate risks in a manner that supports the corporate mission and strategies. ERM requires practitioners to identify and quantify all potential threats and opportunities, because, for ERM, the definition of risk encompasses the potential for losses and gains. According to ERM, risk is any unexpected or unplanned outcome. ERM encompasses another risk management system focused on financial risks: asset-liability management.

Asset-Liability Management

Asset-liability management (ALM) is a cross-functional management system that many types of financial institutions, including life insurance companies, banks, and retirement plans, use to coordinate the risks that simultaneously affect the company's investments and products. ALM practice acknowledges that risks can interact so that their total impact is greater than the sum of their parts.

The purpose of ALM is to make sure that the company always has enough cash to pay all obligations on time, remains solvent, and avoids potential negative financial outcomes. Having enough cash to pay all obligations (liabilities) on time requires a company to have sufficient financial liquidity at all times. The ultimate purposes of ALM are to guard against financial failure and take advantage of opportunities to safely enhance earnings.

ALM is not equally important for all products of insurance companies. For instance, ALM has less importance for coordinating the assets and liabilities of inactive blocks of policies purchased from other companies. Similarly, ALM has less importance for fully reinsured blocks of business, or for separate account products for which all investment risk is passed directly to the customer.

In performing ALM roles, investment and actuarial professionals attempt to achieve a pattern of investment funds flows that will, along with other funds flows, ensure that the company's cash on hand always remains equal to or greater than its outflows of funds.

Example: Roles of Professionals in ALM

Product actuaries involved in ALM for a financial services company focus on properly designing a product so fund flows from assets will be available to support the product.

Investment professionals involved in ALM for a financial services company focus on meeting current demands for cash and investing incoming funds in a manner that supports meeting future demands for funds.

Asset Allocation

Asset allocation, also known as *asset mix*, is the percentage distribution of all portfolio holdings across a specified array of asset classes, such as various sub-categories of stocks and bonds. The asset allocation for any portfolio reflects the objectives and philosophy of the portfolio, as well as financial market conditions. A portfolio manager is responsible for maintaining an appropriate asset allocation.

Example: Asset Allocation

Meteor Total Return Fund is a mutual fund that seeks preservation of capital and maximum returns consistent with a conservative approach to taking risk. Accordingly, Meteor Total Return Fund's assets are allocated in the following proportions to fixed-income securities, equities, and cash:

Fixed-Income Securities	55%
Equities	40%
Cash	5%

In some cases, regulations affect an insurer's asset allocation. For the general account of a life insurance company, regulation strongly influences asset allocation.

Example: Regulatory Requirements Affecting Asset Allocation

In many jurisdictions, insurance companies are permitted to invest no more than a specified percentage of their investments in certain types of securities. Insurance companies are prohibited from investing at all in some indicated types of securities.

A company—when initially constructing a portfolio—purchases assets in specified proportions, according to a planned asset allocation. Over time, after the initial portfolio assets are purchased, market conditions and the values and proportions of portfolio assets change. As time passes, the effort of maintaining a given asset allocation continues. Accordingly, the company periodically takes action to return the portfolio to the required asset allocation.

Portfolio Management

In investments, ***portfolio management*** is the administration of investment policy, strategy, and operations for a specified asset portfolio. Portfolio management includes making decisions about risk, return, and asset allocation, for example. A portfolio manager's work may also involve coordinating the activities of other investment professionals.

Key Terms

institutional investor

trader

portfolio manager

asset-liability manager

analyst

fixed-income investment

equity investment

commodities

derivative security

hybrid security

public offering

private placement

real estate asset

venture capital

corporate bond

government bond

mortgage

tangible asset

intangible asset

capital market

enterprise risk management (ERM)

asset-liability management (ALM)

asset allocation

portfolio management

Endnote

1. Some of the material in this section is based on Patricia Wilson Fridley (Senior Advisor, Center for Financial Stability, LLC), e-mail message to author, 29 September 2011. Used with permission.

Chapter 2

Regulation and Standardization

Objectives

After studying this chapter, you should be able to

2A   Describe the effects on institutional investors of broad and sustained trends toward consolidation, convergence, globalization, and standardization, and identify new opportunities from global expansion of trade

2B   Identify and describe features of a system for governmental regulation of financial services activities, including statutes, administrative agencies, regulations, courts, and branches of government affecting institutional investors

2C   Identify the objectives of market conduct regulation—such as transparency, fiduciary standards, suitability requirements, disclosure regulations, and privacy protection requirements— as well as the objectives of solvency regulation

2D   Describe how companies can proactively manage the risk of changing regulatory requirements and standards

2E   Identify and describe the impact of the federal regulation of securities in the United States on institutional investment activities, with reference to the Securities and Exchange Commission and securities laws

2F   Describe state regulation of insurance as it pertains to the investment activities of insurance companies in the United States, with reference to important model laws and regulations

2G   Describe provincial and territorial regulation of securities in Canada

2H   Describe financial system regulation in the European Union

2I   Describe international non-governmental initiatives affecting institutional investors

Outline

Trends Affecting Regulation and Institutional Investors
- Consolidation and Convergence
- Globalization
- Standardization

Elements of Governmental Regulatory Systems
- Administrative Agencies in Financial Regulation
- Laws and Regulations Affecting Institutional Investors

Objectives of Financial Services Regulation
- Objectives of Market Conduct Regulation
- Objectives of Solvency Regulation

Institutional Investors and Government Relations

Securities Regulation in the United States
- Federal Securities Laws
- Registration of Securities and Market Participants
- Conduct Rules
- Supervision and Record Keeping
- Corporate Reporting and Control
- Proxy Statement Filings
- Forms of Investment Companies
- State Securities Regulation
- State Regulation of Investments of Insurance Companies

Securities Regulation in Canada

Financial System Supervision for the European Union

Nongovernmental Initiatives Affecting Institutional Investors
- Organizations Based in Europe
- Organizations with Roots in the United Nations

Securities and financial services everywhere are highly regulated in an effort to support public confidence in these industries, as well as in the broader economy. Countries and other jurisdictions—including provinces, states, territories, and offshore financial districts—have laws, regulations, regulatory agencies, and courts that support the orderly conduct of securities transactions, insurance, and banking. International advisory boards recommend voluntary standardization initiatives that support consistent rules or regulatory frameworks applicable to a specified industry. Recommendations from these international advisory boards are then disseminated around the globe for local adoption. In turn, many jurisdictions incorporate these standards into their laws and regulations.

For these reasons, an understanding of the financial regulatory environment is critical to an understanding of institutional investing. This chapter is about regulation and standardization as they affect institutional investing.

Trends Affecting Regulation and Institutional Investors

Several broad trends—consolidation, convergence, globalization, and standardization—influence regulation of institutional investors. As financial institutions combine into ever larger organizations, enter into new businesses that may be regulated as a different industry, and conduct business across political boundaries, regulation also evolves.

Consolidation and Convergence

Traditionally, the financial services industry has had three sectors: securities, insurance, and banking. Historically, many smaller businesses engaged in only one of those sectors and faced separate regulatory systems. Now, after more than a decade of pursuing consolidation and convergence, considerably fewer, but larger, corporations, all doing business in more than one sector, dominate the financial services industry. *Consolidation* refers to the combination of financial services institutions within or across sectors. *Convergence* refers to a breakdown of traditional distinctions between sectors of the financial services industry, so that the formerly distinct financial sectors have become less distinct. The broad trends toward consolidation and convergence also extend to initiatives to blend disparate regulatory requirements for the major financial industry sectors.

In practice, regulatory systems focused on a functional separation between financial sectors tend to impose inconsistent requirements across sectors.

- Insurance regulators emphasize disclosure of information that is necessary to verify the solvency of an insurer, whereas securities regulators emphasize disclosure of information necessary to evaluate a business that is expected to continue indefinitely into the future.

- Sales representatives face drastically different disclosure requirements and standards of conduct in the different financial services industry sectors.

- Financial services companies may be required to hold reserves or report asset values on a specified accounting basis—one that is specific to a given financial sector. The accounting basis of financial reporting requirements differs between sectors.

- In some cases, an insurance product and a substantially similar banking product face different capital requirements for the issuer and differing tax treatments for the customer.

- Determining which regulatory agency or agencies have jurisdiction over a given business situation can be problematic.

One common regulatory response to uneven regulation of the industry sectors has been to provide an umbrella type of financial services authority for coordinating the regulation of all three sectors. Several jurisdictions have established a combined financial services regulatory agency, and many more have enacted new laws aimed at cross-sector coordination.

Globalization

Another sustained trend in financial services and other businesses is *globalization*: the increasing potential for businesses to communicate, conduct trade, and move funds with relative freedom across political boundaries. When an institutional investor expands into other countries, each with a unique regulatory environment, the investor's compliance challenges proliferate. To address some of the challenges that companies face in doing business across many political boundaries, important policymaking organizations at the global level support standardization in many areas of regulation and commerce.

When an institutional investor conducts business in a new host country, the investor encounters opportunities as well as challenges. Geographic expansion spreads a company's exposure to geographic risks and currency risk. However, geographic expansion increases a company's total exposure to geopolitical risks. Geographic expansion may permit an institutional investor to gain access to markets with strong potential growth, but in areas with limited infrastructure. In new areas, companies can find customers who have the same financial needs—financing retirement and college educations—as do customers in their traditional areas of operations. Moreover, the company could discover new opportunities, as described in Figure 2.1.

When expanding into a new country, investors need adequate—and, ideally, equal—protection under the local regulatory and enforcement systems. In many host countries, multinational companies find it difficult to obtain fair and equal treatment under local courts and laws. Similarly, investors need reliable lines of communication, as well as reliable credit information from the host country.

Countries and other jurisdictions interested in attracting business activity from outside their political boundaries typically develop regulatory structures that better facilitate business globalization. In making these changes, countries may take guidance from influential national and international policy advisory groups.

Figure 2.1 New Opportunities from Globalization

When financial services companies grow by global expansion, they discover many opportunities, including

- A market need for an entirely new product or service that revolutionizes their future business prospects
- The opportunity to diversify their product portfolio
- A lower labor cost in a new region, potentially giving the company a lower cost of doing business
- An expanded talent pool
- Potential higher demand for product types that are not popular in their home market
- Opportunities to share growth through alliances, joint ventures, or mergers
- The chance to be the first to market in the host country with an impressive new feature
- New opportunities to diversify the institutional investor's portfolio

When financial services companies grow by global expansion, they can also face new risks, such as

- Increased compliance challenges and costs
- Political risk
- Currency risk
- Limited infrastructure in host countries
- Difficulty obtaining fair and equal treatment from regulators, laws, and courts

Standardization

Globalization has been accompanied by a broad trend toward increased standardization. *Standardization* in business consists of a general agreement as to measures, regulations, or specifications designed to achieve an optimum degree of order or uniformity. In theory, standards are helpful when all users can benefit from consistency with all other users of the standard. Figure 2.2 shows examples of standards affecting institutional investors.

Associations of financial professionals, organizations concerned with technology and communications, and organizations recommending global financial policy often set voluntary standards that affect institutional investors. Global standards for professionals in a given profession can help overcome gaps in regulation.

Standardization extends to standards for various aspects of regulation and governance in the financial system. In recent years, principles-based laws incorporate external standards and require adherence to them. In this manner, standards that began as voluntary regulation have become mandatory.

Figure 2.2 Standards Affecting Institutional Investors

Codes of Conduct

- Professional standards of practice and codes of conduct for accountants and actuaries

- A voluntary code of conduct and a code of ethics for investment professionals

- In the United States, market conduct requirements established by the National Association of Insurance Commissioners (NAIC)

- In the United States, a standard of fiduciary duty established under the Employee Retirement Income Security Act (ERISA)

Accounting and Financial Reporting Standards

- Global Investment Performance Standards (GIPS), from the CFA Institute, for consistent reporting of portfolio performance results

- International Financial Reporting Standards (IFRS) from the International Accounting Standards Board (IASB). IFRS are intended to apply without regard to national boundaries.

- In the United States, generally accepted accounting principles (GAAP) from the Financial Accounting Standards Board (FASB) and statutory accounting practices from the NAIC

Elements of Governmental Regulatory Systems

Governmental regulatory systems for the financial services industry generally include statutes, regulations, administrative agencies, and courts.

- Statutes are laws enacted by the legislative branch of government. In many countries, the laws enacted by the legislative branch are compiled and organized into one or more collections of laws known as codes. Statutes typically authorize specific agencies to administer various aspects of the law, issue regulations, oversee conduct addressed in the law, settle disputes under the law, and interpret and enforce the law.

- Regulations are rules or orders that are issued by administrative agencies and that have the force and effect of law.

- Administrative agencies are departments within the executive branch of government.

- Courts are bodies of the judicial branch of government that adjudicate disputes, determine penalties or remedies, interpret statutes and regulations, and administer justice in accordance with the law.

In some cases, governments exercise another avenue of control over financial institutions. When the government has an ownership position in financial institutions, the government is positioned to exercise control directly, without intervention through a regulatory system. Licensing a company to sell products is another way that governments exercise control over companies.

Figure 2.3 illustrates the relationships between these typical elements of a regulatory system. Each political jurisdiction typically regulates corporations, commerce in general, and commerce in financial services.

Administrative Agencies in Financial Regulation

In each jurisdiction, various administrative agencies regulate specific areas of the law. Administrative agencies affecting institutional investing incorporate various descriptive titles, including *commission, ministry, office, department, authority,* and *bureau.* Administrative agencies affecting institutional investors typically include a monetary authority, a banking regulator, an insurance regulator, a securities regulator, a securities exchange regulator, a tax authority, and, in some jurisdictions, a cross-sector financial services regulator.

Examples: Insurance Regulatory Agencies

China Insurance Regulatory Commission (CIRC)

Insurance Regulatory Development Authority (IRDA; India)

National Insurance and Bonding Commission (*Comision Nacional de Seguros y Fianzas*; Mexico)

Examples: Banking Regulatory Agencies

China Bank Regulatory Commission

Bank Regulatory Authority of India

Figure 2.3 Elements of a Governmental Regulatory System

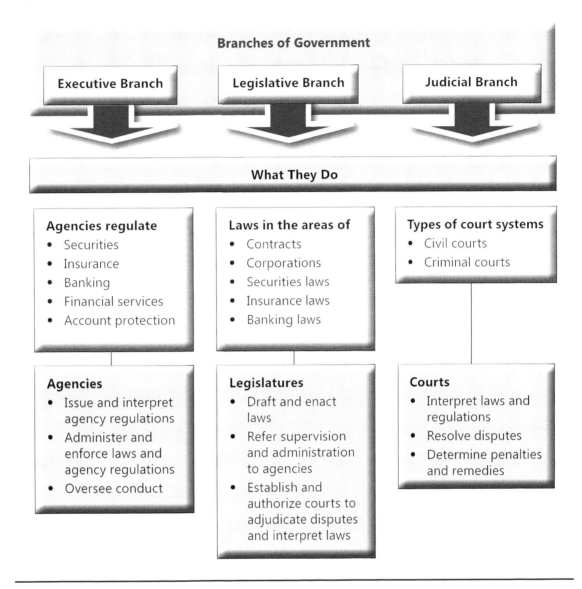

Regulatory authorities continually monitor activities under their jurisdiction to detect developing problems. When problems are detected, regulators can initiate preventive or corrective measures to protect the public interest. For example, financial services regulators are empowered to take over an impaired company and, if necessary, arrange for an orderly dissolution of the business.

When a financial services provider has failed, investors in some jurisdictions have recourse to a kind of financial account protection system designed to recover at least some portion of customer accounts. For securities accounts, protection of investor accounts in this manner generally addresses situations involving fraud and malfeasance, such as when an unauthorized person fraudulently converts funds from a customer's account to the fraudster's own use.

Examples: Investor Account Protection and Recovery Systems

Investor Protection Fund (Bombay Stock Exchange; India)

Canadian Investor Protection Fund (CIPF)

Securities Investor Protection Corporation (SIPC; United States)

Laws and Regulations Affecting Institutional Investors

Political jurisdictions typically have specific laws to address the broad areas of concern, including banking laws, insurance laws, securities laws, and financial services laws.

Financial regulation varies a great deal from one jurisdiction to another. Each political jurisdiction establishes specific criteria for financial institutions operating in that jurisdiction. Financial institutions typically must obtain a certificate of authority, charter, license, or similar document that grants them the right to conduct financial business in a given jurisdiction. In addition, those who distribute financial products also must be licensed by or registered with a specific regulatory agency before conducting business within the jurisdiction. Then, the financial institution must comply with further applicable regulatory requirements.

A functional regulatory system has separate laws specifically for each sector of the financial services industry—securities, insurance, and banking.

■ Securities laws address the issuance, offering, and sale of financial securities; breaches of securities contracts; arrangements for establishment and administration of securities exchanges; transactions in securities; financial reporting and other conduct of issuers of securities; and criminal and civil penalties for regulatory violations.

Investment advisory businesses are regulated under securities laws, as are investment companies, securities exchanges, securities brokers, and some activities of life insurance companies. Separate accounts, subaccounts, variable contracts, and certain deposit-type products of life insurance companies generally are subject to securities laws. Insurance company general accounts are not themselves regulated as securities. However, publicly traded securities held in an insurance company's general account must comply with securities laws.

■ Insurance laws address the formation, licensing, conduct, operation, transfer of ownership, and orderly termination of insurance companies, as well as the issuance, sale, and administration of insurance contracts. Insurance laws, such as India's Insurance Regulatory and Development Act, specify the rights and duties of insurance companies and insurance customers.

Typically, companies that underwrite and issue insurance policies are subject to supervision by authorities. In each country, the primary regulatory goal is the protection of the customers' interests. Regulatory authorities protect customers' interests mainly through regulation and oversight of solvency and capital adequacy of all licensed insurers. As part of their effort to maintain insurer solvency, most jurisdictions impose restrictions on insurance company investments. This text is focused on investment activities and does not attempt to discuss insurance regulation in detail. This chapter addresses the insurance regulations affecting investments by insurance companies.

■ Banking laws address the formation, licensing, operation, conduct, and orderly termination of corporations licensed to take part in the banking business. Not all jurisdictions have passed such legislation. Banking laws typically require banks to hold enough funds to meet their obligations and set limits on interest charges. We do not focus on banking laws in this text.

In recent decades, some jurisdictions have established a single law to address all sectors of financial services under one umbrella—for example, the Capital Market Law and Bapepam in Indonesia. Such laws typically address the formation, licensing, administration, conduct, transfer of ownership, and orderly termination of business entities across all sectors of financial services—banking, insurance, and securities. Figure 2.4 names securities regulatory agencies and securities laws in selected countries.

Objectives of Financial Services Regulation

Financial services regulation generally addresses two broad objectives: market conduct regulation and solvency regulation.

Objectives of Market Conduct Regulation

Market conduct regulation of the financial services industry generally has the objective of ensuring that financial institutions conduct business with customers in a fair, ethical manner. Market conduct requirements are the primary means of customer protection in the securities sector, where solvency regulation is limited. Because investing is, by definition, an activity undertaken to earn compensation for taking financial risk, public policy does not mandate protecting investors from the consequences of taking financial risks. However, public policy does support the orderly conduct of investment transactions by encouraging transparency and full disclosure of risks to potential investors. In financial reporting, *transparency* refers to ease of understanding for users of financial information. Transparency is supported by full, clear, and timely disclosure of relevant information. Investors receive protection from fraudulent and misleading conduct, but not from financial losses due to knowingly taking a financial risk.

Figure 2.4 Selected Securities Regulatory Structures

	Securities Regulatory Agencies	Securities Laws
Brazil	Securities and Exchange Commission National Monetary Council Central Bank of Brazil	Law No. 6,385/76 (Securities Law)
Canada	Provincial and territorial regulatory agencies	Provincial and territorial securities laws
China	China Securities Regulatory Commission	Securities Law Law on Securities Investment Fund Regulation on the Supervision and Administration of Securities Companies
India	Securities and Exchange Board of India	Securities and Exchange Board of India Act, 1992 Depositories Act, 1996 Securities Contract (Regulations) Act, 1956
Indonesia	Bapepam (The financial services agency structure is in transition at the time of publication.)	Law of the Republic of Indonesia Number 8/1995 (Capital Market Law)
Japan	Financial Services Agency Minister of Finance Securities and Exchange Surveillance Commission Certified Public Accountants and Auditing Oversight Board	Financial Instruments and Exchange Act
Malaysia	The Securities Commission Malaysia Bursa Malaysia Bursa Malaysia Securities	Capital Markets and Securities Act 2007
Mexico	National Banking and Securities Commission	Securities Market Law
Philippines	Philippine Securities and Exchange Commission	Securities Regulation Code
Singapore	Monetary Authority of Singapore (MAS)	Securities and Futures Act (2001)
South Korea	Financial Services Commission Securities and Futures Commission Financial Supervisory Services	Financial Investment Services and Capital Markets Act (Capital Markets Act)
United States	Securities and Exchange Commission	Securities Act of 1933 Securities Exchange Act of 1934

As the financial services industry matures in a given jurisdiction, market conduct regulation in that jurisdiction tends to increase. The United States has the most extensive regulation of market conduct in the world. Many countries have enacted market conduct laws similar to those in the United States.

Important aspects of market conduct regulation are standards of fiduciary duty, suitability requirements, disclosure requirements, and customer privacy protections.

Fiduciary Duty Standards

Generally, a *fiduciary duty* is an obligation of a natural person or legal entity, known as a *fiduciary*, to act in the best interest of another party. A person has a fiduciary duty when he holds a special position of trust with regard to another person. In many jurisdictions, investment professionals have a fiduciary duty with regard to clients and end users of investment services. Standards of fiduciary duty applicable to investments typically require making full and complete disclosures to the party whose trust is involved and refraining from taking unreasonable profit at that party's expense.

Example: Standards of Fiduciary Duty

The CFA Institute's professional standards include a standard of fiduciary duty for investment professionals internationally.

In the United States, the Financial Industry Regulatory Authority (FINRA) and the Department of Labor enforce federal regulatory standards of fiduciary duty.

FINRA's conduct rules impose standards of fiduciary duty on securities dealers and brokers with respect to the investors who are their clients.

The U.S. Department of Labor enforces the Employee Retirement Income Security Act (ERISA), which sets a standard of fiduciary duty that includes requiring fiduciaries under qualified plans to act solely in the interest of plan participants and their beneficiaries and with the exclusive purpose of providing benefits to them.

Suitability Requirements

Suitability requirements are market conduct requirements that impose a duty on sales producers or financial services companies to have reasonable grounds on which to believe that a specific product is suitable for a specific customer's needs. Regulators in various jurisdictions apply suitability requirements to sales of securities, annuities, and life insurance. Suitability requirements typically require sales producers—before making any product recommendation—to have a basic understanding of prospective or actual customers' current financial situations and constraints, investment objectives, and future financial needs and obligations. Different regulatory agencies and other authorities may set a variety of suitability standards for different products, sales producers, or customers.

> **Examples: Suitability Requirements**
>
> The CFA Institute sets a standard of professional practice for suitability, in which, before making an investment recommendation to a client, investment professionals must determine that an investment is "suitable to the client's financial situation and consistent with the client's written objectives, mandates, and constraints."[1]
>
> FINRA requires registered securities broker-dealers in the United States to have reasonable grounds for making an investment recommendation to a customer based on the customer's other security holdings, financial situation, and needs.
>
> The NAIC Suitability in Annuity Transactions Model Regulation specifies procedures that producers and insurers must follow when making sales recommendations involving an annuity product to ensure that those recommendations address the insurance needs and financial objectives of investors.

Disclosure Requirements

Regulatory authorities typically require sales producers to make specific types of disclosures, such as those contained in a prospectus for securities or a policy summary or disclosure document for certain insurance company products.

A *prospectus* is a required communication, usually in written form, that offers a security for sale and that must contain detailed information about the issuer of the security and the security itself. A prospectus must be brought up to date annually and provided to existing and prospective investors. *Policy summaries* and *disclosure documents* detail product-specific information that insurers must provide to prospective insurance purchasers.

Privacy Protection Requirements

Privacy protection regulations limit companies' sharing of customers' nonpublic personal information. Privacy protection regulations generally do not limit sharing of publicly available information, such as telephone directories or published government records.

Objectives of Solvency Regulation

Financial institution solvency regulation, sometimes known as *prudential regulation* or *capital adequacy regulation*, addresses the public need for financial institutions to provide financial stability and meet obligations to customers and creditors on time. Solvency regulation and supervision primarily attempt to ensure that banks and insurance companies remain financially healthy. As we have noted, solvency protections are not an element of securities regulations.

Solvency of financial services companies is a complex and technical issue that is subject to ongoing developments in market theory, risk management techniques, and industry best practices. Although solvency restrictions apply to the securities industry and insurance company separate account products, solvency regulations are far more extensive for banking activities and insurance company general accounts. Most solvency regulation sets standards for ensuring that companies hold sufficient assets to support their obligations over an extended time horizon. Solvency regulation typically requires (1) supervisory review that specifies the responsibility of regulators, internal risk management, and governance and (2) disclosures and reporting to ensure that the analysis and governance are adequate and sound. In this context, having sufficient assets means having assets over and above the amount needed to meet the company's direct liabilities. To ensure their ability to determine whether assets are sufficient, regulators can specify a required approach to asset valuation, as well as a required approach to financial reporting. Determining whether assets are sufficient can depend in part on the proper method of valuing the assets. Precise financial accounting and reporting requirements support consistent public presentation of each company's financial status.

Minimum capital standards require companies to hold capital and assets deemed adequate under specified formulas or precise rules. Supplemental capital standards require additional capital specifically to offset certain investment risks.

Some solvency regulations require companies to perform complex mathematical modeling and analysis of the company's future cash flows, including investment cash flows, and future financial condition, including values of assets and liabilities. In this regard, companies must perform quantitative modeling to demonstrate the company's soundness, paired with an actuary's certification that the company's reserves are actuarially sound. Companies are required to exercise care in the valuation of assets as well as liabilities, because these valuations can be controversial.

Figure 2.5 summarizes the approaches that regulators often use to promote the solvency of financial institutions, particularly banks and insurance company general accounts.

Many jurisdictions now employ principles-based regulation to determine financial institution solvency. Under principles-based regulation, illustrated in Figure 2.6, a financial regulatory authority mandates generally accepted principles that companies must adopt and requires the companies to demonstrate that they properly apply the mandated principles to their specific context. The emergence of principles-based regulation places new importance on the many nongovernmental organizations that create industry or professional standards and recommend policy.

In this environment, companies place added emphasis on participation with professional or global organizations in determining or revising the standards. Moreover, nongovernmental organizations may change these standards without going through a legislative or an administrative process.

Solvency standards applied in principles-based regulation are often specified externally to the regulation, such as in a handbook created and maintained by a private, nongovernmental organization. Under such an arrangement, the external standards are subject to continuous updating, while the regulatory requirement does not require updating or amending.

Figure 2.5 Regulatory Approaches to Promoting Solvency

Supervisory review by regulators

Reporting by the financial institutions

Standards for amount and types of assets held

Requirements for valuations of assets

Requirements for valuations of liabilities

Requirements for financial accounting and reporting

Minimum capital requirements

Complex mathematical modeling of future cash flows

Actuarial certification that company reserves are sound

Institutional Investors and Government Relations

Although regulation and standardization arise from forces external to a company, companies can proactively manage their risk from changing regulatory requirements and standards. Compliance with regulations and standards can be costly and thus can diminish a company's profitability. Companies must achieve the right balance between compliance and effectively managing the associated ongoing compliance costs. Companies have the opportunity to proactively manage their risk by helping to shape the direction of regulatory changes and standards, all by participating in the regulatory and legislative approval process.

Financial services companies participate vigorously in the regulatory and legislative approval process. Companies respond to some regulatory initiatives directly with a legislative, regulatory, or judicial authority, whereas they respond to other initiatives through active participation in professional or regulatory associations that shape the public discourse on regulatory issues.

Financial services companies frequently have an opportunity to present their views regarding regulatory issues to the appropriate regulatory authority. In fact, regulators and supervisors encourage the participation and commentary of financial institutions to help them understand proposed regulations' nuances and unintended consequences.

Figure 2.6 Principles-Based Regulation and External Standards

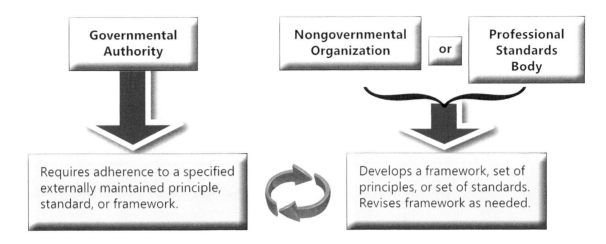

Example: Framework Referenced in Regulations

Insurance regulations in Canada can require adherence to specified standards for accounting and financial reporting, including the International Financial Reporting Standards (IFRS). The IFRS themselves are maintained by an independent accountancy professionalism organization, the International Accounting Standards Board. The IASB may change the contents of its accounting and financial reporting standards without regard to any North American legislative or administrative processes.

In many cases, companies can submit comments or provide testimony to the authority regarding legislative and regulatory proposals. Financial services companies and associations of financial professionals monitor developing regulatory initiatives and may choose to comment on legislation and regulations in their formative stages. Financial services professionals participate in professional organizations and initiatives focused on coordination of industry forces.

Companies have opportunities to join the public discourse about proposed regulatory oversight through the following actions:

■ Participating in public discussions about issues affecting their business

■ Addressing emerging issues by publishing new corporate policy statements before the emerging issues become the focus of legislation, regulation, or standardization

■ Monitoring developing legislation and helping to educate legislators, either on their own or through industry organizations

■ Participating in industry organizations

■ Informing employees about critical issues facing the company and the industry

Securities Regulation in the United States

The primary authority to regulate the U.S. securities industry and the products that qualify as securities belongs to the federal government. For some purposes, individual states also have jurisdiction over securities transactions.

The federal agency responsible for administering and enforcing federal securities laws is the Securities and Exchange Commission (SEC). The mission of the SEC is to protect investors; maintain fair, orderly, and efficient markets; and facilitate capital formation. The SEC is authorized to govern public purchases and sales of securities, whether through a securities exchange or over the counter.

The SEC has jurisdiction over all corporations whose securities are publicly traded in the United States. The SEC also has the authority to set the accounting and reporting methods that public companies use. All publicly traded stock companies, including financial services companies, are subject to SEC regulation. Specifically, SEC regulation applies to companies that issue securities to support their business operations and companies that sell such securities to the investing public. The SEC does not directly supervise the investment decisions or activities of these companies or judge the merits of their securities, however.

Federal securities laws provide a framework for regulation of the securities industry, including (1) registration requirements, (2) reporting and filing requirements, (3) requirements affecting the purchase and sale of publicly traded securities, (4) requirements for periodic examinations of registered entities and individuals, and (5) provisions for enforcement against violators of securities laws.

Federal Securities Laws

U.S. securities laws grew out of reforms in the aftermath of the stock market crash of 1929. The 1929 crash precipitated the Great Depression of the 1930s. The following U.S. laws provide primary federal regulation of the securities industry in the United States: the Securities Act of 1933; the Securities and Exchange Act of 1934, often known as the *Exchange Act*; the Trust Indenture Act of 1939; the Investment Company Act of 1940; and the Investment Advisers Act of 1940. Many securities laws globally are modeled after these laws.

The Dodd-Frank Wall Street Reform and Consumer Protection Act, better known as Dodd-Frank, is more recent financial services legislation also administered in part by the SEC. Dodd-Frank was enacted in 2010 to adopt U.S. financial system reforms in response to the 2008 global financial crisis. The long-term impacts of Dodd-Frank are unknown as this text goes to publication.

The Securities Act of 1933

The Securities Act of 1933 regulates public companies in the United States with two primary objectives:

- Ensuring that investors are provided with financial and other significant information about securities being offered for sale to the public

- Prohibiting deceit, misrepresentation, and fraud in the sale of securities

The Securities Exchange Act of 1934

The Securities Exchange Act of 1934 established the SEC and specified rules for the orderly conduct of securities transactions and securities exchanges. Several securities exchanges operate in the United States. A *securities exchange* is an organized marketplace where specific types of securities, such as common stocks and bonds, are bought and sold by members of the exchange. Over-the-counter (OTC) sales of securities are sales not transacted through a stock exchange, and include sales of securities through a brokerage, sales of variable annuities, and sales of mutual fund shares. Sales on stock exchanges and over the counter qualify as public trades.

The Securities Exchange Act sets additional requirements for participants in the securities industry in the United States, including requirements for registration of securities and market participants, corporate reporting and control requirements, proxy statement filing requirements, disclosure of tender offer requirements, and restrictions on transactions by insiders.

The Trust Indenture Act of 1939

The *Trust Indenture Act of 1939* (TIA) applies to bonds and other debt securities and imposes certain requirements on the issuer, in addition to registration requirements, before the securities can be sold publicly. The issuer of securities subject to the TIA must establish a trust for the benefit of the owner. A trust is an arrangement under the law that is created at the direction of an individual or entity, and designed to allow one party, the trustee, to hold specified property belonging to the individual or entity creating the trust for the benefit of others, the trust beneficiaries.

A **trust indenture**, also known as a *trust deed*, is a formal agreement that establishes a trust and forms the relationship between a trustee and a trust beneficiary. The indenture states the limits of the trustee's authority and conditions governing the trustee's actions in handling the trust assets. The TIA requires a trust indenture to contain certain provisions.

Example: Bond Issue and Trust Indenture

The Nolow Corporation is raising $100 million by publicly issuing bonds subject to the TIA. The TIA requires Nolow to establish a trust and execute a trust indenture for this bond. The trust indenture specifies all particulars of the bond issue, including the maturity date, coupon rate, and any collateral. The trust indenture also appoints a trustee to protect the rights of bondholders.

Certain debt securities, such as municipal bonds and private placement bonds, are exempt from the requirements of the TIA. However, those securities are often issued by means of trust indentures as well.

The Investment Company Act of 1940

The *Investment Company Act of 1940* regulates the organization of investment companies and is designed to protect the interests of investors. An investment company is a company that issues securities and engages primarily in investing, reinvesting, and trading in securities. Investment companies must register with the SEC before conducting business. Today, familiar examples of investment companies include mutual funds, insurance company separate accounts, index funds, and exchange-traded funds.

The Investment Company Act requires investment companies to disclose their financial condition and investment policies to investors when their shares are initially sold, and subsequently on a regular basis. The act focuses on required disclosure to the investing public of information about a fund and its investment objectives, as well as about the investment company's structure and operations. The Investment Company Act contains protections addressing the safekeeping and proper valuation of fund assets, restrictions on transactions among affiliates, and governance requirements. Moreover, the Investment Company Act limits the amount of leverage that funds may bear.

The Investment Advisers Act of 1940

The *Investment Advisers Act of 1940* regulates the activities of individuals and companies compensated for advising others about investments in securities. These individuals or companies must register with the SEC as advisers and meet its requirements for investor protection. Generally, all advisers who have at least $100 million of assets under management or advise a registered investment company must register with the SEC. Many insurance companies, securities brokerages, and asset management companies must register as investment advisers and otherwise meet the requirements of this act.

Other provisions of this act specify record keeping and reporting requirements, requirements affecting advisory contracts, requirements affecting advertising of securities, and requirements for custody of customers' assets.

Dodd-Frank

Dodd-Frank reshaped the U.S. financial regulatory system in a number of areas, including consumer protection, trading restrictions, credit ratings, regulation of financial products, corporate governance, and disclosure. The act also created many new federal agencies, including the Federal Insurance Office (FIO), the Financial Stability Oversight Council (FSOC), the Office of Financial Research, and the Consumer Financial Protection Bureau (CFPB). Dodd-Frank charged various administrative agencies with adopting rules and regulations to carry out its many requirements. Rule-making activities for Dodd-Frank are under way during development of this text. At least some Dodd-Frank provisions are administered by the SEC. Others are administered by the Treasury Department.

The new *Federal Insurance Office (FIO)* is a federal authority mandated to monitor the insurance industry, identify areas with inadequate state regulation, handle international insurance issues, and investigate ways to modernize the state-based system of insurance regulation.

Registration of Securities and Market Participants

The SEC administers registration requirements for securities and market participants:

- A security must be registered with the SEC before it is advertised or offered for sale to the public. Strict registration requirements are designed to ensure adequate disclosure of material information about a security to prospective purchasers. Registration of a security with the SEC consists of filing a preliminary prospectus—known as a *red herring*—and a final prospectus. The prospectus communicates critical information for current and potential investors, and explains the objectives, past performance, costs, and administration of the security. Each year the issuer of a security must provide investors with a current prospectus.

- A variety of securities market participants—including exchanges, brokers, dealers, investment advisers, investment companies, transfer agents, and clearing agencies—must also register with the SEC. Registration of market participants requires filing and regularly updating specified disclosure documents.

Under the Securities Exchange Act, the SEC has the authority and responsibility for registering securities market participants, but, in accordance with the Act, the SEC has delegated much of that authority to the *Financial Industry Regulatory Authority (FINRA)* and the securities exchanges.

FINRA is a nongovernmental, self-regulatory organization empowered by the SEC to license, investigate, and regulate securities firms and their representatives doing business in the United States. More generally, a *self-regulatory organization (SRO)* is a nongovernmental organization that exercises regulatory authority over an industry, a function, or a profession. The securities exchanges and FINRA have registered with the SEC as self-regulatory organizations under the Securities Exchange Act.

In other jurisdictions, SROs sometimes share regulatory authority with a government regulator. When a government delegates regulatory authority to an SRO, that authority is defined by law. However, in other contexts, an SRO can fill an absence of government oversight and regulation.

In addition to registering with the SEC, broker-dealers are required to become members of FINRA and abide by FINRA rules. Individuals who sell securities or are actively involved in a member's security business also must register with FINRA and abide by its rules. Generally, FINRA maintains two levels of qualification and registration for sellers of securities:

- A *registered representative* is a person who is associated with a FINRA member, engages in the securities business on behalf of the member by either soliciting the sale of securities or training securities salespeople, and has passed a special examination administered by FINRA.

- A *registered principal* is generally an officer or manager who is involved in the day-to-day operation and supervision of a company's securities business, has qualified as a registered representative, and has passed additional examinations administered by FINRA.

Conduct Rules

Registered FINRA members—including broker-dealers and the registered persons who are affiliated with those broker-dealers—must conduct business in accordance with all statutory requirements and in compliance with FINRA rules and regulations. FINRA rules impose a variety of requirements on how broker-dealers and registered persons must conduct business.

> **Examples: FINRA Rules**
>
> FINRA Rule 2020 prohibits manipulative, deceptive, or other fraudulent acts.
>
> FINRA Rule 5210 prohibits fraudulent manipulation of the transaction bidding process on securities exchanges.

Supervision and Record Keeping

FINRA rules require broker-dealers to establish and maintain a system to supervise the activities of each registered person to reasonably ensure they comply with applicable regulatory requirements. Each registered person must be assigned to an appropriately registered representative or principal responsible for supervising that person's activities. A registered principal must meet at least once a year with each registered representative to discuss regulatory and compliance matters.

FINRA conducts periodic compliance inspections of all broker-dealers. Examiners review the broker-dealer's books and records, sales practices, and financial condition. The frequency of inspections varies depending on the nature of the broker-dealer's activities.

FINRA has a number of requirements as to advertisements, sales literature, correspondence, and other communications that broker-dealers and registered persons use to communicate with the public about securities offered for sale. FINRA places restrictions on the content of such communications; for example, these materials must not contain certain statements implying guarantees or promises of specific investment results, exaggerations, or opinions for which there is no reasonable basis. A registered principal must review and approve a member's advertisements and sales literature before they are released. Further, broker-dealers must submit certain public communication materials to FINRA for review.

> **Examples: Statements Forbidden for Public Communications about Securities Offered for Sale**
>
> "We expect market interest rates to rise sharply in the next six months."
>
> "We expect a strong market correction in the third quarter."
>
> "Over the long run, you can expect any stock market investment to outperform interest-bearing investments."
>
> "Any investment backed by real estate ownership is absolutely secure."
>
> "If you invest in our target date fund now, you can be sure your retirement savings will meet your future retirement income needs."

Corporate Reporting and Control

SEC-sponsored financial reporting and control standards apply to public companies and companies that issue investment instruments. Companies with more than $10 million in assets whose securities are held by more than 500 owners must file annual and other periodic reports of financial and control information.

The SEC's role in regulation of public companies operating in the United States extends to setting standards for financial accounting and reporting, and for auditing and internal control systems. Most U.S. insurance companies must meet these standards and additional state-level standards specifically for insurance companies.

Under SEC standards, financial reports must conform to *generally accepted accounting principles (GAAP)*. U.S. GAAP is a set of financial reporting standards that all publicly traded companies in the United States follow when preparing their financial statements. The SEC delegates the responsibility for developing, revising, and promulgating U.S. GAAP to the Financial Accounting Standards Board (FASB). To establish and support the use of U.S. GAAP, FASB publishes Statements of Financial Accounting Standards (SFAS), which describe professional standards for financial reporting. FASB is represented at the International Accounting Standards Board (IASB).

For some purposes, companies doing business in Canada follow a Canadian version of GAAP, referred to as *Canadian GAAP* or *C GAAP*. Large Canadian insurance and financial services companies also have implemented International Financial Reporting Standards, known as IFRS, which are sponsored by the IASB.

Required reporting standards can affect the values of invested assets, or they can affect other values that companies must consider in determining their investment strategies, as follows:

- Statutory accounting principles require companies to report bonds at amortized cost and stocks at fair value. For GAAP, companies report both bonds and stocks at fair value.

- Impaired assets are reported at a value lower than book value.

- Under the Minimum Continuing Capital and Surplus Requirements (MCCSR) in Canada, the general account must be invested in low-risk, low-return securities. However, segregated account products may be held in securities with higher risks and potentially higher returns.

The SEC requires executives of public companies to annually evaluate and attest to the effectiveness of their company's internal control over financial reporting according to a suitable, recognized control framework. *Internal control* is an organizational function devoted to verifying that organizational standards, procedures, and other controls are applied as intended and are effective. In this context, a *control framework* is a system of standards for use in an internal control system.

Proxy Statement Filings

Institutional investors can hold large shares in some corporations, and have the opportunity to exercise votes connected with those shares. Corporate shareholders often allow another person to vote on their behalf on issues raised at a corporate meeting. A *proxy* is a written authorization given by one person, such as a corporate shareholder, to another person who is thereby enabled to act on behalf of the first person. A *proxy statement*, also known as a *proxy solicitation* or *proxy materials*, describes matters submitted for a vote in corporation meetings held for the election of directors and the approval of other corporate actions. Proxy statements are disclosures from corporations and intended to solicit shareholders' direction of their votes.

The following requirements apply to proxy statements presented by corporations:

- These materials must be filed with the SEC in advance of any solicitation.

- These materials must disclose all important facts concerning the issues on which shareholders are asked to vote.

Forms of Investment Companies

An investment company is an entity that issues securities and engages primarily in investing and trading securities. For our purposes, investment companies can take one of the following forms: an open-end management company, a closed-end management company, or a type of unit investment trust.

Open-End and Closed-End Management Companies

Some types of investment management companies can operate without necessarily having any connection with insurance companies. Open-end and closed-end management companies are operated by financial services companies that are not insurance companies but are registered as investment advisers. A single financial services holding company can hold an insurance company and an investment management company.

- According to the Investment Company Act, an *open-end management company* establishes a portfolio of securities, issues shares in the portfolio to investors, and redeems investors' shares for cash upon request. Although an open-end company may issue only common stock shares, the number of outstanding shares is flexible. These companies make a continuous public offering of shares, normally issuing more shares as investors request them. Investors trade shares directly with the investment company, and not over the counter or through securities exchanges. Shares in an open-end management company can usually be traded only at the closing price at the end of the market day. On any trading day, a share price is determined by the current value of the investment portfolio. Open-end shares sell at the net asset value (NAV). Mutual funds are the primary type of open-end management company.[2]

- A *closed-end management company* establishes a portfolio of securities and issues a fixed number of shares, but does not redeem shares that are outstanding. Closed-end management companies may issue securities including common stocks, preferred stock, and bonds. Investors typically trade shares on securities exchanges or in the over-the-counter market. In the public trading of these shares, share prices are determined by market forces, not by investment companies. Shares in a closed-end fund can be traded at any time during the market day, meaning that closed-end shares sell at the market price. Accordingly, share prices can trade at a discount or premium to the NAV, depending on market conditions on the exchange.

Unit Investment Trusts and Insurance Company Separate Accounts

According to the Investment Company Act, a *unit investment trust (UIT)* is an investment company that invests only in investment fund shares; is organized under a trust indenture or similar instrument; issues only redeemable securities, each of which represents an undivided interest in a unit of specified securities; does not have a board of directors; and does not include a voting trust.[3] UITs are created for a specified length of time. Insurance company separate accounts usually take the form of a type of UIT.

UITs can also take forms unrelated to insurance company separate accounts, although most UITs today support such accounts.[4] Similarly, not all insurance company separate accounts are designed to support UITs.

In the Investment Company Act, *separate account* is defined as an account established and maintained by an insurance company operating in the United States or Canada and under which operating results from the account's assets—realized or not—are credited to or charged against the relevant account without regard to other income, gains, or losses of the insurance company.[5]

Here, we focus our comments on separate accounts as discussed under the Investment Company Act—those formed to support investment fund options provided under products of insurance companies. Today, separate accounts of insurance companies may also be established for purposes outside of those described in the Investment Company Act.

Each insurance company separate account may be divided into subaccounts—that is, investment funds with distinct investment strategies. Insurance companies must provide prospective separate account product purchasers with prospectuses for the separate account itself and for each relevant underlying subaccount investment option. Figure 2.7 illustrates the configuration of an insurance company's separate account.

Figure 2.7 Zoosk Financial's Separate Accounts

Zoosk Financial is a top-20 U.S. insurance company with more than $100 billion in assets. Zoosk issues variable products that it operates through separate accounts. Zoosk recently created Separate Account G to support a line of variable products.

To support a full array of fund options for investors in Separate Account G, Zoosk established a number of subaccounts:

- Bullseye Target 2030 Fund Option, which Zoosk manages internally
- Quark Global Equities Fund B, which Quark manages for Zoosk

Quark Global Equities Fund B is *subadvised* by Quark Investments; the fund has the same management staff and resources and mirrors the general investing philosophy of the original Quark Global Equities Fund.

In this relationship, Zoosk regards Quark as a service provider, and Quark regards Zoosk as a client.

State Securities Regulation

The United States consists of 50 separate states, each having its own laws and regulations affecting commerce in securities and insurance. Every company doing business in a state must comply with the laws of that state.

Institutional investors overall mainly invest in securities regulated at the federal level, and thus have limited experience with state-regulated securities. For the financial services industry overall, federal regulation of securities has much greater overall impact than does state regulation of securities. Many state securities laws are based on the Uniform Securities Act, created by the Uniform Law Commission. The ***Uniform Law Commission (ULC)*** provides states with nonpartisan, model legislation that brings clarity and stability to critical areas of state statutory law.[6] The ***Uniform Securities Act*** is a longstanding model statute designed to provide a pattern for state legislators to follow in crafting state securities laws.

State securities laws are known informally as *blue sky laws*, so named because these laws are intended to protect the investing public against fraudulent investment schemes—those having "no more substance than a piece of blue sky."

Most state securities laws require new issues of securities to be registered with a specified state agency. State securities laws also generally regulate securities brokers and dealers operating in a state. State securities laws are enforced by a state's attorney general.

State Regulation of Investments of Insurance Companies

The McCarran-Ferguson Act (1945) established the business of insurance in the United States as a matter for state regulation. The differences in insurance regulation from one state to another are many and detailed. Accordingly, here we focus on what is typically true of state regulation of investments of insurance companies.

Each state has an agency for the regulation of insurance, headed by a top regulatory official, usually known as the *insurance commissioner*. State insurance laws are enacted by the state legislatures, and the state office of insurance has the power to make and enforce regulations. State insurance laws are enforced by a state's attorney general, who typically enters enforcement actions at the request of the state's insurance commissioner.

State laws regulating the investments of insurance companies are highly significant for the general account investments of life insurance companies.

State insurance commissioners participate in their influential professional association, the National Association of Insurance Commissioners (NAIC). The NAIC's functions on behalf of state commissioners include information sharing and research, as well as developing model laws and regulations. Most state legislatures refer to the NAIC's models as a basis for the laws and regulations they adopt through legislative processes.

The NAIC provides information-sharing facilities, including but not limited to the System for Electronic Rate and Form Filing, the Financial Standards and Accreditation Program, the National Insurance Producer Registry, and the Securities Valuation Office.

Under state solvency regulation, companies must demonstrate that they have adequate capital to support their business in the long term. State solvency laws have important effects on investments of insurance companies.

State capitalization requirements can highlight a concern that true values of some insurance company assets could be overstated under a given accounting convention. Under state solvency regulation, companies, for purposes of demonstrating capital adequacy, must take a reduction in their reportable capital to offset the effects of assets having reduced or impaired values.

In statutory financial reporting, insurance companies in the United States may not take credit for the full values of certain general account investments on the Assets page of the statutory balance sheet. In this regard, assets can be admitted, partially admitted, or nonadmitted:

- *Admitted assets* are assets for which the full value can be reported on the Assets page of the financial report required for periodic financial reporting to state regulators. Some assets are assigned *partially admitted* status.

- *Nonadmitted assets* are assets for which none of the value can be reported on the Assets page of the financial report required for periodic financial reporting to states.

NAIC Ratings of Securities

The **Securities Valuation Office (SVO)** is a department of the NAIC that publishes designations or unit prices for fixed-income investments of insurance companies.

- The NAIC's designations may be considered a type of rating of the investments.

- The unit prices assigned by the NAIC may be considered a type of valuation of the investments.

NAIC designations of both public and private securities are intended exclusively for statutory accounting and financial reporting purposes in the United States. The NAIC considers its ratings to be regulatory ratings, not public ratings. Therefore, NAIC designations are not intended to aid investment decision making, and are not suited for purposes other than their intended use. Investors also purchase quality ratings and research concerning public companies by subscribing to the services of rating agencies, such as those named in Figure 2.8.

The NAIC's rating system comprises six rating classes, labelled from NAIC 1 at the best end of the scale to NAIC 6 at the weakest end of the scale. Figure 2.9 shows the NAIC's bond rating scale.

NAIC designations and valuations are particularly important for investments that are not actively traded. Insurance companies own substantial amounts of private placement securities that are not actively traded, and are not rated by the commercial rating agencies. Similarly, securities exchanges do not maintain or publish statistics on transactions involving private placement securities.

The goal of the SVO is to set consistent valuations and ratings for bond investments of insurance companies. The SVO provides critical support for solvency monitoring of insurance company investments. The SVO constantly updates the valuations and ratings, which it maintains in an online database for access by interested parties.

- State insurance departments use NAIC valuations and ratings in discharging their obligation to monitor insurer solvency.

Figure 2.8 Private Rating Agencies

A.M. Best Company, Inc.	United States
Caribbean Information & Credit Rating Services Ltd. (CariCRIS)	Trinidad & Tobago
China Lianhe Credit Rating Co. Ltd.	China
CMC International, Ltd.	Nigeria
Credit Analysis & Research Ltd. (CARE)	India
Dominion Bond Rating Service (DBRS)	Canada
European Rating Agency (ERA)	United Kingdom
Fitch Ratings, Ltd.	United States/ United Kingdom
Japan Credit Rating Agency, Ltd. (JCR)	Japan
Moody's Investor Service	United States
Rapid Ratings International, Inc.	Australia/ New Zealand
Standard & Poor's (S&P)	United States

Source: "Credit Rating Agencies—Globally," DefaultRisk.com, http://www.defaultrisk.com/rating_agencies.htm (30 March 2012). Used with permission.

- In statutory reporting, companies must use valuations no less conservative than those provided by the SVO. Notwithstanding the availability of SVO data, companies must use judgment in arriving at appropriately conservative valuations for securities.

Investments of Insurers Model Acts

Many states have adopted important model investment laws for insurance companies. Investments of Insurers Model Acts for regulation of investments of insurance companies in the United States offer two approaches to limiting the investment risks that insurers undertake in the general account:

- Investments of Insurers Model Act–Defined Limits Version, also known as the *pigeonhole version*, specifies the types of assets that insurers are allowed to treat as admitted assets, and imposes quantitative limits on the amount of each type of asset held in an insurance company's general account.

- Investments of Insurers Model Act–Defined Standards Version, also known as the *prudent person version*, specifies that, with respect to an insurer's general account investments, the insurer's board of directors shall exercise the judgment that a person of reasonable prudence would use in similar circumstances.

Figure 2.9 NAIC Designations for Invested Assets

The SVO assigns NAIC 1 and 2 designations to investment-grade securities. Securities with ratings of NAIC 3 though 6 are considered "below-investment-grade." Securities with ratings of NAIC 5 and 6 are in default. The NAIC uses prefixes to indicate certain asset types.

Designation	Meaning
NAIC 1	Highest quality
NAIC 2	High quality
NAIC 3	Medium quality
NAIC 4	Low quality
NAIC 5	Very high probability of default
NAIC 6	In or near default

Prefixes	
P	Perpetual preferred stock
RP	Redeemable preferred stock
NR	Not rated (Quality is in review)
FMC	CMBS*
FMR	RMBS**

*Commercial mortgage-backed securities
**Residential mortgage-backed securities

Source: "NAIC Publicly Traded Securities Listing Definitions," National Association of Insurance Commissioners, http://www.naic.org/documents/svo_naic_public_listing.pdf (26 June 2012). Reprinted with permission of the National Association of Insurance Commissioners.

The Defined Limits Version gives companies specific and narrowly defined limits on specified categories—"pigeonholes," instead of broad discretion—in balancing portfolio risk exposures. In the Defined Limits Version, each pigeonhole represents an acceptable category of securities or issuers. All investment allocations that do not fit the permissible pigeonholes must meet additional limits relevant to their classification.

Examples: Pigeonhole Limitations under the Defined Limits Version

Below-investment-grade securities must not exceed 20 percent of admitted assets.

Investments rated NAIC 5 or 6 by the Securities Valuation Office must not exceed 9 percent of admitted assets.

Investments rated NAIC 6 by the Securities Valuation Office must not exceed 2 percent of admitted assets.

Both model acts have the effect of setting limits on risk taking in the investment activities of insurance companies. These limits are much broader in scope under the Defined Standards Version than in the Defined Limits Version. The Defined Standards Version allows insurers some discretion in selecting prudent investments rather than setting narrowly defined and specific investment limits (pigeonholes). Unlike the Defined Limits Version, the Defined Standards Version does not specify categories of securities and issuers that are acceptable to regulators.

Investment Reserves

State regulations require life insurance companies to hold specific investment reserves: the Asset Valuation Reserve (AVR) and Interest Maintenance Reserve (IMR).

The *Asset Valuation Reserve (AVR)* is a reserve liability intended to absorb realized and unrealized investment gains and losses on assets sold, and potentially arising from changes in the market value of assets and changes in credit ratings on assets. The AVR affects only general account assets that are reported at market value. Realized gains increase the AVR up to a maximum level. Realized losses decrease the AVR. In essence, the AVR is intended to smooth out short-term fluctuations in owners' equity arising from such influences as unrealized gains and losses on equities, unrealized gains and losses on bonds of lower credit quality, and realized capital gains and losses from bonds or equities.

Under the AVR, each asset class is subject to a type of investment reserve. In effect, this reserve diminishes the amount of owners' equity attributable to a given asset. The investment reserve effectively sets aside a portion of the company's surplus to address potential investment losses.[7]

The *Interest Maintenance Reserve (IMR)* is an investment reserve intended to absorb realized gains and losses upon the sale of interest-bearing assets when those gains or losses are attributable to changes in market interest rates, and not to changes in creditworthiness of the assets. Thus, a portion of a realized gain or loss due to fluctuations in market interest rates is reported as a type of reserve, and the amount of the gain or loss is not immediately fully recorded as a gain or loss on the company's financial statements. The overall effect of the IMR is to introduce the effects of fluctuations of market interest rates into financial reporting in as orderly a manner as possible.

As investment reserves, the AVR and IMR are not contractual reserves. These investment reserves apply only for statutory financial reporting and concern only general account assets.

Together, the AVR and IMR serve to reduce the insurance company's exposure to gains and losses arising from fluctuations in market values of assets. Because of the complementary nature of the AVR and IMR, references to the AVR and IMR often group them together as the *AVR/IMR*, or refer to them as simply *investment reserves*.

As is true for all reserves, these investment reserves are intended to support company solvency. The AVR and IMR are both liability accounts. These reserves cushion the asset account and owners' equity account from the full effects of market-value fluctuations.

Derivative Instruments Model Regulation

State securities laws address the holding of derivative securities by insurance companies. The **Derivative Instruments Model Regulation** sets standards for the prudent use of derivative securities by state-regulated insurance companies.

Actions Available to Regulators

When an insurance company becomes unable to meet its financial obligations, state regulators can intervene to safeguard the interests of parties such as customers, investors, and creditors of the insurance company. Although insurance regulators can intervene based on their judgment that a company is impaired, at least three model laws provide guidance in these matters: the Administrative Supervision Model Act, the Insurer Receivership Model Act, and the Risk-Based Capital for Insurers Model Act.

The actions regulators can take in these circumstances involve some focus on the company's investments. Actions that state regulators may take with respect to a financially impaired company typically include

- Requiring the company to take specified corrective actions, such as reducing its liabilities, limiting new business issued, reducing general expenses, suspending or limiting dividend distributions to owners, limiting or withdrawing from specified investments, and reporting asset values to regulators.

- Placing the company under administrative supervision, in which a company must obtain permission from an appointed state administrator before taking any of a number of specified actions, such as selling or transferring assets or in-force business or using assets or in-force business as collateral; withdrawing, lending, or investing funds; entering into a reinsurance agreement; or making any change in management.

- Placing the company in receivership for the purpose of either liquidation or rehabilitation. In rehabilitation, an administrator or conservator, acting for the state, takes control of the company and administers its assets and liabilities. In liquidation, the administrator winds down and terminates the company's operations by transferring or selling assets and liabilities and settling obligations.[8]

Securities Regulation in Canada

The federal government in Canada does not have jurisdiction over securities. The thirteen provincial and territorial governments within Canada regulate the securities industry, each in its own jurisdiction.

Example: Provincial Securities Regulation in Canada

In the Canadian province of Ontario, the Ontario Securities Commission regulates the securities industry under the Securities Act (Ontario); protects investors from unfair, improper and fraudulent practices; and fosters public confidence in capital markets.[9]

This system functions across borders by allowing for a kind of reciprocity in which registration of a person, an entity, or a security with one provincial securities commission accomplishes registration in most other securities commissions. Businesses engaging in broker-dealer transactions in Canada may participate in the appropriate nongovernmental guaranty-type associations, including the Canadian Investor Protection Fund, Mutual Fund Dealers Association, and Mutual Fund Dealers Association Investor Protection Corporation.

For institutional investors in Canada, provincial securities regulation affects the segregated account investments of insurance companies, mutual fund investment operations, and fee-for-service investment advisory services. In contrast, federal regulation of insurance investments primarily focuses on general account investments. Canadian insurance regulation is primarily a federal function, and it addresses solvency supervision, regulation of capital adequacy, and regulation of asset adequacy.

Financial System Supervision for the European Union

The *European Union (EU)* is a governing and lawmaking confederation of member nations in Europe, with provision for oversight of the European Union financial system. The EU has executive, legislative, and judicial branches as follows:

- The executive branch of the EU is the *European Commission*. The European Commission is responsible for proposing legislation, implementing decisions, upholding the EU's treaties, and generally administering the EU.

- The legislative branch of the EU is the *European Parliament*.

- The judicial branch of the EU is the *Court of Justice of the European Union*.

Within a given EU member country, financial institutions comply both with EU regulatory requirements and the given country's regulatory requirements. Financial system supervision for the European Union resides with the European Parliament, with a reporting relationship to the European Central Bank.

The *European Securities and Markets Authority (ESMA)*, which began operating in 2011, is the European Union's supervisory agency for securities markets. ESMA is an independent EU authority that contributes to safeguarding the stability of the European Union's financial system by ensuring the integrity, transparency, efficiency, and orderly functioning of securities markets, as well as enhancing investor protection. As of the publication date of this text, ESMA had not announced its regulatory structure and standards.

The *European Insurance and Occupational Pensions Authority (EIOPA)*, which also began operating in 2011, is an independent advisory body to the European Parliament and the European Commission.[10] EIOPA is responsible for implementing the *EU Directive on the Taking-up and Pursuit of the Business of Insurance and Reinsurance*, commonly known as *Solvency II*. Another initiative of EIOPA is a requirement for companies operating in the European Union to perform an Own Risk and Solvency Assessment (ORSA).[11]

- *Solvency II* is a European-sponsored solvency standard for insurance companies, designed to support solvency testing and solvency supervision in the public interest.

- *Own Risk and Solvency Assessment (ORSA)* is an EU-sponsored approach to a company's internal assessment of the status of its capital adequacy, its risk exposures, and the reporting of its internal risk assessment to relevant solvency supervisors. Although the roots of ORSA are European, as this text goes to publication, regulators in the United States had reached agreement on an ORSA model regulation, but no regulator had enacted an ORSA requirement.

Many multinational companies apply Solvency II and ORSA to their operations in EU member countries and elsewhere.

Nongovernmental Initiatives Affecting Institutional Investors

As you are aware, financial services regulation differs considerably from one jurisdiction to another. As financial companies have achieved global scale, these different regulations and even nonregulatory standards pose complexities that challenge a company's quest for improving operational efficiency. Ideally, voluntary standards and more consistency in regulations could make it easier for companies to control compliance expenses while operating in multiple jurisdictions.

In this section, we review just a few of the international organizations taking an interest in consistency of regulation across the global financial system. Several international bodies recommend policies for governments to apply in the supervision of securities, banking, and insurance activities. In many of these advisory organizations, seats on the board of directors or other governing committee are reserved specifically for people—such as central bank governors or finance ministers—who hold the highest positions of financial power in their home countries, such as central bank governors or finance ministers. At the same time, the home countries of these board members comprise the world's largest and most active economies.

When government officials from multiple countries agree on goals and policy recommendations, the participants, as individuals, may be able to directly implement the policy recommendations in their respective countries.

Furthermore, less developed countries can be highly receptive to policy recommendations from such global organizations, due in part to the prominent positions of the directors. Also, international nongovernmental organizations or their directors may have extended direct economic aid and loans to less developed countries.

The Group of Eight Finance Ministers and Central Bank Governors is commonly known as the *G8*. The G8 is a forum of finance ministers and central bank governors representing eight key countries on matters pertaining to the international financial system. The G8 does not have a charter, and its discussions are private. The G8 member countries are Canada, France, Germany, Italy, Japan, Russia, the United Kingdom, and the United States. G8 participants review policy issues and generally support global financial stability. A larger but otherwise similar forum is the *G20*, or Group of Twenty Finance Ministers and Central Bank Governors. Historically, the size of these groups has fluctuated slightly.

Organizations Based in Europe

The **Bank for International Settlements (BIS)** is a prominent international self-regulatory organization with a primary focus on central banks and the banking industry. The mission of the BIS is to serve central banks globally in supporting monetary and financial stability, fostering international cooperation, and acting as a bank for central banks. The BIS is at the nexus of a network of global policy organizations, including the following organizations:

- Basel Committee on Banking Supervision (BCBS), discussed next in this section, and its affiliates

- International Organisation of Securities Commissions (IOSCO)

- International Association of Insurance Supervisors (IAIS)

- Financial Stability Board (FSB)

- Committee on the Global Financial System (CGFS)

- Committee on Payment and Settlement Systems (CPSS)

- International Association of Deposit Insurers (IADI)

- Financial Action Task Force on Money Laundering (FATF)

The close relationship between the BIS and these other organizations includes a shared website, a shared business address, and interlocking directorates.

Basel Committee on Banking Supervision (BCBS) is a membership organization comprising representatives of bank supervisory authorities and central banks from Argentina, Australia, Belgium, Brazil, Canada, China, France, Germany, Hong Kong SAR, India, Indonesia, Italy, Japan, Korea, Luxembourg, Mexico, the Netherlands, Russia, Saudi Arabia, Singapore, South Africa, Spain, Sweden, Switzerland, Turkey, the United Kingdom, and the United States. The mission of the BCBS is to provide a forum for discussing bank supervision matters worldwide. The BCBS reports to the central bank governors of its member countries, and maintains a close relationship with the BIS. It usually meets at the Bank for International Settlements in Basel, Switzerland. (The BCBS was launched under the auspices of the then-G10—now the G8—as this text goes to publication.)

The BCBS also operates two committees, the *Joint Forum* and the *Coordination Group*, specifically for extending the global banking principles into the securities and insurance sectors.

The BCBS developed and maintains the *Core Principles for Effecting Banking Supervision*, and it also formulates supervisory standards and guidelines and recommends statements of best practice in banking.

The BCBS has broad impact on financial services beyond banking. The BCBS's solvency standards—known as the Basel Capital Accord, Basel II, and **Basel III**—now extend beyond banking and into all financial sectors. Basel III is the common name for a comprehensive set of financial supervision reform measures designed to strengthen the regulation, supervision, and risk management of the banking, insurance, and securities sectors globally. (The Basel III report can be viewed online at http://www.bis.org/publ/bcbs189.pdf .) Basel III formed the basis for the EU's Solvency II standards. The BCBS also develops liquidity standards for banking.

The *Financial Stability Board (FSB)*, also a BIS-affiliated organization, works globally to coordinate effective financial sector policies and publishes the *Compendium of Standards (CoS)*, which it reviews and updates periodically.[12] The CoS lists the various economic and financial standards that are internationally important for financial systems. You can view the CoS online at www.financial-stabilityboard.org.

The International Association of Insurance Supervisors and the International Organisation of Securities Commissions participate with the BSCS's Joint Forum and Coordination Group.

International Association of Insurance Supervisors (IAIS)

The *International Association of Insurance Supervisors (IAIS)*, a participant with BIS initiatives, is an association formed to improve regulatory supervision of the insurance industry; to maintain efficient, fair, safe, and stable insurance markets; to protect policyholders; to promote well-regulated insurance markets; and to support global financial stability. The IAIS members are insurance supervisors and regulators from 190 jurisdictions in 140 countries, comprising most insurance regulators and supervisors from around the world.[13]

Some IAIS standards set best practices for insurance supervisory authorities. Other IAIS standards describe best practices for insurance companies. The IAIS publication *Insurance Core Principles and Methodology* presents fundamental principles of effective insurance regulatory supervision, identifying the areas an insurance supervisor should supervise and the concepts that should form the basis for supervisory standards. The IAIS publishes various other standards that describe best practices for insurance companies and supervisory authorities.

International Organisation of Securities Commissions

The *International Organisation of Securities Commissions (IOSCO)* is the international self-regulatory organization for securities industry regulatory agencies and supervisors. IOSCO develops standards for securities regulation, having notably developed boilerplate language for an agreement between countries as to mutual support for cross-border financial transactions. IOSCO's *Multilateral Memorandum of Understanding (MMoU)* provides assurance that a company's interests can be protected after it invests across a national boundary, and thus paves the way for cross-border investing. Countries that participate as signatories to an accord based on the MMoU agree to mutually support cross-border enforcement investigations and prosecutions by collecting and sharing enforcement-related information.[14]

> **Examples: Information Shared under IOSCO's MMoU**
>
> Witness testimony
>
> Bank account information
>
> Brokerage account information

Organizations with Roots in the United Nations

Several organizations originating from the United Nations (UN) have advisory functions for guiding regulation, supervision, and standardization within the global financial system. These include the International Monetary Fund, the Organisation for Economic Co-Operation and Development, and the World Bank.

The *International Monetary Fund (IMF)* is an organization of 188 countries working to foster global monetary cooperation, secure financial stability, facilitate international trade, promote high employment and sustainable economic growth, and reduce poverty around the world. The IMF's primary purpose is to ensure the stability of the international system of exchange rates and international payments that support cross-border transactions. However, the IMF's mission now extends to the full range of macroeconomic and financial sector issues relevant to global stability. As a UN initiative, the IMF has close ties with the World Bank, including the International Bank for Reconstruction and Development. The IMF works with the World Bank, the Organisation for Economic Co-Operation and Development, regional development banks, various UN agencies, and other international bodies.[15]

The Organisation for Economic Co-operation and Development (OECD) provides a forum in which the governments of its 34 member countries can work together on a wide variety of issues. The OECD published the *Principles of Corporate Governance* and *The Methodology for Assessing Implementation of the OECD Principles of Corporate Governance*—important topics in Chapter 3.[16]

Offshore financial centers have become a major focus of the OECD. An *offshore financial center (OFC)* is defined as a specially regulated commercial territory where most transactions are conducted by nonresident entities, the transactions are initiated elsewhere, and the majority of the financial entities involved are controlled by nonresidents.[17] The OECD increasingly views some OFCs as offering opportunities for money laundering and tax evasion, as well as raising obstacles to anticorruption investigations.

The World Bank is an international institution initiated by the United Nations and having approximately 180 member countries. With reference to the OECD's *Principles of Corporate Governance*, the World Bank conducts assessments of corporate governance policy in various countries at the invitation of country authorities.[18]

Key Terms

transparency
fiduciary duty
suitability requirements
trust indenture
Uniform Law Commission (ULC)
Uniform Securities Act
Securities Valuation Office (SVO)
Asset Valuation Reserve (AVR)
Interest Maintenance Reserve (IMR)
Derivative Instruments
   Model Regulation
European Union (EU)
Solvency II

Own Risk and Solvency
   Assessment (ORSA)
Bank for International
   Settlements (BIS)
Basel Committee on Banking
   Supervision (BCBS)
Basel III
Financial Stability Board (FSB)
Compendium of Standards (CoS)
International Association of Insurance
   Supervisors (IAIS)
International Organisation of Securities
   Commissions (IOSCO)

Key Terms *continued...*

Multilateral Memorandum of Understanding (MMoU)

International Monetary Fund (IMF)

offshore financial center (OFC)

Endnotes

1. CFA Institute, *Code of Ethics and Standards of Professional Conduct* (Charlottesville, VA: CFA Institute, 2010), http://www.cfapubs.org/doi/pdf/10.2469/ccb.v2010.n14.1 (26 September 2012).

2. Investment Company Act of 1940, 15 U.S.C. § 80a-5 (2011).

3. Ibid., 15 U.S.C. § 80a-4 (2011).

4. David Hayter (Executive Vice President and Chief Operations Officer, Liberty Mutual Group Investment Management, Inc.), note to author, March 2012.

5. Investment Company Act of 1940, 15 U.S.C. § 80a-2 (2011).

6. "Home Page," Uniform Law Commission, www.uniformlaws.org (5 June 2012).

7. Diane Bellas (Director, Allstate Corporation), note to author, March 2012; Daniel C. Leimbach (Director of Research, USAA Asset Management), note to author, March 2012; James McClure (Vice President, Investment Accounting and Reporting, Prudential Financial), note to author, March 2012.

8. Harriett E. Jones and Monica R. Maxwell, *Regulatory Compliance: Companies, Producers, and Operations*, 3rd ed. [Atlanta: LOMA (Life Office Management Association, Inc.), © 2009], 158–160. Used with permission; all rights reserved.

9. "About the OSC," Ontario Securities Commission, http://www.osc.gov.on.ca/en/About_about_index.htm (27 September 2012).

10. "About EIOPA," European Insurance and Occupational Pensions Authority, https://eiopa.europa.eu/about-eiopa/index.html (10 September 2012).

11. Global Legal Group, *The International Comparative Legal Guide to: Insurance & Reinsurance 2012* (London: Global Legal Group, 2012), http://www.clydeco.com/uploads/Files/Publications/2012/120322%20-%20ICLG%20-%20Chapter%201.pdf (7 June 2012).

12. "Who Are the Standard-Setting Bodies?" Financial Stability Board, http://www.financialstabilityboard.org/cos/wssb.htm (5 June 2012).

13. "Home Page," International Association of Insurance Supervisors, http://www.iaisweb.org (27 September 2012).

14. Herbert Smith LLP, "China," in *Guide to Financial Services Regulation in Asia*, 5th ed. (Hong Kong: Herbert Smith, 2011), 9, http://www.herbertsmith.com/NR/rdonlyres/055F7368-FAE1-4EFD-84A6-845C6B943C06/17959/GuidetofinancialservicesregulationinAsia2011.pdf (27 September 2012).

15. "About the IMF," International Monetary Fund, http://www.imf.org/external/about.htm (27 September 2012); "The IMF at a Glance," International Monetary Fund Factsheet, International Monetary Fund, August 2012, http://www.imf.org/external/np/exr/facts/pdf/glance.pdf (27 September 2012).

16. Organisation for Economic Co-Operation and Development, *OECD Principles of Corporate Governance* (Paris: OECD Publications, 2004), http://www.oecd.org/dataoecd/32/18/31557724.pdf (27 September 2012); Organisation for Economic Co-Operation and Development, *Methodology for Assessing the Implementation of the OECD Principles of Corporate Governance* (Paris: OECD Publications, 2007). http://www.oecd.org/corporate/corporateaffairs/corporategovernanceprinciples/37776417.pdf (27 September 2012).

17. "Offshore Financial Centers," IMF Background Paper, International Monetary Fund, 23 June 2000, http://www.imf.org/external/np/mae/oshore/2000/eng/back.htm#II_A (27 September 2012).

18. "What We Do," The World Bank Group, http://web.worldbank.org/WBSITE/EXTERNAL/EXTABOUTUS/0,,contentMDK:20103838~menuPK:1696997~pagePK:51123644~piPK:329829~theSitePK:29708,00.html (27 September 2012).

Chapter 3

Governance and Control

Objectives

After studying this chapter, you should be able to

3A Define corporate governance and describe how a company's mission statement and corporate planning and control mechanisms contribute to corporate alignment; and identify signs of corporate misalignment

3B Describe the use of budgets, corporate policies, and standing committees as control mechanisms for the investment function, and describe a risk policy, risk appetite, risk tolerance, and risk limits

3C Identify different types of audits, and describe frameworks used to provide auditing guidance to financial institutions

3D Describe a code of conduct and explain how it contributes to internal control

3E Identify the elements necessary for the control of an investment portfolio, including the investment mission, investment objectives, investment strategies, and investment policies

3F Describe important elements in data governance and data security for the investment function

3G Describe the roles of performance management, job design, authorization limits, and risk limits in the control of the investment function

3H Describe controls at different levels of the organizational hierarchy and how a dashboard is used to display control information for investments

3I Describe types of potentially unethical or illegal practices that the investment function must guard against, including insider trading, front running, late trading, market timing, soft-dollar arrangements, collusion, theft, fraud, and Ponzi schemes

Outline

**Corporate Governance
and Alignment**

Corporate Control Mechanisms
- Budgets
- Standing Committees
  of the Board
- Corporate Policies
- Other Elements of
  Internal Control

**Control Mechanisms in the
Investment Function**
- The Investment Portfolio
- Performance Management
- Data Governance and Data Security
- Job Design and
  Safeguarding of Assets
- Authorization Limits and Risk Limits

**The Control Cycle in
Portfolio Management**

**Abusive and Fraudulent
Investment Practices**
- Insider Trading
- Soft-Dollar Arrangements
- Collusion
- Theft and Fraud

The previous chapter presented regulations and standards that impact institutional investing and are designed to safeguard the public interest. To satisfy regulations and standards, financial institutions must establish a framework of governance. Governance includes plans, policies, and processes designed to accomplish the organization's mission, as well as control mechanisms for detecting illegal or unethical activities and identifying inefficient uses of the company's resources. A good system of governance allows a company to gain and keep the trust of its customers, as well as regulators, employees, vendors, owners, and others.

Corporate Governance and Alignment

Corporate governance is the responsibility and authority of a company's board of directors to direct the company in fulfilling its mission on behalf of its legitimate stakeholders in a legal and fiscally responsible manner. Corporate governance encompasses authority, accountability, stewardship, leadership, direction, and control; it flows from the board's establishment of the company's mission, or reason for existence.

Example: Insurance Company Mission Statement

To protect individuals and businesses from the financial losses associated with certain risks by providing quality products and services at competitive prices.

The board of directors pursues the company's mission by establishing strategic objectives or goals—which are statements of long-term results that a company plans to achieve for every functional area in a company. To be effective, objectives should be (1) clearly stated, (2) specific and measureable, and (3) realistic and actionable.

Corporate alignment refers specifically to the board's efforts to keep all of a business organization's activities, resources, and systems targeted toward achieving the organization's mission, objectives, and strategies. Corporate alignment is the key responsibility of the board of directors.

Misalignment occurs when corporate planning and control mechanisms fail to keep the entire organization aligned correctly with the company's mission, goals, and strategies.[1] Symptoms of misalignment include

■ Missed financial projections. Corporate misalignment is often a major factor in missed corporate financial projections. A significant example of corporate misalignment occurred in 2012 when J.P. Morgan experienced multibillion-dollar trading losses after one of its divisions heavily invested in risky derivatives. These investments appeared contradictory to the company's stated investment goals, which emphasized prudent and safe investment practices.[2]

■ Stalled company growth. Corporate misalignment often results in stagnant or sluggish company growth. Without clear direction, functional areas have difficulties prioritizing and organizing work tasks. For example, work activities may be duplicated within two or more functional areas, resulting in inefficient use of time and resources.

■ Declining employee morale. When employees share common goals, they are generally motivated and more productive in their work activities. Employee morale declines when workers are confused by conflicting goals and strategies.

Misalignment is likely caused by problems in a company's (1) strategic planning process, (2) communication methods, and (3) governance policies. A weak strategic planning process is one of the greatest causes of misalignment. When companies fail to adequately define investment goals with concise and measurable outcomes, operational plans have a tendency to stray from the strategic plan, and investment activities may focus on tasks that do not contribute to the achievement of investment goals. For example, assume that one of an institutional investor's goals is to establish long-term relationships with clients based on mutual trust and integrity. However, the company's compensation program rewards short-term quarterly profits. In such a case, operational areas are likely to focus on short-term quarterly profits rather than the strategic goal of establishing long-term relationships. However, even if strategic plans are well developed, misalignment can creep into functional-area activities if corporate communication is poor, or if functional areas aren't being governed properly through established control mechanisms.[3]

Corporate Control Mechanisms

Corporate control mechanisms are essential to corporate alignment; they allow management to oversee how well functional areas are accomplishing planned objectives and to take corrective action when necessary to bring performance back in line with expectations. A company's control mechanisms, regardless of where they reside in a company's hierarchy, make up a continuous process known as its *control cycle*. As illustrated in Figure 3.1, a control cycle consists of at least three phases: steering controls, concurrent controls, and feedback controls. In real-world applications, a control cycle can contain numerous phases. Many concurrent and feedback controls are automated.

Control mechanisms are in place at all levels of the organizational hierarchy, including the corporate or strategic level, the functional level, and the operational or tactical level. Throughout the remainder of this text, we encounter repeated examples of controls affecting investments from the strategic, functional, and operational levels. Important control mechanisms at the corporate level include corporate budgets, standing committees, and corporate policies.

Figure 3.1. The Control Cycle

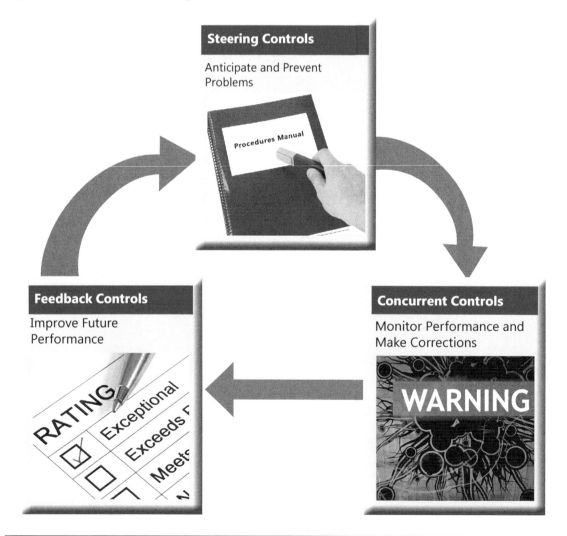

Budgets

A budget is a financial plan of action expressed in monetary terms. Budgeting is necessary at all levels of a financial institution. A company requires a broad corporate budget as well as detailed budgets for each functional and operational area. An insurance company's strategic budget typically shows a monetary value for the estimated net contribution from investment returns. During budgeting, the company estimates an overall percentage rate of return that the investment portfolio is expected to earn on the company's assets under management. This estimated rate of return on invested assets then figures into a company's financial plan for the budget period.

A budget can serve as a steering, concurrent, or feedback control depending upon how it is used. The corporate budget is primarily a steering control that illustrates the board's priorities for the period covered by the budget.

Standing Committees of the Board

Boards of directors of large financial institutions typically delegate ongoing oversight of important company functions, such as investments, to permanent board committees, known as *standing committees*. Standing committees often form working committees that consist of management personnel from involved functional areas. Working committees report to the standing committee about current activities and provide the board with concurrent control over the activities. Standing committees play a critical role in ensuring that the investment function stays aligned with the corporate mission and objectives.

Boards have broad discretion in setting up a company's committee structure. Thus, the names for various committees are not uniform across many financial institutions. However, the following standing committees often exist within financial institutions and play an important role in ensuring corporate alignment of investments:

- An **audit committee** is a standing committee that assists a board of directors in overseeing the internal audit function, independent (external) auditors, financial reporting practices, internal controls, and, in some companies, ethics policy, and compliance with regulations and standards. The investment function is an important focus for the audit committee.

- A *compensation and benefits committee* is a standing committee that assists a board of directors with establishing and supervising compensation policy and strategy for a company's employee compensation and benefits programs, including those for investment professionals.

- An **investment committee** is a standing committee that assists the board of directors in carrying out its governance duties over the company's investments. These duties include reviewing and approving investment policies and procedures, reviewing strategic portfolio composition, ensuring compliance with applicable laws, supervising investment performance and operations, and reviewing and approving major contracts with external providers of investment-related services.

■ A ***corporate governance committee***, also known as a *compliance committee*, is a standing committee that may handle a variety of corporate issues such as corporate privacy policies, data security and usage policies, licensing, market conduct, or general compliance. This committee is often charged with distilling the company's values and expectations for employee conduct into a *code of conduct*.

■ An *information technology (IT) committee* is a standing committee that oversees an organization's technology, systems security, and possibly data governance efforts.

■ A ***risk management committee*** is a standing committee that assists the company's board in supervising the management of the institution's assets, liabilities, capital, and risks. A risk management committee may also be known as an *enterprise risk committee*, a *finance committee*, a *risk committee*, or a *risk and finance committee*. A risk management committee reviews the company's risk management framework, progress of strategic initiatives, annual budget, credit ratings, and any pending mergers or acquisitions. An important responsibility of the risk management committee is to oversee and monitor the company's capital management, asset-liability management (ALM), and enterprise risk management (ERM) efforts. ERM refers to an entire range of processes and techniques for understanding, quantifying, and managing risks and returns at the topmost level of an organization. At least annually, the risk management committee should conduct a review of the effectiveness of all of these management systems. The importance of risk management to investment operations cannot be underestimated as regulators and financial rating agencies focus extensively on risk assessment and risk management. Figure 3.2 describes Standard & Poor's ERM framework.

Figure 3.2 Standard & Poor's Enterprise Risk Management (ERM) Framework

Standard & Poor's ratings explicitly recognize a company's ERM efforts in their rating analysis. According to S&P's ratings framework, a company's ERM system should at least

• Identify and *regularly* monitor risks

• Set and enforce risk limits so that any losses remain within tolerable levels

• Develop pricing approaches and capital allocations that produce a return commensurate to the risk undertaken by the company

The S&P framework goes on to state that ERM should be an enterprise-level endeavor that analyzes risk across all points of a company's exposure. Such a broad focus ensures that losses from all sources are considered when determining and enforcing risk tolerances.[4]

Corporate Policies

Corporate policies outline what needs to be done and guide employees in carrying out work tasks. The board of directors establishes corporate policies that guide investment practices and serve as important steering controls for the investment function.

Risk Policy

A corporate **risk policy** is a policy statement that explains the principles the company will follow for managing risk, outlines the process for managing risk, specifies assignments of authority and responsibility for risk management, and establishes risk reporting and risk controls. The board is responsible for determining the nature and extent of the significant risks the company is willing to take in achieving its strategic objectives. The corporate risk policy should establish clear guidelines for the company's risk appetite and risk tolerance. A company's **risk appetite** is generally viewed as the amount and type of risk that the organization is prepared to seek in the pursuit of profits or other strategic objectives. A company's **risk tolerance** is a broad statement about the organization's capacity and readiness to bear a risk in order to achieve its objectives. In other words, risk appetite is about determining the limits of an organization's *willingness* to bear risk in the pursuit of its strategic objectives, whereas risk tolerance is about determining the organization's *capacity* to bear risk. The risk policy should also include quantitative statements, called **risk limits**, or *risk criteria*, expressing how risk appetite and risk tolerance are to be assessed and monitored.[5] At this level, risk limits translate the company's risk tolerance into guidelines that the company can use on a day-to-day basis. For example, a company may establish an asset concentration limit for lines of business or products. Later, we describe how companies translate these higher-level statements of risk tolerance into appropriate operational limits.

Investment Policy

A company's board establishes an **investment policy**—a policy statement that outlines a set of formal rules and guidelines for investing. Companies establish investment policies at several levels, with broader guidelines at the top of the organization and narrower, more specific guidelines deeper in the organization. A corporate investment policy applies to all company assets. At this level, the investment policy would specify broad guidelines, such as that investment management should follow all applicable laws and regulations. The corporate investment policy might also identify specific corporate investment constraints. For example, a company might prohibit investing in a socially unacceptable industry, such as the tobacco industry. The corporate investment policy is an important communication tool for transmitting the board of directors' priorities for the management of corporate assets to the investment committee and to the investment function.

Compensation and Benefits Policy

A *compensation and benefits policy* is a statement of guidelines and objectives for a company's total package of remuneration to employees. Companies typically have a written compensation and benefits policy for all employees in general, with targeted compensation and benefits policies for executives and investment professionals. In some companies, a large share of compensation for investment professionals is incentive compensation—tied directly to the outcomes achieved in the assets under management. By tying a percentage of an investment professional's compensation to desired outcomes, the board can motivate investment professionals to achieve those outcomes and thus accomplish board objectives.

If properly aligned with relevant objectives, incentive compensation programs help ensure that employees' actions are directed toward appropriate goals. Such programs also serve to motivate employees to greater performance levels. However, employee compensation programs should not encourage employees to engage in unethical behaviors that are not in the best interests of investment clients or the company. Incentive compensation programs should be evaluated periodically to determine their effectiveness in supporting company goals.

Audit Policy

A corporate *audit policy* is a statement about a company's provisions for systematically examining, testing, and evaluating the company's compliance with one or more specified sets of standards. The corporate audit policy describes the company's control framework for audits.

An *audit* is a systematic examination and evaluation of a company's records, procedures, and controls. Audits can serve as steering, concurrent, and feedback controls. Public companies and their officers must proactively demonstrate due diligence in financial reporting and disclosure and provide strong assurances about data accuracy. Auditing procedures must follow an approved control framework in order to satisfy these legal requirements. In the United States, public companies are required to annually evaluate and attest to the effectiveness of their company's internal control processes according to a suitable, recognized control framework. Figure 3.3 provides information about commonly used control frameworks.

Because the audit staff must maintain a high degree of independence and objectivity, their function is separate from those of the departments they examine. They typically present results directly to the audit committee of the board of directors.

A *financial audit* is a systematic evaluation of whether a company's financial information, financial statements, and source documents comply with accounting standards and present a fair and consistent depiction of the company's financial condition and performance. Financial auditing is a review process designed to ensure that

- Quality assurance is maintained.

- Operating procedures, policies, and internal control processes are effective.

A *compliance audit* verifies that company actions adhere to applicable laws and regulatory requirements and to the company's policies and procedures. A *performance audit* measures and evaluates progress toward achieving specific goals or management objectives for a particular function. A performance audit typically explains the processes covered in the audit and reports the auditor's findings and recommendations for process improvement.

Figure 3.3 Control Frameworks for Financial Institutions in the United States

The Public Company Accounting Oversight Board (PCAOB), which oversees audits of public companies, recognizes two frameworks maintained by the Committee of Sponsoring Organizations of the Treadway Commission, known as *COSO*. In addition, PCAOB recognizes the *Statement on Auditing Standards (SAS) No. 70, Service Organizations*, commonly known as *SAS 70*, and a newer *Statement of Standards for Attestation Engagements (SSAE) 16*, commonly known as *SSAE 16*.[6]

- **COSO's 2002 framework** for internal audits, commonly known as the *COSO framework*, defines *internal control* as a process undertaken by a corporation's internal stakeholders that is designed to provide reasonable assurance regarding the achievement of three control objectives: (1) effectiveness and efficiency of operations, (2) reliability of financial reporting, and (3) compliance with applicable laws and regulations. This framework is the most widely used internal control framework in the United States, and it is now popular in many other countries as well.

- **COSO's 2004 Enterprise Risk Management—Integrated Framework**, known as the *COSO ERM framework*, supports the three control objectives from the 2002 COSO framework and adds a fourth objective: assurance of alignment between practices in the audited areas of an organization with the organization's strategic and high-level goals.

- **Statement on Auditing Standards (SAS) No. 70, Service Organizations**, commonly known as *SAS 70*, is an auditing standard developed and maintained for service organizations by the American Institute of Certified Public Accountants (AICPA). Because financial services companies are service organizations, SAS 70 is suited for use by insurance and other financial services companies. Audit reports under SAS 70 evaluate the effectiveness of internal control over financial reporting. An audit conducted under SAS 70 further provides an in-depth examination of the service organization's control objectives and control activities, including controls over information technology and technology-related processes.

- **Statement on Standards for Attestation Engagements (SSAE) 16**, commonly known as *SSAE 16*, is considered by the American Institute of Certified Public Accountants (AICPA) to be an alternative to SAS 70 in many situations. The primary purpose of SSAE 16 is to support proposed international accounting standards. Although similar to SAS 70, SSAE 16 is different in several ways. A major difference between the two is that SSAE 16 requires a written assertion by management that the description in the audit fairly represents the company's control system, and that the control system was operating effectively during the dates described in the audit. In addition, SSAE 16 presents enhanced reporting requirements for *subservice organizations*—third-party service organizations that provide services to another service organization.

Examples: Audit Objectives for the Investment Function

Audit objectives for various activities within the investment function are designed to ensure that

- Investment professionals responsible for investment portfolio monitoring and management properly track investment objectives.

- Asset traders obtain proper authorization for asset purchases and sales.

- Investment professionals perform and use proper analysis and research to support investment decisions.

- External financial account statements from service providers are reconciled with internal records of the same financial assets.

- Physical certificates or other physical evidence of ownership of financial securities are properly safeguarded.

- The valuation of investments is properly determined through sources independent of the investment function.

- The transaction costs for trades are consistent with company policies for best execution and expense management.

Other Elements of Internal Control

A *code of conduct*, also known as an *ethics policy* or a *code of ethics*, is a business policy specifying rules and requirements for ethical behavior for company executives, company employees, and individuals acting as agents for the company. Financial services companies typically have several codes of conduct—a general one for all employees, and supplemental codes of business ethics and conduct for investment employees that specify the company's guidelines for such matters as personal trading, gifts and entertainment, e-mail communications, trade allocations, best execution, trade errors, privacy, and anti–money laundering policies. Typically, investment employees must read and sign all applicable codes of conduct annually, attesting that they understand and are in compliance with all aspects of the code. In addition, many companies require investment professionals to attend annual training in order to ensure their understanding of conduct codes and to reinforce ethical and legal behavior.

Internal codes of conduct may include elements of the Code of Ethics of the CFA Institute, which appears in Figure 3.4.

To be most effective, a code of conduct should illustrate situations that employees might encounter in their work environment, and help employees evaluate the appropriateness of various responses to a given situation. For example, a code of conduct may provide typical examples of situations involving a securities brokerage firm.

Figure 3.4 Code of Ethics of the CFA Institute

Members of the CFA Institute and candidates for the CFA designation ("Members and Candidates") must

- Act with integrity, competence, diligence, respect, and in an ethical manner with the public, clients, prospective clients, employers, employees, colleagues in the investment profession, and other participants in the global capital markets.

- Place the integrity of the investment profession and the interests of clients above their own personal interests.

- Use reasonable care and exercise independent professional judgment when conducting investment analysis, making investment recommendations, taking investment actions, and engaging in other professional activities.

- Practice and encourage others to practice in a professional and ethical manner that will reflect credit on themselves and the profession.

- Promote the integrity of and uphold the rules governing capital markets.

- Maintain and improve their professional competence and strive to maintain and improve the competence of other investment professionals.

Source: CFA Institute, *Standards of Practice Handbook*, 10th ed. (Charlottesville, VA: CFA Institute, 2010), 5, http://www.cfapubs.org/doi/pdf/10.2469/ccb.v2010.n2.1 (20 June 2012). Used with permission.

Examples: Code of Conduct Situations Involving a Securities Brokerage Firm

Situation: An economist for a securities brokerage firm is the featured speaker at a company luncheon for investment professionals. The securities brokerage firm volunteers to provide lunch.

Code of Conduct Analysis: The securities brokerage firm may host the luncheon because the value of the lunch per guest is small.

Situation: A securities brokerage firm offers to host an investment professional on a trip to the US Open golf tournament.

Code of Conduct Analysis: The investment professional should decline the offer because the probability of adding value to investments is low and the value of the event is high.

A code of conduct often provides guidelines for situations involving a conflict of interest or the acceptance of gifts. A *conflict of interest* exists when the interests or actions of one entity, such as an employee, are incompatible with the interests or actions of a related entity, such as an employer.

Example: Violations of Code of Conduct

Code of Conduct Statements:

Employees may never accept cash or cash equivalents during a bidding process or contract negotiation.

Employees may accept gifts or entertainment during the course of employment only if the gift or entertainment is valued at $25 or less.

Situation: Chad works in the commercial real estate department of Emini. His company is seeking a commercial real estate property to fulfill a long-term investment strategy. Bob from Best Buildings sent Chad an $800 iPad with a note that read: "Take a look at the property details and our proposal. Regardless of your decision, the iPad is yours to keep." Chad kept the iPad and decided to purchase the property from Best Buildings.

Code of Conduct Analysis: Chad's acceptance of the iPad represents a conflict of interest. Chad's acceptance of the iPad makes the investment decision questionable. Chad also violated another Code of Conduct guideline against investment professionals accepting gifts or entertainment valued above $25.

A company's organizational culture should act to self-monitor and improve the performance of investment professionals. When a company's culture supports established codes and policies, conforming employees are quick to bring nonconforming employees back in line with the company's policies.

Example: Culture That Fosters Unethical Conduct

Creed Financial suffered significant investment losses related to its proprietary trading. An investigation revealed a culture in which risk measures were ignored. The prevailing culture provided nonconforming employees with the opportunity to incur and conceal losses.

Control Mechanisms in the Investment Function

The feedback loop of planning and control that we saw at the corporate level is repeated in the investment function. An investment unit's objectives, policies, and procedures all are designed to align the investment function with the corporate mission, strategies, and control framework. Since investment activities are organized around managing a portfolio or a composite of portfolios, mechanisms at this level are focused primarily on managing and controlling the investment portfolio.

The Investment Portfolio

Each institutional investment portfolio has its own guidelines and policies. Each investment portfolio has an **investment mission** or reason for existence.

> **Example: Investment Mission for an Endowment Portfolio**
>
> **Investment Mission**
>
> To preserve and enhance the portfolio's returns across all economic scenarios while providing consistent periodic distributions

A portfolio's investment mission is further clarified by one or more investment objectives. **Investment objectives**, also known as *portfolio objectives* or *fund styles*, are the financial goals for an investor to pursue in satisfying the investment mission.

> **Example: Investment Objectives**
>
> To preserve principal value
>
> To preserve purchasing power
>
> To grow capital
>
> To generate steady income

Portfolio managers use an **investment strategy**—a planned approach for dynamically achieving an investment mission or investment objectives. Two important broad categories of portfolio management strategies are passive and active investment strategies.

Active portfolio management involves constantly researching opportunities to add value to a portfolio by making trades and replacing existing assets with new ones.

> **Example: Active Portfolio Management**
>
> Purchasing stocks when their market value is low relative to their book value, and selling them when their market value is high relative to their book value

An active portfolio management style reflects a bias toward the belief that markets are not perfectly efficient. An active portfolio management style involves incurring more commissions on trades and more costs for researching market opportunities than does a passive style. Active management is not suitable for inherently illiquid investments. Active management is suitable only under both of the following conditions:

- The value added to the portfolio by research and trading must exceed the additional costs of research and trading

- Frequent trading must be suitable for the portfolio's objectives

Passive portfolio management is a style or strategy that relies upon careful portfolio construction and infrequent trading.

Example: Passive Portfolio Management

Purchasing a corporate bond and holding it until maturity

A passive style reflects a bias toward the belief that markets are strongly efficient. Trading volume and staff costs are lower for a passive management style than for an active management style. A passive style of portfolio management is consistent with holding assets that may be difficult to resell.

To support asset/liability management (ALM), life insurance companies tend to practice versions of passive management strategies for the general account.

The Investment Policy

At the portfolio level, the *investment policy* is the set of guidelines for managing a distinct investment portfolio or a composite of portfolios. Investment policies vary in their content. An investment policy typically includes the following elements:

- Long-term, broad investment objectives

Example: Investment Objective

The objective is to meet the ongoing income requirements of the Foundation while maintaining the real value of the portfolio.

- *Asset allocation criteria*—also known as *limitations on asset concentrations* or *diversification requirements*—are rules stating limits on the portion of a portfolio that may be invested in a stated category.

Examples: Asset Allocation Criteria

Assets will be diversified so that no single security will have a significant negative impact on the market value of the total portfolio. Assets will be diversified according to asset type, risk characteristics, and number of investments.

- Investments in a single industry or a single company are limited to 20 percent and 5 percent, respectively.

- Total international investments may not exceed 20 percent of the portfolio's investments.

- Total emerging market investments may not exceed 5 percent.

- Authorized investment categories and proportions

> ### Examples: Authorized Investment Categories and Proportions
>
> Between 55 and 85 percent of total funds will be invested in fixed income investments.
>
> Between 15 and 45 percent of total funds will be invested in equity investments.
>
> Between 2 and 10 percent of total funds will be in cash or cash equivalents.

■ A statement of relevant guidelines for portfolio management

> ### Example: Guideline for Portfolio Management
>
> The portfolio must be rebalanced within 90 days of exceeding any guideline.

■ Consistent standards for monitoring and evaluating investment performance and compliance with the investment policy

> ### Example: Standards for Monitoring Performance and Compliance
>
> Total fund performance will be monitored by the investment committee at least semiannually in comparison to the Barclay's Capital Market Index and the S&P 500 Index.

In addition, an investment policy may include criteria for asset trading practices—for example, to seek best execution in all trades and to provide periodic reports on commissions paid for trading. Some criteria may prohibit certain asset trading activities, such as trading in commodities, lending of securities, or exceeding limits on transaction costs. However, these more specific limits may alternatively be included in a separate risk management document that accompanies the investment policy.

Performance Management

The performance of both the investment portfolio and investment professionals must be evaluated periodically to maintain adequate control in the investment function. Figure 3.5 describes the control cycle for performance management in the investment function.

Performance Standards

Whether evaluating the portfolio's performance or the performance of investment professionals, the first step in performance management is establishing performance standards and objectives. A performance standard, often referred to as a *benchmark*, is a previously established level of performance against which actual performance can be measured and evaluated. One of the most important factors in performance evaluation is choosing appropriate benchmarks that can be used as an objective or a target for performance, and against which performance can be compared.

Figure 3.5. The Control Cycle for Investment Performance Management

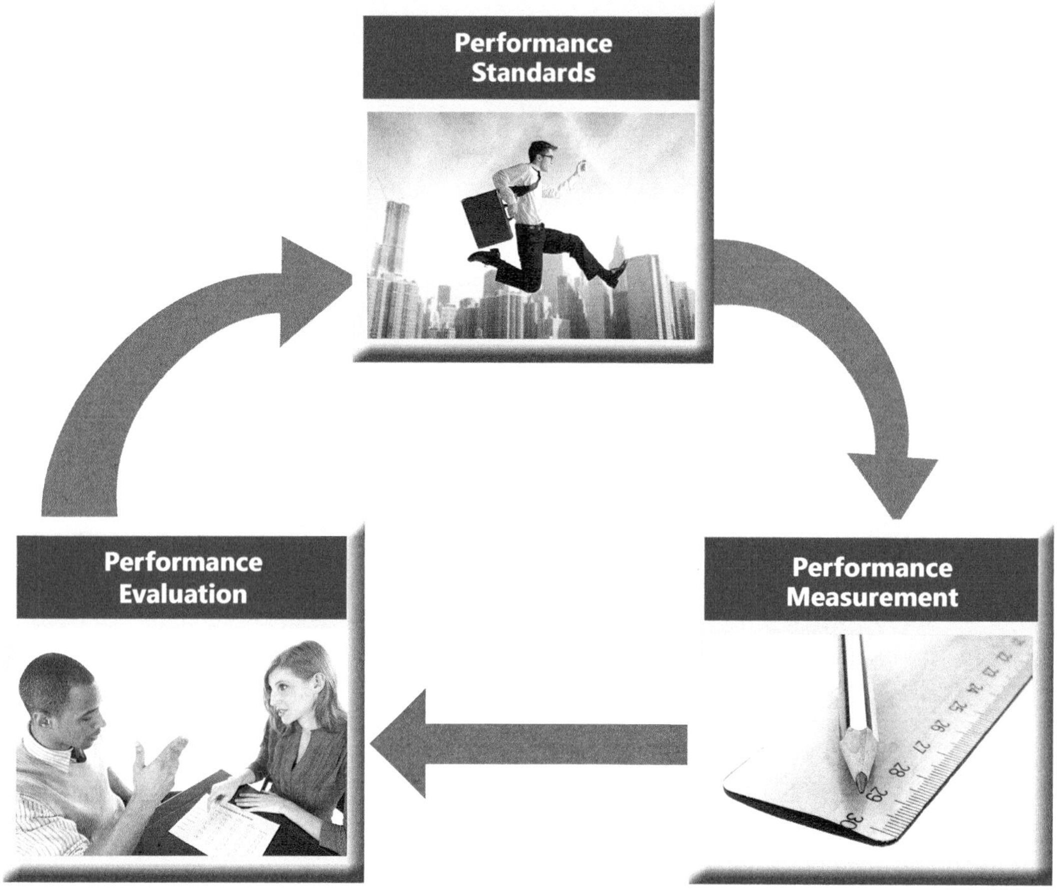

Investment Portfolio Evaluation

Portfolio performance evaluation is an assessment of a portfolio's success in achieving given objectives for asset values, revenues, and expenses over a specified period. *Portfolio performance measurement* refers to any one of several approaches to obtaining and expressing the information that investors need for assessing the effectiveness of their investments. Portfolio performance evaluation focuses on a portfolio's returns as well as its risk exposure. Investment portfolio policies and objectives specify many internal and external standards against which the portfolio's performance is measured. Internal standards include asset allocation and management guidelines.

Portfolio managers continuously monitor their own portfolios, and those of their peers, against established benchmarks. Portfolios are guided by very clear performance targets, which then form the basis for portfolio performance evaluation. We describe portfolio benchmarks and portfolio performance evaluation in greater detail in Chapter 5.

Investment Employee Performance Management

A typical employee performance management process follows the basic control cycle. Objectives are set for an employee at the beginning of an appraisal period. Because they are set at the beginning of the period, these objectives serve as steering controls. During the evaluation period, the evaluator and the employee review the employee's progress toward these objectives—a type of concurrent control. Finally, a formal performance evaluation is conducted at the end of the evaluation period—a type of feedback control.

Attribution analysis of portfolios is an analytical technique that involves assigning components of portfolio returns to specified portfolio management tactics, and in this way, identifies the share of portfolio returns associated with each portfolio management tactic. In other words, attribution analysis attempts to determine whether the portfolio manager added value to the portfolio through investment decisions or the portfolio performance results were merely luck.

Investment Portfolio Performance Reporting

Portfolio performance reporting is a process for regularly communicating the results of a portfolio's investment activity throughout the company's control framework. *Portfolio performance reporting standards* are practices accepted throughout the securities industry for proper reporting of portfolio values as of a specified date. The use of a standard accounting methodology to value and record assets is a critical element in comparing investment performance.

The CFA Institute's **Global Investment Performance Standards (GIPS®)** are standards for consistent reporting of investment performance, designed to ensure fair representation and full disclosure of investment performance across a global market. The GIPS standards provide a universal investment reporting methodology that allows a direct, apples-to-apples comparison of investment performance across different investment management companies, portfolios, portfolio managers, and jurisdictions. In order to claim compliance with the GIPS standards, institutional investors must adhere to the requirements included in the GIPS standards for investment performance measurement and presentation. Compliance includes adhering to certain calculation methodologies and disclosures. The CFA Institute strongly urges investors to undertake independent third-party verifications of their compliance with the GIPS standards. Where laws, regulations, or industry standards already impose requirements related to the presentation of investment performance, investors should comply with the GIPS standards in addition to applicable regulatory requirements.

Recall from Chapter 2 how the International Accounting Standards Board (IASB) maintains a single set of global standards for accounting and financial reporting: the International Financial Reporting Standards (IFRS). In the United States, SEC-sponsored financial reporting and control standards apply to companies that issue investment instruments. In addition, insurance companies in the United States must follow state requirements in the valuation and reporting of securities held in their general account portfolios.

Data Governance and Data Security

The investment function relies heavily on information. ***Data governance*** is a quality control discipline for assessing, managing, using, improving, monitoring, maintaining, and protecting organizational information.[7] Data governance provides a framework for potentially all organizational decisions about how to manage data, realize value from it, minimize its cost and complexity, manage risk, and ensure compliance with ever-growing external requirements for information.

Each organization places data governance into the organizational structure as management sees fit. In some companies, data governance may be included in the responsibilities of the board's standing committees for auditing or information technology (IT). Regardless of organizational structure, to be successful, data governance requires an executive-level sponsor from outside the IT function. In addition, successful data governance requires a senior-management-level advisory committee to support efforts at the functional level and ensure close coordination with IT. Data governance for the investment function includes the following primary elements:

- **Data definitions and standards** address nuances in data. The investment function must publish and maintain a comprehensive data dictionary and other data standards, including standards for understanding, interpreting, and calculating data elements, such as business rules, valid values, and data quality standards.

Example: Importance of Nuances in Data Definitions

Elm Investments owns sovereign bonds issued by Country X. Elm needs to estimate its risk exposure in Country X.

Elm's database includes the following fields: (1) *country of risk*, (2) *country of issue*, (3) *country of issuer*, and (4) *country of ultimate parent*. Data definitions that identify nuances in definitions are essential for Elm to obtain the necessary and correct information to estimate its risk exposure in Country X.

- The **ownership of and accountability for data** should be well defined within investments, with data management roles and responsibilities accepted and endorsed by senior management.

Example: Importance of Ownership and Accountability

Krypton Insurance identified a large and unexpected discrepancy in the Monthly Market Values Comparison Report. By following the trail of data transactions entered into the trading system, auditors identified which portfolio manager had entered an incorrect price. In addition, the supervisor in charge of checking the daily entries had failed to validate the daily trade prices log. The group manager who owned the daily price check process reprimanded the supervisor, and implemented a more effective control that was tested and approved by compliance.

- **Policies and procedures** provide accountability for each aspect of data quality and ensure its accuracy, accessibility, consistency, and completeness. Processes outline how the data is to be used, updated, delivered, and stored. Controls and audit procedures ensure ongoing compliance with established rules.

- **Data integration** addresses enterprise-wide methods, practices, processes, and tools for managing information consistently and effectively across all company functions. These practices include transformation, migration, distribution, utilization, access, and archiving—up to and including retirement and disposal of data.

- **Data delivery** involves strategic planning and alignment of enterprise data structures, processes, tools, and enterprise architecture to support the effective collection and distribution of data and content in a secure and reliable manner through a variety of channels to support and enable information sharing.

- **Data quality** addresses how core information assets achieve and sustain prudent levels of quality across all functions and processes. Data quality includes a balance of the following attributes: accuracy, completeness, timeliness, consistency, and auditability. Data metrics are essential to achieving and sustaining data quality.

The investment function sometimes develops a vision statement for data governance activities.

Example: Vision Statement for Investment Data Governance

Vision: To develop an information environment that balances the three critical components of data—accuracy, consistency, and timeliness—so that data is presented in a form that is easily transformed into information to support the investment decision-making process; and information that is integrated into an organization-wide framework.

In addition, typical data governance goals include

- Protecting the needs of data stakeholders

- Building standard and repeatable processes for managing data quality

- Developing the process and technology infrastructure to support efficient and effective data management and reporting

- Increasing awareness of data and reporting governance throughout the investment function

The investment function is a particularly attractive target for cyber criminals who wish to steal funds, steal information, disrupt normal business operations, and destroy public confidence in financial markets. Figure 3.6 presents protective measures that can help investment operations guard against unauthorized intrusions into information systems.

Figure 3.6 Measures to Protect Against Unauthorized Intrusions into Information Systems

Immediately implement security patches for any known security vulnerabilities

Maintain security programs that detect suspicious programs (malware) and immediately remove from systems or data storage devices

Guard distribution of information by using computer systems that identify when digital information leaves the company and where that digital information goes

Require at least two methods of user verification for individuals authorized to access company information

Ensure that system access authorization is accurately maintained, updated for employee changes, and limited to role-specific access

Block employee access to social media websites, such as Twitter or Facebook

Establish data policy agreements with suppliers and contractors, and monitor adherence to those agreements

Establish policies addressing employees' use of personal electronic devices for business purposes

Incorporate company expectations for how employees should handle and share business information into a Code of Conduct that is reviewed annually by employees, and reinforced as needed with education and training.

Monitor Internet activity with software programs that scan emails for specified terminology, and then automatically block those emails for review before they are allowed to be sent.[8]

Job Design and Safeguarding of Assets

Operational controls are frequently built into job designs. According to the **_principle of segregation of duties_**, also known as the principle of _dual control_, an employer should design jobs so that incompatible functions are assigned to different individuals. In this context, **_incompatible functions_** are job duties in the normal course of employment that, when combined, place an employee in a position where he could commit an illegal act or could conceal errors or irregularities. Segregating duties provides a framework in which a company can safeguard its assets by quickly detecting and correcting errors and irregularities.

Generally, an effective internal control system separates the custodial, authorization, and accounting tasks associated with a company's assets. In this context, *custodial tasks* include the physical or electronic handling of assets. Therefore, an employee who assumes physical or electronic custody of securities should not be the same employee who maintains the accounting records for these securities, nor should either of those employees be authorized to buy, sell, or otherwise dispose of these securities. Institutional investors often use an external provider for custodial tasks. Figure 3.7 provides illustrative control procedures for the safekeeping of securities held in the custody of third parties.

Figure 3.7 Internal Controls for Securities Held by Third Parties

Controls

- Safekeeping or custodial agreements are established with appropriate third parties that provide appropriate controls (i.e., SAS 70 or SSAE 16 reports).
- Investment securities are stored in a bank safe deposit box, bank trust or safekeeping department, fireproof vault, or safe.
- Investments are in the name of the company or nominee name.
- The presence of two or more employees is required for access to vaulted securities.
- Access logs are maintained by personnel who do not have physical access to the vault.

Audit Steps

- Examine custodial agreements.
- Obtain and review SAS 70 or SSAE 16 reports from third-party custodians for indications of control weaknesses.
- Review vault access logs for unauthorized or unusual activity.
- On-site visits of third-party custodians.

Source: LOMA, "325. Securities," in *Business Risks and Controls Handbook* [Atlanta: LOMA (Life Office Management Association, Inc.), © 2001], 325-1–325-10. Used with permission; all rights reserved.

Authorization Limits and Risk Limits

In addition to separating incompatible functions into different jobs, control features can be applied directly to a particular investment professional's job. *Execution of transactions as authorized* is an organizational control principle that concerns the delegation of authority to perform specified tasks and the communication of that authority to designated individuals. According to this principle, no financial transaction should occur without some form of official authorization. Many monetary transactions—such as purchasing and selling securities—require that the employee be authorized to handle the transaction. An *authorization limit* is the maximum monetary amount that a company employee has been granted official power to approve for disbursement without prior approval by someone with higher authority.

Example: Authorization Limits

A less experienced stock trader may have to obtain authorization for all stock purchases or sales in excess of $2 million.

A more experienced stock trader may have to obtain authorization for all stock purchases or sales in excess of $5 million.

Specific risk limits may be applied to the actions of various investment professionals. For example, an investment risk limit may authorize an investment professional to engage in only specific forms of risk taking.

Example: Risk Limits

Risk limits sometimes present an acceptable range of values, with specified upper and lower risk limits for the investment operation. For example, such a risk limit allows an investment professional to cautiously observe a developing risk so long as it doesn't exceed the established upper risk limit. However, corrective actions must be taken immediately when the risk exceeds the upper limit.

Another risk limit in investments is a *stop-loss limit* which indicates an amount of money that a portfolio's single-period market loss should not exceed. The period may be a day, a week, a month, or longer. A limit violation occurs whenever a single-period market loss exceeds a portfolio's stop-loss limit. In such a situation, the investment professional is required to come up with an action plan for bringing the portfolio back to its desired state.[9]

The Control Cycle in Portfolio Management

All of the elements of the control cycle make up a control framework that applies in various ways to different levels within the organizational hierarchy. Figure 3.8 shows the relationships between the corporate, functional, and operational levels of controls for the investment function.

Figure 3.8 Control Framework

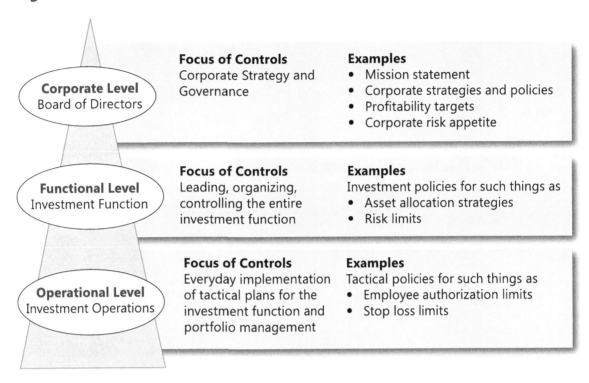

With all of these control mechanisms in place, a portfolio's performance is subject to close—almost minute-by-minute—monitoring. One popular technological tool used in portfolio performance management and control is a ***dashboard***, which is a technology-driven graphical display of the current, real-time status of important performance measures. In the investment function, a dashboard communicates the current status of investment outcomes and controls in a readily understandable format. Dashboards support decision making throughout all levels of an organization, showing a comparison of actual performance to performance standards. Figure 3.9 illustrates a basic dashboard for use in the investment function.

Through portfolio dashboards, portfolio managers have access to the current status of an array of important portfolio performance measures and comparisons to performance standards. Portfolio dashboards provide the following types of information to a portfolio manager:

- Whether all monitored risks are within limits, in a watch zone, or outside of the limits

- How a portfolio is currently performing relative to the performance of established benchmarks

- How well a portfolio's actual asset allocations match planned asset allocations

Figure 3.9 Dashboard for Investment Function

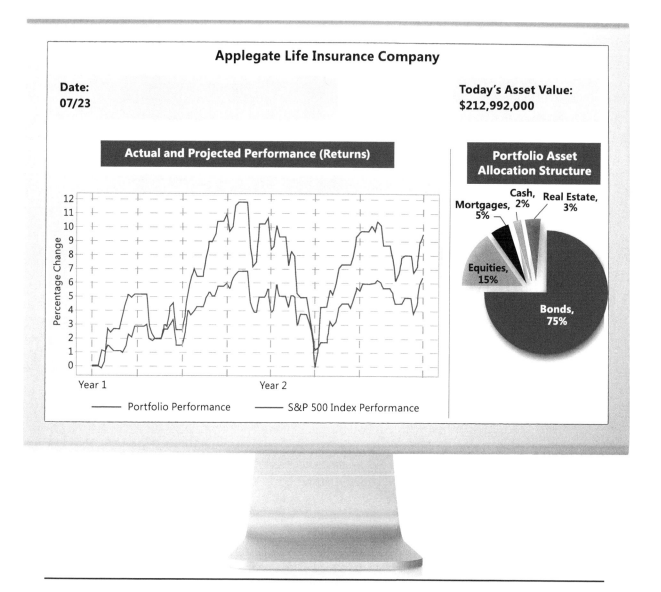

Abusive and Fraudulent Investment Practices

Although organizational planning and control mechanisms are designed to prevent abusive and fraudulent investment practices, a continuous flow of news stories proves that these processes fail. Most efforts toward preventing improper practices involve trying to provide or improve accountability and transparency in investment processes.

■ *Accountability* is the obligation of an organization to be responsible to its stakeholders for the results of its actions. Organizations that focus on accountability find that it leads to increased legitimacy and credibility with stakeholders, and increased employee commitment to doing the right thing. Also, companies that focus on accountability find that, when problems arise, the person or persons responsible for the problem can be identified, and the problem often quickly corrected.

- Transparency is the extent to which stakeholders have ready access to any required information about a company. Transparency helps to prevent the corruption that can occur when a select few have access to important information and use that information for personal gain. An ideal of transparency must be balanced with the need to appropriately protect sensitive information.

When accountability and transparency are impaired, individuals and entities are often able to engage in the following potentially abusive or fraudulent investment practices: insider trading, trading ahead of research reports, soft-dollar arrangements, collusion, theft, and fraud.

Insider Trading

Information about a company's financial performance, innovations, or legal struggles can significantly affect the value of a company's securities. *Material nonpublic information*, also known as *inside information* or *insider information*, is any nonpublic company information that a reasonable person would know might influence the market price of a company's securities. *Insider trading* is buying or selling a company's securities based on material nonpublic information. Insider trading occurs when individuals inside or outside a company take unfair advantage of and profit from material nonpublic information. A person does not have to benefit directly from inside information to be guilty of insider trading. For example, if an employee of a company advises a friend to buy or sell the company's stock, both individuals may be in violation of insider trading rules. Figure 3.10 describes some insider trading cases in the United States.

An individual's sharing of material nonpublic information can also constitute a breach of that individual's duty of confidentiality to the source of the confidential information. In 1997, the U.S. Supreme Court held, "A company's confidential information…qualifies as property to which the company has a right of exclusive use…The undisclosed misappropriation of such information, in violation of a fiduciary duty, constitutes fraud."[10] Since then, the prevailing legal view in the United States is that

Figure 3.10 Insider Trading Violations

Institutional investors have a huge comparative advantage over the average investor because of relationships in the corporate world that provide valuable insights into companies, trends, and potential market-moving events. However, when trades are based on nonpublic information about earnings, forecasts, and mergers, the investor is engaging in insider trading, which is illegal in many jurisdictions. One of the most difficult aspects about prosecuting insider trading is obtaining proof that will stand up in a court of law. Recent court cases in the United States indicate that it may not be so difficult in the future.

In 2011, Raj Rajaratnam, founder of the hedge fund Galleon Group, was found guilty by a New York court on 14 counts of conspiracy and securities fraud and was sentenced to 11 years in prison. In a separate civil case, he was fined $92.8 million for obtaining significant nonpublic information in more than a dozen companies. During his trial, the U.S. government presented recordings that revealed an extensive network of confidential informants that included board members and high-level employees of major companies. One of his informants was Rajat K. Gupta, a former Goldman Sachs board member. Mr. Gupta was found guilty in 2012 of conspiracy and securities fraud. He was convicted based on circumstantial evidence from phone records and trading logs.[11]

anyone who makes investment trades in any stock on the basis of misappropriated (stolen) information is guilty of insider trading.

Example: Insider Trading Using Misappropriated Information

An inventor agrees to sell the rights to a new manufacturing process to Dynamic Enterprises, a publicly traded company. If the inventor's attorney uses that material nonpublic information for the purposes of trading in Dynamic Enterprises stock, the attorney is guilty of insider trading.

In the course of their work, investment professionals often use material non-public information, and they may share such information with people who have a legitimate business need to know the information. Companies must establish procedures that prevent material nonpublic information from being circulated outside or within the company to employees who do not have a need to know. Figure 3.11 provides an example of procedures for preventing and detecting insider trading.

One of the control procedures listed in Figure 3.11 is a review of employee and proprietary trading activities. A **prohibited securities list**, also called a *restricted securities list*, is a list of securities that specified employees of the company, due to their job responsibilities, are prohibited from buying or selling for either their personal accounts or any accounts they control. Specified employees are additionally required to disclose to the employer all purchases and sales of securities for the employees' personal accounts. Such employees also are required to disclose which brokers they will use and then are permitted to use only those disclosed brokers for personal trades. Finally, these employees are required to have all of their personal brokerage confirmations and periodic brokerage account statements sent directly to the company's compliance department.

Trading Ahead of Research Reports

Another control shown in Figure 3.11 is the restriction of interdepartmental communication of material nonpublic information. To comply with regulatory standards, investment companies must establish policies and procedures that restrict or limit the information flow between the research department—or others with reasonable knowledge of what is in research reports—and the trading department. These controls are designed to prevent **trading ahead of research reports**, which occurs when the trading department of an investment company uses nonpublic information in a research report to increase or decrease their inventory positions in a particular security prior to the release of a research report.

Example: Trading Ahead of Research Reports

Traders at the Wallace Firm—a large broker-dealer—know that customer demand for Elegant Securities is likely to be high once a research report is published that reflects favorably on Elegant Securities. The traders purchase shares of Elegant Securities for their own inventory in order to be able to fill these expected customer orders from their own inventory position once the research report is released.

Figure 3.11 Internal Controls for Preventing Insider Trading

Controls

- Explicit insider trading standards, policies, and procedures are established, reviewed regularly, and updated as needed.
- Insider standards, policies, and procedures are communicated to all levels of employees who have access to information related to investments.
- All employees receive mandatory information or educational training about compliance with insider trading policies, which includes signing a code of conduct annually.
- Sensitive documents are safeguarded and secured through (1) restricted physical access to floors or designated areas; and (2) restricted electronic access through password protection.
- Companies safeguard material nonpublic information from internal intrusions by using walls, locks, and passwords.

Audit Steps

- Obtain and review the written policies and procedures.
- Determine that the policies and procedures have been implemented and consistently applied throughout the company, and that the following areas are adequately addressed:
  - Maintain restricted securities lists, watch lists, or rumor lists
  - Maintain an information barrier
- Maintain a system for updating control policies and procedures.
- Determine that policies have been effectively communicated to all employees.
- Document that staff training in policies and procedures was consistent with position or department.
- Confirm that sensitive documents are in a secure environment.
- Review system access documentation and observe IT systems in use.

Source: LOMA, "506. Insider Trading," in *Business Risks and Controls Handbook* [Atlanta: LOMA (Life Office Management Association, Inc.), © 2001], 506-1–506-14. Used with permission; all rights reserved.

Front Running

Front running is a specific type of insider trading that involves the purchase or sale of securities by an unethical investment professional based on advance knowledge of large pending orders from clients. In this manner, the unethical professional is able to personally profit by unfairly making use of nonpublic information. At the same time, front running reduces the clients' potential profits from their order.

Example: Front Running

A portfolio manager purchases a stock for his personal account prior to a large anticipated purchase of those same securities by an account that he manages for a customer. The portfolio manager knows that the large purchase will likely push up that stock's market price, allowing the portfolio manager to profit from purchasing the stock at a lower price prior to the large transaction.

Front running usually involves pending block transactions. Generally, a **block transaction**, also known as a *block trade*, is a securities transaction that is larger than normal given current market conditions—often a minimum of 10,000 shares.

Late Trading and Market Timing Abuses

Late trading is a type of illegal preferential treatment given to some investors who are allowed to trade securities, typically mutual funds, after a stock market closes using that day's closing prices. Late trading shouldn't be confused with *after-hours trading*, in which investors are allowed to trade openly in smaller stock exchanges for a few hours after the close of larger stock exchanges, such as the New York Stock Exchange or the NASDAQ stock market. Late trading is illegal because it allows certain investors to use the day's closing prices to conduct transactions, which are, in turn, based on information that became available only after the market's close. Again, late trading involves using nonpublic information to gain an unfair advantage over other participants in securities markets.

Market timing is investment activity designed to anticipate the future direction of a market, typically through economic data or technical indicators.[12] Although not necessarily illegal, market timing presents significant opportunities for abuse in some markets, particularly mutual funds, because a mutual fund's net asset value (NAV) must be calculated at the close of business each day. Because the NAV is set at different closing times in markets around the world, opportunities exist for investors to use the different closing times to their advantage. For example, investors may purchase mutual fund shares at the end of the U.S. business day after having taken into account material events that will impact markets in other countries. However, since the markets are closed, the prices do not reflect knowledge of the events.[13]

Example: Market Timing

Much can happen during the 15-hour difference between the market close in Japan and the market close in the United States that could affect the price of Japanese securities.

Market timing often results in higher administrative costs for the fund because of increased execution costs. Also, to accommodate the market timers, the affected fund has to keep higher levels of cash on hand than they might otherwise. That cash could instead be invested in securities that could earn more money for the fund—and its shareholders. Companies can counteract the effects of market timers by charging short-term trading fees or by reporting fair-value pricing for fund shares:

■ ***Short-term trading fees***, also known as an *exit fee*, a *back-end load*, a *contingent deferred sales charge*, a *short-term redemption fee*, or a *market-timing fee*, are fees that investment companies charge traders for investments that are not held for a minimum period of time, such as seven or 30 days. Such fees, which may be a specified percentage of an investor's proceeds or a set fee, are designed to discourage investors from making short-term trades.

■ ***Fair-value pricing*** is a practice in which mutual funds adjust their closing prices to reflect significant new information gained from other regions of the globe after the domestic market has closed. Fair-value pricing uses estimates of share values based on what the price would be were there an active market in which to trade.[14]

Soft-Dollar Arrangements

Soft-dollar arrangements consist of situations in which an institutional investor obtains products or services—often research services—from a broker-dealer, and in exchange, the institutional investor directs client brokerage commissions to the broker-dealer providing the product or service. When research services are involved, an argument can be made that the client benefits from the research, so it makes sense to bundle the cost of the research into the client's commission payment. However, ethical issues arise when the client pays more in brokerage commissions than the lowest available brokerage commission rates. Fiduciary responsibility prohibits an investment manager from benefiting from assets entrusted to it by a client. Clients and regulators want to ensure that the higher commission payment is a fair value for the research provided.

To resolve this dilemma, the Securities and Exchange Commission Act contains a "safe harbor" provision that protects investment managers, if they acted in good faith, from claims that they breached their fiduciary duties solely by reason of having caused clients to pay more than the lowest available commission rates for researching and executing a trade. This safe-harbor provision is typically limited to investment research services. The investment manager must make a good-faith determination that the amount of the commission is reasonable in relation to the value of the services provided. The SEC requires investment managers to disclose soft-dollar arrangements to their customers.[15] Complex guidelines surrounding use and disclosure of soft-dollar arrangements are subject to change and are beyond the scope of this text.

Collusion

Other prohibited investment practices, collectively called *collusion*, include

- Coordinating prices (including quotations), trades, or trade reports with other institutions

- Directing or requesting other institutions to alter a price (including a quotation)

- Threatening, harassing, coercing, intimidating, or otherwise attempting to improperly influence the activities of other institutions

    These prohibitions also apply to refusals to trade as well as other conduct that retaliates against or discourages competitive activities of market participants.

Theft and Fraud

Anytime people handle money, there is the potential for theft and fraud. Broadly, *theft* is the unlawful taking of money or property, while *fraud* involves obtaining an unauthorized benefit, such as money or property, by deception. Investment operations provide a great many opportunities for personal or institutional theft and fraud. On an individual level, documents or electronic files can be altered to divert fees for personal use—an example of ***misappropriation of funds***. On an institutional level, an investment company may illegally obtain funds from clients by committing a wide variety of unethical practices, such as overcharging clients for foreign exchange transactions. A much larger example of institutional fraud occurred in 2008 when regulators discovered an approximately $50 billion Ponzi scheme operated by Bernie Madoff.[16]

> **Example: Institutional Fraud**
>
> A ***Ponzi scheme***, also known as a pyramid scheme, is an investment fraud that involves the payment of purported investment returns to existing investors from funds contributed by new investors. A Ponzi scheme will collapse when it becomes difficult to recruit new investors or when a large number of investors wish to withdraw from the investment scheme at one time.[17]

Preventing abusive or fraudulent investment practices requires strong governance and control, and appropriate and enforceable laws, standards, and regulations.

Key Terms

corporate alignment	data governance
misalignment	principle of segregation of duties
audit committee	incompatible functions
investment committee	custodial tasks
corporate governance committee	execution of transactions as authorized
risk management committee	authorization limit
risk policy	stop-loss limit
risk appetite	dashboard
risk tolerance	accountability
risk limit	material nonpublic information
investment policy	insider trading
compensation and benefits policy	prohibited securities list
audit policy	trading ahead of research reports
audit	front running
conflict of interest	block transaction
investment mission	late trading
investment objective	market timing
investment strategy	short-term trading fee
active portfolio management	fair-value pricing
passive portfolio management	soft-dollar arrangements
asset allocation criteria	misappropriation of funds
attribution analysis	Ponzi scheme
Global Investment Performance Standards (GIPS®)	

Endnotes

1. "Symptoms of Corporate Strategy Misalignment," Leading Resources, 26 April 2010, http://corporate-strategy.net/corporate-strategy-misalignment/ (27 September 2012); Joe Evans, "3 Common Causes of Corporate Strategy Misalignment," *Method Frameworks Blog*, 20 April 2010, http://www.methodframeworks.com/blog/2010/3-common-causes-corporate-strategy-misalignment/index.html (27 September 2012).

2. "JP Morgan's $2bn Scandal," *MoneyWeek*, 17 May 2012, http://www.moneyweek.com/investments/stock-markets/us/jp-morgans-2bn-scandal-58905 (9 July 2012).

3. Leading Resources; Evans.

4. Joseph R. Lebens and Francois Morin, *Review and Comparison of Rating Agency Capital Models* (New York: Towers Perrin, 2006), 46–47, http://www.casact.org/research/drm/lebens.pdf (18 July 2012).

5. Institute of Risk Management, *Risk Appetite and Risk Tolerance*, Consultation Paper (London: Institute of Risk Management, 2011), http://www.theirm.org/publications/documents/IRM_Risk_Appetite_Consultation_Paper_Final_Web.pdf (18 July 2012).

6. "SSAE 16 vs. SAS 70: What You Need to Know and Why," NDB Accountants & Consultants, http://www.ssae16.org/white-papers/ssae-16-vs-sas-70--what-you-need-to-know-and-why.html (9 July 2012).

7. "IBM Data Governance," IBM, http://www.ibm.com/ibm/servicemanagement/us/en/data-governance.html (5 June 2012).

8. Rich Baich and Irfan Saif, "Cyber Threats and the Role of Governance" (PowerPoint presentation, Deloitte webinar, 31 May 2012), https://deloitte.zettaneer.com/Subscriptions/default.aspx?eventid=414075 (31 May 2012)

9. Riskglossary.com, s.v. "risk limits," http://www.riskglossary.com/link/risk_limits.htm (3 June 2012).

10. Mortimer B. Zuckerman, "Insider Trading Scandal Shows the Audacity of Greed," iHaveNet.com, http://www.ihavenet.com/United-States-Insider-Trading-Scandal-Shows-the-Audacity-of-Greed-MZ.html (27 September 2012); Peter Lattman and Azam Ahmed, "Rajat Gupta Convicted of Insider Trading," *DealBook*, 15 June 2012, http://dealbook.nytimes.com/2012/06/15/rajat-gupta-convicted-of-insider-trading/ (27 September 2012).

11. United States v. O'Hagan, 521 U.S. 642 (1997).

12. *Investopedia*, s.v. "market timing," http://www.investopedia.com/terms/m/markettiming.asp#axzz1wGfDAF1c (12 June 2012).

13. Ryan Bailey, "Fair Value Priced Mutual Funds and the Benchmarking Issue," J.P. Morgan, http://www.jpmorgan.com/tss/General/Fair_Value_Priced_Mutual_Funds_and_the_Benchmarking_Issue/1306536124638 (27 June 2012).

14. Ibid.

15. "Interpretive Release Concerning the Scope of Section 28(e) of the Securities Exchange Act of 1934 and Related Matters," Securities and Exchange Commission Release No. 34-23170, 17 C.F.R. Part 241 (1986).

16. Robert Lenzner, "Bernie Madoff's $50 Billion Ponzi Scheme," *Forbes*, 12 December 2008, http://www.forbes.com/2008/12/12/madoff-ponzi-hedge-pf-ii-in_rl_1212croesus_inl.html (27 September 2012).

17. "Ponzi Schemes – Frequently Asked Questions," Securities and Exchange Commission, http://www.sec.gov/answers/ponzi.htm (12 June 2012).

Chapter 4

Risk and Return in Investments

Objectives

After studying this chapter, you should be able to

4A Define rate of return, identify potential sources of investment returns, and calculate a rate of return

4B Define total return, risk-free rate of return, historical return, and future returns, and identify the elements of required return—including inflation, disinflation, deflation, the risk-free rate of return, and the risk premium—as well as the arithmetic mean annual return for an investment

4C Explain volatility and its relation to investment risk, discuss how the standard deviation of expected returns relates to risk in investments, and describe the concerns surrounding tail risk

4D Explain the risk-return trade-off, and demonstrate understanding of the concept by providing basic examples

4E Discuss key risk indicators and key performance indicators for investments

4F Explain and differentiate between systemic risk and specific risk; describe diversification; and discuss important sources of specific risk, including interest rate risk, credit risk, real estate risk, currency risk, and liquidity risk

4G Explain the use of duration statistics to measure interest-rate sensitivity, and interpret simple examples using duration statistics

4H Describe the term structure of interest rates and explain its applications to risk and return analysis, including the concepts of the yield curve; the normal, inverted, or flat shapes of the yield curve; and the sovereign yield curve

4I Discuss ways of estimating the loss risk from various known sources of specific risk, and estimate portfolio losses using a duration statistic, expected credit loss rates, loan-to-value ratios, and debt coverage ratios

Outline

People and companies invest to grow their money. To do this, investors take risks with their money. The core objectives of investing focus on earning investment returns and managing investment risks. In this chapter we present various concepts of investment risks and returns.[1]

You might hear investment professionals talk about "returns" when they anticipate the results of their investments. Before their investment results are known, investors expect that their results will be positive. Really, though, they're aware that a loss could materialize, and that they might have overestimated the actual return. These uncertainties represent the risks in investing.

Investment Returns

Investment returns potentially come from two primary sources: income and appreciation.

All investments can experience appreciation or depreciation. Gains from appreciation may be *realized*—if the asset is sold—or *unrealized* while the investor continues to hold the asset. When an investor sells an asset for a price greater than its purchase price, the investor *realizes* a gain on that investment. If an investor sells an asset for a price lower than its purchase price, unless the investment produced returns from other sources, the investor may realize a loss. Note that an investor *realizes* a gain or loss on an asset only when selling or otherwise disposing of the asset. If the market value of an asset increases while the investor continues to hold the asset, the increase in the asset's value is sometimes referred to as an *unrealized* gain.

Assets produce payments to the investor as follows:

- Common stocks can provide dividend payments in cash or securities; dividends from common stock can be increased, reduced, or eliminated while the underlying asset is held.

- Real estate, while the investor holds it, can produce rental payments.

- Bonds can produce periodic interest payments and repayment of principal.

- Mortgages can provide periodic payments of interest and repayment of principal.

- Commodities do not provide interest, dividends, or rent.

Figure 4.1 shows potential sources of income that various investments produce.

Return Concepts

An investment return can be expressed as a monetary amount or a percentage. A *rate of return* is investment earnings expressed as a percentage of the invested principal. Using a ratio or percentage to represent investment return allows investors to compare the returns from a variety of investment opportunities, regardless of differences in type of return, currency, or scale.

To find the rate of return for a specified principal amount and a specified amount of return, the investor divides the monetary amount of return by the principal amount, as represented in the following formula:

$$\text{Rate of return} = \frac{\textbf{Amount of return}}{\textbf{Principal amount}}$$

The following example shows a calculation of the rate of return for an investment.

Example: Rate of Return Calculation

Rhoda invested a principal amount of $10,000. At the end of one year, her investment had earned a return of $750.

$$\text{Rate of return} = \frac{\$750}{\$10,000} = 0.075 = 7.5\%$$

Thus, Rhoda's rate of return on her investment is 7.5 percent.

Figure 4.1. Sources of Income Produced by Various Investments

Although all investments can fluctuate in value, the following sources of income differ by investment type:

Investment Type	Income Type		
	Interest	Dividends	Rent
Common stocks	✗	✓	✗
Directly owned real estate	✗	✗	✓
Bonds	✓	✗	✗
Mortgages	✓	✗	✗
Commodities	✗	✗	✗

✓ indicates Yes; ✗ indicates No

Some investments pay interest to investors at a stated percentage or some other specified amount. In such cases, the stated rate may not be equal to the investor's rate of return, and the specified amount may not equal the investment principal. Such a stated rate of interest is known as *nominal return, nominal interest,* or a *nominal rate*. **Nominal return**, also known as *nominal interest*, or a *nominal rate*, is defined as the stated rate of return on an investment without adjustment for inflation or other factors. Any explicitly expressed rate of return can also be called a nominal rate of return.

Moreover, return can be measured over the entire holding period of an investment, or it can be measured over a uniform time period, usually a year. The *holding period* of an investment is the length of time an investor owns the investment.

Total Return

The **total return** on a single investment or an investment portfolio is the sum of *all* returns from the investment over a given period, typically one year. Thus, total return includes all income as well as realized and unrealized gains or losses. Total return may be historical or expected, and can be expressed as a monetary amount or a percentage. For performance measurement, total return is usually presented as a percentage.

Example: Total Return Calculation

One year ago, Rhoda purchased $10,000 of stock in the Bright Future Corporation.[2] During the year, Rhoda received $750 in dividends on her Bright Future stock, and did not sell any of her shares. Today, Rhoda's stock has a market value of $10,500.

First, Rhoda calculates her unrealized gain on the Bright Future stock as follows:

$$\$10,500 - \$10,000 = \$500$$

To find the total return on her stock, Rhoda applies the total return formula:

Total return = Income + Realized gain or loss + Unrealized gain or loss

$$= \$750 + \$0 + (\$10,500 - \$10,000)$$
$$= \$750 + \$0 + \$500$$
$$= \$1,250$$

Thus, the monetary amount of Rhoda's total return on this investment is $1,250. Next, we find the rate of total return on this investment.

$$\text{Rate of return} = \frac{\$1,250}{\$10,000} = 12.5\%$$

Thus, the rate of the total return on Rhoda's investment is 12.5 percent.

For instructional purposes in this chapter, we focus some examples of investment performance on single assets such as Rhoda's Bright Future stock.

This text's primary concern, however, is institutional investing, and a financial institution views investing in terms of portfolios more than in terms of single assets. Total return for a portfolio encompasses all sources of return for all assets in a portfolio. Calculating total return for a diversified portfolio is considerably more complex than calculating the total return for a single investment. Total return is an important basic tool for evaluating asset classes and portfolios; however, it is not necessarily the best measurement tool for every situation—particularly for measuring performance of institutional portfolios. We discuss portfolio return concepts more in later chapters.

Risk-Free Rate of Return

The risk-free rate of return, also known as the *risk-free rate* or the *riskless rate*, is the return on a risk-free investment. For this purpose, certain investments have no history of default, and thus are used to represent a risk-free investment.

Examples: Risk-Free Investments

The interest rate on a three-month U.S. Treasury bill is commonly used to represent the risk-free rate. Other highly stable examples of sovereign debt securities—debt securities issued by sovereign governments—are sometimes used as a reference for the risk-free rate.

An investor typically requires more than the risk-free rate of return on an investment as incentive for taking an investment risk. For a risky investment, any investment return equal to or lower than the risk-free rate is not reasonable, because the investor could instead get the same or a higher return with no risk by investing in the risk-free investment.

Historical Return

Investment return may be historical, expected, or required. **Historical return**, sometimes referred to as *actual return*, is a known investment performance result. Historical return can be expressed as a monetary amount or a percentage rate of return. Historical return is a measurement of known past performance only. Many approaches to calculating and describing investment returns are compatible with historical returns.

Example: Monetary Return and Rate of Returns

For Rhoda's Bright Future stock, the historical *monetary* return during the previous year was $1,250; the historical *rate* of return on her stock was 12.5 percent.

Future Returns

When considering a future investment result, all investors expect a positive investment return, even while they are aware of the potential for a loss. Otherwise, why would they invest? Two return concepts for expressing attitudes toward future investment returns are expected return and required return. Although these concepts are different, expected and required return can both be expressed as amounts or rates, but they are more commonly expressed as rates of return.

Expected Return

An *expected return* is generally the total amount or annual rate of return an investor expects an investment to earn, given market forces affecting the investment. Institutions take great care in estimating expected returns, often applying quantitative economic and financial models to local and global economic factors.

Required Return

By contrast, required return essentially sets a minimum acceptable value on expected future total return. **Required return**, also known as the *required rate of return* or the *market required rate of return*, is the annual rate of investment return an investor requires as reasonable compensation for a given level of risk and to satisfy the investor's objectives. In this context, a risk premium is the extra compensation an investor requires for taking a specific risk.

> **Example: Establishing Required Return**
>
> Required return = Inflation rate + Risk-free rate + Risk premium
>
> = Inflation rate + T-Bill rate + Risk premium

Investors set significantly different values for required return. For an institutional investor, an organizational value for required return takes into account the organization's growth goals and the minimum rate of return needed to sustain the business.

A **hurdle rate** is the minimum rate of return an institution must obtain in compensation for entering into any investment. In some contexts, required return for an individual or an institution is used as a hurdle rate.

Calculating an expected or a required return typically calls for knowing values for the inflation rate, risk-free rate of return, risk premium, and real return.

Inflation

The presence of inflation in an economy erodes the purchasing power of money. Various statistical services track inflation through price indexes. Up to this point, we have described investment returns without adjusting for the effects of inflation. For investment return calculations, the inflation rate usually expresses the percentage increase in the prices of goods and services during a specific period, typically one year.

> **Example: Erosion of Purchasing Power Due to Inflation**
>
> The annual inflation rate is 4 percent. After one year passes, goods and services will cost an additional 4 percent, which equals 104 percent of their cost today. Note that 104 percent is equal to 1.04. Thus, after one year, an automobile that costs $20,000 today will cost $20,800, calculated as
>
> $$\$20{,}000 \times 104\% = \$20{,}000 \times 1.04 = \$20{,}800$$

As time passes in the presence of inflation, for an investor to maintain the same purchasing power for a given principal amount, the investor's required return must be greater than or equal to the expected inflation rate. Otherwise, the investor loses purchasing power. *Disinflation* is a condition in which the rate of inflation diminishes.

Deflation is also possible. Deflation can be viewed as the opposite of inflation. As time passes during a period of deflation, goods and services drop in price and existing goods lose value.

Risk Premium

In investments, a risk premium is a portion of the investment compensation that investors expect to earn in excess of the risk-free rate and inflation. As such, a risk premium covers compensation for specific sources of investment risk, and each category of specific risk has a risk premium.

- A *credit risk premium* is the portion of investment return greater than the risk-free rate, and it is required to compensate an investor for taking the extra risk in a bond or the credit markets in general.

- An *equity risk premium* is the portion of investment return greater than the risk-free rate, and it is required to compensate an investor for taking the extra risk in an equity investment or the equity market in general.

Real Rate of Return

To determine the loss in purchasing power of an investment in the presence of inflation, investors refer to the *real rate of return,* also known as real return. Real rate of return is the rate of return on an investment after adjustment for inflation and potentially some other systemic effects. The following formula expresses the relationship between the nominal return, the inflation rate, and the real rate of return:

Real rate of return = Nominal return − Inflation rate

Expected and required returns provide only a theoretical guideline for an institutional investor because investors cannot predict with certainty either the inflation rate or the risk premium. In reality, an institutional investor's expected and required return change in response to market conditions, taxes, and economic conditions. Institutional investors use several sophisticated approaches for estimating expected and required returns. Specific components of expected return can differ by the type of asset involved.

Return Concepts Addressing the Investment Period

According to the time period over which the return is calculated or the investment is held, returns can be expressed as a holding period return, an arithmetic mean annual return, and an annualized return.

Holding Period Return

An investor's *holding period* with respect to an investment is the period of time the investor owns that investment. A **holding period return**, also known as a *holding period yield* or *holding period rate of return*, is the rate of return on an investment over the entire period of owning the investment. A holding period return is relevant primarily for investments held for less than a full year.

> **Example: Holding Period Return**
>
> Booking Enterprises paid $250,000 for 10,000 shares of common stock and held the stock for six months, when Booking sold the shares for a total of $252,000. After six months, Booking had collected dividends valued at $1,250. For this holding period of six months, Booking had a total return on this investment of $3,250.
>
> Booking's holding period return on the stock investment is calculated as follows:
>
> $$\text{Holding Period Return} = \frac{\$3,250}{\$250,000}$$
>
> $$= 1.3\%$$

Arithmetic Mean Annual Return

The **arithmetic mean annual return** is the average return of a series of annual investment returns during a multiyear holding period. This measure is not commonly used in published performance presentations.

The arithmetic mean annual return indicates an apparently smooth rate of investment return over a multiyear holding period, regardless of whether the annual returns were actually consistent from year to year. However, the actual magnitude of any fluctuation in returns over a multiyear holding period affects overall return on the investment for that period. Thus, arithmetic mean annual return can be deceptive.

The formula for calculating arithmetic mean annual return is as follows:

Arithmetic mean annual return =

$$\frac{\textbf{Year 1 return + Year 2 return + ...Year } \textit{\textbf{n}} \textbf{ return}}{\textbf{Total number of years, } \textit{\textbf{n}}}$$

The following example demonstrates calculating the arithmetic mean annual return of an investment over a three-year holding period.

Example: Arithmetic Mean Annual Return Calculation

An investment has the following annual rates of return over a holding period of three years:

	Year 1	Year 2	Year 3
Yearly Return	3%	4%	8%

Over three years, the arithmetic mean annual return of this investment is 5 percent, calculated as follows:

Arithmetic mean annual return =

$$\frac{(3\% + 4\% + 8\%)}{3} =$$

$$\frac{15\%}{3} = 5\%$$

An investment that produces consistent returns over a period of time will have a greater value at the end of the period than will an investment that has the same arithmetic mean annual return but greater fluctuation in returns from year to year.

Annualized Return

A variation on a rate of return calculation is the annualized rate of return, also known as a *yearly rate of return* or an *annual rate of return*. An **annualized return** expresses a return for a period longer or shorter than a year as a rate of return for one whole year.

Volatility in Investments

In investments, *volatility* refers to the tendency for an investment's market price—or potentially other aspects of market value, such as bond yield—to change over a specified time period. *Volatility* also is a statistical measure of that tendency in terms of frequency and dispersion of market values. Investments with high volatility can show considerable price fluctuation over a short period. Volatility is an aspect of risk.

Volatility may be historical or implied. *Historical volatility*, also known as *realized volatility*, refers to the known past tendency for market prices to change over a given time period. Implied volatility is a theoretical concept, and we do not discuss it further.

To measure investment volatility, investment professionals refer to standard deviations of asset prices—or, in some cases, bond yields—over time. Historical volatility is measureable as the standard deviation of returns on an investment or investment category over a specified time period.

Standard Deviation of Investment Returns

You probably recall that the standard deviation measures the dispersion of a data set from its mean. Investors can use the mean of a data set consisting of many expected returns as a point estimate for unknown expected returns.

When estimating an expected return for a specified asset, investors take into account historical data for similar assets. If an investor is satisfied to have a point estimate of expected return, then the expected return from a relevant historical data set can support an approximate value for that point estimate. If an investor requires an estimate of expected return that can be attached to a confidence level, the investor probably prefers a range estimate of returns such as one represented by a standard deviation of historical return data.

Figure 4.2 shows the average annual historical return for various asset classes, on the one hand, and the risk for those classes, as measured by standard deviation, on the other hand. In the chart, which is based on a report by New Frontier Advisors, you'll notice that the values for return are consistently lower than the values for risk.

The higher the standard deviation of the historical returns on an investment, the more an actual return can be expected to vary from the expected—or the *mean*—historical return, and, therefore, the greater the investment risk. A higher standard deviation implies greater volatility. The higher the volatility, the greater the uncertainty that the investment's performance will be consistent with its average return.

Figure 4.3 shows normal distribution curves for historical returns from two portfolios with the same value for expected return—that is, they have the same mean—but different standard deviations and, therefore, different risk levels.

Example: Risk and Standard Deviation

Two portfolios have the same mean and the following standard deviations of returns:

Portfolio	Value of standard deviation (%)
A	10.11
B	9.63

This information indicates that the riskier portfolio is Portfolio A, because it has a higher standard deviation of expected returns than does Portfolio B.

Figure 4.2 Risk-Return Comparison for Various Asset Classes

Risk-return estimates are based on historical data and capital market theory.

Asset Class with a representative index	Return*	Risk**
Fixed Income *SBBI 30-day U.S. Treasury Bill* *(1973–2009)*	1.2%	1.2%
U.S. Intermediate-Term Bonds *Barcap U.S. Interm. Gov/Credit Bond* *(1973–2009)*	3.3%	4.7%
U.S. Long-Term Bonds *Barcap U.S. Long Gov/Credit Bond* *(1973–2009)*	4.4%	10.2%
International Government Bonds *Citigroup World Gov Bond ex US* *(1985–2009)*	5.5%	10.8%
U.S. Large Company Stocks *SBBI Large Company Stocks* *(1973–2009)*	6.1%	15.9%
U.S. Small Company Stocks *SBBI Small Company Stocks* *(1973–2009)*	10.4%	21.9%
Emerging Market Stocks *MSCI Emerging Markets* *(1988–2009)*	14.1%	25.0%
U.S. Real Estate *DJ U.S. Select REIT* *(1978–2009)*	8.8%	19.3%

* Return is adjusted for inflation
** Risk is represented by value of one standard deviation

Source: Adapted with permission from Richard Michaud, Robert Michaud, and Elise Schroeder, "Table 2—Annualized CPI Relative Risk-Return Estimates: 1973–2009," in *Fi360 Asset Allocation Optimizer: Risk-Return Estimates* (Boston: New Frontier Advisors, 2010), 5.

Standard deviation can be expressed in the same units as the underlying data. The standard deviation of historical returns is potentially expressed in terms of either basis points or percentages, whichever is consistent with the return itself.

Figure 4.3 Return and Standard Deviation for Investments

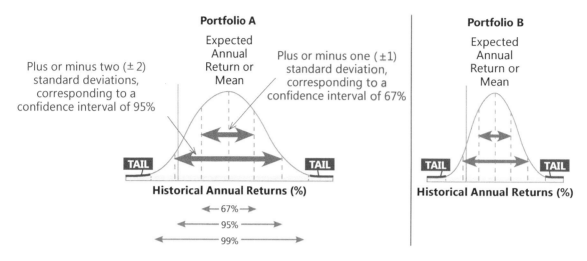

The standard deviation and, therefore, the risk of Portfolio A is greater than the standard deviation and risk of Portfolio B.

Between **plus and minus one standard deviation** corresponds to a confidence interval of **67%**.
Between **plus and minus two standard deviations** corresponds to a confidence interval of **95%**.
Between **plus and minus three standard deviations** corresponds to a confidence interval of **99%**.

By viewing the normal curve, we see another risk concept: tail risk. Tail risk is represented in values in the areas beyond three standard deviations—or for some purposes, two standard deviations—away from the mean of a probability distribution. For a normal curve, we know that the area within plus and minus three standard deviations of the mean amounts to approximately 99 percent of the area under the normal curve. Thus, the area that lies outside plus and minus three standard deviations represents about 1 percent of the area under the curve. This remaining 1 percent is the area in both tails of the curve. Now, although we make reference here to a normal curve for convenience in an educational purpose, most financial risk curves are not normal curves.

The term *tail risk* generally signifies risks of low-probability but high-impact occurrences. The potential financial losses represented in the tails of statistical probability distribution curves are collectively called *tail risks*. The exact interpretation of a tail risk depends on the situation being modeled. When the probability distribution curve represents investment returns, the values to the left of the mean are unsatisfactory returns or even losses, and values to the right of the mean are the more desirable outcomes.

Often, investors are not satisfied with using a point estimate for expected return. A point estimate is necessarily less reliable than a range estimate, also called an *interval estimate*. If we know the mean of expected returns for a type of investment as well as the standard deviation of those expected returns, we can calculate ranges of expected returns. When a confidence estimate can be attached to the range of estimated outcomes, the range is called a *confidence interval*.

A range of potential outcomes is a continuous array of numbers between a lower and an upper limit. For our example, we set the upper and lower limits of the range at plus and minus one standard deviation from the mean.

The range of expected returns is calculated as follows:

Confidence Limits on a Range Estimate

Required information:

Value of the mean of a data distribution

Value of one standard deviation for a data distribution

Equations:

Lower limit of range = Mean minus one standard deviation

Upper limit of range = Mean plus one standard deviation

Consider the following example using these data to estimate risk, or variation in returns.

Example: Calculating Expected Returns for a Specified Risk Level

In this example, we apply the following data to estimate an expected return.

Asset Class with a representative index	Return	Risk
U.S. Long-Term Bonds Barcap U.S. Long Gov/Credit Bond (1973–2011)	4.4%	10.2%

In our data table, U.S. long-term bonds have an expected return of 4.4 percent, with a standard deviation of plus or minus 10.2 percent. Thus, a movement of plus or minus one (+/– 1) standard deviation could cause returns to fall in the range from a loss of 5.8 percent to a gain of 14.6 percent, calculated as follows:

Lower limit of the range:
4.4% – 10.2% = a loss of 5.8%

Upper limit of the range:
4.4% + 10.2% = a gain of 14.6%

If an investor uses one standard deviation in a confidence interval calculation, about a 67 percent confidence level is attached to the estimate. The 67 percent confidence level means that about 67 percent of actual returns are expected to fall within the specified range of expected returns. We can reach this conclusion because, for a normal curve, one standard deviation describes about 67 percent of the estimates or probable outcomes.

Example: Confidence Level and Confidence Interval

Because we calculated our example above with one standard deviation, we can state at a 67 percent confidence level that expected returns will fall in the range—or *confidence interval*—from a loss of 5.8 percent to a gain of 14.6 percent.

To gain greater confidence in an estimate of expected returns, investors can estimate the range of expected returns using two standard deviations. Two standard deviations from the mean describe all estimated outcomes within 95 percent of the area under a normal curve. When an investor uses two standard deviations to set a confidence limit, she can set a 95 percent confidence level on her return estimate.

An investment can fail to achieve its expected return just by having flat returns at a level below its expected return, although other factors can account for a failure to realize expected returns.

The Risk-Return Trade-Off

Companies or institutions must assume risk to achieve an expected return. The ultimate goal of investing is to seek returns while limiting risks to an acceptable level. In general, the greater the risk associated with an investment, the greater the expected return. The interplay between risk and return in investing is known as the risk-return trade-off. The risk-return trade-off affects virtually every financial decision.

Examples: Indicators of Higher Investment Risk

Generally, higher risk is associated with

- Longer investment holding periods
- Lower credit ratings for borrowers
- Higher interest charges to borrowers
- Less knowledge about investment risks
- Less transparency in reporting about investment risks
- Investments with poor liquidity or poor marketability
- Loans made in the absence of security or collateral
- Less knowledge about or certainty of income streams or cash flows

Figure 4.4 shows observable investment characteristics and situations that affect an investment's risks and returns.

As we saw in Chapter 3, a corporate risk committee sets policies addressing a corporation's risk appetite and risk tolerance. These strategic, corporate-level policies articulate the company's acceptable levels of risk across the entire scope of the business. These risk policies are further interpreted for application at each succeeding level of management, as illustrated in Figure 4.5.

Figure 4.4 Trade-Offs Between Risk and Return in Various Investments

Lower Risks Associated with Lower Expected Returns	Higher Risks Associated with Higher Expected Returns
Owning a short-term bond	Owning a long-term bond
Lending to a borrower with a high credit rating	Lending to a borrower with a poor credit rating
Owning an asset that is easy to sell at a fair value	Owning an asset that is difficult to sell at a fair value
Owning a loan that is secured by collateral	Owning a loan that is unsecured by collateral
Owning an investment that pays returns in the investor's domestic currency	Owning an investment that pays returns in a currency foreign to the investor
Owning a corporate bond rated NAIC 1	Owning a corporate bond rated NAIC 3

Figure 4.5. Alignment of Policies in the Corporate Hierarchy

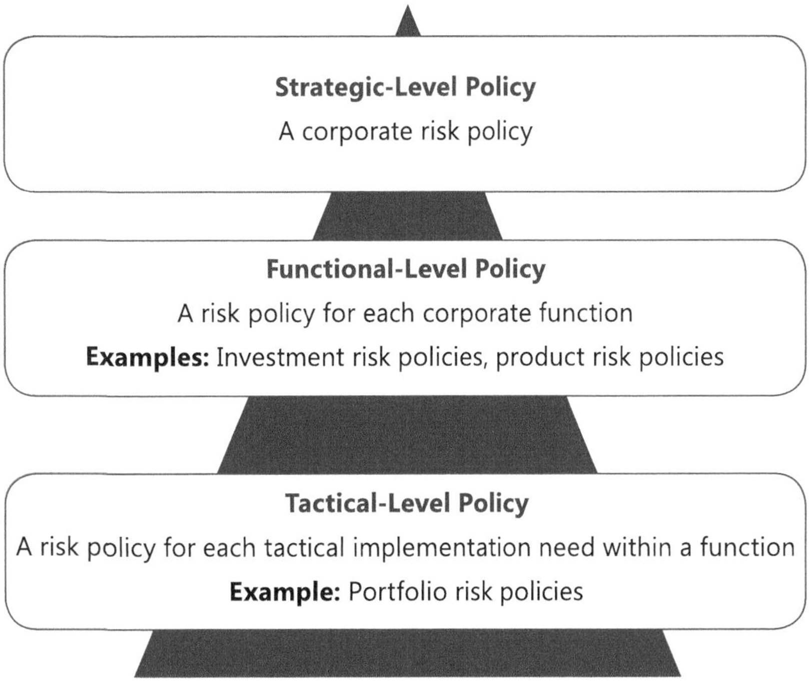

Strategic-Level Policy

A corporate risk policy

Functional-Level Policy

A risk policy for each corporate function

Examples: Investment risk policies, product risk policies

Tactical-Level Policy

A risk policy for each tactical implementation need within a function

Example: Portfolio risk policies

At the strategic level, statements of risk appetite and risk tolerance apply to corporate-level measures of performance, including the company's capital, profits, and return on capital. These corporate-level measures provide a summary view of results from all corporate activities. Corporate policies, including risk policies, are further articulated at the functional level for investments, as well as for company products and other company activities. As illustrated in Figure 4.6, statements of risk appetite and risk tolerance are articulated at a strategic level, a functional level, and an implementation level.

For institutional investors, the ultimate goal of investing is to seek a specified level of returns while meeting specified risk tolerance objectives and capital adequacy goals. An institutional investor's statements of risk appetite and risk tolerance must specify types and amounts of risk, which must be consistent with company objectives.

For operational guidance, the risk tolerance and risk appetite specified for the investment function are often translated into quantifiable key risk indicators and key performance indicators, as follows:

- A *key risk indicator*, known as *KRI*, is a quantitative measure that indicates the level of potential adverse impact in a given activity. A KRI should be readily observable, and should be closely correlated with a likelihood of a risk impact. A KRI directly addresses risk tolerances.

Figure 4.6. Corporate Alignment, Risk Appetite, and Risk Tolerance

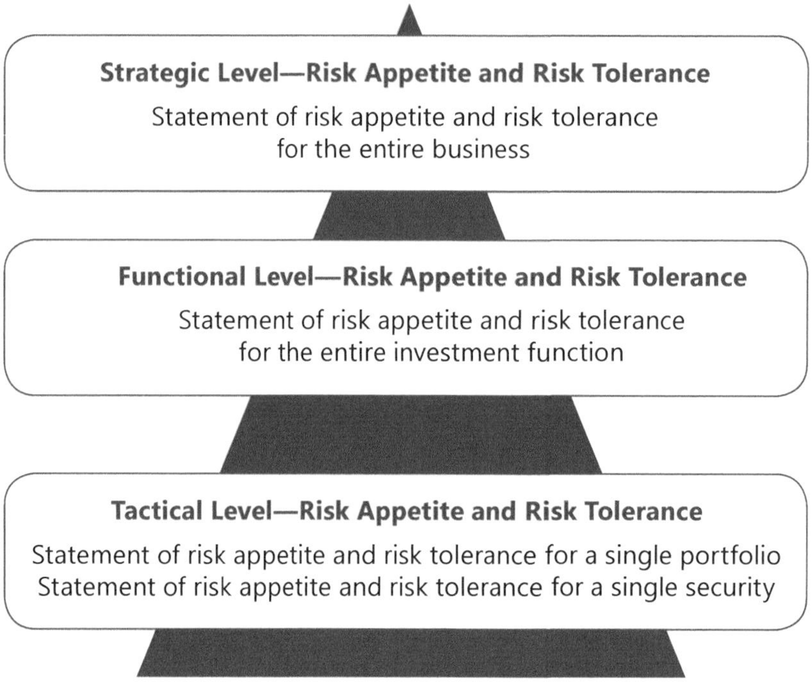

Strategic Level—Risk Appetite and Risk Tolerance
Statement of risk appetite and risk tolerance
for the entire business

Functional Level—Risk Appetite and Risk Tolerance
Statement of risk appetite and risk tolerance
for the entire investment function

Tactical Level—Risk Appetite and Risk Tolerance
Statement of risk appetite and risk tolerance for a single portfolio
Statement of risk appetite and risk tolerance for a single security

- A ***key performance indicator,*** known as ***KPI***, is a quantitative measure that indicates success in the performance attributes of a specified activity. The attributes of a KPI include a target performance value—the goal, the achieved value, the current status value, and potentially a trend. A KPI indirectly addresses risk appetite.

In the investment function, dashboard displays typically indicate relevant KRIs and KPIs.

Because of different inherent qualities of debt and equity securities, investors generally require a lower return for debt securities than for equity securities.

Risk in Investments

For purposes of portfolio management, investment risks may be assigned to one of two categories: specific risks or systemic risks.

The concept of specific risk relies on the concept of diversification. Recall that *diversification* is a defensive principle of investment portfolio construction; it involves balancing the selection of portfolio assets over a variety of types of securities, industries, populations, or geographic areas. Diversification spreads risk across many risk characteristics to reduce the effect of any one risk.

Diversification can reduce or mitigate many types of investment risk in portfolios. We refer to the risks that can be substantially reduced by diversification as ***specific risks*** or, alternatively, *diversifiable risks*. Only risks that can be modeled and managed in a portfolio qualify as specific risks. Because portfolio management techniques can mitigate these risk exposures, estimates of expected returns do not incorporate a risk premium for specific risks.

The alternative category of risks is ***systemic risk***, or alternatively, *nondiversifiable risk*. Systemic risks have broad, similar effects on all elements in an economic system, and cannot be eliminated through diversification.

Figure 4.7 illustrates the notion that total portfolio risk consists of specific risks and systemic risks. The figure also shows that, as more assets are included in a portfolio, the impact of specific risk on returns diminishes. Thus, this figure illustrates the benefits of diversification.

The difference between specific risk and systemic risk hinges on whether the relevant risk can be eliminated from a specified portfolio through diversification. Although we can generalize about which risks are specific or systemic, these distinctions often are not clear in a real-world circumstance.

Examples: Specific and Systemic Risks

Specific risks include interest rate risk, credit risk, real estate risk, liquidity risk, and currency risk. (These categories of specific risk are not mutually exclusive.)

Systemic risks can include the economic impacts of fiscal and monetary policies, interest rate policies, tax policies, inflation, deflation, unemployment, shortages of labor and materials, business cycles, and asset bubbles. We discuss asset bubbles shortly.

Figure 4.7 Total Portfolio Risk

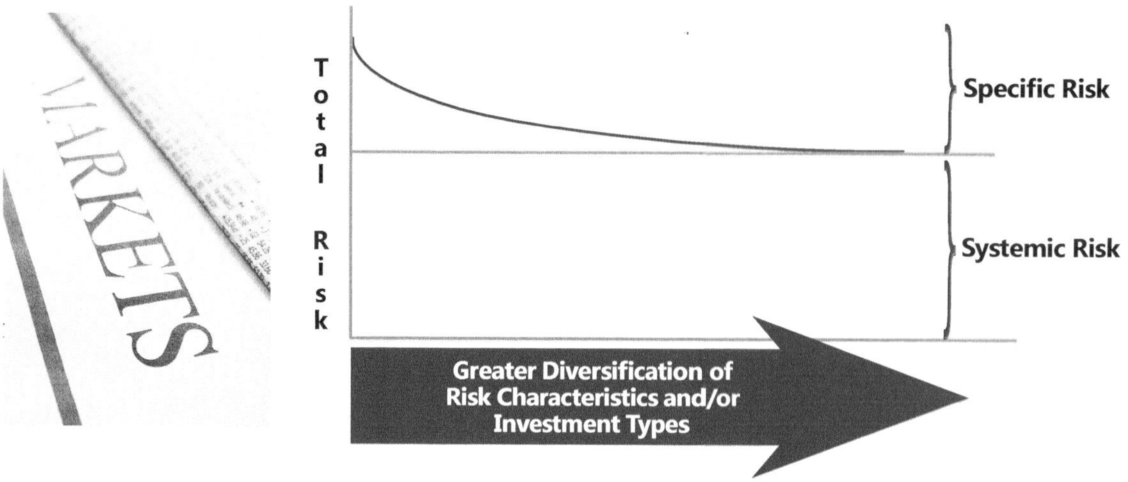

Source: Patricia Wilson Fridley (Senior Advisor, Center for Economic Stability, LLC). Used with permission.

Systemic Risk

Systemic risk is important to institutional investors because it represents the risks that investors cannot diversify away. Investors must address systemic risks through other approaches to risk management. Although we are most aware of the catastrophic effects of systemic risks, these risks do not necessarily have catastrophic impact. Systemic risk can affect securities markets, banking systems, and currencies, resulting in widespread losses across all types of investments.

A *systemic crisis* is a series of adverse events occurring in a significant number of financial institutions or markets. A systemic crisis results in severe impairment of the functioning of the financial system. The impact typically has a ripple effect across several interdependent nonfinancial systems, furthering the damage to the financial systems.

Systemic risk can lead to a systemic crisis. However, in the initial stages, systemic crises can be difficult to distinguish from normal business cycle contractions. Participants in certain sectors of the economy may overlook indicators of a possible systemic crisis and, instead, believe conditions to be normal. Adverse developments in the affected sectors subsequently affect other sectors of the economy.

Sometimes, an asset bubble can lead to a systemic crisis. An *asset bubble*, also known as a *speculative bubble* or a *price bubble*, is a rapid rise in the price of an asset so that the asset's price comes to greatly exceed its fundamental value. Asset bubbles can appear in any market environment, driven by investors' irrational enthusiasm for the affected assets. Eventually, the asset price declines, often rapidly. The bubble "bursts," and investors who own the asset suffer the decline in asset values.

Figure 4.8 presents a series of asset bubbles. A large asset bubble may be so widespread that, in advance of a crisis, its existence is difficult to detect. When the bubble effect is widespread, the eventual price decline may adversely affect an entire economic system.

Figure 4.8 Asset Bubbles in History

Dutch Tulip Bubble
(Burst 1637)

Florida Real Estate Bubble
(Burst 1925)

Asian Currency Bubble
(Burst 1997)

U.S. Dot-Com Bubble
(Burst 2000)

U.S. Housing Bubble
(Burst 2007)

Specific Risks

Important categories of specific risks in investments include interest rate risk, credit risk, real estate risk, currency risk, and liquidity risk.

Interest Rate Risk

Interest rate risk is the risk that the market value of an investment will change due to a change in the absolute level of market interest rates. In general, for bonds and other interest-bearing investments, as market interest rates decrease, the market value of the investment increases, and, as market interest rates increase, the market value of the investment decreases, as summarized in Figure 4.9.

- For bonds, as market interest rates increase, the market value of an existing bond generally decreases.

- For bonds, as market interest rates decrease, the market value of an existing bond generally increases.

- For mortgages, as market interest rates increase, the market value of an existing mortgage generally decreases.

- For mortgages, as market interest rates decrease, the market value of an existing mortgage generally increases.

Interest rate risk affects virtually all investments—not bonds alone. Real estate is subject to interest rate risk, because real estate transactions are typically financed with interest-bearing loans. Some equity market sectors, such as utility stocks and financial institution stocks, are more sensitive to interest rate risk than others. An *interest-sensitive stock* is a stock whose price is extremely sensitive to changes in interest rates.

Interest rate risk is generally the most important risk for debt securities such as high-quality bonds. Approaches to estimating or measuring the impact of interest-rate changes focus on yield curves and durations. The keys to understanding interest rate risk are the duration or average maturity of a debt portfolio; the impact of rising or falling interest rates, and resulting changes in the shape of the yield curve and the term structure of interest rates; and reinvestment risk.

Figure 4.9 Interest-Rate Risk and Market-Value of an Interest-Bearing Security

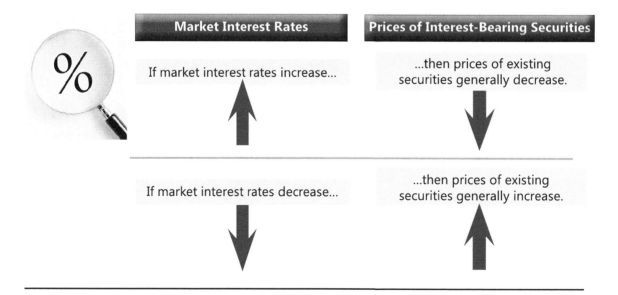

Market Interest Rates	Prices of Interest-Bearing Securities
If market interest rates increase...	...then prices of existing securities generally decrease.
If market interest rates decrease...	...then prices of existing securities generally increase.

Duration and Interest Rates. *Duration* is a statistic that measures the interest-rate sensitivity of an interest-bearing security, and can be defined as the time-weighted value of expected cash inflows, expressed in years. Financial analysts define interest-rate sensitivity as the responsiveness of a security's market price to changes in market interest rates. Interest-rate sensitivity and duration refer to aspects of risk. Duration is typically applied to a stream of known future cash flows, such as bond interest payments or mortgage amortization payments.

The type of duration most commonly used in life insurance companies is known as *modified duration.* However, the actual duration statistics that insurers use vary widely from one company to another.

A duration statistic expresses the responsiveness of a security's price or market value to changes in interest rates. Specifically, a duration statistic of *n* years indicates that, for a change of 1 percent in interest rates, the price or market value of a security will change by *n* percent in the opposite direction.

Interpreting Duration

As the value of duration increases, risk increases.

If two securities are similar except for having different durations, the one with the lower duration is less risky; the lower duration security will also have less potential for appreciation.

If a security's duration is *n* years, then for a change of 1 percent in interest rates, the market price of the security will change in the opposite direction by *n* percent.

Institutional investors have numerous approaches to calculating duration. In a financial context, duration statistics are used to measure an investor's loss potential from an increase or a decrease in interest rates.

Example: Using a Duration Statistic to Estimate Losses

Duration of six years indicates that, for a change of 1 percent in interest rates, the market value of a security will change by 6 percent in the opposite direction.

For a $1 billion portfolio of bonds with an overall duration of six years, the following table shows how the bonds' market value would change in response to specified interest-rate changes:

Beginning Portfolio Value: $1 Billion Duration: 6 years	Change in Market Interest Rate	Resulting Impact on Values of Securities	Projected Ending Bond Portfolio Value
	Increase 1%	Decrease by 6%	$940 million
	Decrease 1%	Increase by 6%	$1.06 billion

For duration of six years and a 1 percent increase in interest rates, the expected decrease in market value of the portfolio is $60 million. On the other hand, if interest rates decrease by 1 percent, the expected increase in the market value of the portfolio is $60 million.[3]

The Term Structure of Interest Rates and Yield Curves. The *term structure of interest rates* is the relationship between interest rates on bonds of the same credit quality but with different maturities.

A graph of the term structure of interest rates is a yield curve. A *yield curve*, also called a *debt curve* or a *bond curve*, is a line graph showing, for a specified date, the relationship between yields of debt securities and the maturities of those securities. The vertical axis of the yield curve represents interest rates, and the horizontal axis represents maturities.

As you can see in Figure 4.10, yield curves generally take on one of three shapes: normal, inverted, or flat. When the yield curve loses its normal shape, corresponding changes in the securities markets become apparent.

■ A *normal yield curve*, an upward slope from left to right, indicates that yields on long-term securities are higher than yields on short-term securities.

■ An *inverted yield curve*, a downward slope from left to right, indicates that yields on short-term securities are higher than yields on long-term securities. For an inverted yield curve, whenever long-term market interest rates become higher than short-term market interest rates, analysts consider that the economy is likely overheating or that financing has become difficult to obtain.

■ A *flat yield curve*, a straight line, indicates that yields on securities are not responsive to an investment's term to maturity. If the yield curve becomes essentially flat, securities markets support essentially the same rate for all bonds, regardless of their term to maturity.

A yield curve for U.S. Treasury bonds generally provides the basis for pricing and valuing bonds issued in the United States. In bond trading, bond prices are quoted in terms of the U.S. Treasury bond rate plus a specified number of basis points.

Figure 4.10 Normal, Inverted, and Flat Yield Curves

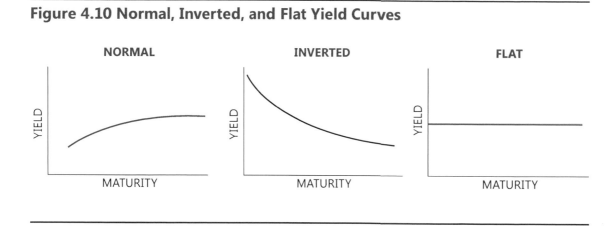

For countries other than the United States, the term structure of interest rates is referred to as the ***sovereign yield curve***, also known as the *sovereign debt curve* or the *sovereign interest curve*. In this context, "sovereign" refers to a nation that rules itself and is not governed by another entity. The horizontal axis of a sovereign yield curve indicates bond maturities, arranged from shortest to longest. The vertical axis of a sovereign yield curve indicates yields for debt securities issued by the sovereign entity. A sovereign yield curve generally provides the basis for pricing and valuing bonds issued in the relevant country. Figure 4.11 shows the yield curve for the United States.

Reinvestment Risk. Generally, ***reinvestment risk*** is the risk that market conditions will be unfavorable when the investor needs to invest the proceeds from a prior investment. Reinvestment risk impacts equity and fixed-income investments. For an interest-bearing security, *reinvestment risk*, along with its subset, *reinvestment-rate risk*, is the risk that a decline in market interest rates will lead to lower interest income after the investor reinvests the proceeds from a matured interest-bearing security.

Example: Reinvestment Risk

A bond typically pays periodic interest coupon payments until the bond's maturity date.

- A $10,000 bond paying 4 percent coupon interest pays the investor $200 every six months until the bond's maturity date.

- A $10,000 bond paying 3 percent coupon interest pays the investor $150 every six months until the bond's maturity date.

Suppose a bond with a coupon of 4 percent matures. On the maturity date, market interest rates have decreased to 3 percent. The investor cannot let the $10,000 proceeds from the old bond sit idle, so he reinvests the proceeds at the new lower rate. After reinvesting, the investor will receive coupon payments of only $150 every six months.

Figure 4.11 Yield Curve for the United States

Source: "Daily Treasury Yield Curve Rates," U.S. Department of the Treasury, http.www.treasury.gov/resource-center/data-chart-center/interest-rates/pages/textview.aspx?data=yield (28 February 2012).

Credit Risk

Credit risk, also known as *default risk*, is the risk that a borrower may default by failing to make payments of principal or interest on time. Credit risk differs according to the type of issuer—corporation, municipal government, government agency, or sovereign nation.

Credit risk affects all types of debt investments: corporate bonds, sovereign bonds, municipal bonds, agency bonds, and mortgages. Further, credit risk affects corporate equity securities, which lose substantial value if the company defaults on its obligations and becomes insolvent.

Corporate credit risk includes components of event risk and financial risk.

- *Event risk* is risk due to unforeseen events associated with an entity, such as a natural disaster that disrupts an entity's operations and increases the probability of a default.

- *Financial risk* is the risk that a debtor may not have adequate cash flow to meet its financial obligations. In general, the more debt instruments a debtor issues, the greater its financial risk. In this text, we refer to the degree to which an entity uses borrowed funds to purchase assets as leverage. Highly leveraged entities borrow money to a greater extent than do other entities, and thus have greater financial risk than other entities.

If a corporation does not repay a loan as promised, creditors have claims against the corporation and its assets. In many jurisdictions, creditors also have certain legal rights against municipal governments in the event of default.

Typically, sovereign debt is the least risky investment to be made in any given economy. *Sovereign credit risk* refers to the risk that a sovereign government will fail to meet its debt obligations, leading to sovereign default or debt restructuring. When analysts evaluate sovereign government credit risk, the sovereign's ability and willingness to repay borrowed money are both important. Risk in sovereign debt arises from a government's inability to favorably exercise the fiscal controls available to a sovereign government, and results in symptoms such as a weak economy, a high tax burden, weak currency, excess money supply, unfavorable demographics, and excess government spending. Governments are also vulnerable to *tax base risk*, a financial risk that tax-paying citizens could move away from or stop paying taxes at the established rates.

Estimating Credit Losses

An important measure of corporate credit risk is the *expected credit loss*, an estimate of the loss from corporate bond defaults. Figure 4.12 describes available data for expected credit loss. Credit default loss or credit default recovery statistics are available for various rating categories of securities. An analyst starting with the original ratings of all bonds in a portfolio can use credit default loss rates and credit default recovery rates by rating category to estimate the amount of loss to expect from a portfolio.

Figure 4.12 Average Credit Loss Rates

Moody's Investor Services maintains detailed statistics on corporate bond defaults. For U.S. corporate bonds from 1982 to 2010, the following table shows the average credit loss rates by bond rating category:

Credit Loss Rates for U.S. Corporate Bonds, 1982–2010	
Moody's Rating Category	Average Cumulative Credit Loss Rate 1982–2010*
Aaa	0.02%
Aa	0.18%
A	0.49%
Baa	1.19%
Ba	6.90%
B	15.57%
Caa–C	35.08%
Investment-Grade	0.60%
Speculative-Grade	14.00%
All Rated Issues	4.85%

* Based on average default rates and senior unsecured bond recoveries within five years of date of default.

Source: Adapted from Moody's Investor Services, *Corporate Default and Recovery Rates, 1920–2010*, Special Comment (New York: Moody's Investor Services, 2011), 21. © Moody's Investors Service, Inc. and/or its affiliates. Reprinted with permission. All Rights Reserved.

An investor can use the information in Figure 4.12 to estimate credit risk for a specific bond investment.

Example: Estimating Credit Losses for a Bond Investment

Manolo owns a corporate bond that was rated Baa at issue. To estimate the potential credit loss associated with that bond, Manolo can find the actual default rate for Baa bonds. In a table of credit default losses, the historical credit loss rate for Baa corporate bonds is 1.19 percent, so Manolo will set the expected credit loss rate at 1.19 percent. To find a monetary amount of expected credit loss, Manolo can apply the credit loss rate to the amount he originally paid for the bond: $10,000.

Estimated monetary credit loss = Bond purchase price × Credit loss rate

$119 estimated monetary credit loss = $10,000 × 0.0119

The expected rate and monetary amount of credit losses for a portfolio of corporate bonds can be estimated in a similar manner. The following hypothetical example features a portfolio of only two assets.

Example: Using Expected Credit Loss to Calculate Losses

Northco Investments has a diversified corporate bond fund with $20 million in assets invested in bonds, as shown:

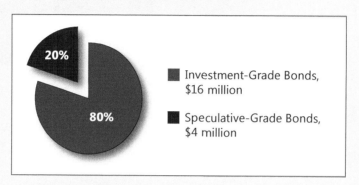

20%

80%

■ Investment-Grade Bonds, $16 million

■ Speculative-Grade Bonds, $4 million

Investment-grade bonds have an expected credit loss rate of 0.60%, and speculative-grade bonds have an expected credit loss rate of 14.00%. Northco can use this information to estimate its credit losses for the next year as follows:

	Investment-grade bond	Speculative-grade bonds	Portfolio totals
Monetary value	$16 million	$4 million	$20 million
% of Portfolio	80.00%	20.00%	100.00%
Expected % credit loss	0.60%	14.00%	N/A
Expected monetary credit loss	$96,000	$560,000	$656,000

As our calculations show, Northco's expected monetary credit loss for this portfolio is $656,000.[4]

Real Estate Risk

Real estate risk is the risk of loss resulting from a decline in the value of real estate. Real estate risk arises from owning real estate directly or from owning debt or equity securities whose value can vary as a result of a change in the value of commercial or residential real estate.

For mortgage analysis, analysts consider two important ratios: loan-to-value and debt service coverage.

■ *Loan-to-value* is the ratio of a mortgage's loan balance to the property's value. Typically, the risk of mortgage default increases as the value of the real estate decreases. For this reason, analysts follow the ratio of a mortgage loan's balance to the property's value.

■   *Debt-to-service coverage ratio* is the ratio of a borrower's monthly interest payments owed or mortgage payments owed to its monthly earnings before interest and taxes. The lower the ratio, the easier for the entity to meet its debt obligations.

Currency Risk

Currency risk is the risk that arises from changes in currency exchange rates. When the value of one currency falls in relation to the value of another, the first currency loses value, and the second currency gains value.

Generally, currency risk can arise from geopolitical factors, supply and demand, inflation, and changes in government leadership. As demand for a country's currency increases, the price of that currency compared to other nations' currency also increases. Manufacturers typically price domestic products in the domestic currency; thus, an increase in demand for a nation's products can result in an increase in demand for that nation's currency.

> **Example: Demand and Currency Exchange Rates**
>
> British manufactured goods typically are priced in pounds sterling. Foreign purchasers must exchange their native currency for pounds sterling in order to purchase those goods. Increased demand for British goods can lead to increased demand for pounds sterling. The value of the British pound would then rise compared to other currencies.

Institutional investors typically estimate expected currency losses by first reviewing the long-term relationship of a foreign currency to their own, and then using a scenarios approach to projecting potential future losses, including an average currency exchange loss scenario and a worst-case currency exchange loss scenario.

Two types of currency risk are transaction risk and translation risk.

Transaction risk is risk resulting from changes in the currency exchange rate between the time of entering into an agreement and the effective time of a transaction. If an investor purchases or sells a security denominated in a foreign currency, the investor may suffer a loss if the exchange rate between the investor's native currency and the foreign currency changes prior to the transaction's being settled or prior to finalizing the transaction.

The greater the time between entering into the agreement and settling the agreement, the greater the possibility of currency rate fluctuation, and thus, the greater the transaction risk.

Translation risk is the risk of loss of value in foreign assets owned as a result of changes in the currency exchange rate. The *book value* of an asset is the balance sheet value shown for the asset. Translation risk primarily affects the book value of a portfolio's foreign assets, because a company must regularly report the value of the asset in the company's domestic currency. The book value of foreign assets fluctuates as a result of changes in the foreign currency's exchange rate. The greater the proportion of asset, liability, and equity classes denominated in a foreign currency, the greater the translation risk.

Translation risk can also affect the gain or loss an investor realizes on the sale of an asset denominated in a foreign currency.

Liquidity Risk

Liquidity risk in investments is the risk that an asset might not be readily sold for its true value. Liquidity risk in investments can arise from lack of buyers, lack of secondary market facilities, or the structure of the investment. Liquidity varies widely among various types of investments. The following situations or investment characteristics are associated with limited liquidity:

■ Private placement securities are not intended for active trading in secondary markets, although these securities are traded. Under securities laws in the United States, securities sold in a private placement are restricted securities, which purchasers cannot freely trade. In many cases, purchasers cannot resell private placement securities for a period of at least one year. However, securities laws allow resales of restricted securities at any time to certain sophisticated investors who manage very large monetary amounts.[5] Restricted securities generally have a legend stamped on the front of the security stating that the security is restricted. Restricted securities, including private placement securities, are not intended for active trading after their initial sale.

■ Small bond issues have limited liquidity. The smaller the size of a bond issue, the smaller the number of bonds in that issue that are readily available for purchase or sale at any particular time. Many institutional investors will not invest in a bond issue of less than $250 million.

■ Institutional investors face regulatory or policy restrictions on investing in particular types of securities. Some institutions' investment policies prohibit investing in bonds with ratings below a specified level. The fewer institutional investors able to invest in a particular security, the less liquid the security.

■ Small capitalization stocks have limited marketability. A company's *market capitalization* is the total market value of all of the company's outstanding shares of stock. The market capitalization equals the number of shares outstanding multiplied by the current market value of one share. In general, the smaller a company's market capitalization, the smaller the dollar amount of stock that is readily available for purchase or sale at any particular time. Many institutional investors set a policy of not investing in the stock of companies with a market capitalization lower than $200 million.

Analysis of Specific Risks for Portfolio Management

In this chapter, we've seen that it's possible to view portfolio management as focusing on analysis of a portfolio's manageable components—asset selection and specific risks. In essence, a portfolio can be viewed as a grouping of specific risks. Institutional investors are able to analyze and estimate the potential losses arising from the relevant specific risks and their components; then, in view of the potential losses, investors are able to compare the amount of each risk to the overall scale of a portfolio to evaluate the reasonableness of the risks contemplated.

■ Interest rate risk in a bond portfolio is generally estimated through the calculation of duration, as well as through understanding of yield curves.

■ Credit risk is usually estimated through analysis of asset quality.

- Real estate risk is usually estimated through probable loss analysis.

- Currency risk is usually approached through analysis of a portfolio's exposure to foreign currency.

- Liquidity risk is usually evaluated by analysis of activity in relevant markets.

Key Terms

rate of return	systemic crisis
nominal return	asset bubble
total return	duration
historical return	term structure of interest rates
expected return	yield curve
required return	normal yield curve
hurdle rate	inverted yield curve
credit risk premium	flat yield curve
equity risk premium	sovereign yield curve
real rate of return	reinvestment risk
holding period return	credit risk
arithmetic mean annual return	sovereign credit risk
annualized return	expected credit loss
volatility	real estate risk
tail risk	currency risk
key risk indicator (KRI)	transaction risk
key performance indicator (KPI)	translation risk
specific risk	liquidity risk
systemic risk	market capitalization

Endnotes

1. Portions of this chapter are based on material provided by Patricia Wilson Fridley, Senior Advisor, Center for Financial Stability, LLC.

2. This and subsequent "Bright Future" examples provided by Patricia Wilson Fridley (Senior Advisor, Center for Financial Stability, LLC), note to author, May 2012. Used with permission.

3. Patricia Wilson Fridley (Senior Advisor, Center for Financial Stability, LLC), note to author, 2 April 2012. Used with permission.

4. Ibid. Used with permission.

5. "Rule 144: Selling Restricted and Control Securities," U.S. Securities and Exchange Commission, http://www.sec.gov/investor/pubs/rule144.htm (29 September 2012).

Chapter 5

Fund Options for Separate Accounts

Objectives

After studying this chapter, you should be able to

5A   Describe separate account customers and clients and identify various types of separate account products that potentially have fund options

5B   Describe fund classifications by style, including equity fund styles by market capitalization, by sector, or by investment goal and fixed-income fund styles by debt instrument or duration; and describe and apply a Morningstar Style Box to equity or fixed-income funds

5C   Describe the use of scorecards in total return fund analysis, including how analysts track the performance of funds relative to peer groups and benchmarks

5D   List and describe qualitative considerations for fund analysis, including governing policies, the portfolio manager and the fund management team, the fund's administrative systems and controls, and external analysts' opinions

5E   Describe the purpose of attribution analysis, explaining the significance of sector selection, security selection, portfolio concentration, momentum, and unexplained residual return, and explain how the results of attribution analysis are used in portfolio analysis

5F   Describe how fund analysts interpret measures of fund risk and return, including beta, tracking error, the information ratio, the Sharpe ratio, and the Sortino ratio

5G   Describe how expense ratios and the portfolio turnover rate are used in portfolio expense analysis

5H   Describe style drift for the investment portfolio; discuss why fund investors have concerns about style drift; and explain how analysts use holdings analysis to identify and evaluate style drift

Outline

Customers and Clients of Separate Account Products

Fund Classifications
- Asset Classes
- Equity Funds
- Fixed-Income Funds
- Other Fund Classifications
- Style Boxes
- Market Indexes

Purposes of Fund Evaluation and Monitoring
- Due Diligence
- Competitive Intelligence

Analysis of Fund Options
- Scorecards
- Governing Policies
- Portfolio Manager and Management Team
- Administrative Systems and Control
- External Analysts' Opinions

Total Return Analysis of Funds
- Performance Comparison to a Benchmark
- Performance Comparison to a Peer Group
- Applying Performance Comparisons

Analysis of Fund Risk
- Standard Deviation of Returns
- Beta

Risk-Return Analysis of Funds
- Tracking Error
- Information Ratio
- Sharpe Ratio
- Sortino Ratio

Analysis of Fund Expenses

Fund Selection, Evaluation, and Oversight
- Style Drift
- Replacing a Fund

Institutional investors, including insurance companies, invest on behalf of the institution to support some portions of their business.[1] For other portions of their business, however, they invest for the benefit of end investors. Many insurance companies offer separate account products and, through these products, offer end investors a menu of fund options. End investors choose various fund options to diversify their investment holdings, benefit from the expertise of skilled portfolio managers, and obtain various associated services. As part of operating a separate account, an insurance company evaluates, selects, and manages the various fund options offered for separate account investment products. This chapter focuses on the fund options offered by insurance companies to support separate account investment products.

Customers and Clients of Separate Account Products

Insurance company separate account fund options may be more accessible if you understand who invests in these fund options. Insurance company separate accounts support products designed for retail customers and institutional clients. Usually, owners of retail investment products are referred to as "customers," whereas institutional contract holders are referred to as "institutional clients." To confound matters even more, both the insurance company and the insurer's institutional clients are regarded as institutional investors.

Figure 5.1 illustrates some examples of the varieties of separate account products that insurers provide to retail customers and institutional clients. Many retail separate account products are individual variable annuities and individual variable life insurance policies. Individual variable products such as these are registered securities for purposes of SEC compliance in the United States.

Institutional separate account products provide asset management services to endowments, foundations, other insurance companies, and other institutional investors, and include the following products:

- *Group benefit products* provide retirement and pension benefits under plans or programs established to provide retirement, pension, or other types of benefits to group members and their beneficiaries. Typically, employers, labor organizations, and professional or trade associations establish group benefit plans on behalf of their employees or members. An insurance company that provides a separate account product for a group benefit plan is called a *plan provider*. The participating employees, plan members, or other plan beneficiaries who are eligible to receive benefits under a plan are *plan participants*.

- *Employer-owned life insurance policies* on certain employees enable an employer to fund the cost of providing employee benefits.

- *Guaranteed investment contracts* typically provide institutional investors with a guaranteed fixed rate of interest.

Figure 5.1 Customers of Separate Account Products

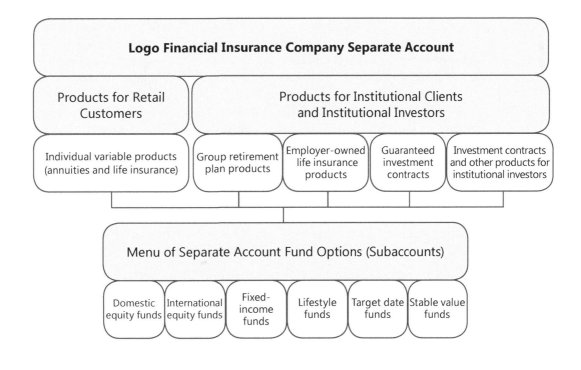

Fund Classifications

As shown in Figure 5.1, the separate accounts of insurance companies provide a menu of separate account fund options known as *subaccounts*. Throughout the remainder of this chapter, following industry convention, we refer to these subaccounts as "fund options" or merely "funds." In this context, you should keep in mind that "fund" is another term for "portfolio."

For fund options, insurance companies can obtain portfolio management services internally or externally. External portfolio managers are consultants known as *subadvisers*. Insurance companies can also gain access to fund options for their customers and clients by adding external funds to their menu of fund options.

Fund options have a fund style. The popularity of fund styles changes with the phases of business cycles, which result in more or less favorable results for various fund styles, and trigger trends in popular interest in various fund styles. To some extent, a fund style classification reflects the perspective of the entity providing the classification. Marketing professionals tend to classify fund options in ways that highlight the fund's intended appeal to end investors. Investment professionals usually categorize fund options according to the observable characteristics of the assets held in the funds. Given these and other perspectives, the classification of fund options can be somewhat arbitrary. Thus, fund options that carry the same label may deploy somewhat different investment strategies.

Two broad categories of funds are based on the primary asset type within a fund: equity and fixed-income funds. As a first approach to understanding funds, we look at an array of broad asset classes.

Asset Classes

Figure 5.2 provides a sample of conventionally recognized asset classes. In addition, some asset classes have characteristics of fixed-income as well as equities, and investors may group them separately from debt or equity. We describe these asset classes, as well as alternative investment classes, in later chapters.

Within the categories of equity or fixed-income funds are many subcategories. For example, an equity fund option may be a U.S.-only stock fund or an international stock fund. Equity funds may be actively or passively managed.

Equity Funds

Equity funds may include common stocks or real estate, but equity funds typically consist of stock investments. Stock funds can be categorized by characteristics of their stock holdings. The most important characteristics for classifying stock funds are market capitalization, industry sectors, and geographic locations.

- *Large-cap funds* invest primarily in the common stock of companies with a large market capitalization—for example, greater than $10 billion.

- *Mid-cap funds* invest primarily in the common stock of companies with a medium market capitalization—for example, $2 billion to $10 billion.

- *Small-cap funds* invest primarily in the common stock of companies with a small market capitalization—for example, less than $2 billion.

Figure 5.2 Broad Asset Classes

Equity Asset Classes	Fixed-Income Asset Classes

I. Common Stocks

Common Stocks by Capitalization

Large-Cap Stocks

Mid-Cap Stocks

Small-Cap Stocks

Common Stocks by Sector

II. Real Estate (Commercial, Residential)

Direct Real Estate Ownership

Real Estate Investment Trusts (REITs)

I. Bonds

Government Bonds

U.S. Treasury Bills

Agency Bonds

Sovereign Debt

Municipal Bonds

Corporate Bonds

II. Debt-Backed Securities

III. Bank Loans

IV. Mortgages and Mortgage-Backed Securities

The capitalization levels that are considered small-, mid-, and large-cap, as well as other potential size categories, are not standardized, and the levels cited here reflect industry custom at the time of publication.

Fund options that invest in stocks of international companies are classified according to the country or region in which those companies are located. A number of classifications describe U.S. funds that invest in stocks of companies based outside of North America. *Global funds*, also known as *world funds*, invest in stocks of companies located both in North America and beyond. *International funds*, also known as *foreign funds*, invest exclusively in stocks of companies located outside the United States. *Regional funds* invest only in stocks of companies located in a particular geographic region, such as Europe, Asia, or Latin America. *Country funds* invest only in stocks of companies located in one particular country. ***Emerging market funds*** invest in stocks of companies located in developing countries, which typically are countries with low per capita income and little industrialization. Although most stock funds invest in companies in a wide variety of industries, ***sector funds*** are equity funds invested in stocks of companies in a particular financial sector or industry. Common types of sector funds include communications funds, energy funds, financial services funds, technology funds, and many others. Sector funds provide less diversification than do other types of funds, but can provide substantial returns or generate higher dividends when the particular sector performs well.

Fixed-Income Funds

Fixed-income funds typically invest in debt instruments and are categorized by the specified type of debt instrument. For example, a fixed-income fund option may be categorized as a *bond fund* or a *government bond fund*. Fund options are further categorized by the expected average durations or expected average maturities of the securities in which the funds invest. For example, *long-term bond funds* invest in bonds with maturity dates far into the future, *intermediate-term bond funds* invest in bonds with medium-term maturity dates, and short-term bond funds invest in securities with maturity dates in the near future. However, no set of definitions for short, medium, and long term is universally observed.

Fixed-income funds are further classified by geographic region or by credit quality. Bond funds are sometimes classified as *investment grade* or *high yield*, depending on published credit ratings of the bonds they own. *Core bond funds* invest in investment-grade credit and government bonds. *Core plus funds* offer investors exposure to high-yield and emerging markets.[2] *Investment-grade bond funds* invest in corporate bonds that have a low risk of default, such as bonds rated BBB or higher by Standard and Poor's. Bonds with a low risk of default pay a lower return than do bonds with a greater risk of default. Some bond funds, known as *high-yield bond funds* or *junk bond funds*, invest in corporate bonds that have a significant risk of default, but these bonds offer significantly higher potential returns than do investment-grade bonds. *Multisector bond funds* invest in the bonds from several fixed-income sectors, including U.S. government obligations, U.S. corporate bonds, foreign bonds, and high-yield U.S. corporate debt securities.

Other Fund Classifications

Sometimes investment funds are classified by such characteristics as the primary investment goal that a fund pursues—such as growth of capital, production of income, or capital protection. Along with other information, the asset classes held in a fund indicate the fund's management approach. A fund's investment category addresses the overall approach the fund uses to set the asset allocation and select specific securities. The fund's investment category helps set expectations for long-term performance and helps market the fund to investors seeking particular types of investments.

- Growth is an investment objective dedicated to growing investment principal or capital by holding stock investments in companies with strong growth prospects. Accordingly, a **growth fund** is a stock fund dedicated to growing investment principal or capital. Growth funds invest in *growth companies*—those for which the stock value is increasing faster than the growth of the overall market. Growth stocks pay little or no dividends; instead, they offer greater potential for capital gains. Growth funds typically have greater volatility than other fund types, such as value funds.

- *Value funds* invest in stocks of companies that are undervalued in relation to the overall market. These stocks, known as *value stocks*, often pay significant dividends. Investors in value funds believe that other investors will eventually realize the fundamental value of these stocks and that their price will rise accordingly. Value funds typically have lower volatility than growth funds.

■   A type of fund that seeks growth *and* value is variously termed a *core fund* or a *blend fund*. Core funds can invest in both stocks and bonds, with the objective of maintaining approximately the same asset allocation between stocks and bonds at all times, such as 60 percent stocks and 40 percent bonds.

■   ***Stable value funds*** are funds that offer fixed, minimum-guaranteed returns, plus a potential for excess interest crediting. This style corresponds to the fixed guaranteed fund option under a variable annuity or variable life insurance contract.

■   An *income fund* is dedicated to earning a reliable income stream from investments that provide interest, dividend payments, or rent.

■   ***Index funds*** seek to produce a pattern of performance similar to that of a specified market index.

■   ***Absolute return funds*** seek to achieve positive returns in all market conditions by investing in alternative investments and derivatives, and employing alternative investment management techniques.

■   *Lifestyle funds*, also known as *risk-based funds*, have the objective of maintaining at all times a specific level of risk. Although a lifestyle fund's asset allocation periodically changes, the fund's overall risk level remains the same.

■   ***Target date funds***, also known as *lifecycle funds*, invest in various asset classes and automatically change the asset allocation over a period of time, with the main objective being to support an investor's goal to accumulate a specified amount of funds by the specified date. Target date funds are designed for accumulating retirement assets to support a person's retirement at the target date. As the target date approaches, the fund's risk level gradually decreases, typically by increasing the ratio of bonds to stocks in the fund's portfolio.

Style Boxes

A *style box* is a standard graphic that is customized to reflect a given purpose. Morningstar (Morningstar.com) popularized the use of style boxes in its mutual fund ratings. The ***Morningstar Style Box*** is a nine-square grid that provides a graphical representation of a fund's investment style. The appropriate box on the grid is blackened or checked to provide a quick visual cue as to the fund's basic classification. Investment professionals readily recognize and understand this simple and familiar nine-cell square box. Analysts may use more complex style boxes for custom applications. Figure 5.3 illustrates equity and fixed-income mutual fund style boxes.

In Figure 5.3, the basic *equity style box* classifies equity funds by market capitalization—large-cap, mid-cap, or small-cap—and by growth, core or blend, and value factors.[3] The basic *fixed-income fund style box* classifies funds by high, medium, or low credit quality and short, medium, or long duration, reflecting the average expected duration in years of the assets held in the fund.[4]

Figure 5.3 Typical Equity and Fixed-Income Fund Style Boxes

Equity Mutual Fund Style Boxes

Basic

Market Capitalization

Fund Style	Large	Medium	Small
Growth			
Blend			
Value			

Complex

Market Capitalization

Fund Style	Large Cap	Mid Cap	Small Cap	Location
Aggressive				Domestic
				Global
				Emerging Market
Growth				Domestic
				Global
				Emerging Market
Blend*				Domestic
				Global
				Emerging Market
Value				Domestic
				Global
				Emerging Market

*Sometimes *core*

Source: Adapted with permission from "The Categorization of Stock Funds," Investing in Mutual Funds, http://www.investing-in-mutual-funds.com/stock-funds.html (2 October 2012).

Fixed-Income Mutual Fund Style Boxes

Basic

Duration

Credit Rating	Short	Medium	Long
Low			
Medium			
High			

Complex

	Corporate			Treasury*			Federal Agency			Municipal		
Duration → Credit Rating	Short	Intermediate	Long	Short	Intermediate	Long	Short	Intermediate	Long	Short	Intermediate	Long
Very high												
High												
Moderate												
Low												
Very low												

* All Treasury bonds have a very high quality rating

Source: Adapted with permission from "The Categorization of Bond Funds," Investing in Mutual Funds, http://www.investing-in-mutual-funds.com/bond-funds.html (2 October 2012).

To indicate a style box classification for a fund, an analyst darkens, marks, or checks the cell of the box at the intersection of the correct fund styles.

Example: Equity and Fixed-Income Style Boxes

Mighty Domestic Mid-Cap Fund's prospectus states that the fund invests in mid-cap stocks of companies with market capitalization below $5 billion. Mighty Domestic's prospectus further states that the fund strategy emphasizes the goal of outperforming the S&P 400 mid-cap index by holding stocks of companies with stronger growth than the S&P 400 mid-cap index.

Sprout Emerging Market Fixed-Income Fund invests in fixed-income securities arising from emerging markets, with an emphasis on generating income by holding bonds with long-term maturities.

Thus, these funds have the following style box profiles:

Mighty Domestic Mid Cap

	Capitalization		
Strategy	Small	Mid	Large
Growth		▓	
Blend or Core			
Value			

Sprout Emerging Market

	Duration		
Credit Quality	Short	Mid	Long
Low			▓
Medium			
High			

Market Indexes

A market index is a statistical measurement system for recording and publishing performance data for a large grouping of similar investments. Generally, each actively traded asset class has at least one associated market index, and such an index is used as a performance standard or benchmark in evaluating a fund's performance for that asset class. In managing funds, market indexes are applied for at least two purposes:

- To ensure that funds conform to their specified fund style

- To serve as a reference for average market performance in a given asset class

Specifically, a market index allows investment professionals to compare the performance of an asset or a portfolio to the average performance for that market. A standard of performance is sometimes known as a benchmark. In this context, market indexes serve as benchmarks for portfolio performance. To serve as an effective investment performance benchmark, an index must closely reflect the long-term behavior of a specified asset class. We discuss market indexes and portfolio performance benchmarks in Chapter 6 and thereafter.

> **Example: Market Index**
>
> The *Standard and Poor's 500 Index (S&P 500 index)* is an index of 500 of the most widely held companies in the United States, chosen for market size, liquidity, and industry grouping. This market index is widely used as a benchmark index or performance standard for large-capitalization U.S. stocks.

Purposes of Fund Evaluation and Monitoring

Insurers are continually evaluating their own menu of fund options as well as potential candidates for possible inclusion in their menu of fund options. Companies must ensure that additional fund options and portfolio managers are available when needed and ensure that the current menu of fund options and portfolio managers are meeting the goals and objectives of their separate accounts.

Insurers' programs for evaluating, selecting, and monitoring fund options and portfolio managers can include routine, ongoing activities, in addition to nonroutine activities required to address specific needs.[5] An insurance company can perform these activities internally or retain external service providers.

> **Examples: External Fund Evaluation Services**
>
> Fund advisory companies monitor and rate funds for retail and institutional customers.
>
> - Morningstar, Lipper, Value Line, and other companies monitor and rate funds and do not sell investment products.
>
> - Wilshire Associates, Fund Evaluation Group, and Massey, Quick, provide data to help companies select fund managers. These firms work primarily for institutional investors, plan sponsors, and high-net-worth individuals.
>
> These service providers have technology and professionals devoted to monitoring overall portfolio performance. Insurers may retain these firms to obtain access for their clients as well as internal access. For their services, including access to their databases, fund advisory companies charge an annual or monthly fee, or both.
>
> For insurance companies and retirement fund managers, retaining an independent entity to provide certain fund analysis and evaluation information precludes a potential for a conflict of interest. Otherwise, the insurance company, as a fund provider, would be in the position of advising customers and clients as to the relative merits of its own products and the alternatives. Using independent providers of fund analysis and ratings to perform this service provides an appearance of impartiality in the analysis.

An insurer's fund analysis programs must (1) support due diligence, (2) exemplify good business practices, (3) comply with regulatory standards, and (4) determine competitive positioning with respect to peers.

Due Diligence

Insurance companies and other institutional investors monitor funds to evaluate whether a fund's performance actually meets current market needs in light of market conditions. In this context, *due diligence* refers to researching, analyzing, and documenting a rationale for selecting and continuing to provide a particular fund option or continuing to employ third parties hired to undertake functions for an investment operation. Typically, in this regard, staff analysts conduct quarterly and annual reviews of at least all funds on the company's menu. Due diligence is particularly important in ensuring that a fund is operating in compliance with regulations and exemplifies best practices.

Due diligence activities often focus on monitoring and investigating the portfolio management team's actions to ensure that they are still following the commitments made in their strategy statements, and are generally meeting the company's expectations. As part of due diligence, the fund analysis team seeks to identify adverse events and situations involving the portfolio management team.

Examples: Adverse Events Involving a Portfolio Management Team

Turnover of critical investment professionals

Ethical incidents involving investment professionals

Changes in ownership of the management organization

Change in adherence to a fund's investment objectives

As described in Chapter 3, companies set investment performance standards for returns, risks, and risk-adjusted returns. These standards apply to funds managed internally or externally. If, over several reporting periods, any fund's investment performance fails to meet minimum performance standards for returns, risk, and risk-adjusted returns, the analysis team investigates the reasons for the subpar aspects of performance. Also, during the evaluation process, a fund analysis team examines the fund's investment decisions for consistency with the portfolio manager's statements about risk management, investment strategy, and management philosophy. Analysts also conduct attribution analysis, described shortly, to identify how the portfolio manager added to or lost value from a fund's performance.

Certain aspects of fund operations are particularly important. Investment professionals monitor a fund's ongoing operations in addition to its investment performance, and they conduct discussions of any areas of interest with fund representatives.

As we have discussed, some separate account fund options are designed for group benefit plans. In the United States, sponsors of group benefit plans have a fiduciary responsibility to plan participants and are accountable for their plan's fund options. A plan sponsor, to meet its fiduciary responsibilities, must offer plan participants a diversified selection of fund options and must have a basis for believing that these funds will perform well and support the plan's investment objective or the sponsor's rationale for including the funds in the plan. Plan sponsors typically maintain a plan investment policy that states, among other requirements, criteria for fund options offered for participants in their plan. An institutional investor's due diligence activities are a necessary support for group benefit products.

Competitive Intelligence

The information gathered as part of monitoring funds can also be applied to competitive analysis. Market awareness is vital to maintaining the right array of fund options and keeping abreast of important trends. To address the need for competitive information, internal analysts continuously track, analyze, rate, and rank a group of peers or competitors in whatever groupings the company finds relevant for internal management purposes. Competitive analysis helps insurance company representatives anticipate fund selection questions from institutional clients and helps them also to develop informative explanations about why the company's menu of funds is a reasonable solution in view of competitors' characteristics and fund offerings.

Analysis of Fund Options

An insurance company's success with separate account products depends on having a menu of fund options that meets the needs of the company, its sales force, institutional clients, and end investors. Insurers constantly analyze the universe of available fund options in an effort to satisfy these needs. Investment professionals undertake a multistep analysis process that covers all aspects of a fund, including many qualitative and quantitative factors.

Scorecards

In one type of analysis, investors typically use a *scorecard*—a type of form, usually with a table or worksheet layout—for analyzing or comparing various funds. Investment analysts, researchers, and other investment professionals use scorecards to build a consistent set of information, record impressions, and communicate with others about each fund or other investment they review.[6] Investment professionals use a scorecard as part of identifying fund option candidates, as well as for ongoing monitoring of a company's menu of fund options. By glancing at a scorecard, investment professionals can see whether a fund option is remaining competitive with its peers. Figure 5.4 presents an example of a scorecard.

Scorecards apply mathematical routines to data inputs and automatically award points for various characteristics; in so doing, they accumulate a score for each fund. As you know, for a score, a high value indicates good quality.

> **Example: Scoring Fund Performance**
>
> In scoring, each fund is typically awarded a predetermined value for each aspect of positive performance. Funds accumulate points based on positive performance in numerous categories. When scoring of an entire peer group is complete, the funds with the best performance of the group will have the highest scores.

Analysts use scorecards to consolidate multiple factors into one metric that demonstrates a fund's standing relative to its peers.

A score can be ranked. For a rank that indicates a fund's sequence in a numerical listing starting with the best score and ending with the lowest score, a low rank value indicates good quality. A rank is one fund's position in a sequence in which all of the funds are ranked from best to worst. For example, a rank of two indicates

Figure 5.4 Scorecard

Fund Name	Ranking vs. Peers*				Criteria										
	1 yr	3 yr	5 yr	10 yr	1	2	3	4	5	6	7	8	9	10	11
Logo Mid Cap	4	2	3	1	✓	✓	✓	✓	✓	✓	✓	✓	✓	✓	✓
Applegate Mid Cap	31	54	41	67	✓	✓	✓	✓	✗	✓	✗	✓	✗	✓	
Overflo Mid Cap	97	57	109	116	✗	✗	✓	✗	✓	✓	✗	✓	✓	✓	✗

*Peers refers to a group of 347 very similar funds. Each rank shows where the given mutual fund's total return ranked within the peer group. In a ranking, a low number indicates better performance than a high number.

Criteria

1 **Inception Date:** The fund must have at least a 3-year track history.

2 **Manager Tenure:** The fund manager must have at least a 2-year track history.

3 **Assets:** The fund must have at least $75 million under management.

4 **Composition:** The fund's allocation to its primary asset class should be $\geq$ 80%.

5 **Style:** The fund's current style box should match the peer group.

6 **Prospectus Net Expense Ratio:** The fund must place in the top 75% of its peer group.

7 **Beta:** The fund must place in the top 50% of its peer group.

8 **Sharpe:** The fund must place in the top 50% of its peer group.

9 **1-Year Return:** The fund must place in the top 50% of its peer group.

10 **3-Year Return:** The fund must place in the top 50% of its peer group.

11 **5-Year Return:** The fund must place in the top 50% of its peer group.

■ = Tier 1
□ = Tier 2
■ = Tier 3

Source: Adapted with permission from fi360, Inc., *Proposal Report* (Bridgeville, PA: fi360, Inc., 2012), 16, http://www.fi360.com/fa/help/Report_Samples/proposal-report.pdf (28 September 2012).

that a fund had the second best performance in its peer group. Scoring and ranking systems indicate the quality of the fund compared to the analyst's standards and potentially to a peer group or a market index benchmark.

Some analysts may assign funds a letter grade or multiple stars rather than a numerical ranking.

For some purposes, analysts calculate the average total return on all portfolios in a peer group, and then group them into percentiles or quartiles. Regardless of the method or notation used, analysts then periodically repeat the scoring and ranking process.

Analysts use scorecards for analysis of a company's existing fund options. If a fund on the menu falls below a specified performance level, it will trigger an investigation into why its relative standing has declined. Such an analysis emphasizes understanding a particular fund's management philosophy and investment and risk management strategies. If the fund does not improve within a designated period of time, it may be removed from the menu of options, and replaced.

Analysts also use scorecards for screening new funds for possible inclusion in a company's menu of fund options. While analysts are identifying the most attractive candidates, they are also eliminating unsuitable candidates. Analysts may reject candidates on the basis of certain factors, such as an inconsistent performance history, excessive management turnover, or legal or regulatory problems. After the screening process identifies a smaller number of likely candidates for fund inclusion, the investment team undertakes a progressively more detailed analysis of the remaining candidates.

Governing Policies

As we discussed in Chapter 3, companies have governance and control structures in place to ensure proper consideration and authorization of important decisions such as those affecting a company's menu of separate account fund options. Companies set policies to guide decisions about their menu of fund options. Such policies set constraints on the menu of fund options and their internal and external administration. These constraints typically address the array of proposed fund categories, number of funds permitted in each category, procedure for approval of a new fund option, and operational controls and limitations.

> ### Example: Policy Constraint on External Fund Options
>
> Typically, to be considered for inclusion in an insurance company's menu of fund options, an external fund must have existed for a minimum time period, typically three to five years, all while adhering to a single management philosophy, and holding assets in excess of a specified amount—often $100 million.

These requirements help to ensure that such a fund has adequate scale to remain viable for the long term.

Portfolio Manager and Management Team

Fund analysts typically prefer portfolio managers with a "disciplined and repeatable process"—a phrase common in due diligence work. When a company selects a portfolio manager and fund, the company needs to feel confident that it has set reasonable expectations and the portfolio manager can meet those expectations. Portfolio managers who lack disciplined processes may surprise analysts and institutional investors with unexpected portfolio results. The presence of disciplined investment management processes indicates that managers are capable of continuing the practices that created their record of successful performance. Otherwise, their past success could have been a matter of unrepeatable good fortune.[7]

Some portfolio managers invest substantial amounts of their own money in the fund so that fund performance directly affects the value of those investments. Investment professionals prefer funds whose portfolio managers invest personal assets in the fund to those whose managers do not; such investments demonstrate that the portfolio manager has a vested interest in the successful performance of the fund. Having such a vested interest in the fund may also discourage a manager from taking excessive risks for the sake of potentially higher compensation.

The analysis of fund management takes into consideration whether the fund has changed managers in the past several years. If so, the analyst compares the fund's performance under the current manager with that under the former manager. Funds having similar performance before and after a change in managers are more likely to have, in practice, a shared management style than are those whose performance changed significantly as a result of the management change. Attribution analysis helps analysts to better understand the portfolio manager's contributions to a fund's performance results.

Attribution Analysis

As we discussed in Chapter 3, attribution analysis describes which of a portfolio manager's strategies were successful in adding value to a portfolio. This analysis involves assigning components of portfolio returns to various portfolio management tactics. Although internal fund analysts have access to adequate internal data for multifactor analysis, similar data may not be readily available for external portfolios. Therefore, this approach may not be useful for analyzing an external fund.

Attribution analysis may be used to gain an understanding of how a manager achieved past performance. It can be part of the analysis to confirm a manager's claims about strategy and how strategy was used to achieve success. Also, it may help to identify whether a manager achieved good performance on the basis of good luck or one highly successful action, rather than by sustaining a pattern of successful behaviors.

Multifactor analysis, also known as *factor analysis*, is the application of advanced quantitative techniques to daily portfolio data for the purpose of identifying which management choices or attribution factors—including risk exposures—most influenced a portfolio's returns. The quantitative techniques used in multifactor analysis incorporate a high degree of estimation, and this degree of estimation can produce a significant residual error in the results. Any attribution analysis presents an attribution factor for unexplained residual return, partly reflecting estimation errors, and possibly partly reflecting returns achieved through luck, not skill.

Typical attribution factors to analyze relative to the investment for equity funds include security selection; sector selection; portfolio concentration; momentum; unexplained residual return; and typical equity valuation ratios such as the price-earnings (P/E) ratio, the price-to-book-value (P/B) ratio, or earnings ranges. We discuss the price-earnings (P/E) ratio and the price-to-book-value (P/B) ratio in Chapter 10.

- **Security selection** refers to a portfolio management tactic of attempting to generate higher returns than the established benchmark index by selecting and overweighting securities having a higher expected return than those in the benchmark allocation.

- **Sector selection** refers to a portfolio management tactic of attempting to generate higher returns than the established benchmark index by selecting and overweighting sectors or industries having a higher expected return than those in the benchmark index. In attribution analysis, *timing* refers to the value added by changing both security and sector weightings during a given performance period.

- *Portfolio concentration*, also known as *asset concentration* or simply *concentration*, refers to allocating a significant share of a portfolio to a few securities, rather than following the broader allocation established by the strategic allocation plan.

- *Momentum* refers to the tendency for a security that is gaining in market value to continue moving in the same direction. Portfolio managers sometimes take advantage of this effect to add value to a portfolio.

- *Unexplained residual return* is the attribution category for the portion of total returns not assigned to other categories. As we have discussed, much of this portion of total return arises from estimation errors associated with the multifactor analysis technique; and a high value for unexplained residual return could indicate that good performance is more a matter of luck than skill.

For fixed-income funds, in addition to unexplained residual return, attribution factors typically include average duration or maturity, sector allocation, and average credit rating. For example, a portfolio manager could attempt to beat a benchmark by using a totally different approach to duration or credit risk than is used in the designated benchmark. Attribution analysis for a fixed-income portfolio would seek to uncover the effect of any such strategy.

Interpretation of Attribution Analysis

In this section, we demonstrate performance attribution analysis using results from multifactor analysis.

Jason, an investment analyst in Logo Financial, compares the overall performance of two similar growth equity funds, the Bola Fund and the Todo Fund. Jason's attribution analysis report shows the following returns for these funds:

	Growth Equity Funds		Benchmark Index
	Bola Fund	Todo Fund	
Attribution Analysis			
Security selection	3.00%	1.05%	
Sector selection	1.50%	1.20%	
Portfolio concentration	0.45%	2.10%	
Momentum	1.00%	0.75%	
Unexplained residual return	0.80%	1.45%	
Total investment return	**6.75%**	**6.55%**	**6.90%**
Derivatives program	0.11%	0.25%	
Securities lending program	NA	0.15%	
Total return	**6.86%**	**6.95%**	**6.90%**
Expense ratio	0.80%	0.95%	
Net return	**6.06%**	**6.00%**	**6.90%**

In the table, notice that the sum of the attribution factors, including unexplained residual return, is *total investment return*. In this analysis, total investment return incorporates all returns from investing. Total investment return excludes operating income, such as income from any derivatives program or securities lending program. However, notice that *total return* incorporates total investment return and income from operating activities. Below the line for *total return*, notice that we subtract an *expense ratio* from the total return, and the result is net return.

■ A fund's expense ratio is the result of dividing the fund's operating expenses during a given period by the average dollar value of its assets during the same period. Fund operating expenses exclude transaction costs for purchasing and selling securities, because the reported total investment return absorbs those costs. Fund operating expenses may comprise costs of paying the portfolio manager, auditing, accounting, other recordkeeping, taxes, custody services, and marketing. Regardless, institutional investors tend to prefer funds that do not incorporate sales loads and/or distribution charges.

■ A fund's net return equals the total return minus the expense ratio. Net return is the portion of total return that is distributable to end investors. All expenses reduce potential returns to end investors.

Jason's Analysis of the Bola Fund: Security selection and sector selection are the main contributors to the Bola Fund's investment returns. For the Bola Fund, security selection contributed 3.00 percent and sector selection contributed another 1.50 percent to the fund's 6.75 percent total investment return. Although some other funds earn additional returns from activities other than investments, this report indicates that the Bola Fund does not take the risk of operating a securities lending program. The Bola Fund limits its derivatives program to hedging its portfolio risks. Finally, the Bola Fund has a slightly lower expense ratio than the Todo Fund.

Jason's Analysis of the Todo Fund: As shown in the data table, total investment return for the Todo Fund is derived mainly from portfolio concentration and momentum. This information indicates that the Todo Fund seemingly emphasizes certain stocks, and also relies to some extent on security selection and sector selection to add to its total investment return. Jason knows that the Todo Fund's manager would not be able to rely on momentum for generating excess returns in a negative market environment.

Jason's Conclusions: Overall, the Bola Fund is a better selection than the Todo Fund. The Bola Fund has a higher total investment return than the Todo Fund because the Bola Fund has slightly higher returns from security selection and sector selection. Security selection and sector selection are repeatable performance attributes because they are derived from a portfolio manager's extensive skill and expertise in certain securities and sectors.

On the other hand, the Todo Fund has a slightly higher total return than the Bola Fund. To achieve much of its total return, the Todo Fund relies on portfolio concentration and momentum, which, together, account for 2.85 percent of its total investment return. Returns based on portfolio concentration or momentum are not reliably repeatable.[8]

Management Team

In addition to gathering information about the portfolio manager, investment professionals gather extensive information about a fund's management team. In a qualitative approach, fund analysts interview key management team members. They ask team members to describe the investment process, their views about other team members, and their philosophy about risk and the measures the fund uses to manage risk. Fund analysts also examine a selection of recent investment decisions and ask the fund's management team members to describe the fund's decision-making process leading to particular trades. Fund analysts look for consistency in all aspects of this close qualitative inspection.

At some funds, management is a team responsibility. The departure of any one team member is unlikely to substantially change the fund's investment decisions. A team approach to fund management can provide continuity after the departure of one team member. On the other hand, a need for consensus could slow the timeliness or limit the quality of decisions. The team structure should be weighed relative to the fund's philosophy and resources.

Figure 5.5 tells the story of a fund analyst who applied skills similar to those described in this chapter to detect a notorious financial fraudster.

Administrative Systems and Control

In addition to evaluating a fund's management team, insurance professionals evaluate the fund's back- and middle-office administrative support with an eye toward evaluating general business risks. Analysts examine systems and personnel to ensure that the fund's administrator is capable of accurately and promptly supporting the fund's activities. In addition, companies must ensure that information technology is compatible between all relevant parties.

Companies examine aspects of a fund's administrative systems and operations, including the fund's

- *Accounting, record keeping, and financial reporting systems.* The fund must be capable of complying with all regulatory requirements and the institutional investor's reporting requirements. All performance calculations must be performed accurately by qualified personnel who are independent of the fund's management.

- *Methods of pricing securities and creating daily fund values.* These methods must be quick, accurate, and compliant with all regulatory requirements.

- *Trading systems and methods.* These systems and methods should ensure that trades are conducted promptly, as ordered, and with minimum total trading costs.

- *Internal risk management framework.* The sponsoring organization should have a well-defined risk management policy with appropriate controls and established limits. The fund should also specify procedures to implement if risk limits are exceeded.

Figure 5.5 The Man Who Figured Out Madoff's Scheme

Harry Markopolos was an obscure financial analyst and mildly eccentric fraud investigator from Boston who most people would never notice on the street.

But today he enjoys an almost heroic status, pursued by journalists and movie producers, and honored by colleagues as the man who went to the Securities and Exchange Commission and blew the whistle on Bernie Madoff and his $50 billion fraud.

It began a decade ago, when Markopolos was working for a Boston investment firm. His boss told him that Madoff, a former chairman of the NASDAQ stock exchange, was running a huge unregistered hedge fund that was producing incredible returns. He wanted Markopolos to reverse-engineer its trading strategy and revenue streams so the firm could duplicate Madoff's results.

"He had the patina of being a respected citizen. One of the most successful businessmen in New York, and certainly, one of the most powerful men on Wall Street. You would never suspect him of fraud. Unless you knew the math," Markopolos said.

Asked how long it took him to figure out something was wrong, Markopolos said, "It took me five minutes to know that it was a fraud. It took me another almost four hours of mathematical modeling to prove that it was a fraud."

It was the performance line that Markopolos said caught his attention. "As we know, markets go up and down, and his only went up. He had very few down months. Only four percent of the months were down months. And that would be equivalent to a baseball player in the major leagues batting .960 for a year. Clearly impossible. You would suspect cheating immediately. No one's that good."

Source: "The Man Who Figured Out Madoff's Scheme," *CBS News*, 1 March 2009, http://www.cbsnews.com/8301-18560_162-4833667. html?tag=contentMain;contentBody (28 September 2012). Used with permission.

- *Regulatory compliance function.* The fund must have adequate systems and personnel to comply with all regulatory requirements.

- *Ethics policy.* The fund should have a comprehensive, established ethics policy. The institutional investor must thoroughly investigate any reported ethical violations or other regulatory or criminal actions brought against the fund or any of its personnel.

External Analysts' Opinions

Insurance companies may not rely solely on their own investment team's findings for fund analysis. Instead, many insurers compile and examine the findings and opinions of external analysts. A number of credible, independent financial analysts evaluate funds and publish their findings and recommendations. These analysts generally have access to the same quantitative information regarding funds as do the insurer's own analysts, but their criteria and opinions can differ from those of the internal analysts. External analysts may also have access to qualitative information such as interviews of managers, and may be able to offer an enhancement to the efficiency of an internal analysis operation. If external analysts reach an opinion opposing that of internal analysts, internal analysts typically consider the reasoning offered by the external analysts.

Total Return Analysis of Funds

An important objective of fund analysis and evaluation is to determine the probability that a fund will be able to meet its stated investment return objectives. In this chapter, our discussion of returns refers only to positive returns. However, it is important to note that some investment outcomes are losses.

Total return for a portfolio in a specified period is the portfolio's investment earnings expressed as a percentage of the portfolio's value at the beginning of the period. Earnings include both price appreciation and distributions. The total annual return for a portfolio is thus the ratio of the portfolio's net investment earnings during the year divided by the portfolio's value at the beginning of the year, as shown:

$$\text{Total annual return for a portfolio} = \frac{\text{Net investment earnings during the year}}{\text{Portfolio value, beginning of year}}$$

Investment analysts typically work with percentages instead of monetary amounts because percentage values are useful for making performance comparisons across different periods and different funds. A fund's total return conveys more meaning when placed in a context of other total returns. Measures that provide a comparison to a useful context are sometimes labeled *relative* measures. We discussed several aspects of fund returns when we discussed attribution analysis earlier in this chapter.

Analysts typically compare the relative performance of a fund to both a benchmark index and a peer group.

Performance Comparison to a Benchmark

As we demonstrated in our example of attribution analysis, analysts typically compare a fund's performance to the performance of a benchmark index, such as a market index. One recognizable example of a market index is the Standard & Poor's 500 Index. We discuss this use of benchmarks in Chapter 6.

Performance Comparison to a Peer Group

One approach to comparing funds is to compare the total returns of comparable funds that have similar investment objectives and similar risk characteristics. A group of funds having the same style and similar risk characteristics is sometimes called a *peer group*. A group of 300 mid-cap growth funds could be used as a peer group category for a given smaller set of mid-cap growth funds. By comparing a fund's total return to the total return results of its peer group, analysts can evaluate the fund's relative performance.

As you saw when we discussed scorecards, a ranking system indicates a fund's relative performance within the peer group. To apply ranking to a group of funds, analysts take the scores they have assigned to a group of funds, and arrange the funds in sequence from highest score to lowest score. Then, they assign a rank to indicate each fund's position in the resulting sequence.

Applying Performance Comparisons

Analysts use different methods to compare a fund's returns to the benchmark returns and peer-group returns. To some extent, this analysis should reflect a fund's management style. For actively managed funds, analysts generally compare the fund's annualized total return to a benchmark return and a peer group return. Investment professionals typically prefer funds that consistently outperform the benchmark and most of the peer group over a period long enough to represent varying market conditions. Over the course of a business cycle, any particular fund style is ordinarily subject to periods that are not favorable for the fund style.

Returns are calculated and evaluated on an annualized basis. In selecting funds for a separate account's menu of fund options, insurers usually evaluate total return for a 10-year period or the lifetime of the fund.

Analysts also evaluate a fund's performance over shorter periods of time representing both favorable and unfavorable overall market conditions.

Analysis of Fund Risk

Risk for an asset or a portfolio is the dispersion of returns, and it is typically viewed in terms of the standard deviation statistic and *beta*, another measure of risk.

Standard Deviation of Returns

In Chapter 4 we discussed standard deviation as the primary approach to measuring risk and volatility. For a given fund, an essential approach to understanding the investment risks is to calculate the standard deviation of returns for that fund over the relevant periods for analysis. For a worthwhile analysis, analysts require a minimum sample size of three years of monthly data.

Actually calculating a standard deviation of returns for a fund relies on having the fund's historical data. Even if the appropriate historical data are readily available, decision makers understand that trends based on historical patterns may not continue unbroken into the future.

Strategies described until this point in our discussion have reflected an underlying belief that the greater the risk, the greater the return. In a climate of persistent low interest rates, measures that analyze just the downside portion of risk have prominence.

Beta

Beta is a measure of market volatility that highlights both return and risk. The applications of beta are, first, to gain understanding of market risk using market beta, and then to gain understanding of a particular fund's overall exposure to market risk. Thus, beta measures market risk. Although beta is potentially applicable to equity and fixed-income markets, beta has far greater usefulness for equities than for fixed-income investments.

The baseline beta for the stock market is 1. A portfolio could have a beta value considerably greater or lower than 1. Beta values greater than 1 indicate more risk than the broad stock market.

Example: Interpreting Betas

The S&P 500 index is the beta baseline. Thus, the S&P 500 index is assigned a beta of 1.00. Thrifty Large-Cap Fund has a portfolio beta of 1.20.

Thrifty's beta indicates that Thrifty is 20 percent riskier than the overall stock market, represented by the S&P 500 index. Accordingly, Thrifty should generate a higher return than the S&P 500 index.

Solo Large-Cap Fund has a portfolio beta of 0.80.

Solo's beta of 0.80 indicates that Solo is 20 percent less risky than the S&P 500 index. Thus, Solo is expected to generate a lower return than the S&P 500 index.

Risk managers look at portfolio betas to express the portfolio's level of exposure to market risk. Beta can be used to estimate the impact of overall market risk on portfolio return. Accordingly, portfolio managers use beta to evaluate market opportunities.

Expected portfolio return using beta

Expected portfolio return =

Risk-free rate + [Beta x (Market return – Risk-free rate)]

Risk-Return Analysis of Funds

Excess return is return that exceeds a fund's performance benchmarks. Excess return for a fund is expressed by the following formula:

Excess return =

Portfolio total return – Benchmark total return

Investors do not, however, consider returns separately from risks. Given two equivalent portfolios with the same return, rational investors prefer the fund with less risk. Thus, investors also consider risk-adjusted returns using measures such as tracking error, the information ratio, the Sharpe ratio, and the Sortino ratio.

Tracking Error

Tracking error is a measure that indicates the closeness of fit between a fund being studied and that investment portfolio's benchmark. Other terms for tracking error are *tracking risk*, *tracking error volatility*, and *active risk*. As you know, a fund's benchmark often is a market index. Tracking error is calculated as the standard deviation of the differences between a fund's investment returns and the investment returns of its benchmark, and the result takes the form of a percentage. A higher value for tracking error indicates a greater degree of departure from the benchmark. Tracking error in a number of its variations can help to indicate whether a fund is achieving the risk exposures it is intended to achieve.

Information Ratio

The information ratio relies on the tracking error. The ***information ratio*** is the ratio of the excess return for a portfolio divided by tracking error, and the result is usually expressed as a percentage. The information ratio compares a fund's excess return over its benchmark return to a unit of tracking error. The information ratio is designed to indicate a portfolio manager's effectiveness in actively deviating from a benchmark to generate a return. The value of an information ratio should be greater than zero. An information ratio is not effective when excess returns are lower than zero. Generally, a higher value for an information ratio indicates greater effectiveness in using risk to generate investment returns. So, all other factors being equal, a fund with a higher result for the information ratio is better at using risk to generate returns than is a fund with a lower result for the information ratio.

The information ratio is expressed as follows:

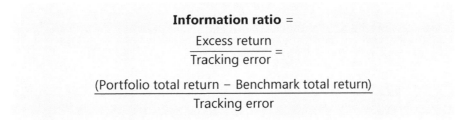

Information ratio =

$$\frac{\text{Excess return}}{\text{Tracking error}} =$$

$$\frac{\text{(Portfolio total return} - \text{Benchmark total return)}}{\text{Tracking error}}$$

Example: Using the Information Ratio

The following table describes information ratios for Funds A and B.

Benchmark Performance	
Benchmark Total Return	9.00%
Standard Deviation	17.00%

Fund Performance	Excess Return	Tracking Error	Information Ratio
Fund A	2.00%	33.00%	00.06
Fund B	1.00%	11.00%	00.09

From this information, we can see that Fund B has a higher information ratio and a lower tracking error than Fund A. Both of these measures indicate that Fund B has slightly better performance than Fund A.[9]

Sharpe Ratio

The *Sharpe ratio* measures a portfolio's returns earned for each unit of risk, when risk is expressed as the standard deviation of portfolio returns. Generally, the higher the Sharpe ratio, the better a portfolio's risk-adjusted return. The Sharpe ratio is ineffective when portfolio returns are lower than the risk-free rate of return.

Investment analysts generally calculate the Sharpe ratio over the same time period as they use for standard deviation calculations. As is true for standard deviations, Sharpe ratio calculations require a minimum sample size of three years of data.

The formula for the Sharpe ratio is

$$\text{Sharpe ratio} = \frac{[\text{Portfolio total return minus risk-free rate of return}]}{\text{Standard deviation of portfolio returns}}$$

Because the Sharpe ratio is based on standard deviation, analysts can use Sharpe ratio results to compare risk-adjusted returns of two or more funds.

Example: Sharpe Ratio Calculation

Steady Growth Fund has published the following information about its performance over the past year.

Total return	8%
Risk-free rate of return	2%
Standard deviation	3%

Steady Growth's Sharpe ratio is 2, calculated as shown:

$$\frac{8\% - 2\%}{3\%} =$$

$$\frac{6\%}{3\%} = 2$$

Analysts can compare a fund's Sharpe ratio to the Sharpe ratio for a benchmark portfolio. The benchmark portfolio could be a market index or another fund. Using the Sharpe ratio to interpret various circumstances, an investment analyst can form the following conclusions:

■ If a portfolio's Sharpe ratio is greater than the Sharpe ratio for a market index, the portfolio has outperformed the market on a risk-adjusted basis.

■ If a portfolio has the same risk, expressed by standard deviation, as a specified benchmark, and also has a higher Sharpe ratio, that portfolio has a greater risk-adjusted return than does the benchmark.

■ Similarly, if a portfolio has the same return as the benchmark, and also has a higher Sharpe ratio, then the portfolio has lower risk than does the benchmark.

Sortino Ratio

As you know, volatility refers to fluctuations in market value. A modification of the Sharpe ratio, the *Sortino ratio* isolates volatility caused by negative portfolio returns from the remaining potential sources of volatility. The Sortino ratio is more effective than the Sharpe ratio because the Sharpe ratio does not consider how often volatility is positive as opposed to how often it is negative. However, the Sortino ratio is ineffective when overall fund returns are below the risk-free rate.

As with the Sharpe ratio, a higher risk-adjusted value for the Sortino ratio represents a lower risk, and a lower risk-adjusted value for the Sortino ratio represents a higher risk.

Analysis of Fund Expenses

Analysts often compare a fund's expenses to those of their peer group by reference to an expense ratio. We discussed the expense ratio earlier in this chapter, where we discussed attribution analysis. An expense ratio is expressed as a percentage, so the fund's level of expenses can be compared across a number of mutual funds.

Institutional investors generally avoid funds that impose sales loads or distribution fees.

In general, analysts prefer funds that have a substantially lower expense ratio than do most other members of the peer group. In addition, analysts examine a fund's expense ratio over time and select funds whose expense ratios have remained consistent or, preferably, have declined over the past several years.

Reflecting a belief that turnover leads to higher fund expenses, some fund analysts evaluate this aspect of fund management by means of the portfolio turnover rate.

The ***portfolio turnover rate*** is the percentage rate at which the fund buys or sells securities, excluding short-term assets.[10] A portfolio turnover rate for a one-year period is calculated according to the following formula:

$$\textbf{Portfolio turnover rate} = \frac{\text{Lesser monetary amount of securities bought or securities sold}}{\text{Average total assets}}$$

Portfolio turnover reflects a fund's investment style. Actively managed funds have a significantly higher portfolio turnover rate than do passively managed funds. In general, analysts assign higher scores or ratings to funds that have substantially lower portfolio turnover rates than do most other members of the peer group. Not all analysis teams use turnover as a scoring standard, however.

Example: Portfolio Turnover Rate Calculation

Last year, the Sunnyside Fund bought $100 million of securities and sold $110 million of securities. The fund's average total asset value for the year was $400 million.

The lesser of assets bought or assets sold is $100 million. The fund's portfolio turnover for last year is 25 percent, calculated as

$$\frac{\$100 \text{ million}}{\$400 \text{ million}} = 0.25 = 25\%$$

Fund Selection, Evaluation, and Oversight

Fund selection, evaluation, and oversight constitute an ongoing process. The investment team seeks to add and maintain fund offerings that meet the company's established parameters and enable the company to provide customers with separate account products that have a high likelihood of performing as expected. The investment team makes recommendations within the company's established reporting structure for adding new fund options and maintaining existing fund options. Company authorities review the recommendations and, if necessary, modify the selection parameters.

To wrap up the evaluation process, the fund analysis team typically prepares a comprehensive analysis report discussing every relevant aspect of a fund—its performance, management, administration, and regulatory compliance. This report helps document that the insurer has conducted a sufficient due-diligence review.

Style Drift

During the selection of or analysis of fund options, investment analysts often observe *style drift*, which is the divergence of an investment fund from its stated investment objective or style. A fund's prospectus or offering circular describes the fund's investment objectives and style. As time passes, funds evolve and exhibit style drift. Analysts seek to understand the degree of style drift more than to detect its presence. Cases of identified style drift merit qualitative and quantitative analysis.

Style drift can occur for a number of reasons. In some cases, a fund's management team changes, and the new management's interpretation of the stated objectives and style differs from that of the former managers. In other cases, the fund's portfolio manager intentionally changes the fund's style in an effort to improve returns.

Example: Style Drift in Equity Funds

Mighty Domestic Mid-Cap Fund's prospectus states that the fund invests in mid-cap stocks. Mighty Domestic's prospectus further states that the fund strategy emphasizes the goal of outperforming the S&P MidCap 400 index. The prospectus does not set a lower limit on a market capitalization for fund investments.

After Mighty Domestic had been operating for several years, the portfolio manager noticed that small-cap domestic stocks were consistently outperforming the S&P MidCap 400 index. The manager invested a small amount of the Mighty Domestic fund in small-cap stocks. Over the next few years, small-cap stocks grew to comprise 35 percent of the total Mighty Domestic portfolio.

Generally, small-cap stocks have substantially higher volatility than mid-cap stocks. By increasing the allocation of a mid-cap fund to small-cap stocks, the portfolio manager increased the risk in the fund.

Investors in Mighty Domestic rely on their mid-cap manager to stay the course in mid-cap stocks. Any Mighty Domestic investors interested in diversifying in the direction of small-cap investments have the option to purposely invest in a small-cap fund.[11]

Actively managed stock funds are generally more susceptible to style drift than are bond funds, money market funds, and passively managed funds. Stock equity funds often must expand their holdings by investing in the stocks of new issuers. As the number of stocks held by a fund increases, the fund can have difficulty finding new stocks that are compatible with the fund's investment style.

For small-cap and mid-cap equity funds, an increasing fund size can lead to style drift. Fund size usually does not present a similar challenge for large-cap equity funds, because large-cap funds generally can purchase substantially larger amounts of stock in some of their existing holdings, if necessary. Due to liquidity concerns, though, small-cap and mid-cap funds face limits in the size of their investment in any particular company. Small-cap and mid-cap funds may proactively close a fund to new entrants before the funds grow too large. To find sufficient additional suitable stocks to purchase, some equity funds invest in stocks from outside their announced style, resulting in style drift. For these reasons, analysts must investigate whether a fund has the capacity to take a substantial influx of new money and new participants. To address this concern, institutions often set a maximum size limit for new small-cap and mid-cap funds.

Because actual fund style is not necessarily the fund style promised in the fund prospectus, analysts make use of investment holdings analysis to determine a fund's actual style. To do so, first they assign every security in a fund to the appropriate style category. For equity funds, the relevant categories would be classified by market capitalization. Then, they calculate the percentage value of securities a fund holds in each style category. For this purpose, returns based style analysis software is widely available in the industry.

Examples: Software for Returns-Based Style Analysis

MPI Stylus is a software package for performing returns-based portfolio style analysis for producing risk analysis, performance attribution, and efficiency measures.[12]

Zephyr StyleADVISOR is a software package for performing returns-based style analysis and reporting applicable to mutual funds. StyleADVISOR is also used for peer group analysis, style attribution analysis, manager search, and asset allocation analysis.[13]

Figure 5.6 shows the results of an investment holdings analysis for a small-cap equity fund. The data table shows that a small-cap fund is drifting into holding large-cap assets.

Figure 5.6 Investment Holdings Analysis—Stars Small-Cap Fund

Measurement Period	Style Category by Capitalization— Stars Small-Cap Fund			Benchmark Index Returns			Weighted Benchmark Index Returns**
	Small	Mid	Large	Small	Mid	Large	
Period 1	100.00%			8.52%	7.92%	7.03%	8.52%
Period 2	96.00%		4.00%	9.00%	8.51%	7.25%	8.93%
Period 3	80.00%		20.00%	8.75%	8.01%	6.75%	8.35%

*The weighted benchmark index returns for each period represent blends of the index returns for the period according to the fund's actual allocations during the same period.

Source: Patricia Wilson Fridley (Senior Advisor, Center for Financial Stability, LLC), notes to author, 30 July 2012 and 16 October 2012. Used with permission.

In Period 1, the Stars Small-Cap Fund holds most of its funds in small-cap equities, so the fund's holdings are completely consistent with the fund's announced small-cap style.

In Period 2, four percent of the Stars Small-Cap Fund is allocated to large-cap equities. Although large-cap equities are not the intended holdings of a small-cap fund, investment policy allows such a small percentage of departure from the small-cap style. However, notice that the benchmark return for large-cap equities was notably lower than for small-cap equities in Period 2.

In Period 3, however, the Stars Small-Cap Fund's style has clearly drifted. Now, only 80 percent of the fund remains in small-cap equities, while 20 percent is in large-cap equities. In Period 3, the benchmark index shows that large-cap equities are performing significantly less well than small-cap equities. With such a high percentage of the Stars fund being held in large-cap equities, the benchmark index for small-cap equities is clearly no longer an appropriate performance standard for this small-cap fund. The weighted benchmark index return for Period 3 blends the small-cap and large-cap benchmark returns for the same period.

Replacing a Fund

Companies replace a fund option for a combination of reasons, including poor investment returns, operational difficulties, legal or regulatory problems, or a change in fund management. To meet their commitment to customers, companies must replace a fund that no longer meets its stated investment objectives.

Companies may place a fund option on a watch list prior to removing it from their menu of funds. In this context, a ***watch list*** is a list of funds that require heightened monitoring.[14] A company typically notifies any fund on the watch list that it has been placed on the watch list, states the reasons for this action, and sets forth requirements the fund must subsequently meet. After that notification, the company documents internal actions regarding any fund on a watch list.

To support the replacement of a fund option, companies offering fund options proactively identify and continuously monitor at least one candidate with potential to replace each fund currently on their menu. In other words, companies have a suitable replacement fund ready to launch on short notice.

Companies offering fund options have a procedure for removing a fund option. Typically, such a procedure requires notifying both internal and external parties affected by the action, potentially including plan sponsors, individual customers, and plan participants.

Example: Changing a Menu of Fund Options

Superlative Financial's Golden Excellence Variable Annuity currently provides a menu of 10 fund options. Superlative Financial retains the right to add new fund options or discontinue current fund options for the Golden Excellence Variable Annuity.

Now, Superlative Financial is enhancing this menu of fund options by adding an international stock fund; dropping one bond fund, and replacing it with another.

Accordingly, Superlative Financial announced the following changes in the menu of fund options:

- Introduce the Small World Fund
- Discontinue the Benevolent Long-Term Bond Fund
- Introduce the Congenial Long-Term Bond Fund

Key Terms

large-cap fund	due diligence
mid-cap fund	scorecard
small-cap fund	security selection
emerging market fund	sector selection
sector fund	portfolio concentration
fixed-income fund	momentum
multisector bond fund	beta
growth fund	excess return
value fund	tracking error
stable value fund	information ratio
index fund	Sharpe ratio
absolute return fund	portfolio turnover rate
target date fund	style drift
Morningstar Style Box	watch list

Endnotes

1. Portions of this chapter are based on notes provided by Leon Osborne, CFA, (Director, Due Diligence, MassMutual Life Investors Services, LLC), March–September 2012. Used with permission.

2. Ibid. Used with permission.

3. "Fact Sheet: The Morningstar Style Box™," Morningstar, Inc., http://corporate.morningstar.com/bf/documents/MethodologyDocuments/FactSheets/MorningstarStyleBox_FactSheet_.pdf (10 August 2012).

4. Morningstar, Inc., *Morningstar Fixed-Income Style Box™ Methodology* (Chicago: Morningstar, 2012), http://corporate.morningstar.com/us/documents/MethodologyDocuments/MethodologyPapers/FixedIncomeStyleBoxMeth.pdf (10 August 2012).

5. Portions of the material in the remainder of this chapter were developed by Patricia Wilson Fridley (Senior Advisor, Center for Financial Stability, LLC). Used with permission.

6. Fi360, *Proposal Report* (Bridgeville, PA: fi360, 2012), 29, http://www.fi360.com/fa/help/Report_Samples/proposal-report.pdf (2 October 2012).

7. Osborne. Used with permission.

8. Fridley, note to author, 30 July 2012. Used with permission.

9. Ibid., note to author, 2 April 2012. Used with permission.

10. Investment Company Institute, *2012 Investment Company Factbook*, 52nd ed. (Washington, DC: Investment Company Institute, 2012), 31, http://www.icifactbook.org/2012_factbook.pdf (4 September 2012).

11. Fridley, note to author, 12 September 2012. Used with permission.

12. "MPI Stylus Suite for Advisors," Markov Processes International, http://www.markovprocesses.com/products/mpistylusa.htm (2 October 2012).

13. "StyleADVISOR," Zephyr Associates, Inc., http://www.styleadvisor.com/products/styleadvisor/index.html (2 October 2012).

14. Fi360.

Chapter 6

Institutional Portfolio Management

Objectives

After studying this chapter, you should be able to

6A Explain the risk management approaches of hedging and diversification; and the bottom-up and top-down approaches to portfolio management

6B Describe the control cycle as it is applied to portfolio management and the role of investment policy and risk in this cycle

6C Describe how investment professionals use peer review analysis, a composite peer portfolio, correlation analysis, an asset-class correlation matrix, mean variance optimization, an efficient frontier, efficient portfolios, standard deviation, beta, and Monte Carlo analysis in identifying appropriate asset classes and developing a strategic asset allocation

6D Describe the data sets that investment professionals use to develop benchmarks for portfolio management, including the strategic portfolio and market indexes; and describe how institutional investors adjust market indexes for use in benchmarking portfolio performance

6E Describe various tactical investment strategies, including contrarian investing, and discuss how these tactical strategies impact the implementation of a portfolio

6F Describe standard approaches to reporting portfolio returns and evaluating portfolio results, and the role of attribution analysis in evaluating a portfolio manager's asset-class allocation and security selection decisions

Outline

In this chapter, we describe institutional processes for the tactical, or operational, level of portfolio management.[1] In previous chapters, we saw that investment professionals in institutions work within their organization's governance and control framework, making use of the information and technology available in an institutional environment. We also reviewed investment risk and returns, including estimating the monetary value of risk exposures. Further, we discussed ways that fund analysts evaluate the fund options offered through separate account products. Because these fund options are investment portfolios seen from a particular viewpoint, that discussion laid significant groundwork for this chapter. We discuss aspects specific to the general account in the next chapter.

Portfolio Management Approaches

Portfolio management applies familiar techniques of risk management, namely diversification and hedging. Using these strategies, investors can take steps to manage investment risk, and also influence investment returns.

- **Diversification.** Investors achieve diversification by purposely spreading the portfolio's holdings to represent a reasonably broad selection of risk exposures, including exposures to various

  - Major asset classes, such as bonds, stocks, mortgages, and real estate

  - Index funds, to achieve diversification within asset classes, and potentially to do so in a cost-effective manner

  - Countries or geographic locales

■ **Hedging.** *Hedging* refers to counterbalancing a given risk exposure against another. As an example, a portfolio could balance stocks that tend to lose value in a recession against stocks that tend to gain value in a recession. Hedging can also take the form of purchasing insurance against a specified risk.

Active and passive approaches to investing, discussed in Chapter 3, are also relevant to portfolio management in institutions. Additionally, investment professionals recognize two extremely different approaches to portfolio management: bottom-up and top-down investing.

■ *Bottom-up investing* consists of selecting individual securities or other assets for a specific portfolio in a manner consistent with portfolio risk guidelines. Bottom-up investors seek asset diversification by selecting one security or issuer at a time.

■ *Top-down investing* consists of starting an investment process by broadly analyzing economic conditions, asset classes, risk exposures, and industries, and then proceeding to build a control framework that addresses this broader environment before finally turning to selecting and purchasing securities.

In an institution, top-down investing consists of setting appropriate constraints on investments, allocating investable funds to classes of assets, setting benchmarks, researching securities markets, planning tactical investment strategies, selecting and then purchasing appropriate securities, monitoring investment risks and returns, reporting performance, comparing performance to standards, and evaluating performance—all in a manner that meets the needs of the portfolio and the organization.

For most purposes, institutional investors generally start with a top-down approach, the topic of this chapter. However, institutional investors also at times borrow from the bottom-up approach.

Figure 6.1 shows a top-down portfolio management process.

Planning for Portfolio Management

Think of institutional portfolio management as a business process that aligns with corporate strategy, applies efficient processes, earns fees for services, and produces investment returns.[2] If you accept this analogy of investment returns as a product of a business process, you can more readily understand the application of performance management concepts to investment portfolios.

Even in institutional contexts, portfolio performance management applies a number of familiar concepts. Any performance management system is cyclical, because this activity is directed toward continuous learning and improvement.

The corporate-level and functional-level controls for portfolio management originate outside the tactical portfolio management context. Here, though, our main focus is the set of control mechanisms directed more narrowly at specific portfolios.

Figure 6.1 Top-Down Portfolio Management Process

1 Select Asset Classes	Identify and analyze appropriate asset classes
2 Set the Asset Class Allocation	Identify the optimum asset class allocation and set the long-term asset class allocation
3 Construct a Benchmark	Develop a composite benchmark for use as a performance standard
4 Plan Tactical Investment Strategies	Analyze the market environment and identify tactical strategies having potential to match or exceed the benchmark
5 Select and Purchase Securities	Analyze securities markets and securities, select securities, and purchase securities
6 Report and Evaluate Performance	Report outcomes, compare outcomes to standards, and evaluate outcomes in view of benchmarks, performance of peers, and tactical strategies

Generally, a long-term control cycle is devoted to setting and communicating performance goals, constraints, and performance standards. When planning for long-term portfolio performance, institutional investors seek to establish:

- Effective determinants of performance that the key decision maker can control—or at least influence to some extent.

- Effective performance goals and constraints expressed in definite, measureable terms.

■ An objective performance standard—a benchmark—for setting performance expectations, guiding tactical decisions, and evaluating performance outcomes.

Planning for institutional portfolio management involves creating an investment policy statement that reflects a particular portfolio's investment objectives and provides guidance as to required returns, risk appetite, risk tolerance, risk limitations, and restrictions on investment practices. For some types of portfolios, such as a pension plan, the investment policy statement may also outline necessary governance arrangements. The investment policy statement should be reviewed periodically to ensure that it accurately reflects the portfolio's circumstances and requirements. Investment professionals then review the risk and reward objectives that are specific to the portfolio they are setting out to manage.

Important outcomes of the planning phase for institutional portfolio management are

■ An investment policy specific to the portfolio that outlines the portfolio's objectives and constraints

■ An *asset-class allocation*—sometimes called a strategic asset allocation—that specifies the long-term targeted mix and proportion of asset classes in the ideal or *efficient* portfolio

■ A benchmark that adequately reflects the asset-class allocation and can be used to evaluate the performance of the tactical portfolio

A portfolio investment policy typically addresses the following issues:

■ The purpose for investing, sometimes known as the portfolio's mission or objective

■ Portfolio risk objectives, potentially expressed in several forms, such as risk appetite and risk tolerance

■ Portfolio return objectives, potentially expressed in several forms, such as absolute and relative return objectives

■ Portfolio constraints, potentially including a time horizon, liquidity needs, income needs, tax considerations, legal and regulatory concerns, and unique needs; such as requirements for socially responsible investing or environmentally responsible investing

■ Portfolio strategy, which is essentially a statement of how to execute the policy

■ A planned asset allocation across broad asset classes, such as 60 percent equities and 40 percent fixed income[3]

Figure 6.2 shows a summary of the investment objectives of a few institutional investors.

During portfolio planning, institutional investors prepare a set of highly specific statements about acceptable levels of risk. For example, a statement may specify the maximum amount of money the given portfolio can lose over a specified period.[4]

Figure 6.2 Typical Investment Objectives of Institutional Investors

Institution	Investment Horizon	Risk Tolerance	Income Need	Liquidity Need
Life insurance company	Long-term	Low	Moderate	High to meet claims
Property-casualty insurance company	Short-term	Low	Low	High to meet claims
Pension plan	Long-term	High	High for mature funds, low for new funds	Low
Endowment or foundation	Very long-term	High	Set to meet spending needs	Low

Source: Adapted with permission from CFA Institute, "Summary of Investment Needs by Client Type," in *Corporate Finance and Portfolio Management* (New York: CFA Institute, 2011), 291–292.

The investment team estimates the potential monetary amounts of losses due to the main sources of specific risk—interest rate risk, credit risk, real estate risk, currency risk, and liquidity risk—for each asset class under consideration. In Chapter 4, we discussed these risks and the processes for estimating monetary losses for them. Asset classes subject to risks that exceed the established risk tolerances are not eligible for inclusion in the development of an asset-class allocation.

Selecting Asset Classes for the Portfolio

When institutional investors set out to construct a specific portfolio, they first identify a set of potentially appropriate asset classes. To select asset classes for a given portfolio, investment professionals consider familiar and new asset classes. For each identified asset class, investment professionals find the expected return and standard deviation of returns from reliable sources, or they estimate these values using reasonably reliable techniques. The initial set of asset classes must show potential for meeting the portfolio's risk and return objectives in the projected economic environment, and should be suited to the available investment management resources.

Investment professionals also evaluate each potential asset class in terms of the company's established risk control framework. Additionally, they evaluate the potential of each asset class to contribute to the portfolio's targeted long-term return objective.

Institutional investors maintain lists of approved asset classes, and portfolio managers must justify and obtain approval for adding any asset class not already on the list. Periodically, institutional investors also specify the *capital market assumptions* that reflect their long-term expectations for the economic environment affecting specified asset classes.

We have previously introduced some broad asset classes. Within those broad asset classes, an institutional investor has available many subcategories of asset classes. In later chapters, we describe many types of asset classes in detail.

In the remainder of this section, we discuss analytical techniques used in identifying a viable set of asset classes for consideration; then, in selecting a set of asset classes for a long-term asset-class allocation; and, finally, in setting the proportions for a long-term asset-class allocation.

An asset-class allocation is designed to give a portfolio the right exposures to particular systemic risks—broad market risks—as well as to balance these risks in the best proportions for the portfolio. Besides addressing the portfolio's investment objectives, the asset-class allocation should incorporate the investor's capital market expectations for the specified asset classes. In the investor's analytical processes, capital market expectations for the specified asset classes are expressed as the expected returns, standard deviations of returns, and correlation coefficients of returns for pairs of asset classes. In turn, investment professionals apply various approaches for developing these capital market expectations.

Important techniques that institutional investors use for identifying appropriate long-term asset classes are peer review analysis, correlation analysis, mean variance optimization, and Monte Carlo modeling.

Institutional investors undertake the necessary analysis in a sequence that brings an increasingly clearer focus on the information they ultimately seek. Generally, first they apply peer review analysis to identify potentially appropriate asset classes; then they refine their understanding of potential asset class combinations by applying correlation analysis; next, they apply mean variance optimization to gain understanding of how various asset-class allocations would perform in different potential future economic environments. Later, using Monte Carlo modeling, they can refine their understanding of potential investment risks and returns.

Peer Review Analysis

Peer review analysis is the most generally accessible approach to creating an asset-class allocation, so institutional investors typically use this approach early in the process, when they are identifying a relatively broad set of appropriate asset classes for further consideration. Institutional investors routinely conduct peer review analysis as described in this section. (In Chapter 5, we discussed a similar activity, the use of peer comparisons as part of analysis of separate account fund options.) Companies use peer comparison information in various contexts, not limited to investments.

For investments, **_peer review analysis_** is a form of quantitative analysis that investment professionals use to initially identify the asset classes their closest competitors use in a similar portfolio. Peer review analysis consists of reviewing the broad asset allocations and published performance data about portfolios operated by the institutional investor's peers.

To apply peer review analysis for identifying suitable long-term asset classes for a new portfolio, an institutional investor

- Identifies a group of about ten or so peer investors and relevant portfolios

- Constructs a *composite peer portfolio* that reflects the mean and median asset mix of the actual portfolios of the peer group

- Analyzes hypothetical results from the composite peer portfolio to estimate an expected return and standard deviation for the asset classes it incorporated into the composite peer portfolio

Limitations of peer review analysis are that

- This approach focuses exclusively on past results

- This approach fails to explicitly address differences in the risk exposures in the various peer portfolios

- An investor using this approach may have difficulty finding public data for closely comparable peers

Still, peer review analysis is useful in verifying that an investment committee's decisions are consistent with other companies' investment decisions.

Building a composite peer portfolio can allow an institutional investor to, eventually,

- Incorporate into the institution's proposed asset-class allocation the insights gained from peer review analysis

- Compare the return and standard deviation of returns for the peer group to the institution's own proposed long-term asset allocation strategy

- Modify the institution's proposed asset allocation strategy to reflect insights gained from peer review analysis

With peer review and other forms of analysis, investment professionals develop an understanding of each asset class and its risk characteristics by considering such factors as the asset sources, types of issuers, the availability of a secondary market, and possible competitive behavior of other investors in the asset class. As the analysis progresses, investment professionals are typically able to remove some asset classes from consideration. A narrower grouping of these asset classes will comprise the investment portfolio when it eventually begins operating.

Investment professionals use the results of peer review analysis when they proceed to perform asset-class correlation analysis.

Correlation Analysis for Diversification

As described in Chapter 4, diversification can be used to reduce or eliminate the impact of sources of portfolio risk. Investment professionals use correlation analysis to determine the potential diversification benefits from including various pairings of asset classes in a portfolio. In this context, *correlation analysis* is a form of quantitative analysis that investment professionals use to determine the potential diversification benefits of various pairings of asset classes. Before we discuss how institutional investors use correlation analysis in setting an asset-class allocation, we briefly discusses correlation concepts.

Generally, *correlation* is the degree of relatedness between two sets of values. The extreme potential correlation conditions are perfect positive correlation, perfect negative correlation, and an absence of correlation, as follows:

- *Perfect positive correlation* between two sets of values exists if an increase in one set of values corresponds to an exactly equal increase in the other and a decrease in one set of values corresponds to an exactly equal decrease in the other.

- *Perfect negative correlation* between two sets of values exists if an increase in one set of values corresponds to an exactly equal decrease in the other and a decrease in one set of values corresponds to an exactly equal increase in the other.

- An absence of correlation between two sets of values exists if a change in one set of values does not exactly equal any change in the other.

The measure that investment professionals use to express the diversification benefit associated with the risk interactions between any pairing of assets is a *correlation coefficient*. Generally, a correlation coefficient indicates how closely movements in two sets of variables track one another. Values of correlation coefficients can range from -1, which represents perfect negative correlation, to +1, which represents perfect positive correlation. Although the extremes of correlation may be the easiest to interpret, in investment markets, investment professionals usually encounter aspects of *partial positive correlation* or *partial negative correlation*.

The following table indicates the strength of risk correlation associated with various ranges of values for the correlation coefficient for a specified pair of risky investments, such as the asset classes we are now discussing.

Correlation Coefficient of Paired Asset Classes	Strength of Risk Correlation
Coefficient between -0.5 and -1.0	Strong negative correlation
Coefficient between -0.5 and 0.0	Modest negative correlation
Coefficient equal to 0.0	No correlation
Coefficient between 0.0 and +0.5	Modest positive correlation
Coefficient between +0.5 and +1.0	Strong positive correlation

Investors obtain the greatest diversification benefits by holding a pair of asset classes having some degree of negative correlation. So long as two asset classes have a correlation coefficient lower than +1, however, investors receive some diversification benefit by including that pairing of asset classes in a portfolio.

The following example describes an effort to improve the diversification of a portfolio consisting entirely of mid-cap U.S. stocks.

Example: Using Correlation Coefficients for Diversification

Portfolio Alpha contains only mid-cap U.S. stocks. Portfolio Alpha's investment goal is to achieve high returns without facing high risk exposures. Pearce, Alpha's portfolio manager, hopes to gain diversification benefits by introducing a new asset class to the asset allocation.

Pearce has access to the following correlation coefficients, each describing a pairing of a proposed new asset class with the existing mid-cap U.S. stock asset class:

New Asset Class	Correlation Coefficients
U.S. corporate bonds	−0.59
U.S. Treasury securities	−0.20
Emerging market stocks	0.25
Large-cap U.S. stocks	0.88

Analysis

U.S. corporate bonds show strong negative correlation with U.S. mid-cap stocks, thus indicating strong diversification benefits. U.S. corporate bonds could substantially improve Alpha's diversification benefits, and thus could stabilize portfolio returns over time.

U.S. Treasury securities show modest negative correlation with U.S. mid-cap stocks. Although this pairing could improve diversification benefits, Pearce knows that the expected return of U.S. Treasury securities is extremely low, and holding these securities would likely reduce portfolio returns.

Emerging market stocks show a modest positive correlation with U.S. mid-cap stocks. Again, although this pairing might improve diversification, Pearce knows that the risks inherent in holding emerging market stocks would violate the portfolio's risk constraints.

Because large-cap U.S. stocks show strong positive correlation to mid-cap U.S. stocks, adding large-cap U.S. stocks to Portfolio Alpha will not produce significant diversification benefits for this portfolio.[5]

An *asset-class correlation matrix* is a table showing the correlation coefficients for all potential pairs of asset classes. For other levels of analysis, investment professionals use a *sector correlation matrix* and a *security correlation matrix*. Figure 6.3 shows a sample correlation matrix for data from several asset classes over a period of five years.

Analysts refer to the results from correlation analysis when they perform mean variance optimization.

Figure 6.3 Sample Five-Year Major Asset-Class Correlation Matrix

ASSET CLASS		UST	USB	EMB	LC	MC	INT
U.S. Treasury	UST						
U.S. Bonds	USB	0.65					
Emerging-Market Bonds	EMB	0.13	0.14				
Large-Cap Stocks	LC	**-0.28**	**-0.37**	**0.19**			
Mid-Cap Stocks	MC	-0.21	-0.28	0.19	**0.93**		
International Stocks	INT	-0.27	-0.42	0.28	**0.85**	0.79	
Real Estate	RE	-0.16	-0.09	0.12	**0.71**	0.74	0.56

Source: Adapted with permission from "Major Asset Correlation Matrix," AssetCorrelation.com, http://www.assetcorrelation.com/majors (15 March 2012).

Mean Variance Optimization

Mean variance optimization (MVO), also known as *mean optimization* or *mean variance analysis*, is a quantitative modeling technique used in generating and analyzing portfolio asset-class allocations. In MVO, each potential mix of asset classes in a portfolio is termed an *asset allocation scenario* or an *asset-class allocation scenario*. MVO attempts to identify asset allocation scenarios that are projected to produce the maximum return for a given risk level.

The output from MVO analysis is a selection of several optimal asset-class allocations. Each optimal asset-class allocation consists of a list of asset classes and proportions, along with projected portfolio returns for each asset class under each of several economic scenarios. Investment professionals use MVO to search for the best possible asset-class allocation scenario within established risk and return constraints, and for the economic scenarios considered most likely to be in effect for the relevant planning period.

Important data inputs to an MVO model are the expected risk and return values of the various asset classes and the correlation coefficients of each potential pair of the asset classes under consideration.

MVO applies a mathematical formula to calculate an *efficient frontier* showing the positions of all hypothetical *efficient portfolios* consistent with the investor's modeling constraints.

■ An ***efficient frontier*** is the set of all potential portfolios having the greatest expected return for different levels of risk.

■ An ***efficient portfolio***, also called an *optimum portfolio*, is a hypothetical portfolio that earns the highest expected return for a given level of risk. In other words, an efficient portfolio represents a theoretically ideal asset allocation.

MVO modeling can produce plots of efficient portfolios on a risk-return graph, as illustrated in Figure 6.4, where the horizontal axis represents risk and the vertical axis represents return.

Figure 6.4 Risk, Return, and the Efficient Frontier

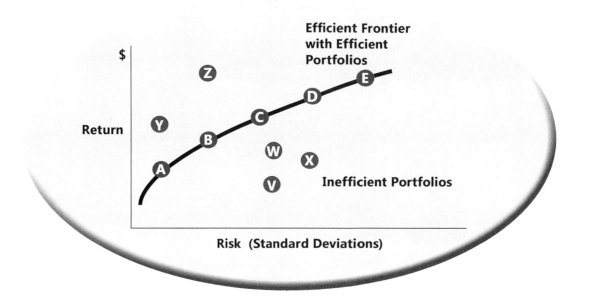

An investor facing this efficient frontier could choose an ideal asset allocation at the points for efficient portfolios A, B, C, D, or E along the efficient frontier, as suited to the investor's risk tolerance and required return.

Source: Adapted with permission from Patricia Wilson Fridley (Senior Advisor, Center for Financial Stability, LLC), note to author, 2 April 2012.

An efficient portfolio, which represents an ideal asset allocation, has the following characteristics:

- An investor cannot add assets to an efficient portfolio to obtain a higher expected return without triggering an increase in portfolio risk.

- Likewise, an investor cannot reduce the risk of an efficient portfolio without decreasing the expected return.

On the risk-return graph, the efficient frontier is represented by a line. Portfolios are represented by dots. The line representing the efficient frontier typically connects all the efficient portfolios. Because the efficient frontier represents the maximum expected return for a given risk level, a rational investor would prefer a portfolio on the efficient frontier. Relative to efficient portfolios, inefficient portfolios can offer the same return for greater risk exposure; lower return for the same risk exposure; or lower return for greater risk exposure.

Investment professionals provide the input data for MVO models and interpret the results of MVO modeling, but they usually do not perform the calculations. The actual computations required for creating MVO scenarios are complex, and are performed electronically. Figure 6.5 presents a simplified example of several MVO-generated scenarios for efficient portfolios with specified asset allocations.

The major limitation of MVO modeling is that small differences in forecasts of return for the asset classes can significantly affect the optimal asset allocation. Also MVO calculations are typically based on historical returns, and historical returns may be poor predictors of future performance.

Instead of relying solely on MVO to suggest an asset-class allocation, investment professionals also conduct a qualitative analysis of different asset classes and apply their judgment to determining the final asset-class allocation. Moreover, investment professionals confirm their impressions of the results of this or any similar model by applying at least one other type of analysis to the problem. In that regard, next we discuss Monte Carlo modeling.

Figure 6.5 Simplified Efficient Portfolio Scenarios

Economic Forecast	Scenario 1	Scenario 2	Scenario 3	Scenario 4
• **Economic growth**	Strong	Average	Slow	None
• **Inflation**	Low	Low	High	Deflation
Asset-class Allocations				
• **Equities**	71.0%	54.0%	48.0%	47.0%
• **Fixed income**	11.0%	14.0%	14.0%	25.0%
• **Hedge funds**	15.0%	20.0%	23.0%	7.0%
• **Real estate**	3.0%	12.0%	15.0%	21.0%
Median Return	9.6%	9.7%	9.8%	9.5%
Standard Deviation	11.7%	9.9%	10.1%	9.0%

A portfolio manager who believes that the new portfolio is likely to initially experience a few years under economic conditions of average economic growth and low inflation would recommend Scenario 2 to the investment committee, because Scenario 2 promises to produce the best results under those conditions. By choosing Scenario 2, the portfolio manager is deciding to use these asset-class proportions to set the new portfolio's SAA.

Source: Patricia Wilson Fridley (Senior Advisor, Center for Financial Stability, LLC), note to author, 25 August 2012. Used with permission.

Monte Carlo Modeling

Monte Carlo modeling is a mathematical modeling process used to approximate the probability of an outcome by running multiple computer simulations that substitute random values for the model's input variables. An institutional investor using Monte Carlo modeling inputs estimated returns, beta, standard deviations, and correlation coefficients for a set of assets, and the model uses these inputs to run potentially thousands of simulations for a specified list of asset classes in various economic scenarios. The investor can then use the model's output to evaluate various potential asset-class allocation scenarios—hypothetical portfolios—to determine which one best fits the company's investment guidelines and risk control framework.

Monte Carlo simulations have applications beyond investment portfolio analysis. Life insurance companies also use Monte Carlo simulations to model product liabilities and satisfy regulatory requirements.

During processing, the Monte Carlo model randomly changes variables such as U.S. Treasury yields, corporate bond rates, the inflation rate, and economic growth. The model then projects investment returns for each set of input factors over various time frames. An investor can then use the results to see, for example, the asset-class mix that would perform best over several years under conditions of high inflation.

Comparing Portfolio Analysis Methods

Peer review analysis, asset-class correlation analysis, MVO, and Monte Carlo modeling have distinctive strengths and weaknesses.

- As we have noted, all of these approaches typically apply historical data as the basis for their modeling results.

- Peer review analysis relies less on software and technical expertise than do MVO or Monte Carlo modeling.

- Monte Carlo modeling is more likely than MVO to effectively address a potential for extremely adverse outcomes.

- Unlike peer review analysis, MVO, and Monte Carlo modeling, asset-class correlation analysis cannot help build an optimal portfolio. Its use is limited to helping companies evaluate the diversification benefits of pairing any two asset classes.

Setting the Strategic Asset Allocation

Investment professionals refer to a long-term asset-class allocation plan as a portfolio's strategic asset allocation. A *strategic asset allocation (SAA)* can be defined as the set of asset-class weights designed to most effectively achieve a portfolio's long-term objectives while remaining consistent with the portfolio's investment policy and investment constraints. A portfolio's SAA represents a version of the efficient portfolio that has been modified to reflect the expert judgment of investment professionals.

Performance Benchmarks

In any performance management context, actual performance is typically evaluated relative to a specified performance standard or benchmark. A good performance standard should not be open to undue influence by the individuals subject to that performance standard, should be relatively easy to access, and should be updated regularly.

In many different performance measurement contexts, managers and analysts compare actual results to performance standards. A standard can indicate results investors would like to achieve or real-world performance results that peers are able to achieve.

Generally, investors expect the actual performance of an actively managed portfolio to beat the relevant securities market overall. They also generally expect the actual performance of a passively managed portfolio to perform close to the securities market overall. Accordingly, performance of a portfolio of securities is typically compared to the performance of the relevant public securities market. In other words, to see if the portfolio did as well as the market overall, investors compare a portfolio's performance against market performance. Later in this chapter, Figure 6.6 discusses considerations in setting benchmarks for portfolios.

The Strategic Portfolio

Having an SAA allows investment professionals to move toward developing a strategic portfolio that can serve as a performance benchmark for a tactical investment portfolio. Central to the development of a strategic portfolio are market proxies. In investments, a ***market proxy*** is a substitute data set that can reasonably be used to represent the primary target of a study, which often may be an entire financial market. Market proxies are used to simplify market studies requiring a market variable, statistic, or comparison. Investors typically use a market proxy to understand the risk and return characteristics of a particular asset class within the SAA. The strategic portfolio thus represents a composite of market proxy results for all of the asset classes in the SAA.

Market Indexes

Investment professionals often use a market index as a market proxy to represent the average of activity for a given asset class. By market index, we mean a statistical measurement system for recording and publishing performance data for a large grouping of similar investments. Generally, each actively traded broad asset class has a market index.

A market index serves as a quantitative record of the average performance of investments in a designated market, and thus allows investment professionals to compare the performance of a portfolio or portfolio segment to the average performance for that market. To function well as a market proxy, an index must closely reflect the long-term behavior of a specified asset class. Figure 6.6 presents a variety of indexes that are commonly used as proxies for various asset classes.

Figure 6.6 Market Indexes for Equity and Fixed-Income Securities

Indexes for Equity Securities Markets

Name	Composition	Unique Risk Profile
S&P 500 (S&P)	Index of the 500 largest companies by market cap in the United States	Benchmark for U.S. large-cap equity
MSCI (US)	Representative indexes for large-, mid-, and small-cap stocks in the United States	U.S. equity benchmark
FTSE Global Equities Series	Representative indexes for developed and emerging markets calculated at regional, national, and sector levels around the world	Benchmark for the largest European equities traded in London
MSCI-EAFE (EAFE)	Representative indexes of the largest companies across Europe, Asia, and the Far East	Benchmark for equities in the developed world, excluding the United States
MSCI All Country Indexes (MCSI-AC)	Representative indexes designed to measure the equity performance of developed and emerging markets around the world	Global equity benchmark

Indexes for Fixed-Income Securities Markets

Name	Composition	Unique Risk Profile
Barclay's Aggregate Bond Index (Barclay Agg)	Fixed-rate, investment-grade bonds, including corporate bonds, U.S. government agency bonds, and mortgage-backed bonds	Broad U.S. bond market index; used as index benchmark for fixed-income portfolios throughout the world
Merrill Lynch High Yield Index (Merrill Junk Index)	Below-investment-grade corporate bonds	Index benchmark for high-yielding, high-risk investments in corporate bonds
JP Morgan Global Government (Global Government)	Foreign-currency-denominated, fixed-income debt instruments in emerging and developed markets	Standard index benchmark for international government bonds

Source: Patricia Wilson Fridley (Senior Advisor, Center for Financial Stability, LLC), note to author, 2 April 2012. Used with permission

Market indexes are useful as market proxies because they conform to specific rules and guidelines, and their results are objectively stated and readily available. Sometimes the statistics from one index are blended with those from another index or indexes to obtain the optimum statistics for use in asset selection and portfolio evaluation. Thus, if appropriate market indexes exist, investment professionals can use these carefully selected market indexes as market proxies for purposes of benchmarking portfolio performance. Other times, investment professionals may have to construct a market proxy by making adjustments to published data or a market index. Still other times, they may have to look beyond market indexes to find suitable market proxies for some asset classes.

Adjustments to Market Index Data

Not all asset classes are traded actively enough to have a single market index suitable to serve as a market proxy. Insurance company general accounts, in particular, typically hold privately traded asset classes for which no public market index exists. And, even when such indexes exist for illiquid assets, they present investors with challenges.

In addition, the market indexes that institutional investors use to create market proxies often have to be adjusted for the following reasons:

- **Mismatched maturities or durations of fixed-income securities.** Bond indexes typically are derived from the behaviors of securities having a much wider variety of expected maturities than those included in a particular institutional portfolio. An institutional investor using a given public market index as a benchmark would make adjustments to the market index data so that the benchmark reflects the expected maturities of bonds similar to those held in its portfolio.

- **Private placement securities.** Most insurance companies and retirement plan funds invest heavily in private placement securities, although market indexes necessarily reflect pricing of securities in public markets. An institutional investor with a large portfolio of private placement securities might choose to refer to a public market index and then adjust the index data to derive a benchmark from the data.

- **Overweighting within an asset class.** Occasionally, one or two individual securities within an asset class may dominate an index, and the institutional analysts may need to reflect this overweighting by adjusting the index.

Example: Adjusting for Overweighted Assets

The NASDAQ 100 Index represents 100 of the largest nonfinancial U.S. and international stocks listed on the NASDAQ. The NASDAQ 100 is often used as a benchmark for these types of assets. However, the performance of one stock—such as Apple—can skew the results of the index.

Therefore, if a portfolio uses the NASDAQ 100 as a benchmark, but does not invest in Apple, the value of the NASDAQ 100 Index will need to be recalculated to reduce the weight given to Apple's results within the index.

■ **Social, ethical, or environmental constraints.** Institutional investors and their stakeholders hold specific beliefs about suitable investments, building asset allocation constraints around those beliefs. An institutional investor using an index that included securities from such restricted companies would adjust the index to remove data representing these companies.

Examples: Social or Ethical Constraints on Investing

Certain insurance companies will not invest in alcohol or tobacco companies because of the harmful effects of such products.

Some benevolent groups prohibit investments on their behalf in companies that design, manufacture, or sell products—such as weapons—that are intended to kill people.

Other Portfolio Benchmarks

Many portfolios have benchmarks that use a target return as the benchmark. In such cases, the target returns may be tied to such factors as inflation, the risk-free rate, or funding requirements.

Example: Target Return as a Benchmark

When a portfolio management system uses target return as a benchmark, a portfolio's benchmark could be to beat the inflation rate by a specified percentage over an established period, such as five to ten years.

Sometimes another operating portfolio with publicly available data and similar portfolio objectives can be used as the benchmark. For example, in the mutual fund business, the performance of an income fund is often compared to other income funds.

Figure 6.7 discusses points to consider in using portfolios as benchmarks for investment performance.

Tactical Investment Strategies

Institutional investors develop an SAA to deliver optimum returns for the long term. In the short term, though, markets can behave erratically. While the SAA does not change in response to short-term market conditions, portfolio managers often use their professional skills to apply a strategy to the tactical portfolio that departs from the SAA to respond to market conditions. All such strategies are designed to optimize returns in accordance with the portfolio's overall investment policy.

Figure 6.7 Considerations for Using Benchmark Portfolios

- A market index used as a data source for a benchmark should be broadly published, measurable, unambiguous, remote from influence by the portfolio managers, appropriate for the intended application, and comprised of securities available for purchase in an active market.

- Benchmark portfolios should be divisible into components, so they can readily be linked to accountabilities in the actual portfolio, and can be used to evaluate portfolio managers responsible for smaller components of a large actual portfolio. For example, a benchmark that combines multiple asset classes should be divisible by asset class, because different portfolio managers likely have responsibility for the various asset classes.

- Benchmark portfolios intended for evaluating the performance of portfolio managers should be disclosed to the portfolio managers far in advance of the performance evaluation.

- A benchmark portfolio should not be regarded as a standalone control mechanism for guiding portfolio management. Instead, portfolio managers should have additional clear policy limitations beyond the benchmark portfolio.

- An ideal benchmark for evaluating a portfolio manager would incorporate all features of the portfolio manager's risk framework.

- A benchmark portfolio chosen for use with a given tactical portfolio should be consistent with the management style and component asset classes of the portfolio.

Source: Patricia Wilson Fridley (Senior Advisor, Center for Financial Stability, LLC), note to author, November 2012. Used with permission.

Besides, to distinguish a portfolio's performance from that of its benchmark, a portfolio manager must employ tactical investment strategies that depart from the strategic asset allocation. The asset proportions in the SAA are expressed as single values, whereas the tactical portfolio is permitted a range of departures from those single values. A portfolio manager's departures from the SAA within these tactical range limits are customarily referred to as "bets."

Example: SAA and Tactical Range Limits

Portfolio A's Investment Goal: *Capital preservation.*

Portfolio A has a low risk tolerance and requires moderate returns at least equal to inflation. Portfolio A also must avoid taking losses. To achieve these goals, the investment committee has approved the following SAA target percentages and related tactical range limits:

	Strategic Asset Allocation	Tactical Range Limits
U.S. Treasury Bills	40%	30% to 60%
High-Grade Corporate Bonds	40%	30% to 50%
Large-Cap Stocks	20%	15% to 30%

The SAA represents the primary means of achieving the investment goal. The tactical range limits formalize the investment team's discretionary limits for diverging from the SAA.

At the beginning of the year, the tactical portfolio holds 28 percent in large-cap stocks. The portfolio manager projects that equity markets will encounter extraordinary volatility during the year, so she reduces the portfolio's equity allocation to 15 percent. If the portfolio ever exceeds the tactical range limits, the portfolio manager is out of compliance and must quickly bring the portfolio back within the tactical range limits.[6]

By using the tactical range limits, a portfolio manager may undertake a strategy of overweighting or underweighting an asset class relative to its weighting in the strategic asset allocation. When a portfolio manager overweights some asset classes, other classes are necessarily underweight. The decisions to overweight or underweight various asset classes can result in positive or negative investment results.

Example: Overweighting or Underweighting an Asset Class

In the SAA, North American corporate fixed-income securities have a weight of 20%, and a permitted tactical range of 15% to 25%.

After the portfolio manager allocates 25% of the portfolio to North American corporate fixed-income securities, the portfolio is overweighted in corporate fixed-income securities. If the market for North American corporate bonds were to fall suddenly and far, the tactical portfolio would perform less well than the SAA because the SAA has only a 20% allocation. The tactical portfolio would have a risk exposure 5% greater than the SAA.

If, however, the portfolio manager had allocated only 15% of the portfolio to North American corporate fixed-income securities, the portfolio would be underweighted in North American corporate fixed-income securities, and would do better in such a bond market downturn.[7]

As time passes and a tactical portfolio gradually loses its original SAA proportions, it is necessary to rebalance the portfolio and return it to the planned asset allocation. Most institutional portfolios are subject to a policy requiring rebalancing at specified intervals. The SAA guides the asset allocation for the tactical portfolio in that, over a long term, the tactical portfolio should remain true to the proportions of the SAA.

In Chapter 5, when we discussed attribution analysis, we saw some strategies that are relevant to tactical management of the investment portfolio, such as timing security selection, sector selection, and momentum. Here, we further consider timing and introduce contrarian investing.

Timing is an investment strategy that attempts to predict future market directions for investment decisions. Although most experts agree that frequently following a timing strategy is statistically a doomed experiment, an experienced investment professional can sometimes forecast when returns for a particular type of investment will improve substantially.

Contrarian investing is an investment strategy that seeks opportunities to buy or sell specific securities when the majority of investors appear to be doing the opposite. Contrarian investors believe that widespread pessimism about a security often drives the price of the security below its intrinsic value and risk levels and thus presents an investor with substantial potential returns. Likewise, contrarian investors believe that widespread market optimism about a particular security or asset class is often followed by a significant market loss in the value of that security.

Although these investment strategies may capitalize on investment opportunities in a current financial market, active portfolio management strategies such as these also involve transaction costs that reduce a portfolio's overall return. The impact of transaction costs on a portfolio's overall return is an important factor in determining investment strategies.

Selecting and Purchasing Securities

Eventually, the institution must purchase the securities to populate the portfolio. In investment jargon, when the portfolio is being populated with securities, the portfolio is being "positioned" into the SAA asset classes. To position a portfolio, the investment team identifies appropriate securities to represent each SAA asset class. Then the team obtains market pricing information for an array of the appropriate securities. With that information in hand, the team is able to rank the available securities in terms of their fit with the portfolio's needs for various risks, returns, and other characteristics. Then, the team purchases the securities that best meet the needs, and continues the search until the portfolio is initially populated. In later chapters, we further discuss the decision process for selecting securities.

Measuring, Reporting, and Evaluating Results

Portfolio performance must be measured and reported regularly, using consistent procedures that comply with all accepted standards and regulations. We have mentioned GIPS as a global standard for performance reporting. Also, regulatory authorities and financial reporting bodies set standards relevant to performance reporting.

Portfolio performance evaluation typically measures two different aspects of portfolio performance: total returns and risk. In many ways, the evaluation of the portfolio and the portfolio manager with regard to performance are one and the same because portfolio measurements typically evaluate the impact of the portfolio manager's actions on the portfolio's total returns.

Performance evaluation includes much of the return and risk analysis described in Chapter 5. Through attribution analysis, institutional investors determine whether any performance gap is due to a portfolio manager's decisions about asset allocation and security selection or, on the other hand, determined by factors outside of the portfolio manager's control. The benchmarks established when a portfolio is created are critical to this determination.

The following data sets are common sources for benchmark data used for evaluating portfolio performance:

- **Strategic portfolio model.** The strategic portfolio illustrates a passive investment strategy because the weightings of the asset classes in the SAA do not change. Thus, any significant differences between the calculated total return of the strategic portfolio model and the tactical portfolio must be the result of the portfolio manager's decisions.

- A **published market index.** When a portfolio, a portfolio segment, or an asset class has the objective of tracking market returns, a market index is an appropriate performance benchmark. Institutional investors often use an index, such as the S&P 500 or the Barclays Capital Aggregate Bond Index, as a performance benchmark during the performance evaluation process. The particular benchmark is typically selected as a market proxy during the asset-class selection process. The asset classes in the index are subject to the same market conditions as those asset classes in the tactical portfolio. Thus, any differences in the total return of the tactical portfolio and the index must be the result of the portfolio manager's decisions.

- **Target returns.** Institutional investors often use as a benchmark a target return based on such factors as inflation, the risk-free rate, or funding requirements.

- **Peer review.** Institutional investors can use the published results of a comparable fund as a benchmark.

When we demonstrated attribution analysis in Chapter 5, we saw that a portfolio's excess return generally is the portfolio's excess performance relative to its benchmark. A portfolio's excess return can be calculated arithmetically or geometrically:

$$\textbf{Arithmetic Excess Return} = \frac{\text{Portfolio Return} - \text{Benchmark Return}}{\text{Initial Portfolio Value}} \times 100\%$$

$$\textbf{Geometric Excess Return} = \frac{\text{Portfolio Return} - \text{Benchmark Return}}{\text{Ending Portfolio Value}} \times 100\%$$

Arithmetic excess return is widely used because it is easier to understand. However, the geometric excess return is used when measuring excess returns over multiple periods or in different currencies.[8]

Risk is a critical component in all performance results. A company's risk committee evaluates observed levels of specific risk against established levels of risk appetite and risk limits so that the portfolio's risk control framework limits the level and types of risks an institutional investor may take in the course of seeking a portfolio's required returns.

At the operational level, portfolio performance should also be evaluated according to certain risk metrics. In Chapter 5, we introduced tracking error, the information ratio, and the Sharpe ratio, which are used to measure the contributions of tactical investment strategies to portfolio performance.

Generally, tracking error indicates whether a portfolio has remained at the same risk level as its benchmark. Portfolio managers are often required to maintain tracking error levels below a certain maximum. Tracking error can also identify inappropriate portfolio manager behaviors such as portfolio churning and aggressive risk-taking. The information ratio typically indicates the additional value and additional risk generated by tactical portfolio management strategies. Institutional monitoring systems generate noncompliance reports if a portfolio manager exceeds risk tolerance limits or otherwise violates established guidelines.

The control cycle involves monitoring the portfolio on an ongoing basis. At the end of each reporting cycle, a portfolio manager and analysts must identify the practices that worked well, failed, and need to be changed. If needed, changes can be made to the long-term investment objectives and risk limits in the SAA. Ongoing controls ensure that a portfolio operates within the risk control framework and attains specific investment objectives. The result of these interactions is a control cycle for the top-down portfolio management process.

Key Terms

bottom-up investing
top-down investing
peer review analysis
composite peer portfolio
correlation
correlation coefficient
asset-class correlation matrix
mean variance optimization (MVO)
efficient frontier
efficient portfolio
Monte Carlo modeling
strategic asset allocation (SAA)
market proxy
contrarian investing

Endnotes

1. Portions of this chapter are based on material provided by Patricia Wilson Fridley (Senior Advisor, Center for Financial Stability, LLC), 2 April 2012. Used with permission.

2. Portfolio management might be described alternatively as a type of long-term *program*, because portfolios have a specified time horizon. For purposes of this chapter, consider that the long time horizon renders portfolio management comparable to a process.

3. CFA Institute, *Corporate Finance and Portfolio Management* (New York: CFA Institute, 2011), 292, 450–452.

4. Ibid., 476–480.

5. Patricia Wilson Fridley (Senior Advisor, Center for Financial Stability, LLC), note to author, 2 April 2012. Used with permission.

6. Ibid. Used with permission.

7. Ibid. Used with permission.

8. Michael McMillan, "Performance Measurement and Attribution: The What, Why, and How of the Investment Management Process," *Enterprising Investor* (blog), CFA Institute, 1 June 2012, http://blogs.cfainstitute.org/investor/2012/06/01/performance-measurement-and-attribution-the-what-why-and-how-of-the-investment-management-process/ (2 October 2012).

Chapter 7

Managing the General Account

Objectives

After studying this chapter, you should be able to

7A Discuss the objectives guiding the general account of a life insurance company

7B Describe the characteristics of the financial obligations of a life insurance company, including how asset risk, credit risk, real-estate risk, and interest-rate risk can affect a company's liabilities, assets, and capital

7C Describe the organizational lines of authority, responsibility, and communication in asset-liability management for a life insurance company, as well as the purposes of and methods for allocating investment income to company liabilities

7D Discuss an integrated portfolio benchmarking system for insurance companies and describe considerations involved in creating a replicating portfolio for insurance company liabilities

7E Discuss investment strategies for managing an insurance company's general account, including duration matching and portfolio immunization; cash-flow matching and portfolio dedication; interest-rate anticipation; and indexing

7F Describe examples of ALM and investment policies for the general account, such as risky asset policies, crediting rate policies, liquidity policies, and duration policies

7G Identify and discuss performance attribution factors applicable to debt portfolios within the general account

7H Identify and describe approaches for analyzing the risks in a company's cash flows and asset adequacy, including cash-flow analysis and asset-adequacy analysis

7I Describe investment risk policies and various types of ALM reports that insurance companies use, including the investment activity report, the investment portfolio performance review, and the duration gap report

7J Discuss ALM system components that require verification as part of an audit of a life insurance company's ALM practices

www.loma.org

Outline

I n Chapter 7, we discuss managing the general account of a life insurance company.[1] Managing the general account of a life insurance company is similar to managing other investment portfolios, with two broad differences:

- An insurance company's overall profitability from the general account comes primarily from the margin between the company's earnings on invested assets and the company's costs to support products and capital obligations. Thus, the management of the general account must be carefully coordinated with the management of the company's liabilities. Companies directly address this unique need through an asset-liability management (ALM) system.

- Although general account portfolios hold some equity investments, the general account holds mainly debt securities.

General Account Objectives

The general account contains assets that back a company's products and other general obligations and fulfill the company's capital requirements. Performance objectives for the general account typically require an insurance company to balance assets with liabilities so that

- The company always has ample capital to protect holders of the company's general account obligations and meet regulatory requirements

- The company's total cash inflows equal or exceed total cash outflows

- The company's operating results provide an optimal risk-adjusted return to the company's owners, within regulatory constraints and the company's chosen performance objectives

- Some interactions between risk exposures in the company's assets and liabilities have the effects of risk offsets or risk hedges, and, thus, one risk exposure somehow mitigates another

- Interactions between some risk exposures in the company's assets and liabilities leave residual risks that the company can actively manage

In pursuit of these and other objectives, companies set numerical performance targets and tolerance ranges around the targets, and then measure performance relative to the targets. Figures 7.1 and 7.2 illustrate a life insurance company's general account performance. A number of aspects of performance, including market value, total returns, duration, and benchmarks have been described earlier in this text. Note that the selection of precisely formulated objectives for financial modeling is a matter for appropriately qualified experts.

Figure 7.1 General Account Objectives and Performance

Risk Snapshot Report Applegate Life Insurance Company Measurement Period 1-1 to 10-31		
Portfolio Total Returns	**Target**	**Actual**
• Debt performance	4.53%	4.60%
• Equity performance	3.45%	3.66%
General Account	4.42%	4.52%
General Account Portfolio Performance		
• Gain in Market Value		10 bp
• General Account Ending Market Value		$1.0 billion
• General Account Beginning Market Value		$960 million
• Debt Portfolio Ending Market Value		$920 million
• Equities Portfolio Ending Market Value		$80 million
Duration Positions		
Liabilities Duration		5.8 years
Assets Duration		6.2 years
Duration Gap		0.4 years

Source: Patricia Wilson Fridley (Senior Advisor, Center for Financial Stability, LLC), note to author, 14 August 2012. Used with permission.

The dashboard display in Figure 7.2 visually summarizes performance data similar to that in the report in Figure 7.1.

Figure 7.2 Dashboard for General Account Objectives

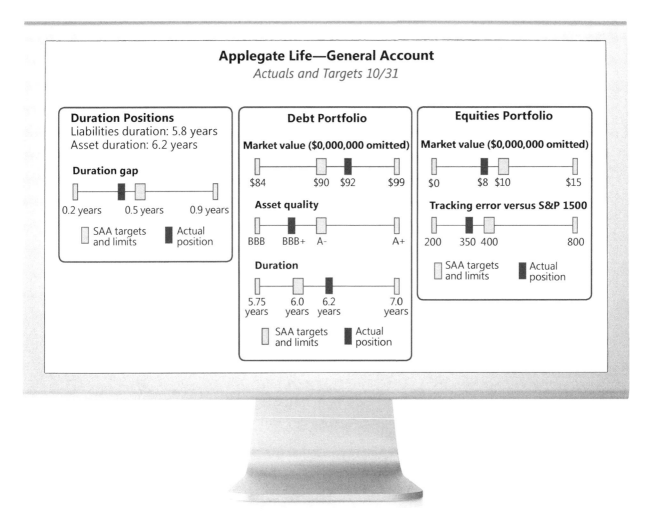

Source: Patricia Wilson Fridley (Senior Advisor, Center for Financial Stability, LLC), note to author, 14 August 2012. Used with permission.

Financial Characteristics of a General Account

For the general account, insurance companies seek to identify asset risk exposures that will earn the financial rewards to compensate them for the risks they have taken. Companies continually monitor these risk exposures and analyze the probabilities and impacts of potential risk events. At the same time, companies work to mitigate any such risk exposures.

To maintain solvency, a company must take prudent risks and earn sufficient asset returns to pay contractual liability obligations and cover company expenses. The investment function's role is to take enough risk to earn adequate returns, but not so much risk that overwhelming losses occur.

Because life insurance companies must meet their obligations in cash, they also monitor their liquidity risk through ALM analysis. (We discussed liquidity risk in a broad context in Chapter 4.)

Asset-liability management risk, sometimes known as *ALM risk*, is the risk that a company's capital could be depleted due to a narrowing of the difference between returns earned on assets and liabilities or a mismatch in cash flows for assets and liabilities. ALM risks arise from interactions between a company's assets and liabilities, including the potential that changes in market interest rates, yield curves, or other market conditions could limit a company's overall potential profitability or threaten its solvency. To address ALM risk, companies use a number of management systems, including their enterprise risk management (ERM) system and their ALM system. In addition, companies set strategic targets for their portfolios and define appropriate benchmarks for investment performance.

A life insurance company's general account supports many of the company's product liabilities and other general obligations. In turn, the general account is affected by the company's liabilities. A company's general obligations have the following broad characteristics:

- They can be lengthy, and sometimes extend beyond 30 years

- They are typically illiquid, and are not easily assigned a market value

- Their values can be sensitive to movements in market interest rates

- Some are specific in timing and amount, so that the company's payouts are highly foreseeable, but, for others, the precise timing or amount of the required payouts is unknown

- They involve some risks that cannot be fully managed by means of diversification and hedging techniques[2]

In actuarial literature and solvency regulation, the four *C risk* categories important to ensuring solvency are asset risk, pricing risk, interest-rate risk, and business management risks. Two C risks are important for managing the general account:

- **Asset risk.** For an insurance company's general account, *asset risk* is the risk that, for reasons other than changes in market interest rates, the company could lose money on its investments and, for that reason, might have to draw on its capital. As one of four C risks, asset risk is also known as C1 risk or credit risk. The regulatory risk-based capital formula in the United States assigns a C1 risk capital charge for each asset, based on the asset type and quality. Asset risk has aspects of liquidity risk, credit risk, real estate risk, and currency risk, all discussed in Chapter 4. Each of these risks has the potential to threaten a company's capital and even its solvency.

- **Interest-rate risk.** For an insurance company's general account, *interest-rate risk* is the risk that market interest rates might shift, causing the insurer's assets to lose value or its liabilities to gain value. Generally, interest-rate risk is the risk that market interest rates, or the uncertainty arising from fluctuations in market interest rates, could work against the insurance company. Within the system of C risks, this risk category is C3 risk. Interest-rate risk has aspects of prepayment risk, reinvestment risk, expansion risk, and contraction risk. Companies typically avoid prepayment and reinvestment risk exposures. We describe expansion risk and contraction risk shortly.

Credit Risk for the General Account

Due to large holdings of debt-related investments in the general account of a life insurance company, credit risk exposures represent the main threats that a company could incur losses on its debt investments. In keeping with the risk-return trade-off, credit risk exposures also represent the company's main opportunities for earning returns on its debt investments. Important aspects of credit risk for the general account of an insurance company are default risk and downgrade risk.

- *Default risk* is an element of credit risk and involves the risk that an issuer of a fixed income security could fail to maintain its obligation under the security. In cases of defaults on debt securities held in an investment portfolio, as we discussed in Chapter 4, an insurance company can expect to regain only a portion of the value of the security. In Chapter 8, we further discuss default situations involving bonds.

- For fixed-income securities, **downgrade risk**, often called *migration risk*, is a type of credit risk that involves the risk of deterioration in a credit rating assigned to an issuer. A credit downgrade or upgrade has no automatic effect on payments of principal or interest to the investor. If an investor holds a security to maturity, then regardless of any downgrade, the investor can expect to collect the fixed income amount originally promised under the security. If the investor must sell a downgraded security before maturity, however, the effect of the downgrade will manifest in a reduced market value for the security.[3]

The ultimate effect of credit risk is that, when an investment is downgraded or goes into default, its market value also decreases. When the market value of an investment decreases, the amount of funds a company could raise by selling the investments also decreases.

Real-Estate Risk for the General Account

As you recall from discussion in Chapter 4, real-estate risk affects all general account investments having a basis in real estate, whether bonds, stocks, mortgage-backed securities, mortgages, partnerships, or outright real-estate ownership. The causative factors for real-estate losses include economic conditions, local new construction, local rents, and local vacancies. Investments based in real estate rely on demand for property, and on the resulting rising or stable property values to create returns or repay principal. If demand for property is low, returns on investments with exposures to real estate risks can suffer. Chapter 9 of this text is devoted to discussion of investments based in real estate.

Interest-Rate Risk for Insurance Companies

Life insurance companies face interest-rate risk in a variety of financial contexts. Movements of market interest rates, whether up or down, can adversely affect assets, liabilities, and capital. Market interest rates influence the market values of bonds, mortgages, and other interest-bearing investments, as well as direct investments in real estate. However, fixed-interest investments are particularly exposed to movements in market interest rates. Market interest rates influence the interest rates that life insurance companies credit to interest-bearing products, such as fixed cash value life insurance and fixed deferred annuity products.[4]

To gain an understanding of interest-rate risk exposures for insurance companies, you can think of the life insurance business as one based on borrowing and lending. In essence, when insurance companies issue cash-value life insurance or annuity contracts supported by their general account, they are borrowing money from policyholders. In these cases, the policy establishes an obligation for insurers to accumulate funds and repay the policyholder, with interest, at a defined point in the future. To meet the contractual obligation and cover their expenses, insurers put the "borrowed" money at risk when they purchase debt securities. The purchase of a debt security is essentially lending money to the issuer of the debt security in order to earn interest on the loan transaction. The resulting high level of debt-like obligations in a company's financial position leaves insurers a narrow margin between the interest rate paid to policyholders and the interest rate earned on debt securities.

Recall from Chapter 4 that the market values of interest-bearing investments move inversely to market interest rates. If market interest rates rise, the market values of existing interest-bearing investments generally decrease. For an entire portfolio of interest-bearing investments, if interest rates rise, the portfolio can lose market value. If market interest rates decrease, however, the inverse relationship still holds: the market values of existing interest-bearing investments generally increase.

The high degree to which the values of existing interest-bearing investments can change in response to market interest rates is an example of *price sensitivity*: the degree to which the demand for a good changes in response to a change in the price of that good. For this purpose, the market value of a financial instrument can be viewed as its price. Price sensitivity of bonds and other interest-bearing investments to changes in market interest rates can be measured using the duration statistics discussed in Chapter 4. In general, it is true that

- The lower the level of market interest rates, the greater an interest-sensitive investment's price sensitivity to increases in market interest rates

- The lower a bond's coupon rate and initial yield to maturity, the greater the bond's price sensitivity to changes in market interest rates

- The longer in the future a bond's maturity date, the greater the bond's price sensitivity to changes in market interest rates[5]

To guard against the negative effects of interest-rate risk exposures, companies can take actions such as disposing of existing interest-bearing investments lacking the desired characteristics; setting highly specific requirements for future acquisitions of interest-bearing investments; and using hedging strategies such as purchasing appropriate derivative securities or obtaining reinsurance.

Effects of Increases in Market Interest Rates

When market interest rates are increasing and bond market values are low, an investor can hold existing bonds to maturity, and avoid selling them under unfavorable market conditions. In such cases, the investor can collect the bonds' full face value, and market interest-rate increases do not affect returns on the bond. Insurance companies generally purchase debt securities with the intention of holding them to maturity.

When market interest rates are increasing, new interest-bearing investments in the general account earn the higher market interest rate. In a period of increasing rates, insurance companies can experience margin compression.

Margin compression refers to the narrowing of an insurer's interest margin, potentially when market interest rates are rising or falling. The *interest margin*, also known as the interest-rate margin or the interest spread, is the share of investment earnings that an insurer retains after crediting a share of investment earnings to policyholders. When market interest rates are rising, policyholders typically immediately demand a higher crediting rate on their accounts. The company's interest-bearing investments, however, continue to earn the older, lower rates that prevailed when the company purchased them. If the company immediately pays the new higher rate on its products, the company's interest margin will narrow. If the company does not pay the new higher rate on its products, the company will likely lose customers and sales producers. To minimize the risk of margin compression, insurance companies typically try to issue products that limit customer withdrawal rights during early years.

Effects of Decreases in Market Interest Rates

The inverse relationship between market values of existing bonds and market interest rates holds true when interest rates are decreasing. An environment of decreasing market interest rates can have the following effects:

■ Because the periodic interest payments on older securities likely reflect higher market interest rates that are no longer available with newly issued securities, the market values of existing interest-bearing investments within an investor's portfolio typically increase. In this setting, investors who sell older bonds before maturity can obtain a higher-than-anticipated price if those bonds offer a higher interest rate than is currently available in the market.

■ In times of decreasing market interest rates, issuers of interest-bearing investments with contractual rights to redeem the investments before maturity may do so. In this case, the owners of any redeemed interest-bearing investments lose an older, higher-yielding investment. Insurance companies typically take steps to avoid significant exposure to this aspect of interest-rate risk.

■ In times of decreasing market interest rates, the liabilities of life insurance companies can lengthen beyond the average life of each liability assumed in financial product design because, if the guaranteed rate on the insurance product is higher than market interest rates customers can obtain elsewhere, customers behaving rationally are likely to keep fixed-rate products in force.

Margin compression and margin expansion also come into play during periods of decreasing market interest rates if asset maturities are not properly aligned with the average life of the liabilities. Margin compression due to falling market interest rates takes effect slowly over time, as the company collects interest and principal payments on older interest-bearing investments, and must reinvest these amounts at lower rates. ***Margin expansion*** refers to an increase in an insurer's profit margin. Margin expansion occurs if the insurer reduces the interest-crediting rates it pays to customers while continuing to earn a higher overall rate of return on its existing invested assets.

Margin expansion can occur when a company experiences an increase in the market value of its existing assets after market interest rates fall. Figure 7.3 summarizes our discussion of the impacts of market interest rates on insurance companies.

Organizational Structures for Managing the General Account

Each company maintains a comprehensive risk management and control system designed and operated to work for the company's unique context. Typically, the important components of this structure are (1) an ALM function, (2) a segmentation plan, and (3) a system of portfolio planning and benchmarking that coordinates portfolio management of general account assets with portfolio management for liabilities, portfolio management for assets combined with liabilities, and residual impacts on capital requirements.

Figure 7.3 Outcomes from Changing Market Interest Rates

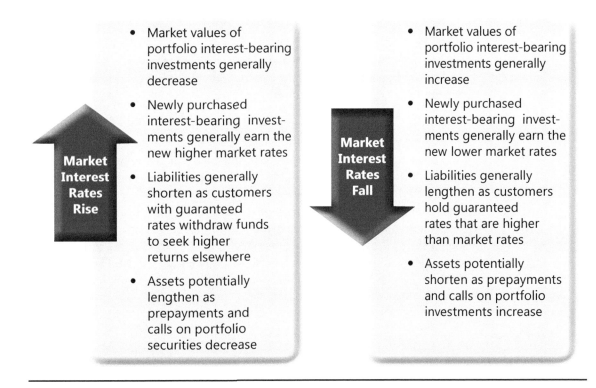

The ALM Function

In many ways, an ALM system functions as the central clearinghouse for any profit-making and financial risk-taking activities of a general account. Organizational structures for accomplishing ALM are not entirely consistent from one company to another. For even the smallest companies, ALM can be complex and requires sophisticated systems. An ALM structure must address each company's internal and external needs for ALM, and must clearly define the authority, roles, and accountabilities at various levels of the ALM process.

The ALM function is responsible for conducting appropriate analysis, communicating the results of the analysis, recommending ALM policy, supporting ALM policy implementation, and establishing systems for ensuring that policies are implemented. ALM practices for life insurance companies are integrated into a company's broader risk management systems, including enterprise risk management (ERM). In practical terms, it can be difficult to distinguish where ALM leaves off and ERM begins, particularly in view of variations in practice from one company to another.

Figure 7.4 illustrates an organizational structure for ALM consisting of a corporate board-level committee, a cross-functional committee, and an ALM unit.

- **Board-Level Oversight Committee.** As we saw in Chapter 3, ALM is sponsored at the level of a company's board of directors, usually through the board's risk committee. In the strategic-level committee that has responsibility for the ALM committee, the ALM committee's accountabilities are coordinated with the company's other management systems for addressing risk management. The board-level committee that oversees the ALM structure, process, and outcomes has a decision making and policy making role. This committee also approves the ALM implementation framework.

- **Cross-Functional ALM Committee.** Reporting to the board-level risk committee is an ALM committee populated with representatives from the investments side and the products side. In other words, an ALM committee has membership consisting of investment professionals and actuarial professionals. An ALM committee makes recommendations concerning important policy matters.

- **ALM Unit.** Most large companies also have an ALM unit reporting to the ALM committee. The ALM operating unit brings together actuarial and investment professionals who perform and interpret the analysis to support decisions affecting ALM risks. Many of these professionals from actuarial or investment backgrounds have an additional specialization in ALM-related professional interests. This operational-level ALM unit directs or performs cross-functional analysis in support of the ALM framework and is accountable for ALM performance outcomes. Although an entire organizational unit may be devoted to ALM support, professionals in asset or liability functional areas are also responsible for much ALM implementation.

Figure 7.4 ALM Hierarchy for Life Insurance Companies

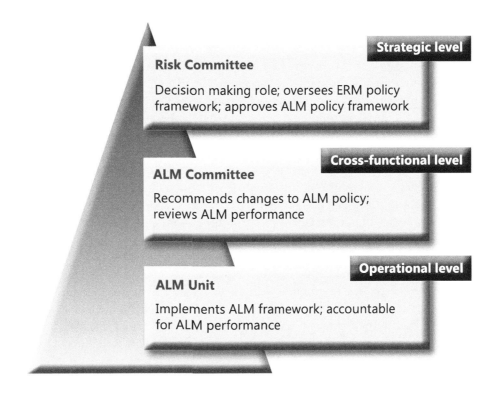

Strategic level

Risk Committee

Decision making role; oversees ERM policy framework; approves ALM policy framework

Cross-functional level

ALM Committee

Recommends changes to ALM policy; reviews ALM performance

Operational level

ALM Unit

Implements ALM framework; accountable for ALM performance

ALM and other risk management systems include establishing frameworks for the general account that

- Associate assets and investment income with various specified products through processes including portfolio segmentation and investment income allocation

- Integrate the strategic asset allocation (SAA) for the general account into a more elaborate portfolio benchmarking system that also incorporates a benchmark portfolio for product liabilities, another for the combination of assets and liabilities, and even one for company capital

Allocating Assets and Investment Income to Liabilities

The general account of a life insurance company contains assets purchased specifically to meet reserve requirements for many different products and product features, all of which represent general obligations of the company. To analyze the effectiveness of these investments relative to the associated products, companies employ frameworks for dividing their assets into appropriate groupings and then assigning certain groupings of assets to specified products.

Segmentation refers to the practice of dividing the general account into *portfolio segments*: smaller groupings of assets to match up with the management objectives for various product lines. Each portfolio segment typically is designated to support a specified product line of the company's general account products, or for another specific purpose, such as to support the company's capital account.

When a company launches a new product, the company dedicates unallocated capital to the product and purchases assets to support the new product. In such a case, the newly purchased assets are assigned to the portfolio segment in the general account specified for the new product.

As you know, an insurance company's primary sources of income are premiums and investments. Premium income is closely identified with a specified product, and allocation of premium income to a product is typically automated within a company's accounting systems. However, investment income may not in all cases be clearly connected with a given product or product line. Thus, for internal purposes, companies establish a reasonable and impartial method for assigning investment income to products or product lines. Various methods for assigning investment revenues to specific products or product lines are known as *investment income allocation methods*.[6]

Figure 7.5 illustrates portfolio segmentation and investment income allocation. Two common investment income allocation methods are the mean liabilities method and the portfolio segmentation method. Companies may use both of these methods, but for somewhat different purposes.

Mean Liabilities Method

Under the **mean liabilities method** of investment income allocation, a company simply assigns investment income to each of its product lines in proportion to the reserves attributed to that product line. At a minimum, the mean liabilities method helps companies in the United States to comply with financial reporting requirements for completing the U.S. Annual Statement. This method may be inadequate in providing needed decision support information.

Portfolio Segmentation Method

In the **portfolio segmentation method** of investment income allocation, an insurance company uses the cash flows associated with a product line, or with a grouping of products that have a need for similar investment strategies, to purchase specific assets for that line or grouping of products. For example, all payout annuities might be grouped together and assets purchased for their support. In essence, the insurer treats each product line as though the product line owned specified investments.

Figure 7.5 Portfolio Segmentation and Investment Income Allocation

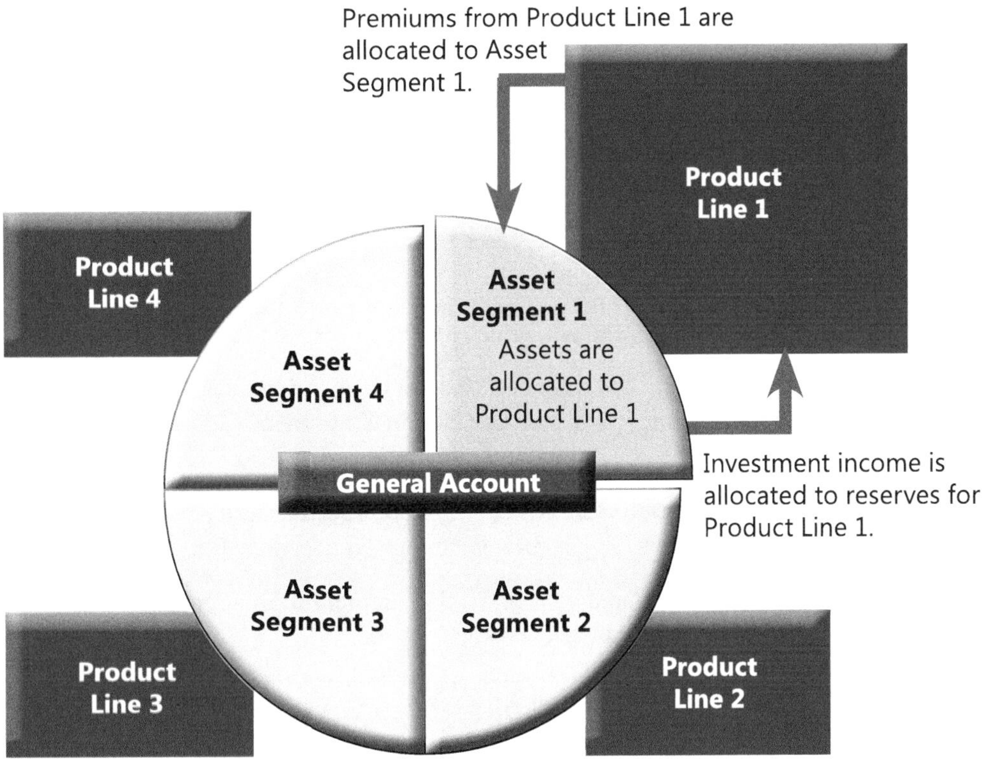

Premiums from Product Line 1 are allocated to Asset Segment 1.

Product Line 1

Asset Segment 1 Assets are allocated to Product Line 1

Investment income is allocated to reserves for Product Line 1.

Product Line 4

Asset Segment 4

General Account

Asset Segment 3

Asset Segment 2

Product Line 3

Product Line 2

Portfolio segmentation and asset allocation. This general account is divided into four portfolio segments corresponding to four product lines. Each portfolio segment is assigned to a product line. In this manner, assets are allocated to products.

Investment income. Each portfolio segment generates investment income.

Investment income allocation. Investment income from each of four portfolio segments is assigned to the associated product line. In this manner, investment income is allocated to specified liabilities.

Premiums. Each product line generates premiums. Premiums are used to purchase assets for the portfolio segment dedicated to the given product line.

For decision-support purposes, when using this method, a company attributes investment income to the portfolio segment that initially acquired the asset. The portfolio segmentation method allows companies to apply distinct investment strategies to different product lines. This characteristic is beneficial because cash flow patterns and investment income requirements differ by product line.

Although a company uses portfolio segmentation for management convenience and decision-making, ultimately, all of the assets of the company's general account remain available to support all liabilities of the general account.

Figure 7.6 shows an example of investment risk constraints for a portfolio segment consisting of a guaranteed deferred annuity product line. As you can see, the insurance company assigns each debt-based asset class to a risk exposure category. The risk exposure categories shown in this example are credit risk, real-estate risk, and interest-rate risk. Currency risk is relevant only for portfolios having assets denominated in a foreign currency. Figure 7.11, at the end of this chapter, presents a narrative investment policy statement designed for all debt investments in the general account. Each portfolio segment is subject to the company's general account investment policies as well as the investment policies distinctive to the given portfolio segment.

Segmentation of the general account portfolio by product line potentially has the following benefits for a company:

■ Portfolio management sets a clear basis for evaluating the performance of each product line relative to its management objectives.

■ For ALM, portfolio segmentation supports efforts to match asset cash flows with liability cash flows, supports required actuarial analysis, and facilitates communication between the actuarial and investment functions.

■ For risk management, portfolio segmentation supports managing the portfolio's exposure to interest-rate risk.

Figure 7.6 Investment Risk Constraints for a Guaranteed Deferred Annuity Portfolio Segment

Risk Exposure and Asset Class	Constraints		
	Target Expected Average Life* (Years)	Credit Quality (Minimum rating)	Other Constraints
Credit Risk Exposures			
Corporate Bonds	8 years	BBB or higher	
High-yield Bonds	7 years		Maximum 15% of the portfolio segment
Interest-Rate Risk Exposures			
U.S. Treasuries	5–10 years	AA	Maximum 5% of the portfolio segment
Agency Mortgage-Backed Securities	7 years	AAA	Under rising interest rates, maximum expected average life 10 years
Real Estate Risk Exposures			
Residential Asset Backed Securities	7 years	AAA	
Commercial Mortgage Loans	5–10 years	BBB or higher	

*Average life of a debt security refers to the length of time the security is expected to remain outstanding.

Source: Patricia Wilson Fridley (Senior Advisor, Center for Financial Stability, LLC), note to author, 7 August 2012. Used with permission.

Example: Managing a Portfolio Segment

Jonah, portfolio manager for a general account portfolio segment, is responsible for investing the universal life (UL) insurance policy premiums and cash inflows to support the UL product line. Jonah continually assesses the suitability of securities held in the UL portfolio segment.

Whenever the portfolio segment accumulates sufficient funds to purchase new assets, Jonah consults with other company professionals to identify specific assets to add to the portfolio segment. Besides investing new money in assets for the portfolio segment, Jonah also has occasion to sell assets from the segment.

- Jonah recently sold investments to obtain cash to fund an unexpected surge in UL policy loans.

- Because Jonah anticipates that conditions in the corporate bond market could deteriorate shortly, he sells the UL portfolio segment's holdings in corporate bonds and purchases U.S. Treasury securities. In this manner, he preserves value in the assets backing the UL product.[7]

An Integrated Portfolio Benchmarking Model

In Chapter 6, we discussed top-down and bottom-up approaches to portfolio analysis, benchmarking, and management. For the general account and the associated insurance liabilities, insurance companies use a similar but more complex approach that supports consistent analysis and benchmarking within one framework of several current or "actual" portfolios and strategic portfolio benchmarks. Such an integrated framework permits companies to also apply the analytical tools of portfolio benchmarking to their liabilities alone; to a combinations of assets and liabilities for testing of ALM alignment; and to their capital alone.

Figure 7.7 depicts an integrated portfolio benchmarking model for insurance companies. The model illustrated there refers to three *actual portfolios* and four *benchmarks*. As the labeling implies, these actual portfolios are managed according to objectives and specifications in a matched set of strategic benchmarks. This arrangement is a more elaborate version of the one described in Chapter 6 and involving an operational portfolio and a strategic benchmark. The benchmarks support purposes of planning, control, and performance analysis.

Several software packages and consulting services offer support to companies in structuring such models to meet a company's unique needs. In this section, we explain one approach to such an integrated benchmarking model, as well as how the integrated portfolio benchmarking approach informs companies about their general account risk exposures and opportunities for earning returns.

Figure 7.7 Integrated Portfolio Benchmarking Model for Insurance Companies

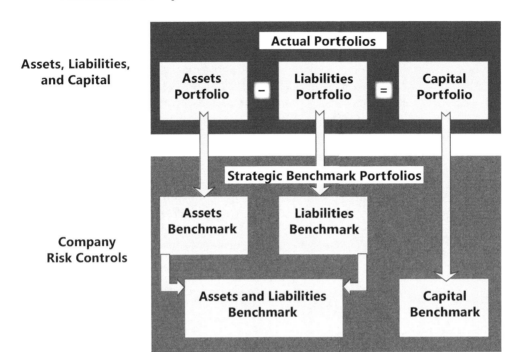

Actual Portfolios in the Integrated Model

In this model, the three actual portfolios are the assets portfolio, the liabilities portfolio, and the capital portfolio. These portfolios are the objects of analysis undertaken in the integrated model:

■ The actual *assets portfolio* contains the insurance company's general account assets. General account assets back both the company's liabilities and its capital. However, for benchmarking, companies can customize their approach to analyzing the assets portfolio.

■ The actual *liabilities portfolio* comprises the insurance company's product reserves. A company's product reserves represent, instead of assets, financial obligations that the company issued against itself. Because these reserve liabilities represent a claim against assets, for some analytical purposes within this benchmarking model, the liabilities are treated as *contra assets*. Broadly, contra assets are offsets against assets. As contra assets, the liabilities take on negative values.

■ The actual *capital portfolio*, sometimes known as the *surplus portfolio*, represents the assets remaining after liabilities are subtracted from general account assets.

Companies differ in how they apply benchmarking information to the assets backing their capital. For purposes of portfolio benchmark analysis, some companies combine the actual portfolios backing liabilities and capital; other companies assign the assets backing capital to an actual capital portfolio and a capital benchmark. In this chapter, we describe a system in which the assets backing capital are subject to a separate capital benchmark.

Benchmarks in the Integrated Model

In this integrated benchmarking model, a company compares the performance of two to three actual portfolios with two to four benchmarks. Here, we describe a full complement of four benchmarks in a fully articulated portfolio benchmarking model. In such a system, first the actual portfolios—using accounting system values for assets, liabilities, and capital—are evaluated and analyzed against the performance results of their respective strategic benchmarks. The actual portfolios consist of one assets portfolio, one liabilities portfolio, and potentially a capital portfolio.

In this phase of performance measurement and evaluation, the analysis of equity investments in the general account closely parallels the portfolio management analysis we described in Chapter 6. However, the general account portfolio that we are discussing here holds predominantly debt-based investments, whereas our Chapter 6 discussion focused on portfolios holding primarily equity investments.

The Assets Benchmark

The *assets benchmark*, a type of strategic benchmark portfolio, serves as the performance standard for a company's general account assets.

To develop the assets benchmark, companies typically assemble a suitable grouping of market indexes, then blend the index performance data in optimized proportions. The resulting blend of market index data from several sources then functions as a performance standard for evaluating the company's similarly allocated assets portfolio.

The Liabilties Benchmark

The *liabilities benchmark* represents a performance standard for comparison to the company's actual liabilities portfolio in this integrated portfolio benchmarking system. Shortly, we devote a section to an approach for creating a suitable liabilities benchmark—developing a replicating portfolio.

The Asset-Liability Benchmark

Next, the modeling software combines the actual assets and liabilities portfolios. Then, the software compares the resulting asset-liability (A/L) portfolio to an integrated *asset-liability (A/L) benchmark*. The A/L benchmark serves as a performance standard for analyzing the company's objectives and performance relevant to potential risk interactions between the actual assets and liabilities portfolios.

When analyzing the integrated A/L benchmark, companies may apply optimization modeling, such as mean variance optimization (MVO), to assets and liabilities, and thus find an efficient frontier for the A/L portfolio.[8] MVO modeling requires users to formulate an objective statement that is designed to achieve some "optimal" value—in other words, a minimum or maximum value. The optimization objective function in MVO analysis for investment portfolios can be set to either minimize a measure of risk or maximize a measure of assets or returns.

The MVO output used for structuring the A/L benchmark represents an optimal target portfolio that differs from the actual assets portfolio and, at the same time, represents the best long-run positioning for general account assets. The company uses the MVO output to set long-term investment strategies designed to reposition the assets so that the assets portfolio will eventually acquire the return-and-risk profile of the A/L benchmark. As the strategy takes hold, the assets benchmark will also migrate, over time, until it more closely resembles the A/L benchmark than it does the strategic asset allocation for the assets alone.

Having both the assets benchmark and A/L benchmark allows companies to conduct performance attribution on the basis of an actual or current asset portfolio that differs from the long-run optimal assets benchmark.

In contrast to the assets benchmark, the A/L benchmark additionally incorporates projected new business or other projected changes in liabilities and the effects of any hedging programs.

As the actual liabilities portfolio's characteristics change over time with the addition of new liabilities, the liabilities benchmark is changed to reflect those changes.

Because the A/L benchmark is established as a long-run target, the liabilities benchmark can be expected to deviate from the long-run A/L benchmark targets. The difference between the A/L benchmark and the liabilities benchmark establishes a basis that allows companies to apply attribution analysis to aspects of portfolio returns that arose from changes in the liabilities and efforts to manage the changes in the liabilities. Later in this chapter, we briefly discuss attribution analysis for debt-based portfolios.

When the actual assets portfolio and liabilities portfolio are combined into an asset-liablity portfolio for comparison to the A/L benchmark, the liabilities are assigned negative values, and thus they offset the values of company assets. In keeping with the basic accounting equation for insurance companies, after liabilities are subtracted from capital, any remaining positive value of the assets represents company capital.

As a final stage in this integrated portfolio benchmarking analysis, the company measures the remaining capital and compares it to the appropriate benchmark, typically a capital benchmark—one constructed using MVO methods, as we have discussed in regard to developing a company's other benchmarks. To develop a capital benchmark, the company uses an MVO objective function that represents the company's performance standards and risk tolerances for its assets backing the company's capital. The resulting benchmark may be called the *capital benchmark* or *surplus benchmark*.

The capital benchmark permits companies to analyze and evaluate performance of company capital on a consistent basis. It also supports important types of analysis that are beyond the scope of this text, including economic value analysis; Value-at-Risk or earnings-at-risk analysis; risk-adjusted return on capital (RAROC) analysis; and solvency assessment.

A Replicating Portfolio for Liabilities

As part of implementing an integrated portfolio benchmarking system for the general account, insurance companies typically use a replicating portfolio as a liabilities benchmark in a system such as the one we have just discussed.[9] Typically, a **replicating portfolio** is a virtual pool of assets created—for purposes of performance measurement, quantitative modeling, and simulations—to reproduce the cash flows and market values observed in a specified pool of assets. When an insurance company develops a replicating portfolio to represent its insurance products, however, the replicating portfolio is a pool of liabilities instead of assets.

Insurance company liabilities are not generally traded in public securities markets, and so published market indexes do not directly establish market values for these financial contracts. Accordingly, a replicating portfolio for company liabilities is necessarily constructed from source data such as published market indexes for publicly traded assets that have no obvious connection to insurance liabilities.

To create a replicating portfolio for liabilities, modelers view insurance products as having an identifiable set of financial risk and return characteristics, such as fixed cash flows, distributions of dividends or excess interest, and minimum guaranteed values. In this view, a modeler can find a publicly traded financial instrument to represent each such identified financial characteristic.

As an early step in creating a replicating portfolio for liabilities, then, companies identify market-traded assets that exhibit the financial risk and return characteristics of the company's liabilities. Then, companies select market indexes that display the relevant characteristics of the selected asset classes. Finally, they assemble the component market indexes in suitable proportions to form a virtual portfolio that reasonably approximates the financial profile of a given product type or even of the company's entire book of liabilities.

Stated somewhat differently, the replicating portfolio uses assets to demonstrate the behavior of liabilities. In replicating a company's actual liabilities portfolio, modelers typically treat the replicating portfolio components as a negative, or *contra*, asset class by changing the positive values from the index to negative values.

A replicating portfolio for insurance liabilities represents the following characteristics of the liabilities:

- Product-related cash inflows generally consist of premiums, other considerations, and deposits, whereas product-related cash outflows consist of payments of benefits and company operating expenses.

- The *average life* of a liabilities segment is the length of time the company's actuaries expect the liabilities to stay on the books. The average life of a policy within a product group is subject to customers' exercising policy surrender rights or other choices. Thus, actuaries use customer behavior assumptions in estimating the average life of liabilities.

- The crediting rate the company pays on liabilities is the rate of return the company credits to the customer's account.

■   For purposes of creating a replicating portfolio, modelers can consider that the company's quality rating indicates the credit risk in the product liabilities.

    •   Typically, the lower an insurance company's quality rating, the higher the commission rate and other sales expenses the company must pay to attract customers and sell products.

    •   Conversely, the higher an insurance company's quality rating, the lower the commission rate and other sales expenses the company must pay to sell its products.

Company management may compare the liabilities replicating portfolio with the assets benchmark, and thus may be able to identify risk offset or diversification effects arising from that pairing of portfolios. In this regard, this pairing of the assets benchmark with the liabilities replicating portfolio should ideally produce a high negative correlation. Recall from earlier discussions that the absence of high positive correlation can indicate some degree of diversification, and the presence of strong negative correlation indicates a strong diversification benefit to holding the specified combination of assets. If the two portfolios have strong negative correlation, we know that the total risk exposure when they are considered in combination is lower than when they are considered separately. The essence of a diversification benefit is a reduction in total risk exposures.

Policy Limitations on Risk Taking

A company's board and its standing committees, notably the investment committee, set corporate investment policies including the company's strategic objectives, cost of capital, risk appetite, and risk tolerance. Policies such as these may be set at the top of the organization for the entire organization, with additional policies being set at the lower levels in the organization, including a profit center, product line, or another business unit. Each portfolio segment is subject to the corporate and general account investment policies as well as the investment policies distinctive to the segment.

    The ALM committee, usually in concert with the risk committee, sets policies constraining risk taking. The ALM committee sets specific numerical objectives and risk guidelines for key risks, including interest-rate risk exposures; excess interest rates on products; a duration gap (mismatch) tolerance; portfolio liquidity policies; and policies governing the use of derivative securities.

    Additionally, the portfolio manager in charge of the general account sets policies for the general account, and the portfolio manager in charge of a portfolio segment may also set policies for the segment.

    We provide examples of such investment policies in Figure 7.11 at the end of this chapter.

Risky Asset Policies

One key aspect of a risk policy is a company's risky asset capacity. A *risky asset* is any asset that carries excess risk or is subject to unusual volatility. Risky asset classes are those for which the investment outcome is uncertain. Risky asset classes comprise public and private equities; below-investment-grade debt securities; real estate owned and other real estate equity positions; and certain other risk exposures.

A company's policy on risky asset capacity sets an upper limit on total allocations to certain designated risky asset classes. ***Risky asset capacity*** is an insurance company's total permitted allocation to risky asset classes, measured at market value. ***Excess risky asset capacity*** is the difference between the policy limit on risky assets and the monetary amount of risky assets currently held.[10]

Crediting Rate Policies

For an interest-bearing product issued by an insurance company, a *crediting rate policy* is a rule governing how much excess interest the board of directors may declare payable to policyholders over and above contractually guaranteed interest. The action a board takes to credit excess interest is called a crediting rate resolution or crediting rate declaration. Some products promise to pay policyholders a guaranteed interest rate plus potential excess interest, if declared by a company's board of directors on eligible products. In this context, we can refer to a guaranteed rate, an excess rate, and a credited rate. The guaranteed rate is the rate the company promises to pay policyholders at specified intervals. The excess rate is any additional interest the company awards to policyholders above the guaranteed rate. The credited rate is the sum of the guaranteed rate and any excess interest, and is the total current interest rate applied to a product's accumulation value.

> **Credited interest rate** =
> Guaranteed interest rate + excess interest rate

Companies set an interest crediting policy within a product's financial design, and they typically adhere to that policy regardless of subsequent changes in market conditions. When designing a crediting rate policy for a given product, companies take into account their risk-adjusted investment returns, prevailing market interest rates, and interest-crediting practices of competitors. Some crediting rate policies specify a minimum interest margin that a product is required to earn before the board will declare excess interest. For this purpose, the interest margin is the difference between the company's return on invested assets allocated to that product and the interest credited to the product's policyholders, both expressed as percentages.

> **Interest margin for an interest-bearing product** =
> Company's return on invested assets allocated to that product −
> Interest credited to policyholders of that product

Liquidity Policies

A ***liquidity policy*** is a formal control that states the minimum monetary amount of cash and near-cash assets a company must hold over a specified time period to meet liabilities. A liquidity policy generally states a requirement for the minimum liquidity needs of the liabilities. Liquidity policies are typically set with the cash-flow testing results as a primary input. A liquidity policy also generally specifies an overall maximum amount of illiquid assets.

Duration Policies

A *duration policy* is a formal control statement of guidelines for asset and liability durations. A *duration gap*, also known as a *duration mismatch*, is the amount by which a company's assets duration exceeds the liabilities duration. A duration policy typically sets an objective that specifies a numerical target for the duration gap and a numerical range of acceptable results around the duration gap objective or target.

> **Example: Duration Policies**
>
> Logo Financial sets a duration gap objective of 0.5 years, ± 0.3 years. In this case, the tolerance range for Logo's duration gap is between a lower limit of 0.2 years and an upper limit of 0.8 years.

Investment Strategies for Managing Debt-Based Portfolios

Strategies for managing portfolios that consist mainly of debt securities include relatively passive strategies as well as more active strategies. Here, we begin our discussion with duration matching and portfolio immunization; next, we discuss cash-flow matching and portfolio dedication; then, we discuss interest-rate anticipation; and, finally, indexing strategy. Life insurance companies may apply aspects of several of these approaches to management of various segments of the general account.

Duration Matching

Duration matching is an ALM strategy that involves matching the duration statistics for fixed-interest assets such as bonds with the duration statistics for the insurance company products that the assets support. Life insurance companies usually set duration objectives in which the assets duration slightly exceeds the liabilities duration. This practice is particularly important when market interest rates are higher for assets with longer maturities than for those with shorter maturities.

Insurance companies steer, track, and control the duration status of the general account's assets and liabilities to ensure that they are accomplishing general account objectives and also so that they can apply a portfolio immunization strategy to segments of the general account. In general, ***portfolio immunization*** refers to any measures taken to protect a portfolio against loss or undue risk.[11] A portfolio of assets constructed to implement an immunization strategy is called an immunized portfolio. *Portfolio immunization* through duration matching refers to initially positioning a portfolio with assets matched to liabilities so that the portfolio's value is insensitive to small changes in interest-rate risk. Companies apply optimization modeling and other quantitative analysis to identify a set of asset and liability portfolio positions that, in theory, maximize portfolio yield subject to a duration constraint.

Cash-Flow Matching and Portfolio Dedication

Cash-flow matching is a technique that involves projecting future patterns of cash outflows for products and matching those patterns with a similar pattern of projected cash inflows from company investments.[12] Companies plan to produce the projected future cash inflows by investing current product-related inflows, such as premiums, through a portfolio segment matched to the relevant liabilities.

The application of cash-flow matching supports a relatively passive portfolio management strategy of *portfolio dedication*. A portfolio dedication strategy consists of deliberately structuring a portfolio of assets so that the anticipated future cash flows from those assets perfectly match the future cash needs that the portfolio was assembled to fulfill. A dedicated portfolio has less risk than an immunized portfolio. However, portfolio dedication can be applied to only a limited set of a life insurance company's products.

Dedicated portfolios generally have limited and predictable transaction costs, because the assets are purchased once. The assets have limited exposure to interest-rate risk because the assets are held to maturity and their cash flows match the liability cash-flows.

A portfolio dedication strategy is best suited for a portfolio that

- Is initially established and positioned in a period of high interest rates, so the portfolio will likely have limited exposure to rising interest rates

- Holds mainly U.S. Treasury bonds, non-callable investment-grade corporate bonds, and high quality municipal bonds

Interest-Rate Anticipation

An *interest-rate anticipation strategy* is generally a very risky active portfolio management strategy for fixed-income portfolios. To apply this strategy, the investor is required to trade securities in anticipation of estimated future changes in interest rates. An interest-rate anticipation strategy has the objectives of preserving capital when interest rates are increasing and achieving capital appreciation when interest rates are decreasing. Here, we do not discuss the considerable intricacies that would be involved in applying these strategies in a general account context, as this approach is not broadly suited to an entire general account.

Interest-rate anticipation objectives can be attained by altering a portfolio's duration. Portfolios with longer durations tend to gain the most in market value when interest rates decrease and lose the most market value when interest rates increase. As we noted earlier in this chapter, when investors expect interest rates to decrease, they should take steps to increase portfolio duration by trading and otherwise repositioning the portfolio. Investors who anticipate an increase in market interest rates should take steps to reduce portfolio duration.

Example: Interest-Rate Anticipation Strategy

Silas expects market interest rates to decrease in the coming three months. As manager of a portfolio of corporate and U.S. Treasury bonds, Silas should undertake trades to increase the duration of the portfolio.

Positioning a Portfolio to Match a Market Index

Indexing strategy refers broadly to a relatively active portfolio strategy that consists of positioning a fixed-income portfolio to approximate the positioning of a market index. The point of an indexing strategy is to match or exceed the risk-adjusted returns of the market index. The effort to replicate the positioning of a large market index encounters a number of practical challenges, so that this strategy has more theoretical than practical potential. After the initial positioning intended to match the index, the investor must periodically rebalance the indexed portfolio to bring it back into line with the index. This relatively active strategy involves elevated transaction costs due to the need for periodic portfolio rebalancing. Although life insurance companies do not use an indexing strategy for overall portfolio management, some techniques loosely related to indexing are employed in the top-down approach to portfolio management.

Portfolio Management for the General Account

Portfolio management for a life insurance company general account incorporates a portfolio management approach common in institutional investing. Management of the general account applies many of the same policies, types of analysis, tools, and strategies that are applied to manage any type of portfolio.

> **Examples: Portfolio Management Techniques**
>
> Investment policies
> Strategic asset allocation
> Peer comparison analysis
> Standard deviation of returns
> Correlation analysis
> Mean variance optimization and other optimization modeling
> Monte Carlo analysis
> Tactical positioning
> Attribution analysis
> Tracking error

The company establishes the asset allocation targets for the general account in much the same manner as it sets an SAA for an equities portfolio in a separate account. A general account, though, is different. Major practical differences are that the general account is heavily invested in debt investments; that the required return on the general account must, to ensure the company's survival, maintain a minimum margin over and above the interest credited to liabilities; and, finally, that a general account requires ongoing ALM analysis and coordination such as we discussed relative to the integrated portfolio benchmarking system.

Understand, however, that the general account is large and complex, and is managed in a context of ever-changing demands on capital, business mixes, product launches, and insurance regulatory requirements—all considerations that do not affect most separate accounts. Whereas the strategic asset allocation for a separate account is typically maintained in an unchanged state for a very long period, the policies and strategic framework for a general account are revised whenever the company's product mix changes or economic conditions change significantly.

Figure 7.8 presents performance results for the debt and equity portfolios within the general account of Applegate Life Insurance Company.

The report shown in Figure 7.8 presents the asset allocation targets and risk tolerances for a debt portfolio within an insurance company's general account. In this report, you can see how the portfolio manager used the risk tolerances as an opportunity to depart from the exact asset allocation target.

Examples: Manager's "Bets" for the Tactical Portfolio

Overweighting. In the row for credit risk exposures and corporate bonds, the SAA target for corporate bonds is 23 percent, the risk tolerance is 15 to 30 percent, the beginning allocation to corporate bonds is 24 percent, and the ending allocation to corporate bonds is 25 percent. These terms indicate that the portfolio manager decided to overweight corporate bonds relative to the SAA.

Underweighting. The row for real estate risk exposures and commercial mortgages shows that the portfolio manager chose to keep the allocation to commercial mortgages slightly lower than the SAA target of 20 percent. Here, the risk tolerance is 10 to 30 percent, the beginning allocation to commercial mortgages is 18 percent, and the ending allocation to commercial mortgages is 19 percent.[13]

Performance Attribution Factors for Debt Portfolios

Attribution analysis is used to learn whether a portfolio manager's or management team's departures from the strategic asset allocation resulted in superior performance for the company's portfolio. In attribution analysis, companies consider various attribution factors one at a time. In this context, an attribution factor is the element that portfolio managers are able to use in an effort to affect portfolio performance. A general account is usually managed by a team of portfolio managers with specific areas of expertise, so that not all accountabilities are assigned to a single person. By the same token, in a general account context, not all attribution factors are useful in measuring the performance of all portfolio managers.

In Chapter 6, we discussed attribution factors for equity portfolios. Many of those attribution factors, as shown below, apply to debt portfolios also:

- Standard deviation of returns

- Information ratio

- Sharpe ratio

- The selection effect

- The sector effect

- Residual returns

However, other attribution factors for debt portfolios differ from those used for equity portfolios.

Figure 7.8 General Account Performance—Targets and Outcomes

Applegate Life Insurance Company
General Account—Portfolio Performance
1-1 to 10-31

Risk Exposure	Debt Allocation Asset Class	Policy Limitations Risk Tolerance*	SAA Target	Tactical Allocations Beginning	Ending
Credit	Corporate bonds	15–30%	23%	24%	25%
	High-yield bonds	0–10%	7%	7%	8%
	Private-placement bonds	15–25%	20%	19%	20%
Real Estate	Asset-backed securities	2–12%	6%	6%	6%
	Commercial mortgages	10–30%	20%	18%	19%
Interest Rate Risk	Mortgage-backed securities	4–14%	10%	10%	10%
	U.S. Treasury bonds	0–10%	4%	1%	4%
Debt Totals			90%	89%	92%
Equity Totals			10%	11%	8%

*Risk tolerance is the range permitted for tactical positioning

Source: Patricia Wilson Fridley (Senior Advisor, Center for Financial Stability, LLC) note to author, 15 August 2012. Used with permission.

The most important controllable returns in bond portfolios are from a portfolio manager's bets on asset allocations to sectors and quality classes. Each of these potential sources of excess returns undergoes attribution analysis.

In attribution analysis for debt portfolios, the share of excess returns that is explained by a given risk factor is called the "effect" of that risk factor. The effects that can potentially permit a bond portfolio to earn excess returns include the quality effect, interest-rate anticipation effect, and analysis effect, as follows:

■ The *quality effect* isolates the share of excess bond portfolio returns attributable to the manager's bets on bonds having different quality ratings

■ The *interest-rate anticipation effect* isolates the share of excess bond portfolio returns attributable to the manager's bets around short-term departures from the duration target for the debt portfolio

■ The *analysis effect* isolates the share of excess bond portfolio returns attributable to the manager's bets around trading in under- or overvalued debt securities[14]

The following potential sources of bond investment returns are not potential sources of excess returns for a bond portfolio:

■ Income from bonds is stable, and generally is not determined by a portfolio manager's skill.

■ Market-value appreciation of bonds, triggered by either movements in the yield curve or changes in the shape of the yield curve, arises from systemic forces, and, thus, these effects are not under a portfolio manager's control.

■ Finally, recall that the yield from bonds is divisible into two components: the risk-free rate of return and a credit-risk premium. The risk-free rate, which is represented by the yield on comparable U.S. Treasury securities, is also a systemic factor, not controlled by a portfolio manager.

ALM Process and Analysis

Life insurance companies stand ready to pay their obligations in cash on short notice. To support this capability, insurance companies monitor their anticipated cash flows and project the future values of their assets, liabilities, and capital. The analytical approach to monitoring this capability is broadly referred to as asset adequacy analysis. ***Asset adequacy analysis*** is defined as an analysis of the adequacy of reserves and other liabilities being tested, in light of the assets supporting those reserves and other liabilities.[15] Asset adequacy analysis can address the sufficiency as well as the liquidity of assets.

The most widely used method of asset adequacy analysis is ***cash-flow testing***, which involves the projection and comparison of the timing and amount of cash flows resulting from economic and other assumptions. Figure 7.9 shows types of insurance company cash flows that potentially require such analysis.

Not all products have features that would require a company to conduct cash-flow testing. Cash-flow testing is generally appropriate where cash flows of existing assets, products, or other liabilities may potentially vary under different interest-rate or economic scenarios.

A company's financial modeling software used for ALM can project financial values for

■ All types of asset adequacy analysis, including multi-scenario cash-flow testing, and interest-sensitive cash-flow testing.

■ Stress tests of asset adequacy under various scenarios for market interest-rates or other economic conditions, and including "shock-rate" tests of extreme changes in market interest rates.

■ Duration analysis to study the sensitivity of financial valuations and cash flows to future changes in market interest rates or other relevant economic variables.

■ Back-testing the company's modeling applications and assumptions—that is, applying the models and assumptions to known past data, to see if the models can produce accurate projections of known data. The purpose of such testing is to validate the models used for making these projections.

Figure 7.9 Cash Flows for Assets and Liabilities

Cash Flows for Assets	
Cash Inflows from Assets	**Cash Outflows for Assets**
Sale of a common stock investment for cash	Purchase of a corporate bond for cash
Collection of interest and principal on bond investments	Purchase of an equity security for cash
Sale of a bond investment for cash	Purchase of a mortgage-backed security for cash
Rental income on property owned	
Interest and principal collected on fixed-income securities	
Dividend payments from stock investments	
Deposits from asset management clients	
Fees from asset management clients	

Cash Flows for Product Liabilities	
Cash Inflows from Product Liabilities	**Cash Outflows for Liabilities and Expenses**
Premiums for insurance policies or retirement contracts	Life insurance benefit payments
Expense charges and transaction fees to customers	Annuity income payments
Reinsurance claims collections	Payments of withdrawal values to customers
	Payment of compensation to employees
	Payment of commissions to sales producers
	Payment of corporate taxes
	Payment of reinsurance considerations

Other Liability Cash Flows	
Cash inflows not directly associated with assets or products:	**Cash outflows not directly associated with assets or products:**
Proceeds from newly issued surplus notes	Payment of company expenses
	Payment of accounts payable
	Debt service on surplus notes or preferred stocks issued by the company
	Payments of shareholder dividends
	Payments of balance sheet items arising from settlements in litigation[16]

To test whether assets are adequate to support liabilities, companies must project both assets and liabilities, as follows:

■ Projecting future values of cash inflows from investments begins with asset values and applies mathematical processes to reflect the company's assumptions as to prevailing market interest rates, inflation or deflation rates, asset prepayment rates, asset default rates, and reinvestment rates.

■ Projecting future values of cash outflows to support products and other outflows begins with data about liability reserve values or other product values; prevailing market interest rates and other relevant economic variables, as well as anticipated product cash outflows, including interest crediting rates on products; and policyholder behavior variables such as withdrawal and surrender rates and annuitization rates.

Example: Projecting Future Assets and Cash Flows

To support its retirement product liabilities, Applegate Life anticipates that, in the year 2025, the company will be required to pay out $4 million per month in retirement income payments. The $4 million represents Applegate's expected future monthly cash outflows. To meet future needs for cash, Applegate invests today in securities that the company expects to produce $4 million per month in investment earnings in the year 2025. These monthly investment earnings are a type of cash inflow. If the company's projections are accurate, the expected 2025 monthly cash inflows for the product will match the expected monthly cash outflows.

To test the adequacy of cash flows, insurance companies must project multiple scenarios of their asset and liability portfolios. In doing so, they test multiple values for the modeling assumptions, and obtain a variety of projected values for asset net cash flows and liability net cash flows. Then, they analyze the different values they derive from the modeling.

Two common approaches to this analysis are scenario testing and sensitivity analysis:

■ *Scenario testing* uses quantitative modeling to develop multiple scenarios, using different values for input variables.

■ *Sensitivity analysis* measures the responsiveness of the outputs from modeling to changes in the values of the model's input variables. Duration analysis, discussed in Chapter 4, is an important type of sensitivity analysis.

Figure 7.10 shows an excerpt from asset adequacy analysis for a pension plan. This figure displays a worksheet of the results for the underlying calculations, a column chart of the results of the shock-rate scenario testing, and a narrative summary analysis of these results.

This analysis demonstrates the pattern of results for scenarios involving a substantial one-time increase or decrease in market interest rates. Although in this table we show results from testing only a one percent increase and a one percent decrease in interest rates, in reality companies test more than just two interest rate scenarios.

This analysis makes use of monetary duration. ***Monetary duration*** expresses the effect of duration on the monetary values of interest-bearing assets. Monetary duration is calculated as the product of duration and the market value of the assets. The use of monetary duration in reporting the results of relative duration analysis allows analysts to present the duration of interest-bearing assets as a monetary value. Two examples of monetary duration are dollar duration and euro duration.

Example: Monetary Durations

Dollar duration expresses the duration of interest-bearing assets as a dollar value.

Euro duration expresses the duration of interest-bearing assets as a euro value.

As you can see, when interest rates decrease, the value of plan assets increases, but when interest rates increase, the value of plan assets decreases. Similarly, when interest rates decrease, the dollar duration of plan assets increases, and the duration gap becomes highly favorable, but when interest rates increase, the dollar duration of plan assets decreases, and the duration gap becomes highly unfavorable.

Insurance companies regularly test product-related cash flows under seven or more interest-rate scenarios. A common pattern of fixed scenarios gives equal consideration to scenarios of rising and falling interest rates. The column chart in Figure 7.10 shows the results of a series of interest rate shock tests. This chart indicates projected effects of specified changes in market interest rates on the market value of portfolio assets.

Scenarios demonstrating the effects of an interest-rate decrease indicate the effects on the dollar duration values of plan assets as well as plan liabilities arising from a one-time event in which market interest rates decrease by the specified amount, such as one percent. The center point of this array of scenarios represents the baseline case, where no change in market interest rates is tested. Scenarios testing the effects of an interest-rate increase indicate the effects on the dollar duration values of plan assets as well as plan liabilities arising from a one-time event in which market interest rates increase by a specified amount, such as one percent.

In addition to selecting an appropriate method of analysis, companies must select appropriate assumptions for use in modeling. Approaches to developing acceptable assumptions include

- Adapting data from company experience or industry studies

- Using a standard set of scenarios

- Applying random variables based on statistical distributions

Figure 7.10 Asset Adequacy Analysis and Duration Gap Report

Asset Adequacy Analysis—Interest Rate Sensitivity

| | | Shock Rate Tests ($) | | |
| | | Down | Flat | Up |
Fixed Income Portfolio	**Duration**	**-1.00%**	**0.00%**	**1.00%**
Short Term Bond Funds (7%)	2.00	307,500,000	300,000,000	295,500,000
Intermediate Bond Funds (23%)	5.00	1,060,000,000	1,000,000,000	960,000,000
Long Term Bond Funds (70%)	13.00	3,450,000,000	3,000,000,000	2,670,000,000
Total Market Value	10.37	4,817,500,000	4,300,000,000	3,925,500,000
Projected Pension Liability	13.00	3,865,653,496	3,381,523,772	2,986,396,601
Dollar Duration of Assets		49,967,558,140	44,600,000,000	40,715,651,163
Dollar Duration of Liabilities		50,256,965,739	43,962,884,713	38,825,836,783
Dollar Duration Gap		(289,407,600)	637,155,287	1,889,814,380
Plan Surplus		99%	101%	105%

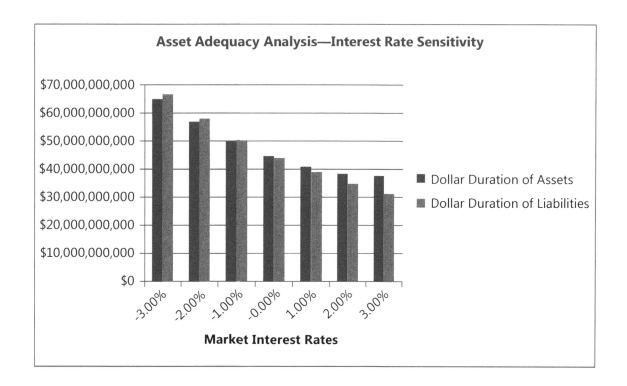

continued...

Figure 7.10 Asset Adequacy Analysis and Duration Gap Report (*continued...*)

Conclusions of Asset Adequacy Analysis

Overall, the analysis indicates that assets and liabilities are well matched and are positioned to weather adverse market conditions.

A straightforward comparison of the plan's asset and liability durations indicates a duration mismatch. The plan has a funding surplus that could be drawn upon if necessary, so any action to correct this mismatch would be unnecessary. The company should not undertake corrective actions to extend duration, because these actions are unnecessary in view of the plan surplus.

Analysis of the dollar duration of projected plan assets and plan liabilities also indicates that, on a dollar duration basis, assets and liabilities are well matched. Essentially, the company holds a surplus of projected plan assets over projected plan liabilities.

Further, under stress testing with shock-rate interest rate scenarios, the plan funding surplus remains relatively intact. The plan funding surplus grows even in an environment of a rapid rise in the market interest rate, largely due to asset positioning relative to market yield curves.

Source: Silas H. Allen (Senior Investment Performance Analyst, USAA Chief Investment Office, United States Automobile Association), worksheet and analysis to author, 26 October 2012. Used with permission.

Internal ALM Reports

Internal ALM reports differ from one company to another but generally have the objective of supporting sound ALM within the particular company. Various reports originate from either liabilities or investments:

- From the liabilities side of ALM, some common internal management reports are a premium income report, a sales commissions report, and a durations report. Less frequently, the liabilities side of ALM reports the liabilities cost of funds and the status of product policies.

- From investments, some common internal ALM reports are an investment activity report, an investment portfolio performance review, a duration gap report, a risk positioning report, and a hedge effectiveness report.

Investment Activity Report

An *investment activity report* specifies the details of all investment portfolio transactions, including all asset acquisitions and dispositions of assets, as well as realized and unrealized capital gain and loss status, estimated returns, and the company's resulting positioning status as to key risk policies, discussed earlier in this chapter.

For each newly acquired debt security, the investment activity report typically gives the asset's yield, term to maturity, duration, and quality rating. Although narrow in scope, this report is typically the most detailed and the most frequently produced of any formal, routine investment report.

Investment Portfolio Performance Review

An *investment portfolio performance review* is typically a quarterly management information report that summarizes a company's investment performance for the company's oversight committees. This report is usually the broadest in scope of any ALM report, but is not the most detailed, because it covers much of the information in summary form. The investment portfolio performance review typically presents quarterly and year-to-date information about the following aspects of investment performance:

■ Overall growth in the portfolio's monetary value, specified in terms of market-value appreciation and income growth; analysis of capital gains and losses; analysis of changes in market values

■ Acquisitions and dispositions by asset type; analysis of the effect on yields of all purchases and sales

■ Narrative discussion of the portfolio composition, known as the asset mix, and the suitability of the asset mix

■ Narrative explanations of key events in the external environment and the company's strategic responses to those events

■ Summary reports on special topics such as problem assets, real estate investments, and international investments

Duration Gap Report

A *duration gap report* provides a snapshot of the asset-liability match at the time of the report. Such a report is typically submitted quarterly to the board of directors. Earlier in this chapter, Figure 7.10 shows a duration gap report for a fund supporting pension benefit obligations. A duration gap report generally describes the results of duration analysis of the company's assets and liabilities and discusses the insurer's current exposure to cash-flow mismatches arising from changes in market interest rates. Even small changes in market interest rates and other economic factors can produce dramatic changes in the asset-liability duration gap, so information in a duration gap report is time-sensitive.

A duration gap report can include

■ Duration statistics and monetary durations for assets and liabilities

■ The book value of the assets allocated to each portfolio segment or line of business, the current market value of the assets, and the book value of the liabilities in each product line

■ Investment returns compared to target investment returns

Risk Positioning Report

A *risk positioning report* for fixed-income assets typically shows the actual quality of securities compared to the targeted quality of securities; duration and the duration gap; performance attribution; and performance relative to overall SAA benchmarks. *Risk positioning analysis* for asset portfolios generally shows for a given period how the tactical portfolio has departed from the company's SAA, and shows the limits placed on such bets.[17]

Hedge Effectiveness Report

When a company holds a derivative security for a hedging purpose, the portfolio position in those derivative securities is a *hedge position*. For the general account, many companies and regulators restrict the use of derivative securities to hedging purposes.

Each general account hedge position is intended to directly offset a specified financial risk. For an established hedge, any change in the underlying risk exposure could also change the effectiveness of the hedge. *Hedge effectiveness* refers to the extent to which a hedge actually reduces risk. To qualify for favorable reporting options under public accounting rules, companies must apply statistical tests at least quarterly to establish the effectiveness of their hedging positions. A *hedge effectiveness report* provides monitoring information for every position established for hedging purposes. For a given hedge, any change in the associated risk posture could cause the hedge to convert from fulfilling its intended purpose of risk reduction to possibly having a risk augmentation effect.

> **Example: Loss of Hedge Effectiveness**
>
> A hedge could lose its effectiveness when the insurance company
>
> - Purchases another derivative security that creates a better match.
>
> - Sells the asset that formerly required a hedge.
>
> - Reinsures a product liability that formerly required a hedge.
>
> - Sells a product line that formerly required a hedge.

Audit Steps for the ALM Function

For any operation, auditors ensure that internal controls are in use, are sufficient to address risk exposures, and that governance processes overall are adequate. As a matter of good business practice and to support appropriate financial reporting, companies must arrange for audits of all ALM functions. Periodic audits of the ALM function should address the following points:

- Review cash-flow analysis of current product obligations; ensure that this analysis has properly assessed the potential cash-flow impact of interest-rate fluctuations; and verify that this analysis tested cash flows associated with projected future product obligations.

- Evaluate the degree of match between assets and liabilities.

- Review cash-flow testing practices. Verify that routine liquidity studies apply an appropriate set of economic scenarios.

- Review the company's investment segmentation plan. Ensure proper groupings of products having similar interest-rate sensitivity; assess whether the number and size of the segments is reasonable; and verify that the aggregate of the segments is consistent with balance sheet amounts.

- Review the investment strategy for the general account and each product segment. Verify that each investment strategy appropriately addresses investment risk.

- For a sample of investment transactions, verify that each transaction was assigned to the appropriate segment.

- For each product group or segment, verify the accuracy of the calculation of net liability. Trace significant liabilities to the source documentation. The total of financial values used in calculating net liability should be consistent with the values found in other financial reporting.

- For investment activity reports, investment portfolio performance reviews, and asset reports, follow source documentation to test for accuracy.

- Sample the company's in-force products to verify that all products were analyzed for interest-rate sensitivity.

- Review the models used for ALM analysis and the appropriateness of any assumptions used in modeling; similarly, review the completeness of scenario modeling as a whole.

- Review the interest coverage ratio calculation.

- Verify that the corporate business recovery plan incorporates ALM as an aspect of recovery.[18]

As part of any audit, a company must ensure that all relevant investment policies have been upheld. Figure 7.11 presents a broad investment policy for debt investments in the general account. In Figure 7.6, you saw a narrower investment policy for a single product segment.

Figure 7.11 Sample General Account and Portfolio Segment Investment Policy Statements

I. Investment Policy Statement: General Account

Investable asset classes: Publicly traded common stocks; REITs; public bonds including corporate bonds, below-investment-grade bonds, bank loans, private placement bonds, commercial mortgages, U.S. government bonds, mortgage-backed securities; asset-backed securities; commercial mortgage-backed securities; and convertible securities. Security types not expressly named are prohibited.

Diversification guidelines. The fixed-income portfolio shall not exceed the following limits without written approval of the board of directors:

- Equities overall: not more than 20 percent at any time
  - Common stocks: 0–20 percent
  - REITs: 0–5 percent
- Public bonds overall: 80–100 percent
  - Investment-grade corporate bonds: 25–40 percent
  - High-yield bonds and bank loans: 0–10 percent
  - Private placement bonds: 10–25 percent
  - Commercial mortgages: 10–25 percent
  - U.S. government bonds: 10–50 percent
  - Mortgage-backed bonds: 25–30 percent
  - Asset-backed securities: 10–20 percent
  - Commercial mortgage-backed securities: 10–15 percent
  - Convertible securities: 0–5 percent

Individual Issuer Limitations

Equities: Not more than 5 percent of the asset class may be held in any one issuer.

Bonds: Not more than 1 percent of any fixed income asset class may be held in one issuer, except for U.S. government bonds, which may be held without limit.

Other Issuer Limitations

The portfolio shall not hold securities for which the issuer derives 25 percent of its revenues from the sale or distribution of tobacco products.

The portfolio shall not hold debt securities for which the rating is less than B.

Total holdings of below-investment-grade securities shall not exceed 8 percent of total assets.

Not more than 10 percent of the account may be committed to any one industry.

Not more than 5 percent of the account value may be committed to any single bond issue.

No foreign securities may be purchased or held. If a security becomes a foreign holding, the investment committee must give specific approval for continuing to hold the security.

Not more than 5 percent of the account may be committed at the time of purchase to the debt securities of any one issuer, except for the United States government or AAA-rated debt securities issued by U.S. government agencies, which may be held without limitation.

This policy does not restrict fixed-income securities in terms of turnover, realized gains and losses, maturities, or coupons.

continued...

Figure 7.11 Sample General Account and Portfolio Segment Investment Policy Statements (*continued*)

Liquidity policy. Illiquid assets comprise commercial mortgages and private placement securities. Total holdings of illiquid assets shall not exceed 25 percent of total assets.

Minimum credit quality. The portfolio may not hold securities that do not meet specified minimum quality rating standards.

If a security held in the portfolio is downgraded, the security must be sold at the best available price within the next three months.

Compliance reviews. The activity and performance of this portfolio will be reviewed quarterly or more often for compliance with this statement. This investment account shall be limited to fixed-income investments, cash, and cash equivalents.

Portfolio policy compliance and risk management reviews. The activity and performance of this portfolio shall be reviewed daily by the designated risk manager.

In addition, the designated risk manager shall quarterly report in a risk management review the portfolio's compliance with investment policies; adequacy of risk policy framework; and emerging risk management practices.

Performance evaluation. Performance will be measured quarterly against a market index and on an absolute basis.

Source: Patricia Wilson Fridley (Senior Advisor, Center for Financial Stability LLC), note to author, 9 November 2012. Used with permission.

Key Terms

asset-liability management risk
asset risk
downgrade risk
margin compression
margin expansion
mean liabilities method
portfolio segmentation method
replicating portfolio
risky asset
risky asset capacity
excess risky asset capacity
liquidity policy
duration policy
duration matching
portfolio immunization
cash-flow matching

portfolio dedication
interest-rate anticipation strategy
quality effect
interest-rate anticipation effect
analysis effect
asset adequacy analysis
cash-flow testing
monetary duration
investment activity report
investment portfolio performance
    review
duration gap report
risk positioning report
hedge position
hedge effectiveness
hedge effectiveness report

Endnotes

1. Portions of this chapter are based on material provided by Patricia Wilson Fridley, Senior Advisor, Center for Financial Stability, LLC, 6 August 2012–9 August 2012. Used with permission.

2. Society of Actuaries, *Society of Actuaries Professional Actuarial Specialty Guide: Asset-Liability Management* (Schaumburg, IL: Society of Actuaries, 2003), 71, http://www.soa.org/news-and-publications/publications/other-publications/professional-actuarial-specialty-guides/pub-asset-liability-guide.pdf (16 August 2012).

3. Mark J. Anson, Frank J. Fabozzi, and Frank J. Jones, *The Handbook of Traditional and Alternative Investment Vehicles: Investment Characteristics and Strategies* (Hoboken, NJ: John Wiley & Sons, 2011), 77, 79–80, 83, 85 –87.

4. John Fenton, Mark Scanlon, and Jaidev Iyer, "Interesting Challenges for Insurers," *Insights*, March 2011, 2–7, http://www.towerswatson.com/assets/pdf/3976/TowersWatson_Low-interest-rate_-NA-2010-18363.pdf (16 October 2012).

5. Anson, Fabozzi, and Jones, 77, 79–80.

6. Society of Actuaries, 29.

7. Patricia Wilson Fridley (Senior Advisor, Center for Financial Stability, LLC), notes to author (7 August 2012). Used with permission.

8. Society of Actuaries, 29; Ellen Cooper et al., *Revisiting the Role of Insurance Company ALM within a Risk Management Framework*, White Paper, (New York: Goldman Sachs, 2010), http://www.goldmansachs.com/gsam/docs/instgeneral/general_materials/whitepaper/wp_revisiting_role_of_ins_co_alm.pdf (8 October 2012).

9. Peter Boekel et al., *Replicating Portfolios, An Introduction: Analysis and Illustrations*, Milliman Research Report, (Seattle: Milliman, 2009) 2–8, http://publications.milliman.com/research/life-rr/pdfs/replicating-portfolios-rr.pdf (2 November 2012); Society of Actuaries, 86.

10. Fridley, note to author, 6 August 2012. Used with permission.

11. Fridley, note to author, 10 November 2012. Used with permission.

12. Society of Actuaries, 29.

13. Actuarial Standards Board, *Analysis of Life, Health, or Property/Casualty Insurer Cash Flows*, Actuarial Standard of Practice No. 7, rev. ed. (Washington, DC: Actuarial Standards Board, 2011) 20, http://www.actuarialstandardsboard.org/pdf/asops/asop007_128.pdf (14 October 2012).

14. Fridley. Used with permission.

15. Actuarial Standards Board, *Statements of Opinion Based on Asset Adequacy Analysis by Actuaries for Life or Health Insurers*, Actuarial Standard of Practice No. 22, rev. ed. (Washington, DC: Actuarial Standards Board, 2011), 3–5, http://www.actuarialstandardsboard.org/pdf/asops/asop022_167.pdf (14 October 2012).

16. Ibid.

17. Fridley, note to author, 2 November 2012. Used with permission.

18. LOMA, "311. Asset Liability Matching," in *Business Risks and Controls Handbook* [Atlanta: LOMA (Life Office Management Association, Inc.), © 2001], 311-1–311-3. Used with permission; all rights reserved.

Chapter 8

Bonds and Bond-Related Investments

Objectives

After studying this chapter, you should be able to

8A Describe important terms and features of bonds, such as type of issuer, whether a bond is secured or unsecured, the industry classification of a corporate bond, its repayment or retirement features, affirmative and restrictive bond covenants, and bond conversion features

8B Identify and describe four principal types of U.S. Treasury obligations—bills, notes, bonds, and TIPS

8C Identify the important characteristics of municipal bonds and Build America Bonds

8D Describe how life insurance companies are required to apply risk capital charges to bond investments

8E Distinguish between primary and secondary bond markets; explain the important characteristics of private placements for bonds; and distinguish between types of domestic and international bonds, including foreign bonds, Yankee bonds, and eurobonds, such as eurodollar bonds and euroyen bonds

8F Describe how institutional investors quote and use corporate bond prices for trading purposes, and explain important controls for maintaining security of bond trading

8G Describe three common investment strategies for bond portfolios: an immunization strategy, a laddered strategy, and a barbell strategy

8H Describe the investment attributes of structured debt securities, including asset-backed securities and collateralized loan obligations; describe the process a loan originator follows to create structured debt securities; describe the role of special purpose entities in structured securities; explain the significance of tranches for investors in structured securities; describe the potential arrangements for enhancing credit of structured securities; and describe potential arrangements for distributions of principal and interest across tranches of the SPE

Outline

Terms of a Bond

Bonds by Issuer
- Corporate Bonds
- U.S. Government–Issued Debt Securities
- Sovereign Debt Securities
- Municipal Bonds

Variations on the Terms of a Bond
- Bond Interest-Rate Features
- Retirement or Repayment Features
- Bond Covenants
- Secured or Unsecured Bonds
- Senior or Subordinated Bonds
- Conversion Features

Bond Risks
- Troubled Corporate Securities
- Risk in Sovereign Debt Issues
- Bond Ratings and Risk Capital Charges in the United States
- Credit Ratings and Coupon Rates

Bond Markets
- Primary Market for Bonds
- Private Placement Bonds
- Secondary Markets for Bonds
- Global Bond Markets

Quoting Corporate Bond Prices

Institutional Bond Purchase Process

Bond Investment Strategies

Securitization and Structured Securities
- Asset-Backed Securities
- Collateralized Loan Obligations

Institutional investors, such as life insurance companies and retirement funds, must reliably preserve principal, cover the expenses of investment administration, and increase the value of their investments. These institutional investors hold a broad variety of investments. However, due to the long-term nature of their liabilities and flows of funds, these institutional investors tend to hold fixed-income debt investments, such as bonds, to a greater extent than they hold equity investments. Insurance companies and retirement funds now hold a variety of fixed-income debt securities.

Fixed-income securities have a significant long-standing role in the portfolios of insurance companies. Over the years, debt-based securities have strongly outweighed equity investments. In recent years, however, companies' allocations to various debt securities have changed somewhat. In 1989, bonds and commercial real estate loans constituted nearly all of insurers' fixed-income investments. By 2010, though, life insurers were investing in a much wider variety of fixed-income securities.[1]

Terms of a Bond

Many different characteristics and features of a bond affect the bond's perceived risk and return. A legally enforceable contract between the bond issuer and the bondholder specifies the promises of the issuer and the rights of the bondholder. This agreement is variously called the *bond indenture, bond contract, bond agreement*, or *note purchase agreement*. If the terms of a bond are amended after the initial formation of a contract, the parties issue a supplemental bond contract. The important characteristics of a bond are also presented in the bond prospectus or similar documents, such as an offering memorandum. Institutional investors typically review the prospectus or memorandum instead of the bond contract.[2]

Important bond features include the bond's par value or principal, its stated maturity date, coupon payments, and coupon rate, as Figure 8.1 illustrates. A bond agreement specifies that the borrower will repay the bond's *par value*, face amount, or principal, to the bondholder at the bond's *maturity date*. Bonds are available with a variety of stated maturity dates, and can carry maturity dates of 20 to 30 years. Bonds may have an actual maturity date that differs from their stated maturity date, because some bonds are *retired*—repaid—before their scheduled maturity date. For this reason, investors sometimes distinguish between a bond's legal maturity and its expected maturity.

Until maturity, the bond issuer usually pays the bondholder periodic payments of the loan interest, known as *coupon payments*, typically at semiannual intervals, that is, every six months. The amount of the periodic interest payment is a percentage—known as the *coupon rate*—of the par value.

Example: Terms of a Bond

A Pearl Sun bond promises that Pearl Sun Corporation will pay bondholders semiannual coupon payments at a 3 percent annual coupon rate on a 15-year, $10,000 bond.

The following table summarizes the terms of the Pearl Sun Corporation bond:

Bond Terms: Pearl Sun Corporation 202X	
Par value	$10,000
Coupon payment	$150
Coupon rate	3%
Maturity date	15 years

Figure 8.1 Bond Basics

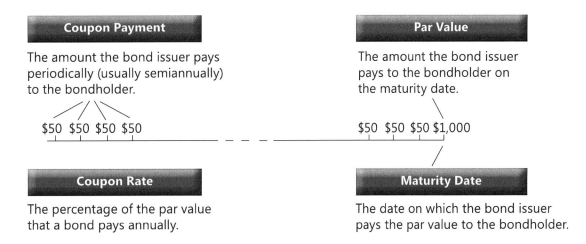

Coupon Payment
The amount the bond issuer pays periodically (usually semiannually) to the bondholder.

$50 $50 $50 $50

Coupon Rate
The percentage of the par value that a bond pays annually.

Par Value
The amount the bond issuer pays to the bondholder on the maturity date.

$50 $50 $50 $1,000

Maturity Date
The date on which the bond issuer pays the par value to the bondholder.

Bonds by Issuer

We can divide the bond market into four categories based on the major issuers: corporations, the U.S. Treasury and other U.S. government agencies, sovereign governments besides the U.S. government, and U.S. state and local governments.

Corporate Bonds

Corporations are the primary nongovernmental issuers of bonds. Corporate bonds are a significant asset class in insurance company general accounts and in many other institutional investor portfolios as well. Corporations typically issue bonds to raise capital to expand their business activities.

Corporate bonds are often classified into the following industry groups:

- *Utility bonds* are issued by providers of utilities, such as telephone and electric companies.

- *Transportation bonds* are issued by providers of transportation, such as airlines, trucking companies, and railroads.

- *Finance bonds* are issued by financial institutions, such as banks and insurance companies.

- *Industrial bonds* are issued by all industries other than the utility, transportation, or financial industries.

U.S. Government-Issued Debt Securities

The U.S. government, including the U.S. Treasury and various federal agencies, is the world's single largest borrower. In the current chapter, we limit our discussion to U.S. Treasury debt securities. The principal types of U.S. Treasury securities are Treasury bills, Treasury notes, Treasury bonds, and Treasury Inflation-Protected Securities (TIPS).

- *Treasury bills*, sometimes referred to as *T-bills*, are short-term Treasury debt securities with a maturity date of one year or less. Treasury bills are commonly issued with maturity dates of 4 weeks, 13 weeks, 26 weeks, and 52 weeks.

- *Treasury notes* are Treasury debt securities with a maturity date between 1 year and 10 years. Treasury notes are commonly issued with maturity dates of 2 years, 3 years, 5 years, 7 years, and 10 years.

- *Treasury bonds* are Treasury debt securities with a maturity date of more than 10 years. In practice, Treasury bonds are issued with much longer maturity dates, usually in the range of 20 to 30 years.

- *Treasury Inflation-Protected Securities (TIPS)* are Treasury securities that provide protection against inflation. The principal amount of a TIPS increases periodically in accordance with the rate of inflation, as measured by the Consumer Price Index. TIPS are issued with maturity dates of 5 years, 10 years, and 30 years. TIPS coupon payments are paid semiannually. These payments reflect the coupon rate multiplied by the inflation-adjusted par value.

The distinctions between these securities are their durations and the presence or absence of inflation protection, as summarized in the following table:

	Time from Issue until Maturity	Inflation Protection?
Treasury Bill	One year or less	No
Treasury Note	At least 1 but not more than 10 years, commonly 2 to 10 years	No
Treasury Bond	More than 10 years, often 20 to 30 years	No
TIPS	5, 10, and 30 years	Yes

Sovereign Debt Securities

To cover the cost of public spending that is not fully supported by tax revenues, many national governments issue bonds in either their domestic currency or a foreign currency. These bonds are traded in either their domestic securities markets or foreign securities markets. Bonds issued by national governments other than the U.S. government are classified as *sovereign debt securities*. Debt of the U.S. government is technically a type of sovereign debt, but U.S. government debt is not usually called "sovereign debt."

Some bonds are issued by multinational or supranational entities such as regional development banks. These bonds are commonly referred to as "super-sovereigns." Also, some jurisdictions that are not sovereign governments but have a great deal of autonomy, such as Canadian provinces, issue bonds that are referred to as "sub-sovereigns."[3]

Municipal Bonds

Municipal bonds, popularly known as *munis*, are debt securities issued by local government agencies and local governments to raise funds for public works, such as schools, parks, bridges, highways, and hospitals. Although municipal bonds are issued by government entities outside of the United States, in this section we refer to municipal bonds issued by U.S. city, county, and state governments.

Generally, investors tend to hold municipal bonds until maturity. Although the size of the U.S. municipal bond market is large, the individual bond issues are typically not very large. Thus, municipal bonds issued in the United States are relatively illiquid.

Two main types of municipal bonds are general obligation bonds and revenue bonds.

- A *general obligation bond* is backed by the full faith and credit of the issuer.

- A *revenue bond* is supported by a specific income-producing project, such as a toll road, as illustrated in Figure 8.2. The issuer of a revenue bond is required to pay the bond's principal and interest only if the project produces sufficient income. Thus, revenue bonds are much riskier than general obligation bonds.

Figure 8.2 Revenue Bond: Lake of the Ozarks Community Bridge

Location	Missouri
Project Sponsors	Missouri Highway Commission
	Lake of the Ozarks Community Bridge Corporation (LOCBC)
	Four Seasons Corporation
Mode	Toll Bridge
Description	The Lake of the Ozarks Community Bridge is a ½-mile toll bridge that improves mobility around Lake of the Ozarks, connecting Horseshoe Bend and U.S. Business Route 54 on the developed east shore to Shawnee Bend and the less developed west shore. The route saves 30 to 50 miles of travel around the lake. Passenger car toll rates vary seasonally (on-season/off-season).
	To finance the bridge's construction, the Lake of the Ozarks Community Bridge Corporation was formed in 1992 under a state law provision enacted in 1990 to allow private, not-for-profit transportation corporations to play a role in developing projects as an alternative to normal funding methods for roads and bridges.
Cost	$25.78 million
Sources of finance	$40.1 million tax-exempt toll revenue bonds, series 1996, sold by LOCBC for construction, contingency funding, capitalized interest and cost of issuance.
	$43 million bridge system refunding bonds sold by LOCBC to refund the series 1996 bonds, fund debt service reserve, and pay cost of issuance of the series 1998 bonds.

Source: "Lake of the Ozarks Community Bridge," AASHTO Center for Excellence in Project Finance, http://www.transportation-finance.org/projects/lake_ozarks_bridge.aspx (28 September 2012). Used with permission.

For purposes of U.S. income taxation, income earned from municipal bonds can be tax exempt or taxable to the investor. Life insurance companies, retirement plans, and foreign investors generally hold municipal bonds that are fully taxable, because these entities do not benefit from the tax exemptions potentially found in municipal securities.

Build America Bonds (BABs) are debt securities issued by a municipal government in the United States, and supported by U.S. government incentives for the issuing municipal government. Unlike many municipal bonds, some BABs can generate taxable income to institutional investors and foreign investors. These BABs are popular with institutional investors because they appear to provide stable income over a long term, they provide attractive total returns, the returns on these bonds are taxable, and they have a strong secondary market.

Variations on the Terms of a Bond

Earlier in the chapter, we discussed the most common features of a bond. Many variations on bond terms are in common use. For example, the coupon interest rate can take several forms. Some bonds even have no coupon.

Bond Interest-Rate Features

Most bonds today have a *fixed-rate coupon*, a coupon having a rate that does not change throughout the bond's term. Sometimes a bond specifies a coupon rate that fluctuates in a specified manner. The rate of a *floating-rate coupon* varies based on changes in a reference index and a spread from the index. A *variable rate* fluctuates based on a reference to a standard other than an index.

In addition, some bonds do not offer periodic coupon interest payments. As Figure 8.3 shows, a **zero-coupon bond** is a bond that does not pay interest coupons during the bond's term. Instead, the bond is sold at a discount to its face value; then the principal is paid in full at the bond's maturity date. U.S. Treasury bills operate in a manner similar to that of a zero-coupon bond. Instead of making interest payments, the Treasury issues bills at a discount to face value and then pays the principal in full at the maturity date.

Holding zero-coupon bonds can reduce reinvestment risk for institutional investors because these bonds do not pay interest during the bond term. Thus, investors do not receive any periodic interest income to reinvest. However, if market interest rates rise, institutional investors cannot gain the potential advantage of reinvesting any interest income at the higher market interest rates. Relative to typical coupon-paying bonds, zero-coupon bonds increase an investor's exposure to credit risk, because a default puts at risk the bond's purchase price and all interest earned on the investment

Retirement or Repayment Features

A bond agreement also states the conditions under which an issuer can retire or repay the bond in the ordinary course of business. In general, bonds are repaid on the maturity date. The most common type of bond, a *term bond*, has one maturity date, upon which the principal is repaid in full.

Figure 8.3 Structure of a Zero-Coupon Bond

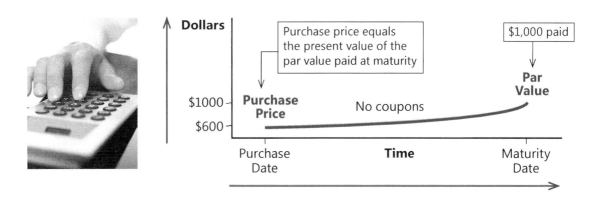

Another type of bond is a *serial bond*, for which the principal is repaid in a series of installments at predetermined dates. In essence, a serial bond has a series of maturity dates. Many U.S. state and local governments issue serial bonds to finance projects with regular income streams, such as toll roads and bridges. Because life insurance companies do not benefit from the tax advantages of tax-exempt municipal bonds to the same extent as do many other institutional investors, they do not usually hold serial bonds.

Some bonds, known as **callable bonds**, include provisions that allow a bond issuer to retire the bond prior to the maturity date at a specified price—the *call price*. If market interest rates fall, a call provision benefits the bond issuer by allowing the issuer to repay a bond with a high coupon interest rate and subsequently issue a similar bond with a lower coupon interest rate. Paying the call price is sometimes known as a **refunding**. Typically, bond provisions do not permit bond issuers to call a bond until after a stated minimum time after issue, such as five years. A provision for early repayment exposes the bondholder to reinvestment risk.

A **sinking fund provision** in a bond requires the bond issuer to follow a particular arrangement for accumulating the amount of the bond's principal over time. At a minimum, a sinking fund provision requires a bond issuer to set aside funds periodically for the repayment of the debt, thus ensuring that money will be available to repay the bond at maturity. A sinking fund provision may also stipulate that the issuer can repay a portion of the bond issue on specified dates before the maturity date. However, the sinking fund never permits full prepayment of the bond issue.

A bond with a sinking fund provision offers a measure of safety for bondholders, as the company issuing the bond is less likely to default, thereby reducing the credit risk exposure for the bondholder. Thus, such bonds typically carry a lower interest rate than comparable bonds without a sinking fund provision.

Bond Covenants

Bond covenants are provisions in a bond agreement intended to protect the interest of the bondholder by limiting the issuer's behaviors. Bond covenants are sometimes classified as affirmative or restrictive.

Affirmative covenants require the issuer to take certain actions, such as meeting stated contractual and legal obligations and maintaining a specified minimum credit rating. Affirmative covenants can also require a bond issuer to produce financial statements for the investor, upon request.

Restrictive covenants, also known as *negative covenants*, restrict the issuer from taking any action that would be harmful to the bondholder. Restrictive covenants commonly set limitations on capital expenditures, declaring and making payments of dividends to stockholders, mergers, acquisitions, and additional debt the firm can incur. Restrictive covenants can also limit the amount of the issuer's total permitted debt. A bond issuer that violates a restrictive covenant may be subject to penalties. For example, a bond issuer that violates a restrictive covenant may be penalized by having to increase the coupon rate for a fixed-rate coupon.

A *financial covenant* is a type of restrictive covenant that, in securities, focuses on particular financial measures and ratios of the issuer. Financial covenants may stipulate that the issuer must maintain a particular level of working capital or ratio of assets to liabilities.

Although all debt securities may contain restrictive or financial covenants, these provisions are most commonly found in bonds with limited marketability, such as private placement bonds, asset-backed securities (ABS), and sometimes high-yield bonds. Investment-grade public bonds do not commonly contain restrictive covenants, because these bonds have ready marketability.

Secured or Unsecured Bonds

A bond may be secured or unsecured. For a secured bond, the bond issuer pledges assets, or *collateral*, as security for the bond. The collateral may be real estate, equipment, or financial assets such as receivables. In the event that the bond issuer does not comply with the bond agreement by failing to make scheduled interest or principal payments, the bondholder can seize and take ownership of the collateral. One common type of secured bond, a **mortgage bond**, gives the bondholder a claim to specified real estate or other real assets in the event that the bond issuer defaults.

Corporate bond issuers with exceptionally good credit are able to pay relatively low interest rates without pledging specific assets as collateral for a bond. Unsecured corporate bonds are known as *debentures*.

Senior or Subordinated Bonds

In the event that a company must be liquidated or reorganized in bankruptcy, certain creditors of the company have priority over others. Debt holders have a claim against the company's assets ahead of the claims of the company's stockowners. Among the debts of a bond issuer, bonds are classified as senior bonds or subordinated bonds, according to their claim priority in the event of a bond issuer's default.

■   A **senior bond** is a bond that has a higher claim of priority in the event of the issuer's default than that of other bonds from the same issuer.

■   A **subordinated bond**, also known as *junior debt*, is a bond that has a lower claim priority in the event of default than that of other bonds from the same issuer.

Typically, in the event of a default, secured bondholders have first priority in satisfying their claims against their collateral, after which unsecured bondholders have a claim against the issuer's residual assets. Thus, secured bonds generally are senior bonds. If the bond issuer does not have any secured debt outstanding, holders of senior debentures have the first claim on the issuer's assets ahead of holders of subordinated debentures. In a default, holders of unsecured bonds are rarely paid the full value of their investment.

Conversion Features

Some securities have features that allow the owner the option of converting the security into the issuer's common stock. These types of securities feature prominently in *mezzanine debt financing*, in which a company issues, through private placement, either unsecured corporate bonds or another form of private placement financing that allows the investor some participation in the equity position of the issuing company. Such securities are often referred to as ***mezzanine debt*** because their claims to an issuing company's assets are senior to those of the company's common stock holders but junior to the claims of the senior bondholders. In this chapter, we focus only on corporate bonds. Preferred stock and other potential venture capital financing arrangements are described in Chapter 10.

Convertible bonds are sometimes included in mezzanine debt financing arrangements. A ***convertible bond*** is a type of corporate bond that pays a fixed interest payment but also gives the bondholder the option of surrendering the bond in exchange for a specified number of shares of the issuing company's common stock. Investors convert such bonds to take advantage of favorable movements in the price of the bond issuer's common stock. If the issuing company's stock price does not appreciate significantly, the convertible bond holder will not exercise the option. Instead the bondholder will continue to receive the coupon payments, and at maturity, the face value of the bond. After a bond conversion is completed, the transaction cannot be reversed. The coupon interest rate for convertible bonds generally is lower than the coupon interest rate for comparable nonconvertible bonds issued by the same company at the same time.

Bond Risks

In Chapter 4, we described credit risk, currency risk, and liquidity risk associated with investments. Other risks specific to debt securities include prepayment risk and extension risk. Insurance companies avoid accepting exposure to prepayment and extension risks, so we do not further discuss these risks.

Troubled Corporate Securities

When investors buy corporate bonds, they expect to receive all coupon payments promised by the issuer as well as a return of the principal. Credit ratings provide information about the likelihood that issuers of corporate bonds will meet these obligations. Unfortunately, some bonds, even those highly rated at the time of purchase, may default.

Bond issuers facing problems meeting a bond's obligations often seek to alter the terms of the debt. ***Debt restructuring***, sometimes known as *rescheduling*, is an agreement by a lender to alter the terms of the debt agreement. Bonds are typically restructured by the bondholder, who might extend the maturity date or accept a lesser amount in repayment of the debt.

In the United States and some other countries, an insolvent company may file for ***reorganization***, a legal proceeding under which the company makes a plan to pay its creditors, in full or in part, and remain in operation. In Europe and certain other countries outside the United States, companies in reorganization are said to be in ***administration***. Frequently, a reorganized company resumes operation on an altered basis, such as under new management or a new ownership structure. After a successful reorganization proceeding, a company's bondholders typically recover some of their investment, either in the form of restructured debt or an ownership interest in the reorganized company, while the company's existing stockholders typically are left with little or nothing.

Example: Effects of Corporate Insolvency

The Ballast Company is no longer able to pay its obligations when due. Ballast has total assets of $120 million. Its total liabilities are $200 million, including liability to bondholders. Ballast's creditors have filed suit to liquidate the company and distribute its assets. Ballast has no secured creditors and no costs are associated with liquidating the company. Thus, Ballast's assets would be distributed to its creditors on a pro rata basis. Each creditor would receive 60 percent of the value of its claim, calculated as follows:

$$\frac{\$120 \text{ million assets}}{\$200 \text{ million liabilities}} = 0.60 = 60\%$$

No assets would remain for distribution to Ballast's equity owners.[4]

Risks in Sovereign Debt Issues

Sovereign debt differs from other types of debt primarily because sovereign debt contracts are not backed by collateral. Also, issues of legal jurisdiction can require a sophisticated approach to any attempt at obtaining enforcement by a court. However, in many cases, investors regard sovereign debt securities as the least risky type of securities because, in theory, governments are able to collect taxes to service their debt. In addition, governments typically are motivated to maintain a good credit rating and thus support their ability to borrow at relatively low interest rates.

Although governments have suspended interest payments or defaulted on their debts, defaults on sovereign debt historically have been rare. Typically, when facing problems with servicing their debt, governments attempt to restructure the debt to make it easier for them to make some payments without complete default. Debt restructuring can take the forms of reducing principal or lowering coupon payments. The International Monetary Fund (IMF) has assisted a number of countries in restructuring sovereign debt by continuing to lend them money.

Bond Ratings and Risk Capital Charges in the United States

We've already mentioned that the NAIC's SVO and private credit rating agencies assign ratings to bonds and other debt securities. As we've seen, in these rating systems, bonds that are rated in the highest rating categories and that have the lowest credit risk are known as *investment-grade bonds*. Bonds that are not investment-grade bonds are *below investment-grade bonds*. Other terms for below investment-grade bonds are *speculative bonds*, *high-yield bonds*, or *junk bonds*. Bonds that are rated in the lowest rating categories are impaired or in default. Although institutional investors use popular credit analysis services, insurance regulators increasingly emphasize that life insurance companies must perform security analysis independently of the ratings agencies, and cannot rely entirely on external services to assess the credit quality of bonds and other debt securities.

As specified in the *Insurance Core Principles* of the International Association of Insurance Supervisors (IAIS), insurance regulators or supervisors must require companies to demonstrate that company assets are adequate for maintaining the company's long-term solvency. Such requirements typically include a mixed focus on both assets and capital.[5] Recall that, in terms of a balance sheet, capital is the residual amount when liabilities are subtracted from assets, as follows:

Capital = Assets – Liabilities

Insurance regulators establish capital adequacy requirements that insurance companies must maintain. In evaluating a company's capital adequacy, insurance regulators in the United States apply *risk capital charges* that in effect reduce the value of the company's assets. The purpose of risk capital charges is to acknowledge that investments are inherently risky, and that these assets can suffer losses.

To address credit risks in a company's investments in debt securities, each bond or fixed-income security is assigned a risk factor—corresponding to the type of security and the security's NAIC rating—that is used to determine the amount of the risk capital charge for that security. The NAIC applies a sliding scale of risk capital charges to investments in fixed-income securities, with lower risk charges being applied to securities in the highest NAIC rating categories, and higher risk charges being applied to investments in lower NAIC rating categories.

Insurance companies face similar requirements from private-sector rating agencies when they hire the rating agencies to assign a quality rating to the insurance company itself. Although rating agencies set slightly different requirements regarding company capital than do regulators, they use an approach consistent with those outlined in the Insurance Core Principles. To earn a quality rating from a rating agency, insurance companies must demonstrate that they set aside adequate capital, called risk capital or *capital at risk,* in view of credit risks in their investments, as well as risks in their liabilities. Rating agencies apply a sliding scale of risk charges to investments in fixed-income securities, with higher risk charges being applied to investments in riskier securities.

Credit Ratings and Coupon Rates

Coupon rates for bonds respond to changes in the issuer's credit ratings. As Figure 8.4 shows, whenever the credit rating of a bond issuer is upgraded, coupon rates on new bonds from that issuer generally decrease; whenever the credit rating of a bond issuer is downgraded, coupon rates on new bonds from that issuer generally increase.

Bond Markets

Whether in New York, London, Singapore, or Beijing, bonds can be initially placed privately or sold to the public in the primary market. Institutional investors, including life insurance companies and retirement plans, participate in many different bond markets. The market in which new issues of securities, including bonds, are sold to the public for the first time is known as the ***primary market***. The primary market includes public offerings and private placements. After the initial sale, all subsequent trading of that issue is done in the ***secondary market.***

Figure 8.4 Relationship between Issuer's Credit Rating and Bond Coupon Rates

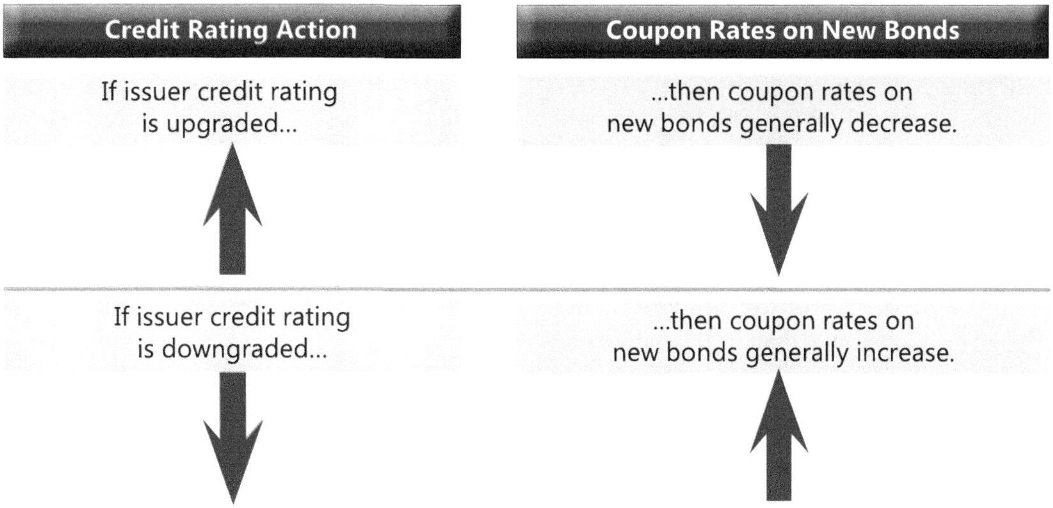

Credit Rating Action	Coupon Rates on New Bonds
If issuer credit rating is upgraded...	...then coupon rates on new bonds generally decrease.
If issuer credit rating is downgraded...	...then coupon rates on new bonds generally increase.

Primary Market for Bonds

The primary market for bonds is the market in which a bond issuer sells newly issued bonds to investors. The primary bond market includes public bond offerings and private placements of bonds. The U.S. Treasury issues bonds and sells them at regularly scheduled public auctions.

Most other public bond issues require the services of an investment bank. Investment banks provide two broad types of services to public bond issuers: underwriting or best efforts.

- An investment bank *underwrites* a bond issue by buying the bonds from the issuer at a specified price, and then selling the bonds to the public at a somewhat higher price.

- An investment bank sells a bond issue on a ***best efforts basis*** by undertaking to sell the issue on behalf of the issuer on the best terms obtainable, in which case the investment bank does not first purchase the bonds from the issuer.

Private Placement Bonds

Bonds that are not publicly issued are known as private placement bonds. Private placement bonds are initially sold in a direct transaction between the bond issuer and the bond purchaser. Private placement bonds make up a significant percentage of the assets in the portfolios of insurance companies and other institutional investors.

Unlike the terms of publicly traded bonds, the terms of a private placement bond can be negotiated between the bond issuer and the purchaser and can also be renegotiated over time, although renegotiations rarely occur. Private placement bonds can include negotiated covenants, which tend to place greater restrictions on issuers than do covenants in publicly offered bonds.[6]

Benefits of Private Placements to Issuers

Private placement bonds offer the following benefits to issuers:

- Lower transaction costs because of less extensive regulatory filings, lower marketing expenses, and lower printing expenses.

- The potential for immediate funding because private placement issues are often conducted quickly between highly sophisticated investors.

- Efficient and quick renegotiations of terms when necessary because renegotiations are conducted between sophisticated investors.

- Greater diversification of issuers because more and different issuers are available than in the public market.

Benefits of Private Placements to Investors

Private placement bonds offer the following benefits to institutional investors:

- Higher returns than for comparable public bonds, reflecting the restricted marketability of private placement bonds.

- Better risk control because stronger covenants protecting the investor and mitigating risks can be included during negotiations. *Make-whole provisions* are call provisions that require the issuer to pay the bondholder a call price derived from a previously agreed-upon formula should the issuer decide to call the bond. The formula takes into account the value of the remaining coupon payments that the bondholder will not receive after the call. If market interest rates have declined since the bond was issued, the call price can be substantially higher than the bond's par value.

Example: Protection for Private Placement Bond Investors

A private placement covenant could restrict the bond issuer from issuing other debt that might put the investment at risk. If the bond issuer violated the covenant, it would be in default, and would be required to pay bondholders the entire principal plus a make-whole premium.

Operational Controls for Private Placement Bond Investments

Life insurance companies and other institutional investors establish specific operational controls for monitoring and controlling private placement bonds in their portfolios. In particular, one important control objective is to monitor and control for the credit quality of these bonds. Investors perform extensive credit analysis on private placement bond issuers. Without public rating agencies to provide supporting information, investors must exercise additional diligence, including site visits, management conferences, and requiring the disclosure of material nonpublic information.

Institutional investors use the following types of operational controls to manage their holdings of private placement bonds. To the extent possible, companies automate such operational controls.

■ As a basic check of appropriate asset allocation, companies calculate the percentage of private placement bonds in the total bond portfolio and compare the result to the authorized maximum percentage of such bonds.

■ Companies also must establish appropriate requirements to ensure the initial and ongoing creditworthiness of private placement bond issuers. In this regard, issuers must initially meet a company's minimum performance standards for bond issuers. In addition, the company must regularly monitor the issuers' adherence to any bond covenants.

■ Companies must perform credit analysis of private placement bonds to uncover any evidence of deteriorating investment quality, and an authorized investment officer must regularly review the quality of all private placement bonds. The investment officer must regularly report the findings from this review to the company's investment committee.

■ Companies must establish systems to ensure that they routinely submit private placement bond information to appropriate regulatory authorities, and also must set controls to ensure that such regulatory filings are current.[7]

Secondary Markets for Bonds

The *secondary market* for previously issued bonds is conducted primarily in over-the-counter (OTC) markets, in which institutional investors typically communicate electronically, including over the telephone, to negotiate trades. In Canada, institutional investors purchase a substantial share of Canadian government bonds in the secondary market. Bonds can also be traded in organized bond exchanges, such as the New York Stock Exchange Bond Platform.

After insurance companies purchase bonds for the general account, they typically hold the bonds to maturity. For separate accounts, companies do not necessarily hold bonds to maturity. Instead, they trade these bonds to take advantage of market opportunities and adjust asset allocations.

Global Bond Markets

Large multinational corporations may issue debt securities in several currencies and several global financial markets. For a variety of reasons, large multinational corporations tend to issue bonds in the United States, the United Kingdom, Europe, Canada, Japan, Australia, and China. To better understand these types of transactions, we must distinguish between domestic bonds and international bonds.

Domestic Bonds

Domestic generally refers to a home base. For any given country, the domestic financial market is the financial market in the home country, and the domestic currency is the home country's currency. An entity is said to be *domiciled* in its home country.

For any given country, a ***domestic bond*** is a bond issued by that country or an entity domiciled in that country, denominated in that country's domestic currency, and traded in that country's domestic financial markets.

Example: Domestic Bonds

The Coca-Cola Company is a large multinational corporation incorporated in the United States. Bonds issued by Coca-Cola that are denominated in U.S. dollars and sold through U.S. bond markets are domestic bonds from the perspective of U.S. investors.

International Bonds

International bonds are bonds issued by any entity other than a domestic entity. International bonds include foreign bonds, Yankee bonds, and Eurobonds.

For any given country, *foreign* refers to people, corporations, currencies, markets, and financial instruments that come from outside that country. ***Foreign bonds*** are bonds issued by an entity domiciled in one country for trading in another specific country's bond market. Foreign bonds are denominated in the currency of the country where they will trade.

Example: Foreign Bond

BMW is a large multinational corporation incorporated in Germany. Bonds issued by BMW in Germany that are denominated in U.S. dollars and sold through U.S. bond markets would be considered foreign bonds from the perspective of U.S. investors.

One of the largest categories of foreign bonds is the Yankee bond. A ***Yankee bond*** is a bond denominated in U.S. dollars that is issued in the United States by a foreign entity but is subject to U.S. regulation.

Example: Yankee Bond

A Japanese corporation issues a Yankee bond in the United States that is denominated in U.S. dollars and will trade in the United States.

A ***eurobond*** is a bond issued in a currency other than the currency of the country in which it was issued. Eurobonds are typically underwritten by an international syndicate of investment bankers and are named after the currency in which they are denominated. So, *eurodollar bonds* are denominated in U.S. dollars, and *euroyen bonds* are denominated in Japanese yen.

Example: Eurobond

A U.S. corporation issued a euroyen bond in Europe, where the bond is denominated in Japanese yen.

Regulations generally limit the amount of international bonds that insurance companies and other financial institutions can own, with more specific limits on the amount an insurance company can hold in the general account. For example, in the United States, investment in bonds issued by foreign entities is limited to about 20 percent of total assets.

Quoting Corporate Bond Prices

For purposes of corporate bond trading, institutional investors quote corporate bond yields in terms of a yield spread over the yield on a comparable U.S. Treasury bond. A *yield spread* is the difference in yields between two debt instruments. In this context, a yield spread usually is quoted in basis points. A *basis point (bp)* is one-hundredth of a percent, or 0.01 percent, or 0.0001. Thus, 100 basis points equal 1 percent. Half a percent is equal to 50 bps, and one and a half percent is equal to 150 bps. If a yield decreases from 4.5 percent to 4 percent, it has decreased 50 bps. Figure 8.5 illustrates the interpretation of basis points.

Figure 8.5 Basis Points

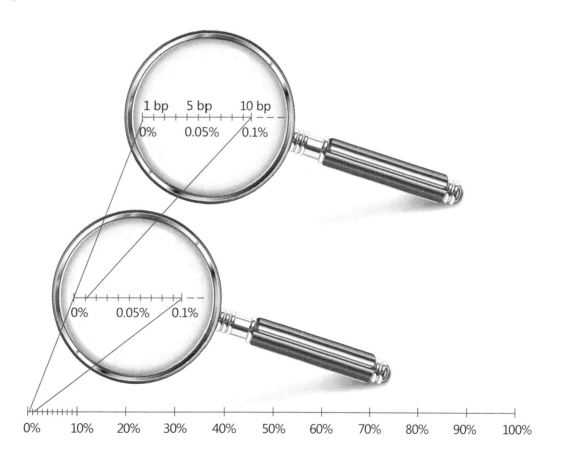

More specifically, a yield spread of 120 basis points over the yield on a given U.S. Treasury security, symbolized as T, is expressed in a quoted yield as follows:

$$T + 120$$

Example: Bond Yield Quoted as a Yield Spread

Stan, a bond trader, obtained a bond yield quote for a Creosote Corporation bond as follows:

$$T + 150$$

Stan knows that Treasury securities comparable in duration to this Creosote Corporation bond are yielding 4.5 percent. Thus, the Creosote Corporation bond is offered at a yield equal to

$$4.5\% + 150 \text{ bps} = 4.5\% + 1.5\% = 6\%$$

A corporate bond with a similar coupon rate and duration often yields 100 bps more than a comparable Treasury bond. This difference is often due to the higher risk and lower credit quality of the corporate bond.

Institutional investors choose bonds based on the relative risks and returns of the bonds, and a comparison between the yield spread and the required return for each bond.

To purchase a corporate bond, institutional bond traders must know that the quoted yield on the corporate bond exceeds the institution's required return and thus provides adequate compensation for the risks inherent in the bond investment. A required return on an investment summarizes the risks inherent in that investment. Institutional investors typically compare the sum of the yield on a comparable Treasury security plus the quoted basis points to the portfolio manager's required return for an investment. If the sum of the rate on a Treasury security and the quoted yield spread equals or exceeds the required return, the bond purchase is acceptable in terms of risk.

Example: Comparing Quotes of Corporate Bonds

Stan has yield quotes for two generally comparable corporate bonds:

10-Year Corporate Bonds

Issuer	Quoted Yields
Sailaway	T + 160
Havisham	T + 200

Havisham has the higher quoted yield. Sailaway has the lower quoted yield. The spread between these quoted yields is 40 basis points. This spread indicates that the Sailaway bond, as the one with the lower quoted yield—is less risky than the Havisham bond.

So, market conditions indicate that the Sailaway bond is less risky than the Havisham bond. Because of the difference in risk levels, Stan must apply different required returns for the two bonds.

continued...

> *... continued*
>
> To determine which bond is the better relative value, Stan then must determine which bond offers a greater yield spread when he compares the bond yield quotes to his required returns. Stan would likely choose the bond with the larger quoted yield—in this case, the Havisham bond.

Market prices for bonds are notably responsive to movements in market interest rates as well as changes in the issuers' credit ratings. As you can see in Figure 8.6, whenever market interest rates go up, prices of existing bonds generally decrease; whenever market interest rates decrease, prices of existing bonds generally increase. Further, as Figure 8.6 illustrates, for outstanding bonds of a corporate issuer, whenever the bond issuer's credit rating is downgraded, the market prices of the corporation's outstanding bonds generally decrease. Similarly, whenever a corporate bond issuer's credit rating is upgraded, the market prices of the issuer's outstanding bonds generally increase.

Institutional Bond Purchase Process

Institutional bond traders typically purchase publicly traded corporate bonds in the secondary market either through bond brokers or directly from other institutional traders by means of electronic trading platforms such as the Bloomberg Professional data service provided by Bloomberg L.P., one of the world's largest mass media companies. Institutional traders use Bloomberg Professional and other trading platforms to research available market pricing, make bids, and conclude purchase transactions with other institutional traders.

On the other hand, the institutional investor purchase process for a private placement bond can differ considerably from one transaction to another.

For proper risk management at the functional level of the organization, the bond purchase process in an institution must apply suitable operational controls. These controls are automated to the extent possible.

- To ensure proper authorization of expenditures, the company maintains up-to-date lists of authorized approvers of transactions and documents the monetary limits of authorization for each approver. Such lists are reviewed regularly by the most senior management in the investment function.

- To support auditing, the company documents all transaction approvals.

- To achieve appropriate segregation of duties, the investments front office communicates bond trades to the operations department for record keeping. Eventually, when the operations department receives account statements from external service providers such as banks, settlement agents, and custodians, the company's operations staff reconciles the external statements with operations departmental records as well as those in the investment department.

Figure 8.6 How Market Interest Rates and Credit Rating Actions Affect Prices of Existing Bonds

Inverse Relationship between Market Interest Rates and Prices of Existing Bonds

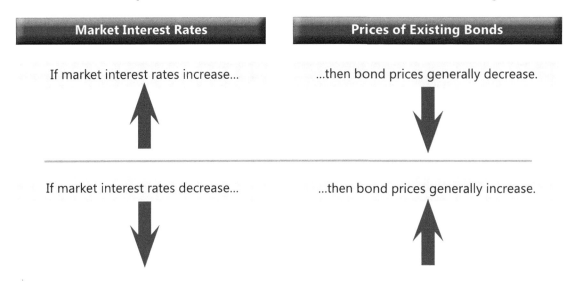

Direct Relationship between Issuer Credit Rating and Prices of Existing Bonds

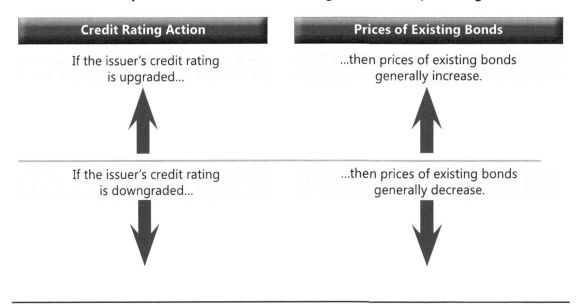

Bond Investment Strategies

Institutional investors employ a variety of useful bond strategies. Passive portfolio management strategies usually are well suited for bond portfolios. Most insurance companies follow a "buy-and-hold strategy" for their bonds, under which they hold all bonds purchased until maturity. So long as bond issuers don't default, insurers know the rate of return they will receive from their bond investments over a given investment period, regardless of market interest rate movements. In effect, by adopting a buy-and-hold strategy, investors can immunize bond portfolios from interest rate risk. Such a strategy is referred to as an *immunization strategy.*

Another passive investment strategy that is a bit more involved than a buy-and-hold strategy is a *laddered strategy,* under which an investor purchases approximately equal amounts of bonds in a series of maturity dates within a given range. The purpose of a laddered strategy is to decrease liquidity risk and interest rate risk. A long-term bond subjects an investor to liquidity risk because, as long as it holds the bond, the investor cannot receive any portion of the principal during the bond's term. In addition, if market interest rates rise during a fixed-coupon bond's term, the investor does not receive a higher coupon rate. However, if the investor buys a series of bonds with differing maturity dates over several years, the investor has greater liquidity and can reinvest at current market interest rates the proceeds of each series of bonds as it matures.

Example: Laddered Bond Portfolio

An insurance company has $100 million to invest. Instead of purchasing $100 million of 10-year bonds, the insurer invests $10 million in bonds maturing each year for the next 10 years, as follows:

$10 million in 1-year bonds
$10 million in 2-year bonds
$10 million in 3-year bonds
$10 million in 4-year bonds
$10 million in 5-year bonds
$10 million in 6-year bonds
$10 million in 7-year bonds
$10 million in 8-year bonds
$10 million in 9-year bonds
$10 million in 10-year bonds

At the end of the first year, the first $10 million of bonds the company purchased will mature, and the company will reinvest the principal it receives by purchasing $10 million in 10-year bonds. Similarly, the company will reinvest each subsequent $10 million of principal it receives in 10-year bonds. Thus, at any time, the company's portfolio will consist of $10 million of bonds maturing in each of the subsequent 10 years.

Another passive bond investment strategy is a *barbell strategy,* under which an investor holds both short-term and long-term bonds, but no intermediate-term bonds. The strategy gets its name from the shape that appears when the bond investments are graphed on a timeline. An investor obtains liquidity from the portfolio's short-term bonds and the potential for higher returns should interest rates rise. However, locking in a minimum interest rate on the long-term bonds minimizes the portfolio's overall interest rate risk.

Securitization and Structured Securities

Securitization is a technique for repackaging forms of credit risk, interest rate risk, and real estate risk in existing investments into a new form of marketable securities. The resulting **structured securities**—sometimes known as *securitizations*, *structured debt*, or *structured debt securities*—promise investors a stream of payments. The credit risk in the securities is backed by collateral.

To securitize debt, a loan originator typically creates a **special purpose entity (SPE)**, also called a *special purpose vehicle*, which is a business organization that is formed for a specific purpose—in this case, debt securitization—and usually for a limited time. A securitization SPE usually is organized in the form of a trust managed by a trustee. We describe other types of SPEs in Chapter 9.

The SPE buys a package of loans to be securitized. The SPE next undertakes actions to enhance the credit of the securities it intends to issue. Then the SPE issues and sells structured securities representing an ownership interest in the packaged loans. The purchasers of these securities include various institutions.

For a fee, the loan originator—or another third party—collects incoming payments on the original loans and distributes the scheduled payouts to the investors in the structured securities. This transaction process involves complex legal and accounting requirements that are beyond the scope of this text. An SPE is unlikely to suffer bankruptcy.

Figure 8.7 illustrates a securitization transaction.

Figure 8.7 A Basic Securitization Transaction

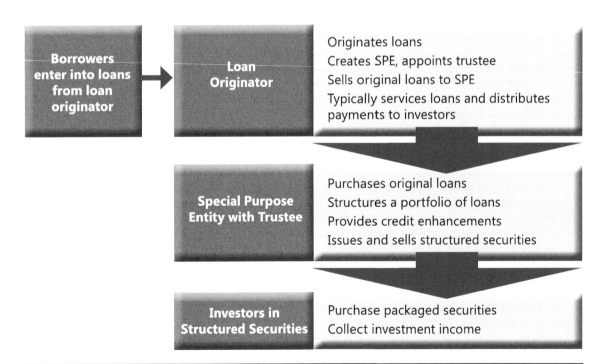

As part of the credit enhancement process for creating structured securities, the SPE typically divides the securities into several ownership classes known as *tranches*, or sometimes known as *tiers*. (*Tranche* is the French word for slice.) Each tranche of a particular debt securitization represents a distinct packaging of investment traits, such as cash flow patterns, credit quality, investment risks, priority given to owners, and others.

Although other configurations are possible, most securitized debt has the following four tranches, presented in order from most senior to least senior.

- The *AAA debt tranche*, said "triple-A debt tranche," is the most senior tranche in that, of all tranches in a given structure, it is the most creditworthy, the first to collect payments from borrowers, and the first to make payments to investors. In view of the senior position of holders of these securities, the interest rate on the securities tends to be lower than on lower tranche securities.

- The *AA debt tranche*, said "double-A debt tranche," is the second most senior tranche. It is second to collect payments from borrowers, and second to make payments to investors.

- The *A debt tranche*, said "single-A debt tranche"—also known as the *subordinated debt tranche*—is the third tranche, and it has the third and lowest priority of the three debt tranches. It is third to collect payments from borrowers, and third to make payments to investors. In view of the subordinated position of holders of these securities, the interest rate on this tranche tends to be higher than on the higher tranches.

- The *equity tranche* is the lowest tranche in a securitization, regardless of the total number of tranches in a given configuration. It has last priority for payment relative to other tranches.[8]

The senior AAA and AA tranches are typically sold to the public in the primary market for new securitizations. The subordinated tranches are typically sold as private placements.

The practice of establishing tranches—some having seniority, the others subordinated—enhances the credit quality of the senior tranche. Frequently, issuers of secured debt undertake credit enhancements to increase the credit rating of the security—as well as to increase its appeal to investors. The following arrangements by the SPE all serve to enhance the credit of structured securities:

- The SPE typically pays rating agencies to rate the top tranches, which are designed to earn high ratings. In turn, high ratings appeal to conservative investors.

- The SPE can design the structured securities so that the total of the face amounts of the underlying pool of loans is greater than the combined value of the new structured securities. This tactic, known as ***overcollateralization***, can protect investors against losses on the secured debt in the event that some borrowers default.

- The SPE can design the structured securities so that the total of the scheduled interest collections from the underlying pool of loans exceeds the total of the interest payment distributions promised to investors in the structured securities.

- Sometimes the SPE provides a *surety bond*—a type of insurance that, in certain circumstances, guarantees payments of interest and principal to the investors in the structured securities.

- Sometimes the SPE obtains a letter of credit from a bank to guarantee some portion of the payment to investors in the structured securities.

In the remainder of this section, we discuss asset-backed securities and collateralized loan obligations, which are secured by various loans other than mortgages on real estate. In Chapter 9, we discuss forms of structured securities involving mortgages.

Asset-Backed Securities

An *asset-backed security (ABS)* is a security backed by debt instruments other than real estate mortgages. Banks, finance companies, and other lenders created asset-backed securities as a way to convert packages of relatively illiquid loans, such as student loans, car loans, and credit card loans, into new structured securities having a liquid market. With an ABS, unlike with a bond, the issuer of the ABS is just an intermediary and the loan is from the bondholder to a borrower, such as a student, the purchaser of a car, or the user of a credit card. Types of loans packaged in ABSs include student loans, home equity loans, loans for manufactured housing, automobile loans, credit card debt, and equipment loans.[9]

As we discuss in Figure 8.8, ABSs may be structured in a number of ways, reflecting how payments on the original loans are allocated between principal and interest. Some of the loans backing structured securities may be *amortizing loans*, which means that each loan repayment reflects both principal and interest. Other loans, such as revolving credit, that back structured securities are *non-amortized loans*, which have repayments that can consist of just an interest payment. Usually, ABSs are payable at par, with no penalty, at any time.

Institutional investors can diversify their portfolios by holding securitized debt investments such as ABSs. In addition, ABSs provide benefits to loan originators and borrowers. Traditionally, when loans such as car loans were financed by banks or other financing companies, the loans remained on the originators' balance sheets. The loan originator had a steady stream of income from the loans, but accounting or regulatory constraints often limited the originator's ability to make additional loans. By bundling and selling these loans, the loan originator can remove these assets from the balance sheet, freeing up capital to make more loans available to borrowers at lower rates.

The market for ABSs is similar to those for other fixed-income securities in the United States. Most ABS trading is done in the secondary market. The issuer of an ABS in the United States must satisfy standard SEC registration and disclosure requirements and file periodic financial statements. Investment banks act as underwriters, and credit agencies rate the securities.

The risks to holders of ABSs are similar to those for holders of bonds, including credit risk, prepayment risk, and liquidity risk. The riskiness of an ABS depends on the creditworthiness of the underlying debt securities. Financial rating agencies publish ratings of ABSs based on creditworthiness, probability of default, and any credit enhancements.

Figure 8.8 Arrangements for Payment of Interest and Principal

With regard to arrangements for payments of interest and principal to various tranches in an SPE, an ABS can have a fully amortized structure, a controlled amortization structure, a bullet payment structure, or a sequential payment structure, as follows:

- **Fully amortized structure.** A fully amortized structured security returns principal over the life of the security. As borrowers on the original loans make more payments, a greater proportion of each payment represents a repayment of principal and less of interest. The maturity date of the structured security is the last possible date that the principal on the original loans may be repaid. However, because the borrowers can pay principal faster than scheduled, the actual maturity may be much shorter and, hence, prepayment risk may be significant. For example, structured securities backed by auto loans tend to have a fully amortized structure.

- **Controlled amortization structure.** A controlled amortization structure is an arrangement used in a structured security to provide investors with a relatively predictable repayment schedule, even if the underlying debt is non-amortizing, such as credit card debt. A structured security with a controlled amortization structure makes payments to investors in two phases, an initial period in which payments comprise only interest, and a final period in which payments to investors comprise both interest and principal.

- **Bullet payment structure.** An ABS with a soft or hard bullet payment structure is designed to return principal to investors in a single payment. With a soft bullet payment structure, the payment date is not guaranteed but is often on the expected maturity date, while a hard bullet payment structure guarantees principal repayment on a particular date.

- **Sequential payment structure.** Within a sequential payment structure, the holders of the most senior tranche receive all principal payments until the tranche is retired. Then holders of the second tranche begin to receive principal payments. This process continues sequentially until the holders of the last tranche are paid.[10]

Collateralized Loan Obligations

A *collateralized loan obligation (CLO)* is a structured security representing an interest in a pool of corporate debt such as commercial loans. As is true of most debt-related securitizations, CLOs are issued by special purpose entities, and the pool of secured debt is divided into multiple tranches.

Key Terms

Treasury bill	reorganization
Treasury note	administration
Treasury bond	primary market
Treasury Inflation-Protected Security (TIPS)	secondary market
	best efforts basis
municipal bond	domestic bond
general obligation bond	international bond
revenue bond	foreign bond
zero-coupon bond	Yankee bond
callable bond	eurobond
refunding	yield spread
sinking fund provision	structured security
mortgage bond	special purpose entity (SPE)
senior bond	overcollateralization
subordinated bond	asset-backed security (ABS)
mezzanine debt	amortizing loan
convertible bond	non-amortized loan
debt restructuring	collateralized loan obligation (CLO)

Endnotes

1. "Interest Rate Risk in 2012: With Low Rates Persisting, Insurance Companies Try to Muddle Through," Standard & Poor's Financial Services, 30 November 2011, http://www.standardandpoors.com/ratings/articles/en/us/?articleType=HTML&assetID=1245325868800 (21 June 2012).

2. Daniel A. Leimbach (Director of Research, Private Placements, USAA Investments), note to author, 26 August 2012.

3. Ivan Francis (Vice President, Bonds, Standard Life Investments, Inc.), note to author, 14 August 2012.

4. Patricia Wilson Fridley (Senior Advisor, Center for Financial Stability, LLC), note to author, 20 September 2012.

5. International Association of Insurance Supervisors, *Insurance Core Principles, Standards, Guidance and Assessment Methodology* (Basel: International Association of Insurance Supervisors, 2011), 221–255, http://www.iaisweb.org/db/content/1/13037.pdf (6 August 2012).

6. Simon Kwan and Willard T. Carleton, "Financial Contracting and the Choice between Private Placement and Publicly Offered Bonds," Working Paper 2004–20, Federal Reserve Bank of San Francisco, November 2004, http://www.frbsf.org/publications/economics/papers/2004/wp04-20bk.pdf (11 July 2012).

7. LOMA, "320. Private Placement Bonds," in *Business Risks and Controls Handbook* [Atlanta: LOMA (Life Office Management Association, Inc.), © 2001], 320-1–320-4. Used with permission; all rights reserved.

8. Fridley, telephone interview with author, 6 August 2012. Used with permission.

9. "US ABS Issuance and Outstanding," Securities Industry and Financial Markets Association, updated 25 September 2012, http://www.sifma.org/research/statistics.aspx (26 September 2012).

10. "About MBS/ABS: How Are ABS Structured?" Securities Industry and Financial Markets Association, http://www.investinginbonds.com/learnmore.asp?catid=11&subcatid=57&id=15 (11 July 2012).

Chapter 9

Investments Based in Real Estate

Objectives

After studying this chapter, you should be able to

9A Distinguish between residential, commercial, and agricultural real estate and identify property characteristics important for real estate investing

9B Describe five approaches for real estate appraisals, including market value appraisals, value-in-use appraisals, investment value appraisals, insurance value appraisals, and liquidation value appraisals

9C Classify and differentiate between types of commercial properties—including multifamily properties, office properties, hotel and resort properties, industrial properties, and retail properties—and identify types of technical services required for real estate investments

9D Describe the basic characteristics of a joint venture and a limited partnership for real estate investing

9E Differentiate between types of mortgages and describe various aspects of mortgage operations

9F Distinguish between an agency mortgage-backed security and a nonagency mortgage-backed security, and describe a collateralized mortgage obligation and a commercial mortgage-backed security

9G Identify the investment characteristics of a real estate investment trust (REIT) and distinguish between an equity REIT and a mortgage REIT

9H Identify different types of real estate market indexes

Outline

Residential, Commercial, and Agricultural Real Estate
- Important Characteristics of Real Estate
- Control Procedures for Income-Producing Properties

Real Estate Appraisals
- Market Value Appraisal
- Value-in-Use Appraisal
- Investment Value Appraisal
- Insurance Value Appraisal
- Liquidation Value Appraisal

Types of Commercial Properties
- Multifamily Properties
- Office Buildings
- Hotels and Resort Facilities
- Light Industrial Properties
- Retail Properties— Shopping Centers

Real Estate Technical Services

Real Estate Ownership
- Joint Ventures
- Limited Partnerships

Mortgages
- Residential Mortgages
- Commercial Mortgages
- Mortgage Operations
- Control Procedures for Mortgages

Mortgage Securities
- Residential Mortgage-Backed Securities
- Commercial Mortgage-Backed Securities

Real Estate Investment Trusts

Real Estate Market Indexes

Real estate can take a variety of roles in an investment portfolio.[1] Real estate can be acquired directly or through joint ventures, limited partnerships, or real estate investment trusts (REITs). In addition, investors can participate in the property markets through direct loans or mortgages to a real estate purchaser or by purchasing mortgage-backed securities. In this chapter, we begin by describing the characteristics of real estate. Then we describe several ways of investing in real estate.

Residential, Commercial, and Agricultural Real Estate

Real estate is generally classified as residential, commercial, or agricultural property, depending on its intended use.

- *Residential real estate* is a single- or multifamily property intended for use as a place of residence.

- *Commercial real estate* is property owned solely for the purpose of producing income. Commercial real estate includes such properties as

  - Multifamily residential properties, such as apartments

  - Office buildings

  - Hotel and resort properties

  - Industrial properties

  - Retail properties, such as shopping centers

■ *Agricultural real estate* is property intended for agricultural use or as undeveloped, open space. Undeveloped land is also known as *raw land*. Important agricultural uses for real estate are ranching, dairy farming, crop production, agribusiness, and timber production.

Important Characteristics of Real Estate

The value of real estate depends on many property characteristics, including location, size, management and maintenance, type of lease, and potential uses.

Location

Property value depends to a large degree on its location. For example, properties in thriving metropolitan areas are typically more valuable than properties in less desirable locations. For this reason, the real estate industry has consistent standards for describing real estate markets. In the United States, real estate markets are classified using the concept of *Metropolitan Statistical Areas*, as described by the federal Office of Management and Budget (OMB). The OMB defines Metropolitan Statistical Areas, Micropolitan Statistical Areas, and Core Based Statistical Areas.[2] The general concept of a *metropolitan area* is that of an urban core having a population of at least 50,000, together with adjacent communities that have a high degree of social and economic integration with that core. Metropolitan areas comprise one or more entire counties.[3] The Core Based Statistical Area is a term for both Metropolitan and Micropolitan Statistical Areas.

A property's location affects its liquidity. Some types of real estate are more liquid than others because of their location.

Example: Liquidity and Location

A secluded rural resort property will have fewer potential buyers than a commercial office space in a growing urban center. However, the resort's remote location and unique characteristics might allow the owner of such a property to sell it for a premium price.

The price of the commercial office space is likely limited by multiple similar commercial office spaces available in the area.

Size

Property size affects value. An apartment with only 15 units must be valued differently than a high-rise apartment building with hundreds of units. Residential and commercial property values are quoted by square footage. For example, a commercial building may be quoted as $100 per square foot.

Management and Maintenance

Investors sometimes directly manage, lease, and maintain real estate properties. In other cases, someone other than the investor performs the day-to-day property management. Proper management and maintenance are required to maintain the value of a property.

Property Leases

Leases on commercial properties take a number of forms and affect the income the property produces, and thus the value of the property. The lease agreement between the lessor/owner and the lessee/tenant specifies the amount the tenant agrees to pay for the use of the property. For investors, the most beneficial leases require tenants to pay a stated rent plus other expenses. Leases that require tenants to bear some responsibility for expenses are called **net leases**. Figure 9.1 describes different types of net leases.

Property Improvements and Uses

Improvements on a property and activities on the property can influence its marketability. A property might have one value as a home and another value if converted to retail or office space. Converting a property from its past use to a new use is likely to change the property's value.

Control Procedures for Income-Producing Properties

Institutional investors with large real estate holdings may have several internal departments for property management, or may hire external parties to perform the administrative duties. Here, we present control procedures for an arrangement in which an institutional investor hires an external property management company.

Control procedures for this situation are designed to ensure that the property is properly safeguarded, rental income payments are promptly and accurately applied, expenditures are legitimate, the property manager follows approved procedures, the flow of funds to the investor is timely and correct, and property upkeep is adequate.

Figure 9.1 Net Leases

	In addition to rent, tenant required to pay		
	Property Taxes	**Building Insurance**	**Repairs and Maintenance**
Single-Net Lease	✓		
Double-Net Lease	✓	✓	
Triple-Net Lease*	✓	✓	✓

*A variation on a triple-net lease is a bondable lease, which requires tenants to pay a stated rent plus every cost possibly associated with the property, including the cost of rebuilding after a fire or other casualty regardless of the insurance proceeds. Tenants may not terminate a bondable lease.[4]

The investor and the property management company usually establish a system for paying management and maintenance expenses and depositing the income generated by a property.

- In most instances, the property manager pays the maintenance expenses from monthly rental income collected, and remits the remainder to the investor.

- Otherwise, at the beginning of each month, the institutional investor sends the property manager an allowance for expenses. In such a case, all income from the property is deposited into the institutional investor's remittance account.

Institutional investors conduct audits that examine the property management company's financial records and compare them to the institution's records. Auditors review operating procedures to ensure that controls are adequate controls and that the property manager has complied with the property management agreement. Auditors also examine the physical condition of a property.

Real Estate Appraisals

In real estate, an *appraisal* is an estimate of a property's value as of a given date, determined by a qualified professional appraiser. A real estate appraisal focuses on a particular standard of value, and appraisers follow professional standards in developing property appraisals suited to each standard of value. The value may be based on replacement cost, the sales of comparable properties, or the property's ability to produce income. Industry professionals can learn real estate appraisal methods through education programs, such as the one sponsored by the Mortgage Appraisal Institute (MAI).

Approaches for establishing the appraised value of real estate—sometimes called a *valuation basis* or an *appraisal basis*—include market value appraisals, value-in-use appraisals, investment value appraisals, insurance value appraisals, and liquidation value appraisals.

Market Value Appraisal

A *market value appraisal* is an appraiser's estimate of the price a buyer would be willing to pay for a property in current market conditions. Real estate appraisers employ three main methods to estimate the market value of a property.

- The *comparables method* attempts to estimate the market value of property by reference to recent selling prices for properties with similar characteristics. Typically, the appraiser looks at similar properties that were sold within the last year and adjusts the prices of those properties for any difference in the age, features, and condition of buildings; any change in the market conditions; and location. Typically, an appraiser estimates market value using the comparables method.

- The *cost method* involves estimating the market value of property by determining how much it would cost to reproduce it. This method considers the cost of the land and any buildings or improvements, adjusting for depreciation.

- The *income capitalization method* involves estimating the value of commercial real estate by first calculating net operating income to determine the capitalization rate (cap rate). The cap rate is then compared to the cap rate for comparable properties.

Example: Calculating Income Capitalization

Net operating income (NOI) = [Potential gross rental income] – [Operating expenses, Maintenance expenses, Insurance expenses, Collections expenses, Property taxes, Loss from vacancies, and Loss from defaults]

$$\text{Cap rate} = \frac{\text{Annual NOI}}{\text{Property value}}$$

When considering a particular commercial property, investors often look at cap rates for comparable property and, using NOI from a particular property, determine the value of the commercial property they're considering.

Note that the cap rate will vary directly with NOI. When the property is generating high income, the cap rate increases; on the other hand, the cap rate varies inversely with the value or price of the property. When the value of the property falls, the cap rate increases.

Value-in-Use Appraisal

A *value-in-use appraisal*, also known as a *use value appraisal*, refers to an appraiser's estimate of the property value to a particular user. Sometimes a property is dedicated to a particular use that is less than the property's highest and best use. Or sometimes a property has special benefits, such as grandfathered zoning rights. In such cases, a value-in-use appraisal can be lower or higher than a market value appraisal for the same property. A property's **value in use** is the discounted value of a cash flow or other benefits that an asset generates for a specific owner under a specific use.

Investment Value Appraisal

An *investment value appraisal* is an appraiser's estimate of the value of the property to a particular investor, with the property valued at its highest and best use. Similar to a value-in-use appraisal, an investment value appraisal is also specific to a given investor. However, unlike a value-in-use appraisal, the specific investor under an investment value appraisal is making the best use of the property. An appraiser typically would estimate investment value using the income capitalization method. An investment value appraisal tends to be higher than a market value appraisal.

Insurance Value Appraisal

An *insurance value appraisal*, also known as a *replacement value appraisal*, is the amount a property insurance company would potentially cover under property insurance if all buildings and fixtures on the property were destroyed. Insurance value of real estate does not include the value of the land. Thus, an insurance value appraisal of a given property is typically lower than a market value appraisal, an investment value appraisal, or a value-in-use appraisal.

Liquidation Value Appraisal

A *liquidation value appraisal* is an appraiser's estimate of the price that a property would bring if the owners were forced to sell it quickly, under distressed circumstances. A liquidation value appraisal for a given property is typically lower than a market value appraisal or an investment value appraisal.

Types of Commercial Properties

Institutional investors tend to focus their expertise on a particular sector of commercial property.[5] Real estate investors traditionally classify properties into three classes on the basis of risk characteristics: core properties, value-added properties, and opportunistic properties.

- *Core properties* comprise multifamily properties, office buildings, light industrial properties, and retail properties. Core properties are the ones that institutional investors are most likely to hold for long periods of time to take advantage of the stable lease and rental cash flows that they provide to an investment portfolio. Core properties are the most liquid in that they can be sold more easily than other types of commercial property.

- *Value-added properties* either require specialty management in order to achieve full income potential or may require significant repositioning, renovation, or redevelopment. Value-added real estate investing typically focuses on potential for both income and capital appreciation. Hotels are a type of commercial property that often qualifies as a value-added property.

- *Opportunistic properties* offer an investor significant potential for capital appreciation, and potentially require extensive development over an extended time period. Such properties have a high-risk, high-return investment profile.

Multifamily Properties

The demand for apartment housing tends to increase with population growth and population mobility. Because renting an apartment may be a substitute for home ownership, rents and demand for apartments vary directly with the cost of homeownership. In other words, all other factors being equal, as the cost of home ownership increases, rent levels and demand for apartments increase; conversely, as the cost of home ownership decreases, rent levels and demand for apartment rentals decrease.

Example: Apartment Housing

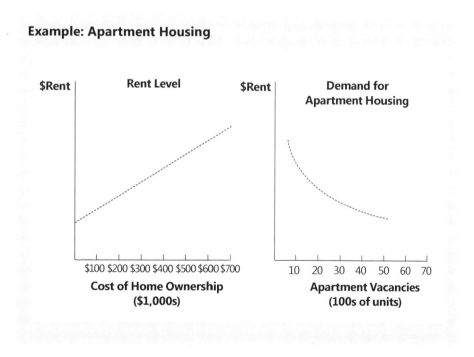

Demand for apartments is subject to boom-and-bust cycles depending on the supply of apartment buildings in an area. In general, apartment buildings cannot be developed quickly. Developers often find it difficult to obtain the approval of local governments and local residents, who may believe that an apartment building will overwhelm municipal services, especially schools, and possibly diminish home prices.

A common indicator of the demand for apartments is the vacancy rate, which measures the percentage of property that is unoccupied and not producing income. The value of an apartment building is directly related to the net cash inflows associated with the property's rental income. As a rule, when vacancy rates exceed 20 percent, an excess supply of apartments exists. In excess supply conditions, rents typically begin to decline. Vacancy rates lower than 5 percent indicate excess demand. In such situations, rents typically rise.

Apartment properties are classified as garden, midrise, and high-rise apartments: garden apartment properties are typically low-level buildings that have direct access to a yard or garden through balconies or patio areas; mid-rise apartment properties have from four to six levels; high-rise apartment properties have more than six levels.

Office Buildings

Office buildings appeal to tenants primarily on the basis of location. Thus, the ability of an office building to provide stable rental income depends heavily on its location in prime real estate markets. However, the characteristics and amenities of the building are also important in generating lease income. The Building Owners and Managers Association International (BOMA; www.boma.org) identifies three classes of buildings, shown in Figure 9.2, using Metropolitan Base Definitions.[6]

The demand for office buildings is cyclical and depends upon the national and regional business cycle, the local office building cycle, changes in geographical preferences, and changes in industrial work. The low point of the demand cycle for office buildings provides an opportunity for investors to either develop an office building or buy one that is already built, but in financial trouble. In an economic recovery or growth period, demand for office space is high. When demand is high, office building vacancy rates fall and rents rise. In a financial recovery phase of the business cycle, Class A buildings tend to fill up first, then Class B buildings, and finally Class C buildings. In this phase, developing new office space becomes profitable. Typically, rents continue to rise during the period between the decision to build and when the building becomes available for occupancy. However, as new buildings become available to tenants, the pressure on rents will ease, and vacancy rates will rise again. In an economic slowdown, office building vacancy rates rise, and rents fall.

Hotels and Resort Facilities

Hotels and resort facilities are the main property types in the lodging industry. Although hotels and resort facilities generate revenues mainly from daily room rentals, they frequently also have restaurant, meeting, and convention facilities, which can be leased to third parties, and generate lease income to the hotel or resort owner. The lodging industry is sensitive to economic downturns. During an economic downturn, hotels and resorts may be converted to apartments, condominiums, or time shares.

Figure 9.2 Metropolitan Base Definitions of Building Classes

		Class A Buildings	Class B Buildings	Class C Buildings
	**Building Characteristics**	• High-quality standard finishes • State-of-the-art systems • Exceptional accessibility • A definite market presence	• Fair to good finishes for the area • Adequate systems	• Functional space
	**Target Tenants**	Premier office tenants who will pay rents above average for the area	A wide range of tenants who will pay rents that are average for the area	Tenants who will accept fewer amenities to pay below average rents for the area

A standard measure of the success of investments in the lodging industry is *revenue per available room*, abbreviated as *RevPAR*. RevPAR is determined by two component factors, average occupancy rate and average daily room rate.

■ *Average occupancy rate (AOR)* is the percentage of days a room is occupied during a specified period.

■ *Average daily rate (ADR)* for a room is the average of rates charged for a room during a specified period.

We calculate the revenue per available room (RevPAR) as follows:

$$\text{Revenue per Available Room} = $$
$$\text{RevPAR} = \text{AOR} \times \text{ADR}$$

Total room revenue for a hotel per period is RevPAR multiplied by the number of days in that period multiplied by the number of rooms. For a given property over a given period,

Total room revenue = RevPAR × number of days × number of rooms

Example: RevPAR and Total Room Revenue

The SleepTight Hotel has an average occupancy rate of 82 percent, an average daily rate of $112, and 1,000 rooms.

RevPAR = .82 × $112 =$91.84
Total room revenue = $91.84 × 365 × 1,000 = $33,521,600

Investment-value appraisals for hotels are often set at between two and four times the total room revenue per year, with potential adjustments depending on any nonroom revenue associated with the property, the potential for growth in AOR and ADR, and the physical condition of the property.

Light Industrial Properties

Light industrial properties are typically buildings with very high ceilings throughout, a small office configuration, and ample loading bays for trucks. Light industrial buildings are most often used for assembly, freight forwarding, shipping, and warehousing.[7] Light industrial property occasionally houses some light manufacturing if such activities do not require reconfiguring the space. Reconfiguring a building space is both costly and time consuming, and if the tenant for whom the space was configured leaves, the owner may find it difficult to find another tenant who wishes to occupy the same space configuration.

In valuing light industrial properties, investors typically consider whether the property has appropriate zoning permits and easy highway access, is close to airports or seaports, and whether it satisfies environmental protection regulations.

Retail Properties—Shopping Centers

Retail properties—typically shopping centers—include a variety of types of stores. A *shopping center* is a group of retail and other commercial establishments, with on-site parking, that is planned, developed, owned, and managed as a single property. A shopping center is typically owned by an investor and managed by a property management company. The terms of a tenant's lease in a shopping center often include details such as hours of operation and signage requirements. Shopping center rental agreements frequently require tenants to pay a base rent plus a fixed percentage of gross sales, usually ranging from 2 percent to 8 percent.

Successful shopping centers retain successful tenants. An ***anchor tenant*** is a major department store or store from a major retail chain that will attract customers to the shopping center. A successful anchor tenant can offer benefits to other tenants, and the loss of an anchor tenant can negatively impact other tenants. Shopping center tenants share common resources, such as a parking lot, security, and marketing, as well as sharing a market segment of customers.

Shopping centers vary greatly in size and come in a variety of types: strip shopping centers, neighborhood shopping centers, community shopping centers, inner-city shopping centers, and regional or superregional shopping centers. A neighborhood shopping center can be one of the safest property types to include in a real estate portfolio. Figure 9.3 identifies five basic types of shopping centers.

Real Estate Technical Services

Support for investments based in real estate requires technical services that an institutional investor may obtain from internal resources or hire from external resources.

■ **Economic research.** An economic research staff develops macroeconomic and microeconomic demand and supply analysis for various geographic markets and all major property types. This unit conducts both macroeconomic research and local area research to help forecast any trends that may influence investment decisions.

■ **Appraisal services.** Staff appraisers independently review external appraisals and also participate in tax appeals, real estate consulting, litigation, and hiring external appraisers.

■ **Engineering services.** Engineers advise the investment staff on engineering issues related to commercial properties, including physical design, construction, environmental impact, seismic risk, risk management, and operations. Specialized engineering consultants provide technical expertise in local markets.

Figure 9.3 Basic Types of Shopping Centers

• A *strip shopping center* houses 3 to 10 small independent stores clustered on a heavily traveled road. The independent stores may be convenience stores, fast-food restaurants, dry cleaners, and specialty stores.

• A *neighborhood shopping center* houses 5 to 10 small independent stores similar to those in strip shopping centers and is typically anchored by a supermarket. Such centers are usually located close to apartment complexes and businesses with many employees.

• A *community shopping center* houses a major anchor tenant and from 5 to 25 small stores, and is typically located at a major intersection along a heavily traveled road. The anchor tenant is likely a discount department store, drugstore, or grocery supermarket.

• An *inner-city shopping center* is located on the street-level floor or lowest floors of a large building in a city, and serves local residents as well as visitors to the city.

• A *regional or superregional shopping center* houses a large concentration of retailers—perhaps 25 to 50 stores, and is located near major interstate highways. Such shopping centers typically include more than one anchor tenant.[8]

- **Legal services unit.** Lawyers and legal assistants on staff provide support throughout all phases of the real estate investment process. When needed, outside counsel provides support for in-house counsel.

- **Information technology (IT) services.** A unit of real estate IT professionals sets up hardware and software, develops customized software, consults, provides educational support, and administers the local area network file servers, PCs, and workstations. This group develops proprietary or acquires third-party software applications, such as a real estate and mortgage loan system, a sophisticated discounted cash flow model, quality-rating models, loan loss forecast models, and portfolio-monitoring systems. Figure 9.4 illustrates a dashboard designed for displaying the status of commercial real estate investments.

- **Accounting and financial reporting.** An accounting unit specializing in real estate provides portfolio performance reports. These reports include budgeting, variance analysis, financial projections, valuation, and performance measurement in various financial reporting systems.

Figure 9.4 Commercial Real Estate Dashboard

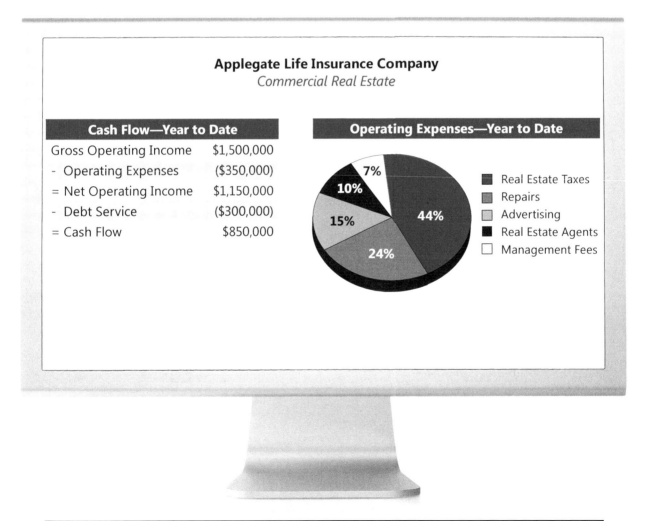

Applegate Life Insurance Company
Commercial Real Estate

Cash Flow—Year to Date	
Gross Operating Income	$1,500,000
- Operating Expenses	($350,000)
= Net Operating Income	$1,150,000
- Debt Service	($300,000)
= Cash Flow	$850,000

Operating Expenses—Year to Date

7%, 10%, 15%, 24%, 44%

- Real Estate Taxes
- Repairs
- Advertising
- Real Estate Agents
- Management Fees

Real Estate Ownership

Real estate ownership provides several potential benefits to an institution's investment portfolio. Real estate ownership can provide a return in the form of rental income and the opportunity for appreciation in the property's value. The risk-adjusted returns for real estate over the past 20 years compare very well to stocks and bonds. Also, commercial real estate investments typically outperform other investments when inflation is rising. However, the income stream can be unpredictable because of the possibility of vacancies. If an economic downturn occurs, property valuations decrease and vacancies increase, and the negative impact on an investment portfolio's returns can be significant. In addition, real estate property investments are not as liquid as most other types of investments. Commercial properties also must be managed effectively to produce maximum benefits for the investor.

Recall from Chapter 8 that special purpose entities (SPEs) have a role in debt securitization. SPEs also have a role in real estate investing. Two commonly used types of SPEs are joint ventures and limited partnerships. Smaller institutional investors often use joint ventures or limited partnerships for participation in sizeable real estate investments.

Joint Ventures

A *joint venture* is a legal agreement between two otherwise independent businesses that agree to undertake a specific project together for a specified time period. Commercial properties often involve a joint venture between several partners. Typically, one or more partners own and develop the property, and one or more other partners, such as an institutional investor, supply most or all of the funds necessary for the project. Other partners may provide specialized services such as property management, architectural services, or legal services. Typically, the members of the joint venture intend to sell the property at the conclusion of the development phase of the project.

The legal documents that establish the joint venture describe its legal form, the specific purpose for forming it, the ownership interest of each joint venture member, the contributions of each member, the manner of profit distribution, the share of profits to be distributed to each member, the liability of each member, and the manner of terminating the joint venture.

Example: Real Estate Joint Venture

The Kennington Foundation entered into a real estate joint venture with Fast Moving Developers. Under the joint venture agreement, Fast Moving will build a shopping center on vacant land it owns. Kennington will supply 90 percent of the funds for the project. Fast Moving will supply the remaining 10 percent of the funds and will manage the construction of the shopping center. After the shopping center is complete, Kennington and Fast Moving will sell the property. After expenses, Kennington and Fast Moving will each receive 50 percent of the profits.

Limited Partnerships

A *limited partnership* is a form of business organization consisting of one or more general partners who manage and control a business and are legally liable for all the debts and obligations of the business, and one or more limited partners who are liable only to the extent of the amount of money invested in the business. Limited partners usually do not have control over the day-to-day operations of the business.

A limited partnership operates in a similar manner as a joint venture, with one major exception. A limited partnership is an ongoing business organization that continues until it is dissolved. Limited partnerships generally have an expected life of 10 years, with an option to extend the limited partnership for another one to five years. In contrast, a joint venture generally concludes at the end of the project for which it was formed.

Limited partnerships are often used as special purpose vehicles for institutional investing. For example, a real estate limited partnership often buys commercial real estate, manages it, and receives rental income on an ongoing basis, which is then divided among several partners as specified in the partnership agreement.

Example: Real Estate Limited Partnership

Reliable Properties formed a real estate limited partnership to buy the currently vacant Western Office Park. Applegate Life participated with nine other limited partners to provide $1 million for the purchase price and an additional $200,000 to renovate the property.

Reliable, as general partner, negotiated with the property owner, closed the sale, supervised the renovation of the property, recruited tenants, entered into leases, and subsequently manages the property. Operating profits will be divided so that Reliable will receive 25 percent of the proceeds and the limited partners, together, will receive 75 percent.

As a limited partner, Applegate's potential liability in this property is limited to the amount of money invested. In contrast, Reliable, as a general partner, is fully liable for any claims against the partnership or any obligations of the partnership.

In the United States, limited partnerships can arrange to avoid registration as an investment company and thus avoid the negative impact of certain regulations. In addition, when certain conditions are fulfilled, all of the income and capital gains earned by a limited partnership investment fund flow through the partnership to the partner investors and the partnership itself is not taxed. We describe venture capital funds in Chapter 10.

Mortgages

Some institutional investors supply funds to borrowers through mortgages for purchases of property. The income collected from a mortgage provides a predictable stream of cash flows that is a good match with an insurer's obligations for fixed-income annuity products, as well as some common obligations of retirement plans.

The level of protection provided by a mortgage depends upon whether the loan is a nonrecourse loan or a recourse loan.

■   If the mortgage loan is a ***nonrecourse loan***, and the borrower fails to pay the loan, the lender is allowed to seize the property used as collateral for the loan and sell the property to satisfy the outstanding liability. If the property's value does not satisfy the outstanding loan, the lender must take a loss on the investment, and cannot pursue the borrower for the additional funds. Nonrecourse mortgages do not provide the lender with court-enforced payment of the entire debt.

■   A ***recourse loan*** allows the lender to seek financial damages if the borrower fails to pay the loan, and if the value of the asset is not enough to cover the outstanding liability. The lender can obtain a legal action known as a *deficiency judgment* to enforce collection of the outstanding amount owed to the lender from the borrower's other assets.

Mortgages tend to be somewhat riskier investments than bonds, and are also less liquid than bonds. Although both investments are subject to default risk, mortgages are not rated by agencies. Thus, evaluating the default risk in a mortgage is more challenging than evaluating default risk in a bond. In addition, bondholders can, in most instances, pursue effective legal claims against a borrower that defaults.

Residential Mortgages

A ***conventional mortgage loan*** is a residential mortgage loan that is made on the basis of the borrower's credit level and the value of the collateral that is the basis for the mortgage. ***Nonconventional mortgage loans*** are residential mortgage loans that do not necessarily satisfy conventional mortgage requirements, but do satisfy U.S. government–specified criteria—such as those specified by the Veterans Administration (VA) or Federal Housing Administration (FHA)—and thus qualify for government-provided mortgage insurance that guarantees the mortgage. Approximately 35 percent to 50 percent of the mortgages issued in the United States are conventional mortgage loans.[9]

Upon application for a residential mortgage, the borrower undergoes an underwriting process to determine if the borrower has the ability to repay the loan. The borrower's credit rating and current income factor heavily into the loan origination process. Subprime loans are mortgages made to borrowers who do not meet traditional underwriting standards, and these loans represent additional risk to a lender. When less qualified borrowers meet relaxed standards set by a residential mortgage lender, the resulting loans can fail to meet the loan purchasing standards set by important government mortgage agencies. A ***nonconforming loan*** is one that does not meet the mortgage purchasing standards maintained by Fannie Mae and Freddie Mac for conventional residential mortgages, and the lender cannot then sell the mortgage to these agencies. The following examples of problematic or "subprime" loans fall into the category of nonconforming loans:

■   *Negative amortization loans* have such low introductory interest rates that the principal on the loan increases during the introductory period.

- *Low-documentation loans* are originated without the documents necessary to provide reasonably reliable evidence of the borrower's ability to pay.

- *Alt-A loans* are made to borrowers with a good credit history but on loans having one or more other risk factors and that do not conform to accepted mortgage standards. For example, the proposed term of the mortgage could be longer than 30 years or the LTV ratio could be too high.

Commercial Mortgages

A *commercial mortgage loan* is a loan secured by commercial real estate properties or other types of commercial property. Although commercial mortgages can be structured in a variety of ways, a typical commercial mortgage is a nonrecourse, fixed-rate loan with a partial repayment of interest and principal during the loan period, and a balloon payment on a specified date. A **balloon payment** is a lump-sum payment of the final amount of the loan. Many borrowers attempt to refinance at the time the balloon payment is due. This need to refinance exposes the original lender to a risk of deterioration of the borrower's credit. In case of poor credit, the borrower may have limited options for obtaining a new loan.

Example: A Typical Commercial Mortgage

The Metcalfe Company obtained a commercial mortgage loan in which the principal and interest payments are amortized over a 20-year period. However, at the end of the loan's 10th year, Metcalf must make a balloon payment of the remaining principal and interest due on the loan.

Mortgage Operations

In addition to the real estate technical services required for investments discussed earlier in the chapter, mortgage investments require additional administrative activities, such as mortgage underwriting, origination, closing, servicing, and asset preservation. The activities of origination, underwriting, and closing are often done all at once, and sometimes by a single unit. Similarly, mortgage servicing and asset preservation may be performed by a single unit.

Mortgage Underwriting

Mortgage underwriting refers to evaluating the credit risk of a potential borrower. Mortgage underwriters participate in all stages of mortgage transactions. They also monitor assigned geographic territories to maintain (1) detailed market knowledge and (2) strong relationships with mortgage brokers and borrowers in each area. Mortgage underwriters also evaluate a property's value in relation to the loan value. A loan-to-value (LTV) ratio, introduced in Chapter 4, is often used to evaluate real estate investments. Basically, the greater the LTV ratio, the riskier the mortgage loan. Life insurance companies rarely make loans on commercial real estate with an LTV ratio greater than 60 percent. Generally, after the LTV ratio exceeds 80 percent, loan repayment is considered extremely risky. Figure 9.5 shows the historical distribution of LTV ratios for general account investments of U.S. life insurance companies.

Example: Calculating LTV

If a building worth $1 million has a $700,000 mortgage, the loan-to-value ratio on the property is 70 percent, calculated as shown:

$$\text{LTV} = \frac{\$700,000}{\$1,000,000} = 70\%$$

The *debt-to-service coverage ratio*—the ratio of the property's net operating income divided by its total debt servicing for interest, principal, or lease payments—is another ratio useful in commercial real estate valuations. The higher this ratio, the easier for the entity to cover its debt obligations.

For commercial mortgages, lenders typically look to the rental income stream to secure repayment of the loan. As described earlier, the location of the property and its ability to attract and sustain tenants over time are particularly important during this analysis. The work of a commercial mortgage underwriter is somewhat similar to that of a bond analyst, and the two functions typically work together. Financial analysts on staff continuously research all major industries. The mortgage underwriting area consults with industry-sector analysts with respect to the strength of major industries. The mortgage underwriters must evaluate the quality of the income streams from the industries that rent the buildings which secure the commercial mortgages.

Figure 9.5 Mortgages Held by U.S. Life Insurance Companies by LTV Ratio

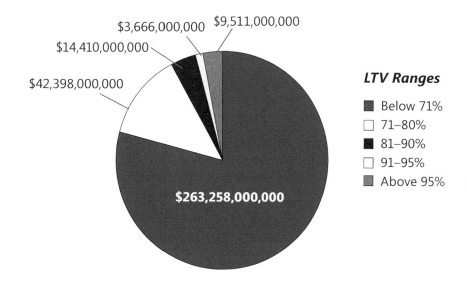

LTV Ranges
- ■ Below 71%
- □ 71–80%
- ■ 81–90%
- □ 91–95%
- ▨ Above 95%

$3,666,000,000
$9,511,000,000
$14,410,000,000
$42,398,000,000
$263,258,000,000

Source: American Council of Life Insurers, *ACLI, Life Insurers Fact Book 2012.* Used with permission.

Mortgage Origination

Mortgage origination refers to the process of creating a mortgage loan, and sometimes encompasses the activities of mortgage underwriting and mortgage closing. Because mortgage origination is labor-intensive, many smaller institutional investors choose to let external entities fulfill the mortgage origination function. Many larger institutional investors have the size and expertise to originate mortgage loans internally, and they may sell this service to other companies for fee income.

Most insurers in the United States employee a *mortgage correspondent*—a real estate professional who originates mortgage loans in a local area. Correspondents are familiar with local markets and typically offer real estate investors non-recourse loans of five to 20 years. Outside the United States, most mortgages are recourse loans, and borrowers are responsible for the full value of the loan. Correspondents also can collect principal and interest payments, and sometimes also collect property taxes and insurance.

Mortgage Closing

Mortgage closing is an event in which property ownership is transferred by deed, the purchase price is paid, and a promissory note and deed of trust are executed. In a mortgage closing department, lawyers and paralegal staff negotiate, document, and close mortgages. The closing department supports mortgage underwriting and provides considerable input into loan applications and loan closings.

Mortgage Servicing

Mortgage servicing consists of collecting payments, keeping records, and sending statements. A mortgage servicing department provides mortgage services to borrowers and monitors loan performance and compliance.

- *Loan performance* refers to timely payment of principal and interest. Overdue mortgages are subdivided into classifications of slow-pay loans and nonperforming loans. Loans that generally pay 60 to 90 days late are considered slow-pay loans. Loan payments that are past due by at least 90 days generally are said to be *nonperforming loans* and are subject to foreclosure. See Figure 9.6 for a description of mortgage performance quality.

- *Loan compliance* refers to the borrower's adherence to provisions in the mortgage agreement. These provisions can restrict the amount of additional debt the borrower may assume, require the property owner to pay property taxes, and require the property owner to maintain property and liability insurance coverage.

- *Asset preservation* refers to identifying and monitoring loans for slow payment and resolving problems with delinquency. Asset preservation specialists have expertise in law and mortgage underwriting. Options for resolving problem mortgage loans are (1) restructuring the loan with new terms of interest, principal, and term to maturity; (2) negotiating an immediate loan payoff at a reduced amount of principal and interest; (3) facilitating borrower bankruptcies; and (4) handling foreclosures.

Figure 9.6 Mortgage Performance Quality

Mortgages are classified according to quality in the following classes, given in order from best quality to lowest quality.

- **Mortgages in good standing**—mortgages on which borrowers are current with interest and principal payments. The mortgages held in life insurance company portfolios are overwhelmingly in good standing.

- **Restructured mortgages**—mortgage agreements that were at one time overdue and in danger of foreclosure, but which have been renegotiated as to interest rate, term to maturity, and principal due.

- **Overdue mortgages**—mortgages on which the borrower is 30 through 90 days delinquent in payment.

- **Mortgage in process of foreclosure**—a nonperforming mortgage loan on which the borrower is more than 90 days delinquent in payments and a foreclosure procedure is under way.

- **Foreclosed property**—an equity real estate asset that a lender acquired by foreclosure on a mortgage after a borrower defaulted on the terms of the mortgage.

Example: Asset Preservation

PDQ Real Estate Investors owns and operates 10 commercial office buildings. In a recessionary economy, PDQ is unable to make the required mortgage payments to its lender, Hull Investments, on two of the 10 properties.

PDQ's Proposal: PDQ asked Hull Investments to modify its terms for two delinquent loans. PDQ proposed to make interest-only payments for six months. PDQ posited that the time would allow them to bring in new tenants. PDQ further stated that its alternative course of action would be to cease making payments and default on the mortgages.

Renegotiated Agreement: Hull Investments authorized a three-month modification of payment terms. Further, Hull required PDQ to deposit the difference between the new and the old loan payment in an account designated for improvements on behalf of prospective tenants. Such a provision increases the likelihood that PDQ will attract the needed new tenants.

Analysis: Hull Investments could have ignored the request from PDQ and foreclosed on the two properties when they went into default. However, Hull might have realized even larger losses by foreclosing if Hull were unable to sell the property or step in and manage the property effectively. Hull felt that its approach improved the probability that the loan would be repaid, or, if PDQ did eventually default, that the losses might be smaller than otherwise.

Control Procedures for Mortgages

Institutional investors that originate and service their own mortgage loans must have appropriate control systems and procedures for these operations. Such control procedures are designed to ensure that mortgage loans and advances have proper documentation of appraisals, are properly authorized by the investor, and are properly recorded. Moreover, these procedures are designed to ensure that the company's mortgage documents are registered, the underlying assets are protected, the transaction complies with both the investor's and governmental regulatory mortgage investment policies and guidelines, and the overall administration, servicing, collection, and discharge functions are complete and comprehensive. The following aspects of mortgage loans typically have specific controls:

- **Acquisition.** Loan underwriting and procedure manuals must specify a loan approval structure and segregation of duties for underwriting, loan approval, and collection and disbursement of funds. Systems should provide for edit checks of data entered, and any movement of funds should require authorization and approval.

- **Registration and protection of assets.** Procedures must ensure that (1) the property description details in the registered title deed agree with the appraisal report property description, (2) the mortgage document is a recorded registered lien against the listed property, and (3) the borrower has a clear title to the property and evidence of proper insurance by the mortgagor.

- **Collection and servicing.** Procedures must ensure that (1) periodic mortgage repayments are received on or before the due date and banked promptly, (2) legal documentation is properly maintained and access is appropriately restricted, (3) delinquencies are handled appropriately.

Investors or their representatives must conduct periodic audits or reviews to verify all of the different stages of the mortgage loan process. For example, an audit might trace a sample of mortgage loans for completeness and accuracy through the mortgage accounting process, beginning from the time the funds are advanced, and ensuring that the mortgage servicing records captured the correct loan amount, as well as the correct amortized repayment amounts and dates necessary to ensure effective servicing of the mortgage loan. LTV ratios might be conducted to ensure compliance with applicable regulations. All accounting and financial reports are reviewed periodically for accuracy.[10]

Mortgage Securities

In Chapter 8, we described the pooling of assets and the division of the pool into shares that—through the creation of a special purpose entity (SPE)—can be sold as structured securities. In this chapter, we address structured mortgage securities that are created when holders of mortgages form a pool of mortgages and sell shares in the pool to investors.[11]

When mortgage income is packaged into securities, investors in mortgage securities can benefit from the potential price appreciation of the securities, the ability to trade the securities in an active secondary market, and a steady return. Mortgage securities can be classified as either residential or commercial mortgage-backed securities.

- A *residential mortgage-backed security (MBS)* is a type of mortgage-backed security that is secured by a pool of residential real estate loans.

- A *commercial mortgage-backed security (CMBS)* is a type of mortgage-backed security that is secured by a pool of various commercial mortgages.

Residential Mortgage-Backed Securities

The two primary types of MBSs are agency mortgage-backed securities and nonagency mortgage-backed securities. Collateralized mortgage obligations (CMOs) are another type of security created from agency mortgage-backed securities and high-quality nonagency mortgage-backed securities.

Agency Mortgage-Backed Securities

Agency mortgage-backed securities, better known as *agency MBSs*, are securities based on portfolios of residential mortgages that meet the guidelines as to credit quality, underwriting standards, and other risk factors of one of several U.S. government agencies. Three relevant U.S. government agencies that participate in the creation of agency MBSs are the Government National Mortgage Association, the Federal National Mortgage Association, and the Federal Home Loan Mortgage Corporation.

The Government National Mortgage Association, known as *Ginnie Mae*, explicitly backs its MBSs with the full faith and credit of the U.S. government because the pooled loans are primarily Veterans' Administration (VA) loans and Federal Home Association (FHA) loans. Because VA and FHA mortgages are insured by the U.S. government, Ginnie Mae guarantees the payment of principal and interest on these securities. Like Treasury securities, Ginnie Mae securities are viewed as risk-free in terms of default risk. The Federal National Mortgage Association, known as *Fannie Mae*, and the Federal Home Loan Mortgage Corporation, known as *Freddie Mac*, are U.S. government–sponsored entities that also issue MBSs. Even though Fannie Mae and Freddie Mac are not agencies of the U.S. government, their issues are considered agency MBSs. The creditworthiness of these types of agency MBSs is considered less secure than those guaranteed by Ginnie Mae. Figure 9.7 shows the first page of a Fannie Mae MBS prospectus, including the wording, "The certificates and payments of principal and interest on the certificates are not guaranteed by the United States and do not constitute a debt or obligation of the United States or any of its agencies or instrumentalities other than Fannie Mae." Still, the U.S. federal government has ensured that these two entities satisfy their obligations.

Figure 9.7 Fannie Mae MBS Prospectus

 **FannieMae.**

**Guaranteed Mortgage Pass-Through Certificates
(Single-Family Residential Mortgage Loans)**

The Certificates

We, the Federal National Mortgage Association, or Fannie Mae, will issue the guaranteed mortgage pass-through certificates, or certificates. Each issuance of certificates will have its own identification number and will represent beneficial ownership interests in a distinct pool of residential mortgage loans that are secured by single-family (one-to four-unit) dwellings, or in a pool of participation interests in loans of that type. The mortgage loans or participation interests are held in a trust created under a trust agreement.

Fannie Mae Guaranty

We guarantee to each trust that we will supplement amounts received by the trust as required to permit timely payments of principal and interest on the certificates.

We alone are responsible for making payments under our guaranty. The certificates and payments of principal and interest on the certificates are not guaranteed by the United States and do not constitute a debt or obligation of the United States or any of its agencies or instrumentalities other than Fannie Mae.

Consider carefully the risk factors section beginning on page 12. Unless you understand and are able to tolerate these risks, you should not invest in the certificates.

The certificates are exempt from registration under the Securities Act of 1933, as amended, and are "exempted securities" under the Securities Exchange Act of 1934, as amended. Neither the Securities and Exchange Commission nor any state securities commission has approved or disapproved these certificates or determined if this prospectus is truthful or complete. Any representation to the contrary is a criminal offense.

The date of this Prospectus is February 1, 2012.

Source: Fannie Mae, *Guaranteed Mortgage Pass-Through Certificates (Single-Family Residential Mortgage Loans)*, Single Family MBS Prospectus (Washington, DC: Fannie Mae, 2012), http://www.efanniemae.com/syndicated/documents/mbs/mbspros/SF_February_1_2012.pdf (1 October 2012).

Major financial publications publish the cash flow yields for MBSs of all three U.S. agencies. Although MBSs typically produce a slightly higher yield than U.S. Treasuries, additional risks are associated with MBSs. The primary risk is prepayment risk—when current mortgage interest rates are lower than the contract rates of the mortgages in the pool, the borrowers are likely to refinance at the lower rate. A secondary risk associated with MBSs is reinvestment risk—the risk that the investor will lose the cash flows associated with MBSs at a time when interest rates on other potential investments are low. These risks are essentially the same ones potentially facing bond investments.

To help distribute prepayment risk and reinvestment risk for investors, some securities structure the debt into tranches, which you learned about in Chapter 8. A collateralized mortgage obligation (CMO) is another securitized financial instrument developed to lessen the effects of these types of risk.

Nonagency Mortgage-Backed Securities

A **nonagency MBS**, also called a *private-label MBS*, contains home loans that do not qualify as agency MBSs. Nonagency MBSs are issued by private institutions, such as investment banks, financial institutions, and home builders. The loans held in a nonagency MBS can represent significantly more default risk than agency MBSs. Nonagency MBSs may include subprime residential loans with negative amortization, low-documentation loans, and alt-A loans.

Figure 9.8 illustrates the structure of a nonagency MBS, in which the principal and interest associated with the underlying loans has been divided into seven tranches. The first tranche receives the first set of payments and the seventh tranche the last set of payments. Because the investors of the first tranche receive their money first, they receive the lowest return because of their lower risk of loss. Holders of riskier tranches carry more risk of defaults, and are paid a higher return. The various tranches in these securities appeal to different investors and are rated by credit rating agencies.

Collateralized Mortgage Obligations (CMOs)

Collateralized mortgage obligations (CMOs) are structured mortgage securities that use a portfolio of agency MBSs and high-quality nonagency MBSs as collateral. CMO issuers include government agencies and private issuers. The rules for distributing interest and principal to a CMO's bond classes are fairly complex and are set forth in the prospectus.

Because CMOs usually only involve high-quality mortgages or those guaranteed by the government, CMOs are particularly attractive to institutional investors, including life insurance companies and retirement plans. CMOs have credit ratings, their ratings are generally high, and they have little default risk. Also, within a range suited to high-quality loans, these securities offer investors various levels of exposure to prepayment risk and credit risk.

Figure 9.8 Structure of a Nonagency MBS

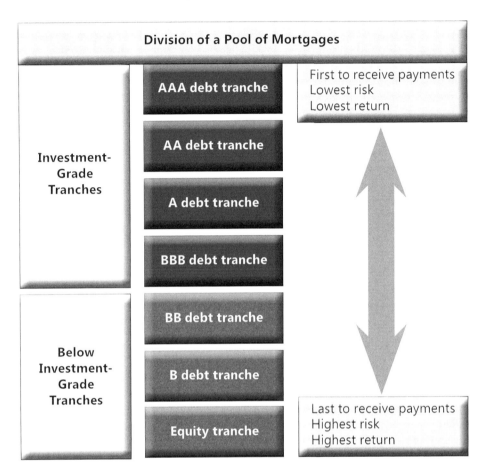

Commercial Mortgage-Backed Securities

Commercial mortgage-backed securities (CMBSs) are fixed-income securities backed by commercial loans. Specifically, in a CMBS, many single commercial mortgage loans of potentially varying size, property type, and location are pooled and transferred to a trust. In the trust, the securities are divided into tranches that differ in yield, duration, and payment priority. Each tranche is usually assigned a rating from a credit rating agency. Each month, the interest and principal collected from the pooled loans is paid to the investors, starting with those investors holding the most senior tranches. Then interest is paid to the holders of the next-highest-rated bonds and so on.[12]

CMBSs issued in the United States have limited prepayment risk because they include *make-whole provisions* that discourage prepayments. If a borrower chooses to prepay a loan and remove property from the pool, it must purchase and pledge to the trust a collection of high-quality government securities that will generate enough cash to make all monthly payments due on the loan, including any balloon payments. Otherwise, the borrower must pay the CMBS holders a penalty.

The administration of CMBSs differs from the administration of MBSs in that CMBSs are generally noncallable and the cash flows associated with CMBS are reasonably predictable. The LTV and the debt-to-service-coverage ratio are used in determining the credit risk associated with the properties in the pool.

Real Estate Investment Trusts

A *real estate investment trust (REIT)* is a corporation or trust that uses the pooled capital of a number of investors to purchase and manage real estate property or mortgage loans. A REIT combines capital from many investors and invests in a pool of real estate.

Investors can purchase shares in a REIT through either public exchanges or through nonpublic transactions. Public REIT stock shares are listed on major stock exchanges. Investors who might otherwise be unable to invest in real estate can do so by purchasing public shares of REIT stock. However, the vast majority of REITs, known as *private REITs*, are privately traded and limited to institutional investors and other affluent investors.

Whether the REIT is public or private, shareholders in a REIT are similar to corporate stockholders in that they earn a share of the income that the investment generates. REITs often specialize in a single type of real estate, such as apartment, retail, office, residential, or industrial properties. Although the United States remains the largest market for REITs, many other countries have REIT markets or are considering adding such a market. A REIT may invest in a single city or throughout the world.[13] The two primary types of REITs are equity REITs and mortgage REITs.

- Equity REITs use pooled capital to purchase income-producing assets, such as apartments or office buildings. The REIT is the owner of the property in the REIT portfolio, and is also responsible for managing the property. The REIT produces revenue for investors by collecting lease and rental payments. Because rental and lease payments can increase with inflation, equity REITs are a potential hedge against inflation.

- Mortgage REITS invest in loans to borrowers who wish to purchase real estate. A mortgage REIT can invest in mortgages or mortgage-backed securities. The REIT earns income from the interest on the loans.

Private REITs generally are closed-end funds with a specific term, usually 10 to 12 years. At the end of the specified term, the REIT either liquidates its assets and distributes the proceeds to its investors or goes public. During its lifetime, a private REIT typically pays investors periodic cash dividends that generally are higher than the dividends paid by publicly traded REITs. Private REIT investors can redeem their shares during the REIT's lifetime, but REITs typically impose restrictions on redemptions, including waiting periods and financial penalties.

REITs offer several advantages to investors. One benefit of REITs is that they use professional real estate managers who know how to acquire, finance, develop, renovate, and negotiate leases to get the most return for the shareholders. In addition, REITs pay a consistent dividend yield regardless of how the REIT shares perform. The REIT dividend is important to retired shareholders or shareholders living on a fixed income. However, REITs do not provide the opportunities for price appreciation possible with a pure real estate investment.

Real Estate Market Indexes

Several important market indexes reflect market returns on investment properties held by institutional investors, notably the NPI, the LifeComps Index, and the FTSE NAREIT Index Series. These indexes are used to facilitate asset allocation in the investment portfolio and as benchmarks for measuring performance, as well as offering insight for estimating losses.

- The *NCREIF Property Index*, known as the *NPI*, is a quarterly time-series composite index based on a total-rate-of-return measure of investment performance of a very large pool of individual commercial real estate properties acquired in the private market for investment purposes only. All properties in the NPI have been acquired, at least in part, on behalf of tax-exempt institutional investors, with the great majority being pension funds. As such, all properties are held in a fiduciary environment.[14]

- *LifeComps Index*™ provides an investment performance index for use in comparing returns on life insurance company investments in private commercial real estate loans with those of other investment asset classes—such as public and private bonds, or equities—and to serve as a benchmark for privately held commercial real estate mortgages, as described in Figure 9.9.[15]

- The *FTSE NAREIT Real Estate Index Series* comprises a U.S. and a global index. The *FTSE NAREIT US Index* is a comprehensive family of benchmarks for REITs and publicly traded real estate. The index series provides investors with exposure to all investment and property sectors. In addition, the more narrowly focused property sector and subsector indexes allow for concentrated commercial real estate exposure in more selected markets. The *FTSE EPRA/NAREIT Global Real Estate Index Series* is designed to represent general trends in eligible real estate equities worldwide. The index series covers global, developed, and emerging real estate equities markets.[16]

Figure 9.9 LifeComps Index

Eight major life insurance company investors maintain a robust database to capture commercial real estate whole loan performance data over time, along with that of the underlying real estate collateral. LifeComps participants currently represent about 29 percent of the total life insurance company investment in the commercial mortgage market, with approximately a $90.09 billion principal balance in 4,984 loans at December 31, 2011.

Using the LifeComps Index, an owner of commercial mortgage whole loan instruments can compare its investment performance with that of an aggregate life insurance industry commercial mortgage portfolio.

For commercial real estate whole loans, the LifeComps Index captures both loan performance and the underlying real estate collateral performance, and supplies the required data for the long-run correlation of credit losses on the mortgages to the underlying cycles within the real estate market. Each quarter, LifeComps calculates time weighted total return, income and appreciation returns, cash yields, and duration adjusted yields, and performs attribution analysis, delinquency, and basis point loss analysis for each Participant and for the Aggregate for the total portfolio and for property type, region, loan size, origination year, duration bucket, and delinquency status subportfolios.

Source: "Frequently Asked Questions," LifeComps Commercial Loan Index, http://lifecomps.com/FAQs/ (1 October 2012). Used with permission.

Key Terms

net lease
appraisal
market value appraisal
comparables method
cost method
income capitalization method
value-in-use appraisal
value in use
investment value appraisal
insurance value appraisal
liquidation value appraisal
average occupancy rate (AOR)
average daily rate (ADR)
total room revenue
anchor tenant
joint venture
limited partnership
nonrecourse loan
recourse loan
conventional mortgage loan
nonconventional mortgage loan

nonconforming loan
balloon payment
mortgage underwriting
debt-to-service coverage ratio
mortgage origination
mortgage correspondent
mortgage closing
mortgage servicing
loan performance
nonperforming loan
loan compliance
asset preservation
residential mortgage-backed security
    (MBS)
commercial mortgage-backed security
    (CMBS)
agency MBS
nonagency MBS
collateralized mortgage obligation
    (CMO)
real estate investment trust (REIT)

Endnotes

1. Portions of this chapter are based on James Manzi, Diana Berezina, and Mark Adelson, "Commercial Mortgage-Backed Securities," in *Handbook of Finance*, ed. Frank J. Fabozzi (Hoboken, NJ: John Wiley & Sons, 2008), 1:367–375; Frank J. Fabozzi, Anand K. Bhattacharya, and William Berliner, "Introduction to Mortgage-Backed Securities," in *Handbook of Finance*, 1:347–354; and Mark J. Anson, Frank J. Fabozzi, and Frank J. Jones, *The Handbook of Traditional and Alternative Investment Vehicles: Investment Characteristics and Strategies* (Hoboken, NJ: John Wiley & Sons, 2011), 106–107, 278–279, 285–293, 299–302, 374–375.

2. OMB Bulletin No.10–02, Update of Statistical Area Definitions and Guidance on Their Uses (1 December 2009), http://www.whitehouse.gov/sites/default/files/omb/assets/bulletins/b10-02.pdf (25 September 2012).

3. "State and County QuickFacts: Metropolitan Statistical Area," U.S. Census Bureau, http://quickfacts.census.gov/qfd/meta/long_metro.htm (25 September 2012).

4. USLegal, s.v. "bondable lease," http://definitions.uslegal.com/b/bondable-lease/ (1 October 2012).

5. Portions of this section are based on G. Timothy Haight and Daniel Singer, *The Real Estate Investment Handbook* (Hoboken, NJ: John Wiley & Sons, 2005).

6. "Building Class Definitions," Building Owners and Managers Association International, http://www.boma.org/Resources/classifications/Pages/default.aspx (1 October 2012).

7. Portions of this section are based on Patricia Wilson Fridley (Senior Advisor, Center for Financial Stability, LLC), note to author, 31 August 2012. Used with permission.

8. International Council of Shopping Centers, *ICSC Shopping Center Definitions* (New York: International Council of Shopping Centers, 1999), http://www.icsc.org/srch/lib/SCDefinitions99.pdf (1 October 2012).

9. *Investopedia*, s.v. "conventional mortgage," http://www.investopedia.com/terms/c/conventionalmortgage.asp#axzz25RGukOpH (1 October 2012); Karen Lawson, "What Is a Conventional Mortgage?" eHow, http://www.ehow.com/facts_5031554_conventional-mortgage.html (1 October 2012).

10. LOMA, "318. Mortgage Loans," in *Business Risks and Controls Handbook* [Atlanta: LOMA (Life Office Management Association, Inc.), © 2001], 318-1–318-14. Used with permission; all rights reserved.

11. "Asset Backed Securities and Structured Finance," Credit and Finance Risk Analysis, http://credfinrisk.com/assetsecure.html (25 September 2012).

12. Commercial Mortgage Securities Association and Mortgage Bankers Association, *Borrower Guide to CMBS*, (New York: Commercial Mortgage Securities Association, 2004), http://www.crefc.org/CMSA_Resources/Borrowers_Page/Borrower_s_Page/ (1 October 2012).

13. "Global Real Estate Investment," National Association of Real Estate Investment Trusts, http://www.reit.com/REIT101/REITFAQs/GlobalRealEstateInvestment.aspx (1 October 2012).

14. "FAQs: Property Level Data and Indices," National Council of Real Estate Investment Fiduciaries, http://www.ncreif.org/faqsproperty.aspx (1 October 2012).

15. "Home Page," LifeComps Commerical Mortgage Loan Index, http://www.lifecomps.com (1 October 2012).

16. "Index Data," National Association of Real Estate Investment Trusts, http://www.reit.com/DataAndResearch/IndexData.aspx (1 October 2012).

Chapter 10

Stocks, Derivatives, and Alternative Investments

Objectives

After studying this chapter, you should be able to

10A   Distinguish between common stock and preferred stock

10B   Describe types of common stock dividends and the process for declaring, paying, and controlling dividend payments

10C   Calculate various stock ratios, including the earnings per share, price/earnings ratio, and the price-to-book ratio, and describe how investors use such ratios

10D   Describe how institutional investors buy and sell stocks in auction-based, dealer-based, and alternative electronic markets

10E   Describe important regulatory restrictions on common stocks and derivatives in the general account of a life insurance company

10F   Describe and differentiate between types of put and call options, swaps, and futures contracts; explain the operation of put and call options; and explain how life insurance companies use options, swaps, and futures

10G   Describe the primary characteristics of alternative investments

10H   Describe a hedge fund and identify four types of hedge funds: market-directional hedge funds, corporate restructuring hedge funds, convergence trading hedge funds, and opportunistic hedge funds

10I   Describe private equity and distinguish among different types of private equity investments, including venture capital funds, leveraged buyout funds, mezzanine debt funds, and distressed debt funds

Outline

Stock as an Investment

Common Stock
- Dividends
- Analysis and Valuation of Common Stocks
- Buying and Selling Stocks
- Primary and Secondary Markets
- Trading Orders
- Stock Trading Costs
- Common Stocks in the General Account

Derivative Securities
- Options
- Option Trades
- Swaps
- Futures
- Restrictions on Derivatives in the General Account

Alternative Investments
- Hedge Funds
- Private Equity Funds

Stock is an equity security that represents an ownership interest in a corporation. A stock investment potentially provides earnings in the form of dividends as well as price appreciation. In Chapter 10, we primarily focus on stock investments. We also look at derivative securities and alternative investments.

Stock as an Investment

Stocks make up a large share of the assets held in life insurers' separate account portfolios and the investment portfolios of many other institutional investors. Stocks are also included in life insurers' general account portfolios. Traditionally, life insurance companies supported their products with returns from fixed-income investments. However, prolonged low-interest rate environments have significantly limited returns from fixed income investments. In such conditions, institutional investors must seek enhanced investment returns from other sectors.

As you know, the historical return on stocks generally has been substantially higher than the historical return on fixed-income investments such as bonds. Generally, though, the risk associated with stocks is also higher than that associated with fixed-income investments.

Corporations issue two basic types of stock: common and preferred. These types of stock differ primarily in how an owner participates in distributions of a company's earnings and the priority given to each over debt holders in the distribution of assets in the event of the company's liquidation.

	Debt Holders	Preferred Stockholders	Common Stockholders
Have an ownership interest in the company?	No	Yes	Yes
Have the right to vote for Board of Directors and other company matters?	No	No	Yes

Have the right to receive dividends when declared by the Board of Directors?	No	Yes	Yes
Have a guaranteed stock dividend rate?	N/A	Yes	No
Priority in payment of stock dividends	N/A	1st	2nd
Priority in claims on assets in case of liquidation	1st	2nd	3rd

Like the convertible bonds described in Chapter 8, preferred stock is a type of hybrid security that has characteristics of both equity and debt. Convertible bonds and preferred stock both have fixed-income characteristics: convertible bonds offer a fixed interest payment, and preferred stock offers a fixed dividend rate. Both offer the potential for price appreciation:

■ A convertible bond gives the holder an option to convert the bond to a stated number of shares of the issuing company's stock.

■ Preferred stock may result in capital gains when sold.

However, the potential for a preferred stock's price appreciation is typically less than that for common stocks. Accordingly, when the investment objective is to gain an enhanced level of returns by seeking enhanced risk, institutional investors focus on common stock, not preferred. Insurance companies typically own very little preferred stock.

Common Stock

A company's common stock, sometimes known as *voting stock* or *ordinary share stock*, may provide the same benefits of ownership to all common stockholders. On the other hand, a corporation can issue common stock known as ***classified common stock***, which entitles different share classes to distinctive stockholder rights, such as those relating to dividend rights and rights in a liquidation proceeding.

Example: Stockholder Rights by Share Class

Forthright Enterprises issued classified common stock in two share classes: Class A and Class B. Class A and Class B shareholders all have the rights to receive dividend distributions and periodic financial reports. However, Class A shareholders have 100 votes per share, whereas Class B shareholders have only one vote per share.

Share Class	Votes per Share	Full Dividend Distribution	Financial Report
Class A	100	Yes	Yes
Class B	1	Yes	Yes

Dividends

Companies generally are not required to pay any dividends on common stock. A company's board of directors determines whether to declare a dividend, and, if so, the amount, form, and date of the dividend payment. Typically, companies follow an established dividend payment pattern. If a corporation pays a dividend, the company usually will continue to pay dividends regularly in roughly the same pattern unless extraordinary circumstances force the company to reduce or cut the dividend. When a public company is forced to reduce or cut a dividend, the company's share price usually falls.

Types of Dividends

Companies can pay cash dividends, stock dividends, or special dividends. Most dividends on common stock take the form of a cash dividend. A *cash dividend* is a cash payment to stockholders in proportion to the shares owned.

Example: Cash Dividend

Bright Future Corporation's board of directors declared a stock dividend of 50 cents per share. Bright Future has 1 million shares of common stock in circulation.

Because Margie Miller owns 100 shares of Bright Future common stock, she will receive $50 from Bright Future, calculated as follows:

$$100 \text{ shares} \times \$0.50 = \$50$$

A *stock dividend* is a distribution of additional shares of stock to stockholders. When a company issues a stock dividend, each stockholder's proportionate share of ownership in the company remains the same. For example, if an investor owns 2 percent of a company before the stock dividend, the investor will own 2 percent of the company after the stock dividend is distributed. A stock dividend is expressed as

$$\text{Stock dividend shares} = \text{Shares currently owned} \times \text{Dividend percentage}$$

Example: Stock Dividend

Instead of issuing a cash dividend, Bright Future's board of directors declared a 10 percent stock dividend.

In this situation, Ms. Miller will receive 10 shares of additional stock, calculated as follows:

$$10 = 100 \times 0.10 = 100 \times 10\% = 10 \text{ shares}$$

Bright Future must issue each stockholder one additional share of Bright Future stock for each 10 shares the stockholder currently owns. To pay the stock dividend, Bright Future must issue an additional 100,000 shares of common stock. After the stock dividend, Bright Future will have 1.1 million shares of common stock outstanding.

A *special dividend*, sometimes referred to as an *extra dividend*, is a nonrecurring dividend that is usually paid in cash. A special dividend generally is considerably larger than the normal dividend a company pays. Companies declare special dividends when earnings are exceptionally strong in order to maintain good relationships with stockholders and generate favorable publicity, but without creating an expectation that the company will continue to pay such a dividend amount regularly.

Dividend Declarations and Payments

Companies can declare and pay a dividend at any time but typically do so on a quarterly basis. A declared dividend is paid to a designated *stockholder of record*—a party the corporation has recorded as owning stock in the corporation. Four important dates affect stockholders' rights to a declared dividend.

- The **declaration date** is the date when the board of directors announces to stockholders and the public that it intends to pay a dividend. On this date, the board announces the amount of the dividend, the date of record, and the payment date. Also, on this date, the company creates a liability on its books for the amount of the dividend.

- The *record date*, or *date of record*, is the date specified by the board of directors to determine who will receive the dividend. A stockholder must be a registered stockholder in the company's records on this date to be entitled to receive a dividend.

- The **ex-dividend date**, also known as the *ex-date*, is the date that determines which investors actually receive a declared dividend. The ex-date is typically two business days prior to the record date. Any investor who owns the stock the day before the ex-date receives the dividend. Any investor who buys the stock on or after the ex-date does not receive the dividend. Because stock can be traded frequently and companies require time to register a new stockholder in their records, the ex-dividend date is used to determine who is eligible to receive a declared dividend.

- The *payment date* is the date on which a declared dividend is scheduled to be paid. For a stock dividend, the payment date is the date when the additional shares of stock are distributed to the stockholder.

Example: Who Gets the Dividend?

On May 1, the board of directors of the Challenger Company declared a dividend of $1.00 per share to common stockholders of record as of Friday, May 11, with a payment date of May 15. In this situation, the declaration date is May 1, the record date is May 11, the payment date is May 15, and the ex-dividend date is May 9.

Dividend declared	ApLIC buys Stock	Ex-dividend date	Record date	Payment date
May 1	May 7	May 9	May 11	May 15

Applegate Life purchased Challenger common stock on May 7. Because the stock was purchased before the ex-dividend date, Applegate Life is eligible to receive the declared dividend. If Applegate Life had purchased the stock on the ex-dividend date or thereafter, it would not have been eligible to receive the dividend.

Dividend Yield

Dividends contribute to an investor's total rate of return from a stock investment. The *dividend yield* is the ratio of a company's annual dividend payments to stock price.

> ### Example: Dividend Yield
>
> For the past five years, Challenger Corporation has paid a quarterly dividend of $0.50 per share. The current price of Challenger stock is $40 a share. Thus, Challenger's annual dividend yield is 5 percent, calculated according to the following formula:
>
> $$\text{Dividend yield} = \frac{\text{Annual dividend per share}}{\text{Price per share}}$$
>
> $$= \frac{\$0.50 \times 4}{\$40} = \frac{\$2}{\$40} = 5\%$$

When market interest rates are low, stocks that have a high dividend yield can be an attractive investment alternative to debt securities, especially for investors seeking current income. Potential investors can compare a company's dividend yield to the market interest rate available on a fixed-income investment to help determine which investment will likely provide the higher current income yield.

Operational Controls for Dividends

Institutional stockholders establish operational controls over dividend collections. To the extent possible, companies typically design and deploy automated forms of operational controls. An important focus of managing common stock holdings is to collect and record dividends so that dividend income is

- Received and collected as it was declared

- Collected in a timely fashion

- Recorded properly and accurately in the company's systems

- Properly valued, in the case of stock dividends

- Accurately reported in all required financial reporting, such as the Annual Statement filing, Schedule D, for insurance companies in the United States[1]

Analysis and Valuation of Common Stocks

For various management and reporting purposes, companies can use different concepts of value for stocks, including book value and market value:

- The **book value** of a stock is the value at which it is reported in financial records. Under statutory accounting principles applicable to insurance companies in the United States, the book value of a publicly traded stock is the closing price of the stock on the last day of the reporting period.

- The **market value** of a publicly traded stock is the currently quoted price at which investors buy or sell the stock. Investors use the market value of a stock to determine the unrealized gain or loss on the stock and its rate of return.

In determining whether to buy or sell a stock, institutional investors usually compare the intrinsic value of a stock to its market value. The **intrinsic value of a stock** is the value of the stock based on a valuation of all aspects of the issuing company's business, including both tangible and intangible factors. Investors generally seek to buy stocks whose intrinsic value exceeds their market value.

To estimate the expected return on a stock, institutional investors often attempt to estimate the future intrinsic value of the stock. For many reasons, the market value of a stock often differs substantially from its intrinsic value. By estimating a stock's intrinsic value, investors also estimate the stock's likely future market value.

Institutional investors typically attempt to understand the intrinsic value of a stock by examining the company's financial records and calculating various ratios derived from those records, including common ratios such as earnings per share, the price/earnings ratio, and the price-to-book ratio.

Earnings Per Share (EPS)

Earnings per share (EPS) is the portion of a company's profit that can be allocated to each outstanding share of common stock. Investors calculate earnings per share according to the following formula:

$$\text{Earnings per share} = \frac{\text{Total profit}}{\text{Number of outstanding common stock shares}}$$

Price/Earnings (P/E) Ratio

The **price/earnings (P/E) ratio** is a stock's price per share divided by the earnings per share, as shown:

$$\text{Price/earnings ratio} = \frac{\text{Market price per share}}{\text{Earnings per share}}$$

Example: Earnings per Share and Price/Earnings Ratio

Last year, Sailaway Corporation earned a total profit of $10 million. Sailaway has 5 million shares of outstanding common stock. The current market price of Sailaway stock is $20 per share.

Thus, Sailaway had $2 EPS in the last year, calculated as shown:

$$\text{Earnings per share} = \frac{\$10,000,000}{5,000,000} = \$2$$

The result shown is Sailaway's *historical* EPS.

Analysts can apply the same formula to estimate a future EPS. If an analyst believes Sailaway will earn a profit of $10 million next year also, then estimated EPS for Sailaway's stock for next year would also be $2.

Sailaway's P/E ratio is 10, calculated as shown:

$$\text{Price/earnings ratio} = \frac{\text{Market price per share}}{\text{Earnings per share}} = \frac{\$20}{\$2} = 10$$

When the P/E ratio of Sailaway stock is 10, an analyst can conclude that Sailaway Stock is currently trading at 10 times the company's current earnings.

Analysts use the P/E ratio to determine if the market share price is reasonable relative to the earnings of the company. A stock with a high P/E relative to stocks of firms in the same industry may be overpriced. Conversely, a stock with a low P/E may be a good value.

Price-to-Book (P/B) Ratio

The *price-to-book (P/B) ratio* for a stock is the stock's market price per share divided by the stock's book value per share, as shown:

$$\text{Price to book (P/B) ratio} = \frac{\text{Market price per share}}{\text{Book value per share}}$$

A company's book value is the accounting value of its owners' equity. Thus, the book value per share is owners' equity divided by the number of shares of common stock outstanding.

Example: Calculating a P/B Ratio

The common stock of Sparkle Consumer Finance is trading at $30 per share. The book value per share of Sparkle's stockholders' equity is $25. We calculate Sparkle's P/B ratio as follows:

$$\frac{P}{B} = \frac{\$30}{\$25} = 1.2$$

This information shows that Sparkle's stock is trading above its book value.[2]

A P/B ratio can be useful for identifying stocks for which the market price does not fully represent the asset value in the company, particularly for companies that hold mostly liquid assets, such as investment firms. A P/B ratio lower than 1.0 can indicate that a stock's market price has room to grow. A P/B ratio greater than 1.0 may indicate that a stock's market price is too high.

Example: Interpreting P/B Ratio

Because the P/B ratio of Gizmo Investments is 0.65, an analyst knows that Gizmo's shares are currently trading at 65 percent of Gizmo's stockholders' equity. If the P/B ratio of other companies in the same industry as Gizmo is lower than 65 percent, then Gizmo stock may represent a good value, in that Gizmo stock may be undervalued for its industry.

Investors can use dashboards to display the results of such ratios and to monitor the performance of various stocks against the company's operational-level risk limits. A rule might require the company to sell a particular stock if the price of the stock increases so that the company's investment in that stock exceeds a specified percentage of the total equity allocation for the portfolio. A dashboard display can show a warning condition as a stock approaches its allocation limit. Figure 10.1 illustrates a stock dashboard.

Buying and Selling Stocks

Stocks are typically bought and sold in equity markets known as stock exchanges. A stock that is traded on a particular exchange is said to be *listed* on that exchange. Companies must meet the listing requirements of a particular stock exchange in order for their stock to be traded on the exchange. There are two primary types of stock exchanges: auction-based markets and dealer-based markets. In addition, alternative electronic markets have become major markets for equity trading. Figure 10.2 identifies the largest stock exchanges in the world.

Auction-Based Market. A trade occurs in an auction-based market if the highest bid price equals the lowest ask price. If the highest bid price is less than the lowest ask price, no trade occurs. The New York Stock Exchange (NYSE) is primarily an auction-based market.

Example: Auction Market

The stock of Sailaway Enterprises trades in an auction market. Potential buyers and sellers enter the following bids and offers for one share of Sailaway stock.

Seller	Ask	Bid	Buyer
Mancini	$51.00		
Lopez	$50.50		
Rushton	$50.00	$50.00	Nadri
		$49.50	Chomsky
		$49.00	Lambert

Rushton sells his share of Sailaway to Nadri for $50. If Nadri had not submitted a bid, no trade would have occurred because the highest bid price would have been lower than the lowest ask price.

Figure 10.1 Stock Dashboard

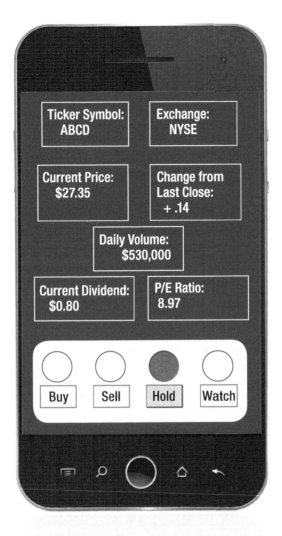

Dealer-Based Market. A dealer-based market is often referred to as a "quote-driven" market because buyers and sellers trade with dealers who publicly post bid and ask prices for an inventory of securities that they hold and stand ready to trade at those prices. A **_market maker_** is a dealer who holds an inventory of a particular stock and stands ready to buy and sell shares of that stock continuously at published bid and ask prices. Because market makers agree to buy and sell shares of stock continuously, trades at posted bid and ask prices are always conducted immediately. The NASDAQ is an example of a dealer-based market.

Example: Dealer-Based Market

Positron Financial is a market maker for Caesar Corporation, whose stock is traded in a dealer-based market. Positron posts the following quotation for Caesar stock.

Bid Price: $29.90
Ask Price: $30.10

Positron stands ready to sell Caesar stock from its inventory to anyone immediately at $30.10 a share. Positron also stands ready to buy Caesar stock from anyone immediately at $29.90 a share.

Figure 10.2 World's Largest Stock Exchanges

Stock Exchange	Country	Total Market Capitalization***
1. New York Stock Exchange	United States	$13.4
2. NASDAQ	United States	$4.5
3. London Stock Exchange	United Kingdom	$4.1
4. Tokyo Stock Exchange	Japan	$3.5
5. Hong Kong Stock Exchange	China	$2.6
6. Shanghai Stock Exchange	China	$2.6
7. Euronext*	Netherlands	$2.6
8. TMX Group**	Canada	$2.0
9. Deutsche Borse	Germany	$1.4
10. Australian Stock Exchange	Australia	$1.3

    * Euronext is a European electronic stock exchange based in Amsterdam with subsidiaries in several European countries.
  ** Includes Toronto Stock Exchange and Montreal Stock Exchange.
 *** (Trillions of US dollars, as of April 2012)

Source: "Latest Statistics," World Federation of Exchanges, http://www.world-exchanges.org/statistics/monthly-reports (21 May 2012).

Alternative Electronic Markets. In addition to auction-based and dealer-based markets, alternative markets allow buyers and sellers to conduct trades directly with one another without an intermediary. Institutional investors place orders directly in an electronic trading network, and the network, whenever possible, automatically matches buy and sell orders.

Many traditional stock exchanges, like the NYSE, now offer electronic trading. The NYSE offers electronic trading through its NYSE Hybrid Market. Buyers and sellers have the option of trading most stocks listed on the exchange either directly on the trading floor or electronically.

In some electronic markets, investors are able to view pending orders and, as a result, can enter a corresponding order to any pending order at a matching price.

Two major alternative electronic stock markets are the Better Alternative Trading System (BATS) exchange and the Direct Edge exchange.[3] Trades conducted via alternative electronic markets have the following characteristics:

- Trading costs in these markets are often lower than they would be for trades conducted on a traditional exchange.

- Large institutions can use these facilities to resell private placement securities to other qualified institutions.

- When institutions trade anonymously in these markets, they can avoid signaling the company's intent to the market and thereby impacting the prices of securities they may be trading in large volume.

Stocks not listed on any type of organized exchange are traded in the *over-the-counter (OTC) market*. The OTC market is loosely defined as a decentralized market in which market participants trade over the telephone, facsimile, or electronic network. Alternative electronic markets do trade in OTC stocks as well as in stocks listed on organized exchanges.

Primary and Secondary Markets

Recall from Chapter 8 that newly issued securities are initially bought and sold in the primary market. Stocks are initially offered for sale through an initial public offering (IPO), a rights offering to existing stockholders, or a private placement.

- A company selling its stock through an IPO works with an investment banking firm that sets the price of the stock and helps determine the size of the potential market for the stock.

- An issuing company provides a *rights offering* to existing stockholders to give them the first opportunity to purchase new shares of stock in proportion to their current ownership position.

- A private placement of stock takes place in the primary market.

After the initial sale, any further trading in the stock takes place in the *secondary market*, and the issuer of the stock does not receive any further payment on the basis of trades in the secondary market. The majority of stock trading takes place in the secondary market through stock exchanges and alternative electronic markets.

Institutional investors occasionally sell large blocks of outstanding stock by means of a secondary offering in the secondary market. A **secondary offering**, also known as a *secondary distribution*, is a sale of a large block of registered securities by a private investor through an investment banking company, typically at a set price. Generally, the stock sold in a secondary offering is stock that institutional investors previously acquired in a private placement.

Trading Orders

Investors generally trade stock by placing various types of orders either with brokers or through an electronic trading network. Each order specifies a *bid size* or *ask size*, which is the number of shares of stock the investor is seeking to buy or sell. Two types of trading orders are market orders and limit orders.

Market Order

A *market order* is an order to buy or sell a stock immediately at the best available price. Market orders have priority over all other types of orders. As a result, market orders for most stocks are executed almost immediately. However, investors have no control over the price at which a market order is executed; in some circumstances, the actual trading price can differ significantly from the price when the investor placed the order. For this and other reasons, for institutional investors, market orders generally are inconsistent with best practices for trade execution and risk control.

Limit Order

A *limit order* is an order to buy a set number of shares of a particular stock at or below a stated price, known as the *limit price*, or to sell a set number of shares of a particular stock at or above the limit price. A *buy limit order* is a limit order for the purchase of stock, and a *sell limit order* is a limit order for the sale of stock. The limit price for a buy limit order is typically lower than the current price of the stock, while the limit price for a sell limit order is typically higher than the current price of the stock.

> **Example: Limit Buy Order**
> Buy 500 shares of Challenger stock at or below $150 per share.

A limit order that is not executed immediately remains in effect until it expires. If the price of the stock subsequently reaches the limit price while the order remains in effect, the order is then executed. A limit order typically expires at the end of the trading day on which it is placed.

Stock Trading Costs

Trading commissions, custodial fees, transaction fees, and taxes are common investment costs. In addition to these costs, stocks involve certain other transaction costs. *Investment delay* costs result from being unable to execute a stock order immediately. Normally, a delay occurs between when the decision is made to place an order and when the order is filled in the market. If the price of the stock changes during this period, any resulting costs are investment delay costs. *Market timing* costs result when the price of a stock changes at the time of the transaction due to the actions of other market participants or general market volatility.

Common Stocks in the General Account

From our Chapter 5 discussion of managing fund options, you're aware that common stocks are a mainstay of separate account investments. For a number of reasons, common stocks also have a significant role in an insurance company general account. As mentioned, equity investments generally offer the potential for additional returns above those available with fixed-income debt securities. In addition, holding common stocks in the general account provides diversification because of the negative correlation between stocks and debt securities.

Regulatory authorities in the United States and elsewhere restrict common stock ownership for the general account, including the following restrictions:

- State insurance codes prohibit insurers from investing more than a stated percentage, typically 10 percent to 20 percent, of their admitted assets in common stocks. These codes typically limit common stock investment to U.S. and Canadian companies.

- Common stocks are subject to an asset valuation reserve (AVR), and the AVR required for common stocks is generally significantly higher than the AVR for investment-grade bonds.

- Authorities impose distinctive requirements on the statutory reporting and valuation of common stock. For regulatory financial reporting, listed common stocks held in the general account are reported at their fair value.

- For some purposes of monitoring the company's capital adequacy, life insurance companies also must apply a risk capital charge to common stocks held in the general account. For the United States, most publicly traded common stocks have a basic risk capital charge factor of 30 percent, subject to further adjustments.

Derivative Securities

Derivative securities have no inherent value. A derivative's value is based on an underlying security or the credit quality of an entity referenced in the contract. Institutions pursue a number of investment strategies that employ types of exchange-traded derivatives to maximize return and minimize risk, including various types of options, swaps, and futures contracts.

Options

An *option* is a type of derivative security that gives the holder the right to either buy or sell a specified security, such as a stock or bond, at a stated price on or before an expiration date. Options give investors an opportunity to (1) reduce the risk of holding the underlying instrument or (2) profit from an expected change in the underlying instrument's market values.

One party, known as the option *writer*, sells an option to an investor, known as the option *holder*. The option writer must either purchase the underlying security from the holder of the option or deliver the underlying security to the holder of the option, according to the terms of the option contract. The price at which the option holder can buy or sell the underlying security is called the *strike price*. Options generally are not written by the company that issued the underlying security. An option contract that has not expired and has not been exercised is an open contract. If the holder does not exercise an option by the expiration date, the option expires and has no further value.

Options are either puts or calls, as shown in Figure 10.3, depending on whether the contract is a commitment for the writer to purchase or sell an underlying security:

- A *put option*, or *put*, gives the holder the right, but not the obligation, to *sell* the underlying security at the strike price on or before the option's expiration date.

- A *call option*, or *call*, gives the holder the right, but not the obligation, to *buy* the underlying security at the strike price, on or before the expiration date.

Options are further classified by the type of underlying security. Common types of options include stock options, bond options, futures options, and currency options. So, for example, a currency option would allow the holder the right to either purchase or sell a foreign currency at a specified price on or before the expiration date of the option. A bond option would allow the holder the right to either purchase or sell the underlying bond at a specified price on or before the expiration date of the option. Figure 10.3 illustrates the difference between put and call options.

Figure 10.3 Difference Between Put and Call Options for an Underlying Security

	Put	Call
Writer	Must purchase at strike price	Must sell at strike price
Holder	May sell at strike price	May purchase at strike price

Option Trades

Options are traded in the same manner as any other security. Most common types of securities options are publicly traded on exchanges. For simplicity, we limit our discussion in this section to stock options.

To facilitate trading, exchanges standardize option terms relating to a particular asset that underlies the option. For example, in the United States, each stock option contract is a contract for the purchase or sale of 100 shares of stock.

The price quoted for a particular option, referred to as the *option price* or *option premium*, is the price per share of the option; thus, the total cost of an option is 100 times the premium. Options also have a standard expiration schedule. Investors can purchase options with expiration dates up to three years in the future. Stock options scheduled to expire in a given month usually expire on the Saturday following the third Friday of that month.

The cost of an option is calculated using the following formula:

$$\text{Option cost} = \frac{\text{Price per}}{\text{stock share}} \times \frac{\text{Shares per}}{\text{contract}} \times \frac{\text{Number of}}{\text{contracts}}$$

Example: Purchasing Options

Applegate Life buys 5 September 60 put contracts for Bright Future stock at $2.00 per share.

The options give Applegate the right to sell 500 shares of Bright Future stock on or before the Saturday following the third Friday of September at a price of $60 per share.

Applegate paid a total cost for the put options of $1,000, as shown:

$2.00 per share × 100 shares per contract × 5 contracts = $1,000

If the strike price of a call option is *lower* than the current price of the underlying security or the strike price of a put option is higher than the current price of the underlying security, the option is said to be in the money. When an option is *in the money*, the option holder will realize a profit from exercising the option. Of course, the option seller hopes that the option will remain *out of the money* and not exercised.

Example: In-the-Money Option

The Nightingale Fund holds a call option for Sailaway stock at a strike price of $50 per share. If the current price of Sailaway stock is $55 per share, Nightingale's option is in the money.

Nightingale can exercise its option, buy the Sailaway stock for $50 per share, and then sell the stock in the open market at $55 per share—for a profit.

The ***intrinsic value of an option*** is the difference between the strike price and the price of the underlying security.

- The intrinsic value of a call option is the price of the underlying security minus the strike price.

- The intrinsic value of a put option is the strike price minus the price of the underlying security.

Institutional investors typically use options to hedge portfolio risks.

Swaps

A ***swap***, or *swap contract*, is a contract in which two parties exchange one asset, liability, security, or cash flow for another. Unlike options, which typically are standardized contracts traded on exchanges, swaps usually are traded over-the-counter, and the exact terms of a swap often are individually negotiated between the parties to the swap. Institutional investors often use swaps for hedging purposes. Institutional investors commonly use credit default swaps, interest-rate swaps, and currency swaps.

A ***credit default swap (CDS)*** is a type of derivative financial instrument used primarily to protect its owner against an investment's credit risk. A CDS can be thought of as a form of insurance or hedge against the risk that the issuer of a security, such as a bond or mortgage-backed security, will default. The purchaser of a CDS makes premium payments to the seller, or *writer*, of the CDS. In return, the writer promises to pay a benefit to the purchaser of the CDS, if the purchaser experiences the specified credit default defined in the agreement. Often, the benefit is a lump-sum cash amount.

The *International Swaps and Derivatives Association (ISDA)* is an association that supports orderly OTC transactions in swaps and derivatives. The ISDA specifically supports a master agreement for these transactions as well as a broader framework of standard documentation. Most transactions worldwide involving CDSs and other OTC-traded swaps and derivatives follow the documentation standards maintained by the ISDA. The *ISDA Master Agreement* is the boilerplate agreement for these transactions.[4] A parallel standard agreement for similar transactions in Islamic financial markets is the *Tahawwut Master Agreement*.

An ***interest-rate swap*** is an agreement between two parties to exchange a set of cash flows, typically with one based on a fixed interest rate and the other based on a variable, or floating, interest rate. Interest rate swaps generally expire after a specified period of time.

A ***currency swap*** is an agreement to exchange principal and interest payments on a particular debt instrument payable in one currency for principal and interest payments on a similar debt instrument payable in another currency. Parties to a currency swap exchange the principal and the interest payments.

Although institutional investors can reduce certain types of risk through the use of swaps, they must carefully consider the level of counterparty risk associated with using swaps. ***Counterparty risk*** is the risk that one party to a contract will not fulfill its contractual obligations to the other party. Investors face counterparty risk in all financial contracts, but counterparty risk is an especially important concern in swap contracts.

Exchange-traded derivatives have minimal counterparty risk because the exchange itself serves as the counterparty and fulfills the contract if the original counterparty defaults on a derivative contract. However, swaps are over-the-counter derivatives rather than exchange-traded derivatives. Because an institutional investor usually enters into a swap directly with a counterparty, the exposure to counterparty risk can be significant in such agreements. Institutional investors often limit their counterparty risk by (1) contracting only with highly solvent, reliable counterparties, and (2) entering into master contracts that contain terms affording them additional legal protection in the event of counterparty default. Figure 10.4 lists common CDS counterparties.

Futures

Futures, or *futures contracts*, are contracts for the sale of an asset, usually a physical commodity or financial instrument, at a specified future date and price. The underlying asset in a commodity futures contract is typically something that has an economic value, but does not yield an ongoing income stream. The underlying asset in a financial futures contract is a financial instrument such as a stock, or in many cases an intangible asset such as a currency, a stock index, or an interest rate.

Like options, futures contracts are traded on organized exchanges; they have uniform contract size and terms, and daily liquidity. Unlike options, which give the holder the right to buy or sell an asset up to an expiration date, futures contracts impose on the parties the *obligation* to buy or sell the asset. However, futures

---

Figure 10.4 Common CDS Counterparties

US Counterparties	Other Counterparties
JP Morgan Chase	Deutsche Bank
Citigroup	Barclays Bank
Goldman Sachs	CreditSuisse
Morgan Stanley	BNP Paribas
Bank of America (Merrill Lynch)	HSBC
	Royal Bank of Canada (RBC)

Source: "Insights into the Insurance Industry's Derivatives Exposure," Capital Markets Special Report, National Association of Insurance Commissioners, www.naic.org/capital_markets_archive/110610.htm (1 June 2011). Reprinted with permission of the National Association of Insurance Commissioners.

---

contracts rarely result in the actual delivery of an asset. Investors typically purchase an offsetting futures contract that will close out the initial contract before the delivery date arrives.

Futures contracts are often used for hedging and speculation. The following examples describe investment strategies that employ futures:

- Commodity prices usually increase during an inflationary period, and when commodity prices increase, the prices of commodities futures also increase. By purchasing commodities futures, an institutional investor can offset lower rates of return during inflationary periods with gains from commodity price increases that also occur during inflationary periods.

- By purchasing currency futures, an investor can determine the exact rate at which it can exchange one currency for another in the future, thus limiting its exposure to currency risk. For example, a currency futures contract might require one party to buy 125,000 euros from another party on a specified date at an exchange rate of 1.3 U.S. dollars per euro.

Restrictions on Derivatives in the General Account

Regulatory authorities in many jurisdictions impose various restrictions on insurance company investments in derivatives for the general account.[5]

Consistent with the *Investments of Insurers Model Acts*, insurers in the United States can purchase or sell derivatives for hedging purposes up to a stated maximum percentage of the insurer's admitted assets—usually less than 10 percent. Insurers must be able to demonstrate the intended hedging characteristics and ongoing effectiveness of the derivative transaction.

Typically, insurers in the United States must maintain an AVR for derivatives. The AVR for most exchange-traded derivatives is considerably lower than the AVR required for equity securities.

Before engaging in any derivative transactions, companies must adopt and obtain regulatory approval for their written guidelines, commonly referred to as a *derivative use plan (DUP)*, for handling transactions in derivatives. The DUP typically provides information about

- Company objectives for engaging in derivative transactions, derivative strategies, and risk constraints

- Exposure limits for counterparty risk exposures and credit quality standards

- Permissible derivative transactions, including identification of the risks being hedged against in a transaction

- Internal control procedures and practices for derivative transactions

- Management oversight standards for transactions in derivatives and a description of how these standards relate to the company's risk management program

- Documentation and reporting procedures and standards for derivative transactions

- Procedures for assessment of internal controls related to derivatives

In recognition of the high level of risk that many derivative transactions carry, regulators impose additional requirements on insurance companies in regard to derivative transactions, as follows:

- Companies must adopt a methodology for determining the effectiveness of hedging transactions involving the use of derivatives.

- Companies must certify that they have adequate professional staff, technical expertise, and systems to engage in derivative transactions in accordance with the DUP.

- Company boards of directors must review whether derivative transactions are made in accordance with the DUP and the investment objectives, and must maintain appropriate internal controls relative to derivatives.[6]

Alternative Investments

The term *alternative investment* is subject to interpretation because the distinction between traditional and alternative can be a matter of opinion. Historically, any investment not classified as stocks, bonds, or cash equivalents has been referred to as an alternative investment.[7] Using this definition, real estate, REITs, and derivatives can all be considered alternative investments. To institutional investors, however, real estate, REITs, and derivatives are commonly considered traditional investments.

In this section, we focus on two categories of alternative investments that are important to institutional investors: hedge funds and private equity funds.

- A hedge fund invests in mostly public securities and some private securities. Hedge funds do not typically invest in property. Hedge funds have lower returns and much lower risk and volatility than do private equities and public equities.

- A private equity fund invests in companies and property. Private equity funds can achieve higher returns, expressed in terms of a median long-term performance, than do comparable public equities.

Institutional investors often choose alternative investments because they seek higher returns than they can expect to obtain from traditional investments. Alternative investments also potentially provide institutional investors and other affluent investors with favorable accounting treatment, enhanced opportunities for diversification, and the ability to invest in social causes.

Alternative investments generally have the following characteristics:

- Investors in alternative investments have limited ability to liquidate the investment on demand. Some alternative investments require investors to make a commitment to a defined term, usually several years. Others permit early liquidation with advance notice. By contrast, an investment in public stock permits an investor to sell the stock and liquidate the investment in about three days.

■ Participation in alternative investments is open mainly to sophisticated investors who must meet requirements of a minimum net worth and minimum income. In effect, some alternative investments are established entirely for participation by institutional investors holding at least $100 million of assets under management. Such alternative investments require investors to be qualified institutional buyers (QIBs), a special status under U.S. securities laws. QIBs meet a number of tests, including holding a minimum of $100 million of assets under management.

■ Alternative investments provide investors with access to strategies or securities not readily available elsewhere, thus supporting diversification.

■ Each purchase agreement for an alternative investment is unique, and each requires due diligence and deliberation. Potential investors are responsible for obtaining adequate information about the arrangement, and may, for example, wish to obtain such additional information as an independent audit and on-site inspection of facilities and records.

■ Ongoing due diligence regarding an alternative investment management company is required to verify that the management company maintains the conditions of the purchase agreement. Such ongoing due diligence has added importance because performance can differ considerably from one management company to another.

■ The management company does not face specific regulatory minimum disclosure requirements, but the management company is subject to a requirement of accurate reporting.

■ Typically, alternative investments charge investors a base management fee plus potentially an incentive management fee.

  • The base management fee is a specified percentage, typically 1 to 3 percent, of the amount of capital an investor commits to the fund. So, for example, if a fund earns no returns in a given period, the fund management company still collects a percentage of the total amount of funds committed by the investor.

  • After the investment returns a specified minimum profit, usually in a range from 6 to 8 percent, investors owe an incentive management fee, which is a percentage of the profit above the minimum. Fund investors pay this fee to the fund manager. If the fund does not realize a profit in excess of the specified minimum, investors do not pay the incentive fee.

Hedge Funds

A hedge fund is a privately organized investment arrangement available to certain sophisticated investors who participate in a portfolio of mostly public and some private securities. A hedge fund typically concentrates on only one economic sector or market segment. Hedge funds in the United States are available only to high-net-worth investors, such as foundations, endowments, and pension funds. Many hedge funds invest in private placement securities that do not require a prospectus and do not have an SEC review.

Hedge funds typically require a minimum initial investment of $200,000 or more. Hedge funds severely restrict fund redemptions, particularly in the period immediately after the investor purchases shares.

Hedge funds are often assigned to style categories similar to style categories for mutual funds. Hedge fund styles are subject to trends in popularity as markets change. Here we discuss four broad styles of hedge funds: market-directional hedge funds, corporate restructuring hedge funds, convergence trading hedge funds, and opportunistic hedge funds.

- *Market-directional hedge funds*, also called *long/short funds*, retain some of the systemic risk exposure associated with the stock market. These hedge funds purchase stocks that appear to be good long-term investments and options on other stocks that are expected to decline in value. These hedge funds often invest in emerging markets or public companies that benefit from activist involvement to achieve better governance of the corporation.

- *Corporate restructuring hedge funds*, also called *merger arbitrage funds*, focus on investing in companies that are undergoing mergers, acquisitions, or bankruptcies. Such events often provide investment opportunities. Managers of corporate restructuring hedge funds develop specialized knowledge regarding one or two industry sectors and the companies operating in those sectors. Corporate restructuring hedge funds are subject to event risks consisting of the potential that an expected event won't occur. For example, a company heading into bankruptcy may be able to turn its situation into a recovery. Also, companies planning a merger may call off the merger or turn to a different merger partner.

- *Convergence trading hedge funds* seek to purchase and sell similar investments, with the hope of buying low and selling high. The hedge fund manager waits for the undervalued security to increase in value or the overvalued security to decline in value, or perhaps for both to occur.

- *Opportunistic hedge funds* invest broadly across financial, commodity, and futures markets with macroeconomic strategies, or they invest in other hedge funds.

  - A *global macro fund* is a type of opportunistic hedge fund that, principally through futures markets, takes large positions on changes in interest rates, currency movements, monetary policies, and other macroeconomic indicators. These hedge funds offer a wide exposure and involve substantial risk.

  - A ***fund of funds*** is a type of opportunistic hedge fund that invests exclusively in other hedge funds. A typical fund of funds might invest in ten other hedge funds. The purpose of a fund of funds is to diversify the sophisticated investor's risk exposure by investing a given monetary amount in multiple hedge funds instead of only one or a very few. In this regard, a fund of funds typically has turnover in the range of 20 to 30 percent annually, so that the investor does not have a long-term stake in a single option. The major disadvantage to investing in a fund of funds is that investors in these funds pay management fees to both the fund of funds and the underlying hedge fund. For these fees, though, fund investors obtain the benefit of an additional layer of intensive fund monitoring.

Private Equity Funds

A *private equity fund*, by definition, is a privately organized investment arrangement designed to facilitate the participation of certain sophisticated investors in ownership of equities—either companies or property—that are not publicly traded. Investments in private equity funds are illiquid, and investors must be prepared to hold such investments for long periods, perhaps as long as 5 to 10 years.

When target companies have not been able to list their stock on any exchange, they can sometimes obtain private equity funding. Private equity funding can be used to take publicly traded companies private. Venture capital funds, leveraged buyout funds, mezzanine debt funds, and distressed debt funds are types of private equity fund investments.

Venture Capital Funds

A **venture capital fund** is a private equity investment arrangement that provides capital to target companies. Some institutional investors provide venture capital directly to startup companies or other small companies. Venture capital funds offer investors strong diversification benefits by investing in multiple companies. As we described in Chapter 9, limited partnerships organized as special purpose entities are the primary form of venture capital investing for institutional investors.

The venture capital fund typically takes an active role in the management of the target company by providing advice and incentive plans to management, and goals for the company to achieve. During their initial few years of operation, most venture capital funds do not earn any significant returns or distribute payouts to investors.

Most venture capital funds invest in start-up companies for a substantial number of years. Thus, venture capital funds must have an *exit strategy*. Common exit strategies for venture capital funds are

- Taking an IPO of common stock to market, which allows the venture capital fund an opportunity to convert its preferred stock to common stock

- Selling the startup company directly to an outside investor or to another venture capital fund

- Requiring the startup company's management to buy the venture capital fund's stock holdings before a certain date

Leveraged Buyout Funds

A *leveraged buyout fund*, known as an *LBO fund*, is a type of venture capital fund designed for participation by sophisticated investors and uses debt financing to purchase shares of target companies. LBO funds exist to offer investors an opportunity to participate in potential investment returns connected with leveraged buyout transactions. A *buyout* is a purchase of a company's outstanding stock with the intention of taking a public company private. In most cases, LBO fund investors do not borrow all of the funds for purchasing the target company. In most cases, however, the target company is bought through a leveraged buyout (LBO), where value in the target company is used to secure debt financing to purchase the outstanding equity of the company.

In an LBO fund, investors typically supply a small portion, usually 10 percent to 30 percent, of the money required to purchase the target company. The LBO fund typically obtains the rest of the purchase price either by borrowing the money from lending institutions and other institutional investors, by issuing bonds, or both. The target company's cash flows are used to make coupon or loan payments on the outstanding debt until the debt is repaid.

LBO transactions are conducted through an SPE fund structure that is very similar to a venture capital fund. Like venture capital funds, LBO fund managers charge investors a management fee between 1.25 percent and 3.00 percent for arranging and conducting the LBO transaction. In addition, LBO funds collect incentive fees if the investment prospers. LBO funds also typically collect fees for arranging the sale of the target company when the buyout is complete. Figure 10.5 contrasts the typical characteristics of venture capital funds with those of leveraged buyout funds.

Figure 10.5 Venture Capital Funds and Leveraged Buyout Funds

Venture Capital Funds	Leveraged Buyout Funds
Target company needs start-up capital	Target company can support a high debt load and has potential for creating operating efficiencies
Target company is idea-driven and has an unproven product	Target company has an established product
Target company has not established predictable revenues	Target company produces predictable revenues
Fund investors obtain a significant equity stake in the target company	Fund investors obtain all equity in the target company

Mezzanine Debt Funds

Mezzanine debt funds exist to participate in potential investment returns connected with mezzanine debt transactions. Mezzanine funds look for investment opportunities in well-run companies that have a high potential for growth and earnings.

Distressed Debt Funds

A **distressed debt fund**, often known as a *vulture fund*, invests in bonds and other debt securities issued by target companies in financial distress. Distressed debt funds purchase distressed debt as a long-term investment in a target company with the potential for significant future returns. Sometimes distressed debt is undervalued, and the fund purchases it to quickly resell it at a higher price after a company turnaround. Other times the fund purchases distressed debt to obtain an equity stake in a target company after a bankruptcy reorganization. Senior bonds are often converted to equity during a bankruptcy. In both cases, investors primarily consider the target company's business risks and whether the company has a viable business plan for continued operations.

Key Terms

classified common stock	strike price
stock dividend	put option
special dividend	call option
declaration date	intrinsic value of an option
ex-dividend date	swap
dividend yield	credit default swap (CDS)
book value	interest-rate swap
market value	currency swap
intrinsic value of a stock	counterparty risk
earnings per share (EPS)	futures
price/earnings (P/E) ratio	fund of funds
price-to-book (P/B) ratio	venture capital fund
market maker	leveraged buyout fund
secondary offering	distressed debt fund
option	

Endnotes

1. LOMA, "313. Bond Interest and Stock Dividend Income," in *Business Risks and Controls Handbook* [Atlanta: LOMA (Life Office Management Association, Inc.), © 2001], 313-1–313-4. Used with permission. All rights reserved.

2. Patricia Wilson Fridley (Senior Advisor, Center for Financial Stability, LLC), note to author, 20 September 2012. Used with permission.

3. Mark J. Anson, Frank J. Fabozzi, and Frank J. Jones, *The Handbook of Traditional and Alternative Investment Vehicles: Investment Characteristics and Strategies* (Hoboken, NJ: John Wiley and Sons, 2011), 30–31.

4. "About ISDA," International Swaps and Derivatives Association, http://www2.isda.org/about-isda (1 October 2012).

5. Portions of this section are based on "Insights into the Insurance Industry's Derivatives Exposure," Capital Markets Special Report, National Association of Insurance Commissioners, ww.naic.org/capital_markets_archive/110610.htm (1 October 2012).

6. LOMA, "312. Derivatives," in *LOMA Business Risks and Controls Handbook* [Atlanta: LOMA (Life Office Management Association, Inc.), © 2001], 312-1–312-14. Used with permission; all rights reserved.

7. Portions of this section are based on Anson, Fabozzi, and Jones, 313–453.

Glossary

ABS. *See* **asset-backed security.**

absolute return fund. A fund option or mutual fund that seeks to achieve positive returns in all market conditions by investing in alternative investments and derivatives, and employing alternative investment management techniques. [5]

accountability. For institutional investors, the obligation of an organization to be responsible to its stakeholders for the results of its actions. [3]

active portfolio management. A broad category of portfolio management strategies that involves constantly researching opportunities to add value to a portfolio by making trades and replacing existing assets with new ones. [3]

active risk. *See* **tracking error.**

actual return. *See* **historical return.**

administration. In debt restructuring in Europe and certain other countries outside the United States, a legal proceeding under which an insolvent company makes a plan to pay its creditors, in full or in part, and remain in operation. Known as *reorganization* in the United States and some other countries. [8]

ADR. *See* **average daily rate.**

agency MBS. A security based on a portfolio of residential mortgages that meet the guidelines as to credit quality, underwriting standards, and other risk factors set by one of several U.S. government agencies. Also known as an *agency mortgage-backed security.* [9]

agency mortgage-backed security. *See* **agency MBS.**

ALM. *See* **asset-liability management.**

ALM risk. *See* **asset-liability management risk.**

amortizing loan. A loan for which each repayment reflects both principal and interest. [8]

analysis effect. For debt investment portfolios, the share of excess bond portfolio returns attributable to the manager's bets around trading in under- or overvalued debt securities. [7]

analyst. An investment professional responsible for monitoring issuers of securities and making buy-hold-sell recommendations as to future trading activity. [1]

anchor tenant. In a shopping center, a major department store or store from a major retail chain that will attract customers to the center. [9]

annual rate of return. *See* **annualized return.**

annualized return. For investments, a variation on a rate of return calculation that expresses a return for a period longer than a year as a rate of return for one whole year. Also known as a *yearly rate of return* or an *annual rate of return.* [4]

AOR. *See* **average occupancy rate.**

appraisal. In real estate, an estimate of a property's value as of a given date, determined by a qualified professional known as an appraiser. [9]

arithmetic mean annual return. The average return of a series of annual investment returns during a multiyear holding period. [4]

asset adequacy analysis. In asset-liability management for insurance companies, an analysis of the adequacy of reserves and other liabilities being tested, in light of the assets supporting those reserves and other liabilities; a broad actuarial practice undertaken to ensure that the assets backing reserves meet established standards. [7]

asset allocation. In portfolio management, the percentage distribution of all portfolio holdings across a specified array of asset classes, such as various subcategories of stocks and bonds. Also known as *asset mix.* [1]

asset allocation criteria. An element in an investment policy that consists of rules stating limits on the portion of a portfolio that may be invested in a stated category. Also known as *diversification criteria* or *limitations on asset concentrations.* [3]

asset-backed security (ABS). A structured security backed by debt instruments other than real estate mortgages. [8]

asset bubble. A rapid rise in the price of an asset so that the asset's price comes to greatly exceed its fundamental value. Also known as a *speculative bubble* or *price bubble.* [4]

asset-class correlation matrix. For a defined set of asset classes, a table showing the correlation coefficients for all potential pairs of asset classes. [6]

asset concentration. *See* **portfolio concentration.**

asset-liability management (ALM). A cross-functional management system that many types of financial institutions, including life insurance companies, banks, and retirement plans, use to coordinate the risks that simultaneously affect the company's investments and products. [1]

asset-liability management risk. The risk that a company's capital could be depleted due to a narrowing of the difference between returns earned on assets and liabilities or a mismatch in cash flows for assets and liabilities. Also known as *ALM risk.* [7]

asset-liability manager. A financial professional who monitors a company's assets supporting a specified product line, such as annuities. [1]

asset mix. *See* **asset allocation.**

asset preservation. A process of identifying and monitoring mortgages for slow payment and resolving problems with delinquency. [9]

asset risk. For an insurance company's general account, the risk that, for reasons other than changes in interest rates, the company could lose money on its investments and, for that reason, might have to draw on its capital. Also known as *C1 risk* or *credit risk*. [7]

Asset Valuation Reserve (AVR). For insurance companies in the United States, an investment reserve liability intended to absorb realized and unrealized investment gains and losses on assets sold, and potentially arising from changes in market value of assets and changes in credit ratings on assets. [2]

attribution analysis. In portfolio management, an analytical technique that involves assigning components of portfolio returns to specified portfolio management tactics, and in this way, identifies the share of portfolio returns associated with each portfolio management tactic. [3]

audit. A systematic examination and evaluation of a company's records, procedures, and controls. [3]

audit committee. A standing committee that assists a company's board of directors in overseeing the internal audit function, independent (external) auditors, financial reporting practices, internal controls, and, in some companies, ethics policy, and compliance with regulations and standards. [3]

audit policy. A corporate statement about a company's provisions for systematically examining, testing, and evaluating the company's compliance with one or more specified sets of standards. [3]

authorization limit. In financial control systems, a maximum monetary amount that a company employee has official power to approve for disbursement without prior approval by another company employee with higher authority. [3]

average daily rate (ADR). The average of rates charged for a hotel or resort room during a specified period; one factor used in measuring the success of investments in the lodging industry. [9]

average occupancy rate (AOR). The percentage of days a hotel or resort room is occupied during a specified period; one factor used in measuring the success of investments in the lodging industry. [9]

AVR. *See* **Asset Valuation Reserve.**

back-end load. *See* **short-term trading fee.**

balloon payment. In a mortgage, a lump-sum payment of the final amount of the mortgage, payable on a specified date. [9]

Bank for International Settlements (BIS). A prominent international self-regulatory organization with a primary focus on central banks and the banking industry, with a mission to serve central banks globally in supporting monetary and financial stability, fostering international cooperation, and acting as a bank for central banks. [2]

Basel Committee on Banking Supervision (BCBS). A membership organization comprising representatives of bank supervisory authorities and central banks from countries with prominent economies, with a mission to provide a forum for discussing bank supervision matters worldwide. [2]

Basel III. The common name for a comprehensive set of financial supervision reform measures designed to strengthen the regulation, supervision and risk management of the banking, insurance, and securities sectors globally. [2]

BCBS. *See* **Basel Committee on Banking Supervision.**

best efforts basis. A service in which an investment bank undertakes to sell a bond issue on behalf of the issuer on the best terms obtainable, but does not first purchase the bonds from the issuer. [8]

beta. For investment analysis, a popular measure of financial market volatility that highlights both return and market risk. [5]

BIS. *See* **Bank for International Settlements.**

block trade. *See* **block transaction.**

block transaction. Generally, a securities transaction that is larger than normal given current market conditions—often a minimum of 10,000 shares. Also known as a *block trade*. [3]

bond curve. *See* **yield curve.**

bond fund. *See* **fixed-income fund.**

book value. For a stock, the value at which the stock is reported in financial records. [10]

bottom-up investing. In portfolio management, a practice of selecting individual securities or other assets for a specific portfolio in a manner consistent with portfolio risk guidelines; bottom-up investors seek asset diversification by selecting one security or issuer at a time. [6]

buy-and-hold strategy. *See* **passive portfolio management.**

call. *See* **call option.**

callable bond. A bond that includes provisions that allow the bond issuer to retire the bond prior to the maturity date at a specified price—the *call price*. [8]

call option. A type of derivative security that gives the holder the right, but not the obligation, to *buy* an underlying security at a specified strike price, on or before the expiration date. Also known as a *call*. [10]

capital market. The aggregate of all marketplaces, participants, and activities that move funding in a given economic system from net suppliers of capital to net users of capital. [1]

cash-flow matching. A portfolio management technique that involves projecting future patterns of cash outflows for products and matching those patterns with a similar pattern of projected cash inflows from company investments. [7]

cash-flow testing. A method of asset adequacy analysis; a modeling exercise involving the projection and comparison of the timing and amount of future cash flows resulting from economic and other assumptions. [7]

CDS. *See* **credit default swap.**

classified common stock. A type of common stock that entitles different share classes to distinctive stockholder rights, such as dividend rights and rights in a liquidation proceeding. [10]

CMBS. *See* **commercial mortgage-backed security.**

CMO. *See* **collateralized mortgage obligation.**

coefficient of variation. *See* **correlation coefficient.**

collateralized loan obligation (CLO). A structured security representing an interest in a pool of corporate debt such as commercial loans. [8]

collateralized mortgage obligation (CMO). A structured mortgage security that uses a portfolio of agency residential mortgage-backed securities and high-quality nonagency residential mortgage-backed securities as collateral. [9]

commercial mortgage-backed security (CMBS). A type of mortgage-backed security that is secured by a pool of various commercial mortgages. [9]

commodities. Primary products traded in bulk on commodities exchanges or in spot markets and comprising natural resources that have been mined or extracted—such as metals, coal, and petroleum—and agricultural products and livestock—such as grains, coffee, sugar, orange juice, and pork.[1]

comparables method. A real estate appraisal method that requires estimating the market value of a property by reference to recent selling prices for other properties having similar characteristics. [9]

Compendium of Standards (CoS). Maintained by the Financial Stability Board, a list of various economic and financial standards that are internationally important for financial systems. [2]

compensation and benefits policy. A statement of guidelines and objectives for a company's total package of remuneration to employees. [3]

compliance committee. *See* **corporate governance committee.**

composite peer portfolio. In connection with peer review analysis of investment portfolios, a hypothetical portfolio having the mean and median asset mix of the sampled peer portfolios. [6]

concentration. *See* **portfolio concentration.**

C1 risk. *See* **asset risk.**

conflict of interest. A situation where the interests or actions of one entity, such as an employee, are incompatible with the interests or actions of a related entity, such as an employer. [3]

contingent deferred sales charge. *See* **short-term trading fee.**

contrarian investing. An investment strategy in which the investor seeks opportunities to buy or sell specific securities when the majority of investors appear to be doing the opposite. [6]

conventional mortgage loan. A residential mortgage loan that is made on the basis of the borrower's credit level and the value of the collateral that is the basis for the mortgage. [9]

convertible bond. A type of corporate bond that pays a fixed interest payment but also gives the bondholder the option of surrendering the bond in exchange for a specified number of shares of the issuing company's common stock. [8]

corporate alignment. A consistent targeting of a business organization's activities, resources, and systems toward achieving the organization's mission, objectives, and strategies. [3]

corporate bond. A bond issued by a corporation. [1]

corporate governance committee. A standing committee that may handle a variety of corporate issues such as corporate privacy policies, data security and usage policies, licensing, market conduct, or general compliance. Also known as a *compliance committee.* [3]

correlation. In descriptive statistics, the degree of relatedness between two sets of values. [6]

correlation coefficient. A measure in descriptive statistics that indicates how closely movements in two variables track one another; in investments, a measure used to express the risk correlation for any pairing of assets. Also known as the *coefficient of variation, covariance,* or *correlation factor.* [6]

correlation factor. *See* **correlation coefficient.**

CoS. *See* **Compendium of Standards.**

cost method. A real estate appraisal method that requires estimating the market value of a property by determining the cost of reproducing that property. [9]

counterparty risk. The potential that one party to a contract might not fulfill its contractual obligations to the other party. [10]

covariance. *See* **correlation coefficient.**

credit default swap (CDS). A type of derivative security in which the contract writer promises to pay a benefit to the purchaser if the purchaser experiences the credit default defined in the agreement; used primarily to protect the purchaser against credit risk in an investment. [10]

credit risk. The risk that a borrower may default by failing to make payments of principal or interest on time. Also known as *default risk.* [4]

credit risk premium. The portion of investment return greater than the risk-free rate, and required to compensate an investor for taking the extra risk in a bond or the credit markets in general. [4]

currency risk. The financial risk that arises from potential changes in currency exchange rates. [4]

currency swap. An agreement to exchange principal and interest payments on a particular debt instrument payable in one currency for principal and interest payments on a similar debt instrument payable in another currency. [10]

custodial tasks. In the context of a company's operational control system, job duties that include the physical or electronic handling of assets. [3]

dashboard. In portfolio performance management and control, a technology-driven graphical display of the current, real-time status of important investment performance measures. [3]

data governance. A quality control discipline for assessing, managing, using, improving, monitoring, maintaining, and protecting organizational information. [3]

debt curve. *See* **yield curve.**

debt restructuring. An agreement between a debt issuer and a lender, typically representing the lender's concession to extend the maturity date, accept a lesser amount in repayment of the debt, or otherwise alter the terms of the debt agreement. Also known as *rescheduling*. [8]

debt-to-service coverage ratio. For valuations of commercial property, the ratio of the property's net operating income to its total debt service for interest, principal, and lease payments. [9]

declaration date. For stock companies, the date on which a company's board of directors announces to stockholders and the public that it intends to pay a dividend. [10]

default risk. *See* **credit risk.**

Derivative Instruments Model Regulation. A securities model law that sets standards for the prudent use of derivative securities by state-regulated insurance companies in the United States. [2]

derivative security. A financial security that derives its value from other securities; for example, an option. [1]

distressed debt fund. A type of private equity investment fund arrangement that invests in bonds and other debt securities issued by target companies in financial distress. [10]

diversifiable risk. *See* **specific risk.**

diversification criteria. *See* **asset allocation criteria.**

dividend yield. The ratio of a company's annual dividend payments to stock price. [10]

domestic bond. For any given country, a bond issued by that country or an entity domiciled in that country, denominated in that country's domestic currency, and traded in that country's domestic financial markets. [8]

downgrade risk. For fixed-income securities, a type of credit risk that involves the risk of deterioration in a credit rating assigned to an issuer. Also known as *migration risk*. [7]

dual control. *See* **principle of segregation of duties.**

due diligence. In monitoring and evaluating a fund option or mutual fund, the research, analysis, and documentation of a rationale for selecting and continuing to offer a particular fund option or continuing to employ third parties hired to undertake functions for an investment operation. [5]

duration. 1. In finance, a statistic that measures the interest-rate sensitivity of an interest-bearing security, and can be defined as the time-weighted value of expected cash inflows, expressed in years. 2. Generally, simply the term to maturity of a financial obligation. [4]

duration gap report. A report that provides a snapshot of a company's asset-liability match at the time of the report. The report describes results of duration analysis of the company's assets and liabilities and the institution's current exposure to cash-flow mismatches. [7]

duration matching. An asset-liability management strategy that involves matching the duration statistics for fixed-income assets such as bonds with the duration statistics for the insurance company products that the assets support. *See* **duration**. [7]

duration policy. A formal control statement of guidelines for asset and liability durations. *See* **duration**. [7]

earnings per share (EPS). The portion of a company's profit attributable to each outstanding share of the company's common stock; calculated by dividing the company's total profit by the number of outstanding common stock shares. [10]

efficient frontier. In mean variance optimization (MVO) for a given set of portfolio modeling inputs, the set of all hypothetical portfolios having the greatest expected return, each for a specified level of risk. [6]

efficient portfolio. In mean variance optimization (MVO) for a given set of portfolio modeling inputs, the hypothetical portfolio having the highest expected return for a given level of risk. Also known as *optimum portfolio*. [6]

emerging market fund. A fund option or mutual fund that invests in stocks of companies located in developing countries, which typically are countries with low per capita income and little industrialization. [5]

enterprise risk committee. *See* **risk management committee.**

enterprise risk management (ERM). A cross-functional and comprehensive management system for coordinating management of all corporate risks in a manner that supports the corporate mission and strategies. [1]

EPS. *See* **earnings per share.**

equity investment. An investment that represents ownership of assets; for example, ownership of common stock or real estate. [1]

equity risk premium. The portion of investment return greater than the risk-free rate, and it is required to compensate an investor for taking the extra risk in an equity investment or the equity market in general. [4]

ERM. *See* **enterprise risk management.**

EU. *See* **European Union.**

EU Directive on the Taking-up and Pursuit of the Business of Insurance and Reinsurance. *See* **Solvency II.**

eurobond. An international bond issued in a currency other than that of the country in which it was issued, and typically underwritten by an international syndicate of investment bankers. Typical examples are the eurodollar bond and euroyen bond. [8]

European Union (EU). In Europe, an influential governing and lawmaking confederation of member nations with provision for oversight of the European Union financial system. [2]

excess return. In portfolio performance measurement, the share of a fund's total investment return that exceeds the return from the fund's benchmark. [5]

excess risky asset capacity. The difference between an investor's policy limit on risky assets and the monetary amount of risky assets currently held. [7]

ex-date. *See* **ex-dividend date.**

ex-dividend date. Following a declaration of a dividend on common stock, the date that determines which investors actually receive the recently declared dividend; typically two business days prior to the record date. Also known as the *ex-date.* [10]

execution of transactions as authorized. An organizational control principle that concerns the delegation of authority to perform specified tasks and the communication of that authority to designated individuals. [3]

exit fee. *See* **short-term trading fee.**

expected credit loss. A measure of corporate credit risk that is an estimate of the loss from corporate bond defaults. [4]

expected return. Generally, the total amount or annual rate of return an investor expects an investment to earn, given market forces affecting the investment. [4]

extra dividend. *See* **special dividend.**

fair-value pricing. A practice in which mutual funds adjust their closing prices to reflect significant new information gained from other regions of the globe after the domestic market has closed. [3]

fiduciary duty. An obligation of a natural person or legal entity, known as a *fiduciary*, to act in the best interest of another party. [2]

finance committee. *See* **risk management committee.**

Financial Stability Board (FSB). An organization that works globally to coordinate effective financial sector policies and publishes the Compendium of Standards (CoS), which it reviews and updates periodically. Affiliated with the *Bank for International Settlements (BIS).* [2]

fixed-income fund. A fund option or mutual fund that typically invests in specified debt instruments and is categorized by the specified type of debt instrument; for example, a *bond fund* or a *government bond fund.* [5].

fixed-income investment. An investment that typically provides a predictable stream of income; for example, bonds or mortgages. [1]

flat yield curve. For a yield curve, a line graph showing a horizontal straight line, and thus indicating that yields on securities are not responsive to an investment's term to maturity. [4]

foreign bond. A bond issued by an entity domiciled in one country for trading in another specific country's bond market. [8]

front running. A specific type of insider trading that involves an unethical investment professional's securities trade based on advance knowledge of large pending orders from clients. [3]

FSB. *See* **Financial Stability Board.**

fund of funds. A type of opportunistic hedge fund that invests exclusively in other hedge funds. [10]

futures. Contracts for the sale of an asset, usually a physical commodity or financial instrument, at a specified future date and price. Also known as *futures contracts*. [10]

futures contracts. *See* **futures.**

general obligation bond. A type of municipal bond that is backed by the full faith and credit of the issuer. [8]

GIPS. *See* **Global Investment Performance Standards.**

Global Investment Performance Standards (GIPS®). Standards for consistent reporting of investment performance sponsored by the CFA Institute and designed to ensure fair representation and full disclosure of investment performance across a global market. [3]

government bond. A bond issued by a government, including federal, sovereign, state, provincial, county, city, and other local governments, and local government agencies or projects. [1]

government bond fund. *See* **fixed-income fund.**

growth fund. A type of fund option or mutual fund dedicated to investing in stock and growing investment principal. [5]

hedge effectiveness. The extent to which a hedge position actually reduces risk in a portfolio. [7]

hedge effectiveness report. An institutional investment report that provides monitoring information for every position established for hedging purposes. [7]

hedge position. A portfolio position in a derivative security held for a hedging purpose. [7]

historical return. A known investment performance result, expressed as a monetary amount or a percentage rate of return. Also known as *actual return*. [4]

holding period rate of return. *See* **holding period return.**

holding period return. The rate of return on an investment over the entire period of owning the investment; relevant primarily for investments held for less than a full year. Also known as a *holding period yield* or a *holding period rate of return*. [4]

holding period yield. *See* **holding period return.**

hurdle rate. The minimum rate of return an institution must obtain in compensation for entering into any investment. [4]

hybrid security. A financial security that has characteristics of both equity and debt securities; for example, a preferred stock or convertible bond. [1]

IAIS. *See* **International Association of Insurance Supervisors.**

IMF. *See* **International Monetary Fund.**

IMR. *See* **Interest Maintenance Reserve.**

income capitalization method. A real estate appraisal method that involves estimating the value of commercial real estate by first calculating net operating income to determine the capitalization rate (cap rate), then comparing that cap rate to the cap rate for comparable properties. [9]

incompatible functions. In the context of internal financial controls, duties in the normal course of employment that, when combined, place an employee in a position where he or she could commit an illegal act or could conceal errors or irregularities. *See* **principle of segregation of duties**. [3]

index fund. A fund option or mutual fund that seeks to produce a pattern of performance similar to that of a specified market index. [5]

information ratio. The ratio of the excess return for a portfolio divided by tracking error, and the result is usually expressed as a percentage. The information ratio indicates a portfolio manager's effectiveness in using risk to generate returns. [5]

inside information. *See* **material nonpublic information.**

insider information. *See* **material nonpublic information.**

insider trading. The prohibited act of buying or selling a company's securities based on knowledge of material nonpublic information. [3]

institutional investor. Generally, any organization devoted to holding financial assets and trading securities in large volume; for example, insurance companies, mutual funds, retirement plans, and pension funds. [1]

insurance value appraisal. In real estate, the amount a property insurance company would potentially cover under property insurance if all buildings and fixtures on a property were destroyed. Also known as a *replacement value appraisal*. [9]

intangible asset. An asset that represents ownership of a legal right or another nonphysical resource; for example, securities, patents, copyrights, computer software, leases, and licenses. [1]

Interest Maintenance Reserve (IMR). For insurance companies in the United States, an investment reserve intended to absorb realized gains and losses upon the sale of interest-bearing assets when those gains or losses are attributable to changes in market interest rates, and not to changes in creditworthiness of the assets. [2]

interest-rate anticipation effect. For bond investment portfolios, the share of excess bond portfolio returns attributable to the manager's bets around short-term departures from the duration target for the debt portfolio. [7]

interest-rate anticipation strategy. Generally, a very risky active portfolio management strategy for fixed-income portfolios in which the investor trades securities in anticipation of estimated future changes in market interest rates. [7]

interest-rate swap. A type of derivative security consisting of an agreement between two parties to exchange a set of cash flows, typically with one based on a fixed interest rate and the other based on a variable, or floating, interest rate. [10]

International Association of Insurance Supervisors (IAIS). An association formed to improve regulatory supervision of the insurance industry; to maintain efficient, fair, safe, and stable insurance markets; to protect policyholders; to promote well-regulated insurance markets; and to support global financial stability. [2]

international bond. A bond issued by any entity other than a domestic entity; includes foreign bonds, Yankee bonds, and eurobonds. [8]

International Monetary Fund (IMF). An organization representing many countries working to foster global monetary cooperation, secure financial stability, facilitate international trade, promote high employment and sustainable economic growth, and reduce poverty around the world. [2]

International Organisation of Securities Commissions (IOSCO). The international self-regulatory organization for securities industry regulatory agencies and supervisors; develops standards for securities regulation. [2]

intrinsic value of a stock. The value of a stock based on a valuation of all aspects of the issuing company's business, including both tangible and intangible factors. [10]

intrinsic value of an option. In securities options, the difference between the strike price and the price of the underlying security. [10]

inverted yield curve. For a yield curve for a given date, a line graph that shows a downward slope from left to right, indicating that yields on short-term securities are higher than yields on long-term securities. [4]

investment activity report. A formal periodic report that specifies the details of all investment portfolio transactions, including all asset acquisitions and dispositions of assets, as well as realized and unrealized capital gain and loss status, estimated returns, and the company's resulting positioning status as to key risk policies. [7]

investment committee. A corporate standing committee that assists a company's board of directors in carrying out governance duties over the company's investments. [3]

investment mission. For an investment portfolio, a statement that explains the portfolio's reason for existence. [3]

investment objective. Statements that clarify a portfolio's investment mission by specifying the financial goals for an investor to pursue in satisfying that mission. [3]

investment policy. Established by an institutional investor's board of directors, a policy statement that outlines a set of formal rules and guidelines for investing. [3]

investment portfolio performance review. A management information report that presents a portfolio's investment performance for presentation to the company's oversight committees. [7]

investment strategy. Used by investment portfolio managers, a planned approach for dynamically achieving an investment mission or investment objectives. [3]

investment value appraisal. A real estate appraiser's estimate of the value of a property to a particular investor, with the property valued at its highest and best use. [9]

IOSCO. *See* **International Organisation of Securities Commissions.**

joint venture. A legal agreement between two otherwise independent businesses that agree to undertake a specific project together for a specified time period. [9]

junior debt. *See* **subordinated bond.**

key performance indicator (KPI). A quantitative measure that indicates success in the performance attributes of a specified activity. [4]

key risk indicator (KRI). A quantitative measure that indicates the level of potential adverse impact in a given activity. [4]

KPI. *See* **key performance indicator.**

KRI. *See* **key risk indicator.**

large-cap fund. A fund option or mutual fund that invests primarily in the common stock of companies with a large market capitalization—for example, greater than $10 billion. [5]

late trading. A type of illegal preferential treatment given to some investors who are allowed to trade securities, typically mutual funds, after a stock market closes using that day's closing prices. [3]

LBO fund. *See* **leveraged buyout fund.**

leveraged buyout fund. A type of venture capital fund that is designed for participation by sophisticated investors and uses debt financing to purchase shares of target companies. Also known as an *LBO fund.* [10]

lifecycle fund. *See* **target date fund.**

limitations on asset concentrations. *See* **asset allocation criteria.**

limited partnership. A form of business organization consisting of one or more general partners who manage and control a business and are legally liable for all the debts and obligations of the business, and one or more limited partners who are liable only to the extent of the amount of money invested in the business. [9]

liquidation value appraisal. A real estate appraiser's estimate of the price that a property would bring if the owners were forced to sell it quickly, under distressed circumstances. [9]

liquidity policy. A formal control that states the minimum monetary amount of cash and near-cash assets a company must hold over a specified time period to support liabilities. [7]

liquidity risk. In investments, the risk that an asset might not be readily sold for its true value. [4]

loan compliance. For mortgages, a borrower's adherence to provisions in the mortgage agreement. [9]

loan performance. For mortgages, the timely payment of principal and interest. [9]

margin compression. The narrowing of an insurer's interest margin, potentially occurring when market interest rates are rising or falling. [7]

margin expansion. An increase in an insurer's profit margin, potentially occurring when market interest rates are rising or falling. [7]

market capitalization. The total market value of all of a company's outstanding shares of stock. [4]

market maker. A securities dealer who holds an inventory of a particular stock and stands ready to buy and sell shares of that stock continuously at published bid and ask prices. [10]

market proxy. In investments, a substitute data set that can reasonably be used to represent the primary target of study, which often may be an entire financial market; used to simplify market studies requiring a market variable, statistic, or comparison. [6]

market required rate of return. *See* **required return.**

market timing. An investment activity designed to anticipate the future direction of a market, typically through economic data or technical indicators; not necessarily illegal but presents significant opportunities for abuse in some markets, particularly mutual funds. [3]

market-timing fee. *See* **short-term trading fee.**

market value. For a publicly traded stock, the currently quoted price at which investors buy or sell the stock. [10]

market value appraisal. In real estate investing, an appraiser's estimate of the price a buyer would be willing to pay for a property in current market conditions. [9]

material nonpublic information. Any nonpublic company information that a reasonable person would know might influence the market price of a company's securities. Also known as *inside information* or *insider information*. [3]

MBS. *See* **residential mortgage-backed security.**

mean liabilities method. For insurance companies, a method of investment income allocation in which a company simply assigns investment income to each of its product lines in proportion to the reserves attributed to that product line. [7]

mean optimization. *See* **mean variance optimization.**

mean variance analysis. *See* **mean variance optimization.**

mean variance optimization (MVO). A quantitative modeling technique used to identify portfolio asset-class allocations that represent efficient portfolios. Also known as *mean optimization* or *mean variance analysis*. [6]

mezzanine debt. A type of debt obligation for which claims to the issuing company's assets are senior to those of holders of the company's common stock, but junior to those of senior bondholders. [8]

mid-cap fund. A fund option or mutual fund that invests primarily in the common stock of companies with a large market capitalization—for example, $2 billion to $10 billion. [5]

migration risk. *See* **downgrade risk.**

misalignment. In business strategy, a situation that occurs when corporate planning and control mechanisms fail to keep the entire organization aligned correctly with the company's mission, goals, and strategies. [3]

misappropriation of funds. A fraud that occurs when an individual authorized to handle funds alters documents or electronic files to divert fees for personal use. [3]

MMoU. *See* **Multilateral Memorandum of Understanding.**

momentum. The tendency for a security that is gaining in market value to continue moving in the same direction; portfolio managers sometimes take advantage of this effect to add value to a portfolio. [5]

monetary duration. The expression of the effect of duration on the future monetary values of interest-bearing assets; calculated as the product of duration and the market value of the assets. Typical examples are dollar duration and euro duration. [7]

Monte Carlo modeling. A mathematical modeling process used to approximate the probability of an outcome by running multiple computer simulations using random values for the input variables. [6]

Morningstar Style Box. A nine-square grid that provides a graphical representation of a fund's investment style; the appropriate box on the grid is blackened or checked to provide a quick visual cue as to the fund's basic style classification. [5]

mortgage. A debt obligation secured by a pledge of specified real property; all mortgages represent debt secured by real estate. [1]

mortgage bond. A type of secured bond that gives the bondholder a claim to specified real estate or other real assets in the event that the bond issuer defaults. [8]

mortgage closing. An event in which property ownership is transferred by deed, the purchase price is paid, and a promissory note and deed of trust are executed. [9]

mortgage correspondent. For most United States insurance companies, a real estate professional who originates mortgage loans in a local area. [9]

mortgage origination. The process of creating a mortgage; sometimes encompasses the activities of mortgage underwriting and mortgage closing. [9]

mortgage servicing. An administrative process that consists of collecting payments, keeping records, and sending statements for mortgages. [9]

mortgage underwriting. For mortgages, the process of evaluating the credit risk of a potential borrower. [9]

Multilateral Memorandum of Understanding (MMoU). Document with standard language that provides assurance that a company's interests can be protected after it invests across a national boundary; the MMoU paves the way for cross-border investing. [2]

multisector bond fund. A fund option or mutual fund that invests primarily in bonds from several fixed-income sectors, including U.S. government obligations, U.S. corporate bonds, foreign bonds, and high-yield U.S. corporate debt securities. [5]

municipal bond. A debt security issued by local government agencies and local governments to raise funds for public works, such as schools, parks, bridges, highways, and hospitals. Also known as a *muni*. [8]

muni. *See* **municipal bond.**

net lease. A type of real estate lease that requires commercial property tenants to pay a stated rent plus other expenses. [9]

nominal interest. *See* **nominal return.**

nominal rate. *See* **nominal return.**

nominal return. The stated rate of return on an investment without adjustment for inflation or other factors. Also known as *nominal interest*; *nominal rate*. [4]

nonagency MBS. A security that is based on a portfolio of residential mortgages and that does not qualify as an agency residential mortgage-backed security; the nonagency MBS is issued by a private business entity, such as an investment bank, financial institution, or home builder. Also known as *private-label MBS*. [9]

nonagency mortgage-backed security. *See* **nonagency MBS.**

non-amortized loan. A loan that has repayments that can consist of an interest payment only. [8]

nonconforming loan. In real estate, a residential mortgage that does not meet the mortgage purchasing standards that government-sponsored agencies such as Fannie Mae and Freddie Mac set for conventional residential mortgages issued by banks, and thus the lender cannot then sell the mortgage to these agencies. [9]

nonconventional mortgage loan. A residential mortgage that does not satisfy lender requirements for conventional loans, but does satisfy U.S. government-criteria—such as those specified by the Veterans Administration (VA) or Federal Housing Administration (FHA)—and thus qualifies for government-provided mortgage insurance that guarantees the mortgage. [9]

nondiversifiable risk. *See* **systemic risk.**

nonperforming loan. Generally, a mortgage or another loan for which payments are past due by a specified number of days, usually at least 90 days, and that is subject to foreclosure. [9]

nonrecourse loan. A mortgage or another secured loan in which, if the borrower fails to pay the loan, the lender is allowed to seize the property used as collateral and sell the property to satisfy the outstanding debt. If the property's value does not entirely satisfy the debt, the contract does not permit the lender to pursue the borrower for the additional funds, and the lender must take a loss. [9]

normal yield curve. Relative to a yield curve, a line graph showing an upward slope from left to right, indicating that yields on long-term securities are higher than yields on short-term securities. [4]

OFC. *See* **offshore financial center.**

offshore financial center (OFC). A specially regulated commercial territory where most transactions are conducted by nonresident entities, the transactions are initiated elsewhere, and the majority of the financial entities involved are controlled by nonresidents. [2]

optimum portfolio. *See* **efficient portfolio.**

option. A type of derivative security that gives the holder the right to either buy or sell a specified security, such as a stock or bond, at a stated price on or before a specified expiration date. [10]

ORSA. *See* **Own Risk and Solvency Assessment.**

overcollateralization. A tactic in which a special purpose entity designs structured securities so that the total of the face amounts of the underlying pool of loans is greater than the combined value of the new structured securities, thereby protecting investors against losses on the secured debt in the event that some borrowers default. [8]

Own Risk and Solvency Assessment (ORSA). An approach to a financial institution's internal assessment of the status of its capital adequacy, its risk exposures, and the reporting of its internal risk assessment to relevant solvency supervisors. [2]

passive portfolio management. A broad category of portfolio management strategies that relies upon careful portfolio construction and infrequent trading. Also known as a *buy-and-hold strategy.* [3]

P/B ratio. *See* **price-to-book ratio.**

peer review analysis. A form of competitive analysis that consists of reviewing the broad asset allocations and other public data about the institutional investor's closest competitors. [6]

P/E ratio. *See* **price/earnings ratio.**

Ponzi scheme. An investment fraud that involves the payment of purported investment returns to existing investors from funds contributed by new investors. Also known as *pyramid scheme.* [3]

portfolio concentration. An active portfolio management tactic of allocating a significant share of a portfolio to a few securities, rather than following the broader allocation established by the strategic allocation plan. Also known as *asset concentration* or simply *concentration*. [5]

portfolio dedication. A relatively passive portfolio management strategy consisting of deliberately structuring a portfolio of assets so that the anticipated future cash flows from those assets perfectly match the future cash needs that the portfolio was assembled to fulfill. [7]

portfolio immunization. Generally, any measures taken to protect a portfolio against loss or undue risk, and typically achieved through a technique of duration matching. [7]

portfolio management. In investments, the administration of investment policy, strategy, and operations for a specified group of investments. [1]

portfolio manager. An investment professional with broad authority and accountability for fulfilling the mission and objectives of an investment portfolio, usually across asset classes. [1]

portfolio segmentation method. A method of investment income allocation in which an insurance company uses the cash flows associated with a product line, or with a grouping of products that have a need for similar investment strategies, to purchase specific assets for that line or grouping of products. [7]

portfolio turnover rate. For an investment portfolio or mutual fund, the percentage rate at which the fund buys or sells securities, excluding short-term assets; for a one-year period, calculated as the ratio of the lesser monetary amount of securities bought or securities sold to the fund's average total assets. [5]

price bubble. *See* **asset bubble.**

price/earnings (P/E) ratio. A stock's market price per share divided by the earnings per share; used to determine if a stock's market price per share is reasonable relative to the earnings of the company. [10]

price-to-book (P/B) ratio. A stock's market price per share divided by the stock's book value per share; used to identify stocks for which the market price does not fully represent the asset value in the company. [10]

primary market. The market in which new issues of securities, including bonds, are sold to the public for the first time. [8]

principle of segregation of duties. A principle of control under which an employer should design jobs so that incompatible functions are assigned to different individuals. Also known as the principle of *dual control*. [3]

private-label MBS. *See* **nonagency MBS.**

private placement. A method of issuing securities in which the issuer sells the entire issue directly to one or more qualified investors. [1]

prohibited securities list. A list of securities that specified company employees, due to their job responsibilities, are prohibited from buying or selling for either their personal accounts or any accounts they control. Also known as a *restricted securities list*. [3]

public offering. A method of issuing securities in which securities are sold to the public, usually through the services of an investment banking firm. [1]

put. *See* **put option.**

put option. A type of securities option that gives the holder the right, but not the obligation, to sell the underlying security at the strike price on or before the option's expiration date. Also known as a *put.* [10]

pyramid scheme. *See* **Ponzi scheme.**

quality effect. For debt investment portfolios, the share of excess bond portfolio returns attributable to the manager's bets on bonds having various quality ratings. [7]

rate of return. Investment earnings expressed as a percentage of the invested principal. [4]

real estate asset. An equity investment consisting of real property, buildings, and fixtures on the property. [1]

real estate investment trust (REIT). A corporation or trust that uses the pooled capital of a number of investors to purchase and manage either real estate property or mortgages. [9]

real estate risk. The potential for loss resulting from a decline in the value of real estate. [4]

real rate of return. The rate of return on an investment after adjustment for inflation and potentially some other systemic effects. Also known as *real return.* [4]

real return. *See* **real rate of return.**

recourse loan. A mortgage or another secured loan that allows the lender to seek financial damages if the borrower fails to pay the loan, and if the value of the asset is not enough to cover the outstanding liability. [9]

refunding. For bonds, paying the call price for a callable bond. [8]

reinvestment risk. Generally, a risk that market conditions will be unfavorable when the investor needs to invest the proceeds from a prior investment; for an interest-bearing security, the risk that a decline in market interest rates will lead to lower interest income after the investor reinvests the proceeds from a matured interest-bearing security. [4]

REIT. *See* **real estate investment trust.**

reorganization. In debt restructuring in the United States and some other countries, a legal proceeding under which an insolvent company makes a plan to pay its creditors, in full or in part, and remain in operation. Known as *administration* in Europe and certain other countries outside the United States. [8]

replacement value appraisal. *See* **insurance value appraisal.**

replicating portfolio. 1. Generally, a virtual pool of assets created—for purposes of performance measurement, quantitative modeling, and simulations—to reproduce the cash flows and market values observed in a specified pool of assets. 2. As used for managing the general account of an insurance company, a virtual pool of assets created—for purposes of performance measurement, quantitative modeling, and simulations—the cash flows and market values observed in a specified pool of liabilities. [7]

required rate of return. *See* **required return.**

required return. The annual rate of investment return an investor requires as reasonable compensation for a given level of risk and to satisfy the investor's objectives. Also known as the *required rate of return* or the *market required rate of return*. [4]

rescheduling. *See* **debt restructuring.**

residential mortgage-backed security (MBS). A type of mortgage-backed security that is secured by a pool of residential real estate loans. [9]

restricted securities list. *See* **prohibited securities list.**

revenue bond. A type of municipal bond that is supported by a specific income-producing project–for example, a toll road. [8]

risk and finance committee. *See* **risk management committee.**

risk appetite. The amount and type of risk that an organization is prepared to seek in the pursuit of profits or other strategic objectives. *Contrast with* **risk tolerance**. [3]

risk committee. *See* **risk management committee.**

risk criterion. *See* **risk limit.**

risk limit. In a company's risk policy, a quantitative statement that expresses how the company's risk appetite and risk tolerance are to be assessed and monitored. Also known as *risk criterion*. [3]

risk management committee. A standing committee that assists a company's board of directors in supervising the management of the institution's assets, liabilities, capital, and risks. Also known as *enterprise risk committee, finance committee, risk committee,* or *risk and finance committee*. [3]

risk policy. A corporate policy statement that explains the principles the company will follow for managing risk, outlines the process for managing risk, specifies assignments of authority and responsibility for risk management, and establishes risk reporting and risk controls. [3]

risk positioning report. For fixed-income assets, a report that typically shows the actual quality of securities compared to the targeted quality of securities; duration and the duration gap; performance attribution; and performance relative to overall performance benchmarks. [7]

risk tolerance. An organization's capacity and readiness to bear a risk in order to achieve its objectives. *Contrast with* **risk appetite**. [3]

risky asset. For institutional investors, any asset that carries excess risk or is subject to unusual volatility, and for which the investment outcome is uncertain. [7]

risky asset capacity. An institutional investor's total permitted allocation to risky asset classes, measured at market value. [7]

SAA. *See* **strategic asset allocation.**

scorecard. In investment applications, a table or worksheet form used for analyzing or comparing various fund options or mutual funds. [5]

secondary distribution. *See* **secondary offering.**

secondary market. The market in which issues of securities, including bonds, are subsequently traded after the initial sale. [8]

secondary offering. A sale of a large block of registered securities by a private investor through an investment banking company, typically at a set price. Also known as a *secondary distribution.* [10]

sector fund. A fund option or mutual fund that invests in stocks of companies in a particular financial sector or industry. [5]

sector selection. A portfolio management tactic of attempting to generate higher returns than the established benchmark index by selecting and overweighting sectors or industries having a higher expected return than those in the benchmark index. [5]

Securities Valuation Office (SVO). A department of the National Association of Insurance Commissioners that publishes designations or unit prices for fixed-income investments of insurance companies. [2]

securitizations. *See* **structured security.**

security selection. A portfolio management tactic of attempting to generate higher returns than the established benchmark index by selecting and over-weighting securities having a higher expected return than those in the benchmark allocation. [5]

segregation of duties. *See* **principle of segregation of duties.**

senior bond. A bond that has a higher claim of priority in the event of the issuer's default than that of other bonds from the same issuer. *Contrast with* **subordinated bond**. [8]

Sharpe ratio. A measure of a portfolio's returns earned for each unit of risk, when risk is expressed as the standard deviation of portfolio returns; generally, the higher the Sharpe ratio, the better the portfolio's risk-adjusted returns. [5]

short-term redemption fee. *See* **short-term trading fee.**

short-term trading fee. A fee that investment companies charge traders for investments that are not held for a minimum period of time, such as 7 or 30 days. Also known as an *exit fee*, a *back-end load*, a *contingent deferred sales charge*, a *short-term redemption fee*, or a *market-timing fee.* [3]

sinking fund provision. In a bond agreement, a provision requiring the bond issuer to follow a particular arrangement for accumulating the amount of the bond's principal over time. [8]

small-cap fund. A fund option or mutual fund that invests primarily in the common stock of companies with a small market capitalization—for example, less than $2 billion. [5]

soft-dollar arrangement. A situation in which an institutional investor obtains products or services—often research services—from a broker-dealer and, in exchange, the institutional investor directs client brokerage commissions to the broker-dealer providing the product or service; can sometimes raise ethical issues. [3]

Solvency II. A European-sponsored solvency standard for insurance companies, designed to support solvency testing and solvency supervision in the public interest. Also known as the *EU Directive on the Taking-up and Pursuit of the Business of Insurance and Reinsurance*. [2]

sovereign credit risk. The risk that a sovereign government will fail to meet its debt obligations, leading to sovereign default or sovereign debt restructuring. [4]

sovereign debt curve. *See* **sovereign yield curve.**

sovereign interest curve. *See* **sovereign yield curve.**

sovereign yield curve. For countries other than the United States, the term structure of interest rates. Also known as *sovereign debt curve* or *sovereign interest curve*. [4]

SPE. *See* **special purpose entity.**

special dividend. A nonrecurring dividend that is usually paid in cash and generally is considerably larger than the normal dividend a company pays. Also known as an *extra dividend*. [10]

special purpose entity (SPE). A business organization that is formed for a specific purpose–for example, debt securitization–and usually for a limited time. Also known as a *special purpose vehicle*. [8]

special purpose vehicle. *See* **special purpose entity (SPE).**

specific risk. An investment risk that can be substantially reduced by diversification. Also known as *diversifiable risk*. [4]

speculative bubble. *See* **asset bubble.**

stable value fund. A fund option or mutual fund that offers fixed, minimum-guaranteed returns, plus a potential for excess interest crediting; this style corresponds to the fixed guaranteed fund option under a variable annuity or variable life insurance contract. [5]

stock dividend. A type of dividend in which a company distributes additional shares of its stock to stockholders. [10]

stop-loss limit. In investments, a risk limit that indicates an amount of money that a portfolio's single-period market loss should not exceed. [3]

strategic asset allocation (SAA). The set of asset-class weights designed to most effectively achieve a portfolio's long-term objectives while remaining consistent with the portfolio's investment policy and investment constraints; the mechanism that investment professionals use for specifying a long-term asset-class allocation plan. Also known as *target asset allocation* or *strategic asset allocation plan*. [6]

strategic asset allocation plan. *See* **strategic asset allocation (SAA).**

strike price. In options contracts, the price at which the option holder can buy or sell the underlying security. [10]

structured debt. *See* **structured security.**

structured security. A security in which forms of credit risk, interest rate risk, and real estate risk in existing investments have been repackaged into a new form of marketable security that generally promises investors a stream of payments. Also known as *securitization* or *structured debt*. [8]

style drift. The divergence of an investment fund from its stated investment objective or style. [5]

subordinated bond. A bond that has a lower claim priority in the event of default than that of other bonds from the same issuer. Also known as *junior debt*. *Contrast with* **senior bond**. [8]

suitability requirement. Market conduct requirement that imposes a duty on sales producers or financial services companies to have reasonable grounds on which to believe that a specific product is suitable for a specific customer's needs. [2]

SVO. *See* **Securities Valuation Office.**

swap contract. *See* **swap.**

swap. In investments, a derivative security in which two parties agree to exchange one asset, liability, security, or cash flow for another. Also known as a *swap contract*. [10]

systemic crisis. A series of adverse events occurring in a significant number of financial institutions or markets. [4]

systemic risk. An investment risk that has a broad, similar effect on all elements in an economic system, and cannot be eliminated through diversification. Also known as *nondiversifiable risk*. [4]

tail risk. Generally, a reference to risks of low-probability but high-impact occurrences; also the potential financial losses represented in the tails of statistical probability distribution curves. [4]

tangible asset. An asset that has a physical form; for example, cash, real estate, automobiles, collectibles, commodities, equipment and machinery. [1]

target asset allocation. *See* **strategic asset allocation.**

target date fund. A fund option or mutual fund that invests in various asset classes and automatically changes the asset allocation over a period of time, with the main objective being to support an investor's goal to accumulate a specified amount of funds by the specified date. Also known as a *lifecycle fund*. [5]

T-bill. *See* **Treasury bill.**

term structure of interest rates. The relationship between interest rates on bonds of the same credit quality but with different maturities; illustrated by a yield curve. [4]

TIPS. *See* **Treasury Inflation-Protected Security.**

top-down investing. In portfolio management, a practice of starting an investment process by broadly analyzing economic conditions, asset classes, risk exposures, and industries, and then proceeding to build a control framework that addresses this broader environment before finally turning to selecting and purchasing securities. [6]

total return. For a single investment or an investment portfolio, the sum of all returns—including all income as well as realized and unrealized gains or losses—from the investment over a given period, typically one year. [4]

total room revenue. For a given hotel or resort property over a given period, the revenue per available room (RevPAR) multiplied by the number of days in that period multiplied by the number of rooms. [9]

tracking error volatility. *See* **tracking error.**

tracking error. In portfolio analysis, a measure that indicates the closeness of fit between a fund being studied and that investment portfolio's benchmark. Also known as *tracking risk, tracking error volatility,* and *active risk.* [5]

tracking risk. *See* **tracking error.**

trader. An investment professional responsible for executing purchases and sales of publicly traded securities under instructions from portfolio managers. [1]

trading ahead of research reports. An unethical activity that occurs when, prior to the release of a research report, the trading operation of an investment company uses nonpublic information in a research report as a basis for increasing or decreasing their inventory position in a particular security. [3]

transaction risk. The risk resulting from changes in the currency exchange rate between the time of entering into an agreement and the effective time of a transaction. [4]

translation risk. The risk of loss of value in foreign assets owned as a result of changes in the currency exchange rate. [4]

transparency. In financial reporting, ease of understanding for users of financial information, made possible by full, clear and timely disclosure of relevant information. [2]

Treasury bill. A short-term U.S. Treasury debt security with a maturity date of one year or less. Also known as a *T-bill.* [8]

Treasury bond. A U.S. Treasury debt security with a maturity date of more than 10 years. [8]

Treasury Inflation-Protected Security (TIPS). A U.S. Treasury security that provides protection against inflation, because the principal amount increases periodically in accordance with the rate of inflation. [8]

Treasury note. A U.S. Treasury debt security with a maturity date between 1 year and 10 years. [8]

trust deed. *See* **trust indenture.**

trust indenture. A formal agreement that establishes a trust and forms the relationship between a trustee and a trust beneficiary. Also known as a *trust deed.* [2]

Uniform Law Commission (ULC). Provides U.S. states with nonpartisan, model legislation that brings clarity and stability to critical areas of state statutory law; created the *Uniform Securities Act.* [2]

Uniform Securities Act. A longstanding model statute created by the Uniform Law Commission and designed to provide a pattern for U.S. state legislators to follow in crafting state securities laws. [2]

use value appraisal. *See* **value-in-use appraisal.**

value fund. A fund option or mutual fund that invests primarily in value stocks: stocks of companies that are undervalued in relation to the overall market, and that often pay significant dividends. [5]

value in use. In real estate, the discounted value of a cash flow or other benefits that a property generates for a specific owner under a specific use. [9]

value-in-use appraisal. A real estate appraiser's estimate of a property's value to a particular user. Also known as a *use value appraisal.* [9]

venture capital. An investment of capital in a new and usually risky enterprise. [1]

venture capital fund. A type of private equity fund arrangement that provides capital and management expertise to the startup companies that are the targets of such a fund. [10]

volatility. In investments, the tendency for an investment's market price—or potentially other aspects of market value, such as bond yield—to change over a specified time period; also a statistical measure of that tendency in terms of frequency and dispersion of market values. [4]

watch list. In the context of replacing a fund option or mutual fund, a list of funds that require heightened monitoring and must subsequently meet specified performance requirements. [5]

Yankee bond. A foreign bond denominated in U.S. dollars that is issued in the United States by a foreign entity but is subject to U.S. regulation. [8]

yearly rate of return. *See* **annualized return.**

yield curve. A line graph showing, for a specified date, the relationship between yields of debt securities and the maturities of those securities; illustrates the term structure of interest rates. Also known as a *debt curve* or a *bond curve.* [4]

yield spread. The difference in yields between two debt instruments, and which, for bonds, usually is quoted in basis points. [8]

zero-coupon bond. A bond that does not pay interest coupons during the term of the bond; instead, the bond is sold at a discount to its face value and the principal is paid in full at the bond's maturity date. [8]

Index

bond indenture, 8.2
bond options, 10.15
bond prospectus, 8.2
bonds, 1.12–1.13, 1.14
    conversion features of, 8.9–8.10
    global markets for, 8.15–8.17
    income from, 4.2
    institutional investors' holdings in, 8.2
    institutional purchase process for, 8.19
    interest-rate features of, 8.7
    investment strategies for, 8.19–8.21
    markets for, 8.12–8.17
    market value of,
        interest rates' effect on, 4.20
    prices for, 8.17–8.19, 8.20
    relative value of, 8.18–8.19
    retired, 8.3
    ratings, 2.26, 4.25, 8.11
    retirement or repayment
        features of, 8.7–8.8
    risk associated with, 8.10–8.12
    risk capital charges and, 8.11
    sale and purchase of, 1.18, 8.18
    secondary markets for, 8.15
    standard deviations of yields on, 4.10
    terms of, 8.2–8.3, 8.7–8.10
    yield spread on, 8.18
book value, 4.27, 10.7
bottom-up investing, 6.3
bp. See basis point
broker-dealer distribution, 1.12
broker-dealers, 1.12, 1.19, 2.19, 2.20
bubble, 1.3, 4.17–4.19, 4.30
    Asian currency bubble, 4.19
    asset bubble, 1.3
    bubble effect, 4.18
    Dutch tulip bubble, 4.19
    Florida real estate bubble, 4.19
    price bubble, 4.18
    speculative bubble, 4.18
    U.S. dot-com bubble, 4.19
    U.S. housing bubble, 4.19
budget, 3.4–3.6, 9.3
    Budget, Office of Management and,
        (OMB), 9.3
Build America Bonds (BABs), 8.6
Building Owners and Managers Association
    (BOMA), 9.8
bullet payment structure, 8.25
Bursa Malaysia, 2.10
Bursa Malaysia Securities, 2.10
business cycles, 4.17, 4.18, 5.4, 5.21, 9.8
business management risks, 7.5
business recovery plan, 7.35
buy-and-hold strategy, 8.19–8.21
buy limit order, 10.13
buyout, 10.24

C

call, 10.15, 10.17
callable bond, 8.8
call option, 10.15, 10.17
call price, 8.8
Canada, 1.17, 1.22, 2.10, 2.21, 2.23, 2.27,
    2.30–2.33, 8.15, 10.11, 10.18
    insurance regulation in, 2.31
    secondary market in, for government
        bonds, 8.15
    securities regulation in, 2.30–2.31
Canadian, 2.8, 2.21, 2.30, 8.5, 10.14
Canadian GAAP, 2.21
Canadian Investor Protection Fund, 2.8, 2.31
capital, 1.16
    standards for, 2.13
    state requirements for, 2.26
    unallocated, 7.12
capital adequacy
    oversight of, 2.9
    regulation of, 2.12.
        See also solvency, regulation of
    requirements for, 8.12
capital benchmark, 7.18
capital gains and losses, internal reporting of,
    7.32
capitalization (cap) rate, 9.5
capital management, 3.6
Capital Market Law (Indonesia), 2.9
capital markets, 1.16–1.17
    assumptions for, 6.6
    buyers in, 1.19, 1.20
    facilitators for, 1.19
    participants in, 1.19–1.21
    sellers in, 1.19, 1.20
    transactions in, 1.17–1.18
Capital Markets and Securities Act 2007
    (Malaysia), 2.10
Capital Markets and Securities Act 2007
    (Mexico), 2.10
capital portfolio, 7.16
capital at risk, 8.12
CARE. See Credit Analysis & Research Ltd.
Caribbean Information & Credit Rating
    Services Ltd. (CariCRIS)
    (Trinidad & Tobago), 2.27
cash dividend, 10.4
cash-flow analysis, 7.34
cash-flow matching, 7.22, 7.23
cash flows, 1.21–1.24, 7.19, 7.28, 7.29
cash-flow testing, 7.21, 7.27–7.30, 7.35
cash forecasting, 1.10
cash management, 1.10
CDS. See credit default swap
Central Bank of Brazil, 2.10
certificate of authority, 2.8
Certified Public Accountants and Auditing
    Oversight Board (Japan), 2.10

Deutsche Borse, *10.11*
Direct Edge exchange, 10.12
disclosure, 1.25, 2.3, 2.9, 2.11–2.13, 2.17–2.19,
2.22, 3.8, 3.17, 3.29, 8.4, 8.24, 10.21
documents, 2.12
requirements, 2.12
disinflation, 4.7
dissolution, 2.7
distressed debt fund, 10.25
distribution fees, 5.25
diversifiable risks, 4.17
diversification, 6.2, 6.8, 7.20
benefit, 6.9–6.10
requirements for, 3.14–3.15
dividend income, 1.14
dividends
on common stock, 4.2, 10.4–10.6
operational controls for, 10.6
dividend yield, 10.6
Dodd-Frank (Dodd-Frank Wall Street Reform
and Consumer Protection Act [2010]),
2.16, 2.18
dollar duration, 7.30
domestic bonds, 8.15–8.16
Dominion Bond Rating Service (DBRS)
(Canada), *2.27*
dot-com bubble (U.S.), *4.19*
double net lease, *9.4*
downgrade risk, 7.6
dual control, 3.20–3.21
due diligence, 3.8, 5.10, 5.11, 5.14, 10.21
due-diligence analysts, 1.7
due-diligence review, 5.26
DUP. *See* derivative use plan
duration(s), 4.20, 4.21, 5.4, 5.6–5.7, *5.8*, 5.9,
5.16, 6.17, *7.3*, *7.4*, 7.23, 7.27, 7.29,
7.30, *7.31–7.32*, 7.33–7.34, 8.5, 8.18,
9.24, *9.27*
and bond funds, 5.4, 5.6, 5.7
and interest-rate anticipation, 7.23, 7.26
and interest rate risk, 4.20
and portfolio immunization, 7.22
monetary, 7.30
portfolio, 7.23
positions, *7.3*, *7.4*
dollar, 7.30
euro, 7.30
statistic(s), 7.7
used to estimate losses, 4.21, 4.29
duration analysis, 7.27, 7.29
duration gap, *7.3*, *7.4*, 7.20. 7.22, *7.31–7.32*,
7.33–7.34
duration gap report, *7.31–7.32*, 7.33
duration gap tolerance, 7.20
duration matching, 7.22
duration mismatch, 7.22
duration mismatch tolerance, 7.20
duration policy, 7.22
durations report, 7.32
Dutch tulip bubble, *4.19*

E

earnings, 1.14, 1.24, 1.26, 3.25, 4.2, 4.3, 4.27,
5.7, 5.15, 5.20, 6.3, 7.2, 7.6, 7.8, 7.15, 7.18,
7.29, 10.2, 10.5, 10.7–10.8, 10.25
earnings ranges, 5.15
earnings-at-risk analysis, 7.18
earnings per share (EPS), 10.7, 10.8
economic aid, 2.32
economic constraints, 6.6–6.7
economic research, 9.11
economic value analysis, 7.18
efficient frontier, 6.11–6.12, *6.13*, 7.18
efficient portfolio, 6.11–6.12, *6.13*
EIOPA. *See* European Insurance and
Occupational Pensions Authority
electronic, *3.20*, 3.21, 3.27, 3.30, 8.19, 10.9,
10.11, 10.12, 10.13
access, restricted, 3.27
custody of securities, 3.21
handling of assets, 3.21
Electronic Rate and Form Filing, System
for, (NAIC), 2.25
market, alternative, 10.9, *10.11*, 10.12
network, 10.12
stock market, 10.12
trading network, 10.13
trading platform, 8.19
emerging, 1.3, 2.15, 3.14, 4.11, 5.5–5.6, 5.9,
6.10, *6.11*, *6.16*, *7.37*, 9.26, 10.22
emerging market fund, 5.5
Employee Retirement Income Security Act
(ERISA), *2.5*, 2.11
employees, morale of, 3.3
employer-owned life insurance, 5.3
endowment(s), 1.2, 1.16, 1.19, *1.20*, 1.25, 3.13,
5.3, *6.6*, 10.21
energy fund, 5.5
engineering services, 9.11
enterprise risk committee, 3.6
enterprise risk management (ERM), 1.26, 3.6,
7.5., 7.10
environmentally responsible investing, 6.5,
6.18
environmental
constraints, 6.6–6.7, 6.18
impact, 9.11
protection regulations, 9.10
EPS. *See* earnings per share
equities, 1.14. *See also* equity investments;
stocks
equities trader, 1.5
equity analysts, 1.7
equity fund, 5.4–5.5
equity investments, 1.13
equity REITs, 9.25
equity risk premium, 4.7
equity securities, 1.12, 4.17, 6.16
equity style box, 5.7–5.9

internal control requirements for, 2.21
Public Company Accounting Oversight Board
(PCAOB), *3.9*
public equities, 1.13, 7.20
public offering, 1.13
public securities, 1.13
public stocks, 1.13
public trades, 2.17
purchasing power, loss of, 4.6–4.7
put option, 10.15, 10.17
pyramid scheme, 3.30

Q

QIBs. *See* qualified institutional buyers
qualified institutional buyers, 10.20
qualified plans, 2.11
quality effect, 7.26
quality rating, 1.20, 7.20
quantitative analysts, 1.7
quote-driven market, 10.10

R

Rajaratnam, Raj, *3.25*
range estimate, 4.10, 4.12–4.13
rank, *5.12*, 5.21
ranking, 5.12–5.13, 5.21
Rapid Ratings International
(Australia/New Zealand), *2.27*
RAROC analysis. *See* risk-adjusted return on
capital analysis
rate of return, 4.3–4.6
rating(s), 1.7, 1.10, 1.20–1.21, 2.18, 2.26–2.27,
2.28, 2.29, 3.6, *4.14*, *4.15*, 4.28, 5.6–5.7,
5.8, 5.10, 5.16, 5.25, 7.6, *7.14*, 7.20, 7.26,
7.32, *7.36–7.37*, 8.8, 8.10–8.12, *8.13*, 8.14,
8.19, *8.20*, 8.23, 9.12, 9.15, 9.23–9.24
rating agency (-ies), 1.20, 2.27, 4.25
raw land, 9.3
real estate, 1.12, 1.13, 1.14, 7.20
appraisal of, 9.5–9.6
characteristics of, 9.3–9.4
commercial property types, 9.7–9.11
income-producing, control procedures for,
9.4–9.5
ownership of, 9.13–9.14
rental payments on, 4.2
subject to interest rate risk, 4.20
technical services for, 9.11–9.12
types of, 9.2
real estate analysts, 1.7
real estate assets, 1.14
real estate investment trust (REIT), *4.11*, *5.15*,
7.11, 9.2, 9.25–9.26, 10.20
equity, 9.26
index, 9.26
mortgage, 9.25
private, 9.25–9.26

real estate joint venture, 9.13
real estate limited partnership, 9.14
real estate risk, 4.19, 4.26–4.27, 4.29, 6.6, 7.5,
7.6, 7.14, 7.25, 8.22
realized volatility, 4.10
real rate of return, 4.7
real return, 4.7
rebalancing, 6.21, 7.24
receivership, 2.30
record date, 10.5
recourse loan, 9.15, 9.18
red herring, 2.19
refunding, 8.8
regional fund, 5.5
regional shopping center, *9.11*
registered principals, 2.19, 2.20
registered representatives, 2.19, 2.20
registration requirements, 2.17, 2.19
Regulation on the Supervision and
Administration of Securities
Companies (China), *2.10*
regulation, 2.6
evolution of, 2.2
focused on function, 2.3
global, consistency in, 2.32
of insurance company investments, by the
states, 2.25–2.30
of securities, by the states, 2.25
regulatory systems
elements of, 2.6–2.9
organized by function, 2.8
rehabilitation, 2.30
reinsurance companies, 1.19
reinvestment-rate risk, 4.23
reinvestment risk, 4.20, 4.23, 7.5, 9.23
REIT. *See* real estate investment trust
relative measures, 5.20
rental income, stream of, 9.17
reorganization, 8.10
replacement value appraisal, 9.6
replicating portfolio, 7.19–7.20
request(s) for proposal (RFP), 1.11
required rate of return, 4.6
required return, 4.6, 4.8, 6.5
rescheduling, 8.10
research reports, trading ahead of, 3.26
research services, soft-dollar arrangements
and, 3.29
residential mortgage-backed security, 9.21–
9.23
residential real estate, 9.2
residual returns, 7.25
resort facilities, 9.8–9.10
restricted securities, 3.26, 4.28, 6.18
See also prohibited securities list
restrictive covenant, 8.8–8.9
restructured mortgage, *9.19*
retail financial products, 1.16

stress tests, 7.27
strike price, 10.15, 10.16
strip shopping center, *9.11*
structured debt, 8.22
structured securities, 8.22–8.23, 9.20
style box, 5.7–5.9
style drift, 5.26–5.29
subaccount(s), 1.24. 2.23, 2.24, 5.3, 5.4.
    See also fund option; fund; portfolio
subadvisers, 5.4
subordinated bond, 8.9
subordinated debt tranche, 8.23
subprime loans, 9.15–9.16
subservice organizations, *3.9*
sub-sovereigns, 8.5
suitability requirements, 2.11–2.12
super-regional shopping center, *9.11*
super-sovereigns, 8.5
supplemental capital standards, 2.13
surety bond, 8.24
surplus benchmark, 7.18
surplus portfolio, 7.16
SVO. *See* National Association of
    Insurance Commissioners,
    Securities Valuation Office
swap(s), 1.13, 10.17
swap contract, 10.17
System for Electronic Rate and Form Filing
    (NAIC), 2.25
systemic crisis, 4.18
systemic risk, 4.17–4.18, 6.7

T

tactical investment portfolio, 6.15
tactical portfolio, 6.5, 6.19
tactical positioning, 7.24
tactical range limits, 6.20
Tahawwut Master Agreement, 10.17
tail risk, 4.12
tangible assets, 1.15
target company, 10.23–10.25
target date fund, 5.7
target returns, 6.18, 6.22
tax-base risk, 4.24
T-bills, 8.4–8.5
technology fund, 5.5
tender offers, disclosure of, 2.17
term bond, 8.7
term structure of interest rates, 4.22–4.23
theft, 3.30
third-party distribution, 1.12
TIA. *See* Trust Indenture Act of 1939
tier, 8.23
timing, 5.15, 6.21
TIPS. *See* Treasury Inflation-Protected
    Securities

TMX Group, *10.11*
Tokyo Stock Exchange, *10.11*
top-down investing, 6.3
total investment return, 5.17
total return, 4.4–4.5, 5.17, 5.20, 6.22
total room revenue, 9.10
tracking error, 5.22, 5.23, 6.23, 7.24
tracking error volatility, 5.23
tracking risk, 5.23
trade management systems, 1.10
trader(s), 1.5, 1.10, 1.23, 1,24, 3.22, 3.26, 3.29,
    8.18–8.19
trade settlement. *See* settlement
trading ahead of research reports, 3.26
trading commissions, 10.14
trading orders, for stock, 10.13
tranche(s), 8.23, *8.25*, 9.23, *9.24*
transaction risk, 4.27
transactions
    basics of, 1.17–1.18
    costs of, 6.21, 7.23, 10.14
translation risk, 4.27
transparency, 2.9, 3.25
transportation bonds, 8.4
Treasury bills, 8.4–8.5
Treasury bonds, 8.4–8.5
Treasury Inflation-Protected Securities,
    8.4–8.5
Treasury notes, 8.4–8.5
treasury operations, 1.10
triple net lease, 9.4
trust, 1.2, 1.19, 2.11, 2.16–2.17, 2.22–2.23,
    3.21, 8.22, 9.18, *9.22*, 9, 24, 9.25.
    See also real estate investment trust
    (REIT), unit investment trust (UIT)
    beneficiary, 2.17
    deed, 2.17, 9.18
    indenture, 2.17, 2.23
trustee, 2.17
Trust Indenture Act of 1939, 2.16, 2.17
turnaround, 10.25

U

UIT. *See* unit investment trust
ULC. *See* Uniform Law Commission
underweight, underweighting, 6.20, 7.25
underwriting
    of bond issues, 8.13
    for mortgages, 9.16–9.17
unexplained residual return, 5.15, 5.16
uniform contract size and terms
Uniform Law Commission (ULC), 2.25
Uniform Securities Act, 2.25
unit investment trust, 2.22, 2.23
United Nations, 2.35
United States (U.S., USA)